KU-498-292

# Luxembourg

# WORLD BIBLIOGRAPHICAL SERIES

General Editors:
Robert G. Neville (Executive Editor)
John J. Horton

Robert A. Myers                Hans H. Wellisch
Ian Wallace                Ralph Lee Woodward, Jr.

**John J. Horton** is Deputy Librarian of the University of Bradford and was formerly Chairman of its Academic Board of Studies in Social Sciences. He has maintained a longstanding interest in the discipline of area studies and its associated bibliographical problems, with special reference to European Studies. In particular he has published in the field of Icelandic and of Yugoslav studies, including the two relevant volumes in the World Bibliographical Series.

**Robert A. Myers** is Associate Professor of Anthropology in the Division of Social Sciences and Director of Study Abroad Programs at Alfred University, Alfred, New York. He has studied post-colonial island nations of the Caribbean and has spent two years in Nigeria on a Fulbright Lectureship. His interests include international public health, historical anthropology and developing societies. In addition to *Amerindians of the Lesser Antilles: a bibliography* (1981), *A Resource Guide to Dominica, 1493-1986* (1987) and numerous articles, he has compiled the World Bibliographical Series volumes on *Dominica* (1987), *Nigeria* (1989) and *Ghana* (1991).

**Ian Wallace** is Professor of German at the University of Bath. A graduate of Oxford in French and German, he also studied in Tübingen, Heidelberg and Lausanne before taking teaching posts at universities in the USA, Scotland and England. He specializes in contemporary German affairs, especially literature and culture, on which he has published numerous articles and books. In 1979 he founded the journal *GDR Monitor*, which he continues to edit under its new title *German Monitor*.

**Hans H. Wellisch** is Professor emeritus at the College of Library and Information Services, University of Maryland. He was President of the American Society of Indexers and was a member of the International Federation for Documentation. He is the author of numerous articles and several books on indexing and abstracting, and has published *The Conversion of Scripts and Indexing and Abstracting: an International Bibliography*, and *Indexing from A to Z*. He also contributes frequently to *Journal of the American Society for Information Science*, *The Indexer* and other professional journals.

**Ralph Lee Woodward, Jr.** is Professor of History at Tulane University, New Orleans. He is the author of *Central America, a Nation Divided*, 2nd ed. (1985), as well as several monographs and more than seventy scholarly articles on modern Latin America. He has also compiled volumes in the World Bibliographical Series on *Belize* (1980), *El Salvador* (1988), *Guatemala* (Rev. Ed.) (1992) and *Nicaragua* (Rev. Ed.) (1994). Dr. Woodward edited the Central American section of the *Research Guide to Central America and the Caribbean* (1985) and is currently associate editor of Scribner's *Encyclopedia of Latin American History*.

VOLUME 23

# Luxembourg

## Revised Edition

Jul Christophory
and
Emile Thoma

*Compilers*

CLIO PRESS
OXFORD, ENGLAND · SANTA BARBARA, CALIFORNIA
DENVER, COLORADO

© Copyright 1997 by ABC-CLIO Ltd.

All rights reserved. No part of this publication may be reproduced, stored in any retrieval system, or transmitted in any form or by any means, electronic, mechanical, photocopying or otherwise, without the prior permission in writing of the publishers.

British Library Cataloguing in Publication Data

Christophory, Jul.
Luxembourg. Rev. ed. – (World bibliographical series; v. 23)
1. Luxembourg – Bibliography
I. Title   II. Thoma, Emile
016.9'4935

ISBN 1–85109–249–8


ABC-CLIO Ltd.,
Old Clarendon Ironworks,
35A Great Clarendon Street,
Oxford OX2 6AT, England.


ABC-CLIO Inc.,
130 Cremona Drive,
Santa Barbara,
CA 93117, USA.

Designed by Bernard Crossland.
Typeset by Columns Design Ltd., Reading, England.
Printed and bound in Great Britain by Bookcraft (Bath) Ltd., Midsomer Norton.

# THE WORLD BIBLIOGRAPHICAL SERIES

This series, which is principally designed for the English speaker, will eventually cover every country (and some of the world's principal regions and cities), each in a separate volume comprising annotated entries on works dealing with its history, geography, economy and politics; and with its people, their culture, customs, religion and social organization. Attention will also be paid to current living conditions – housing, education, newspapers, clothing, etc. – that are all too often ignored in standard bibliographies; and to those particular aspects relevant to individual countries. Each volume seeks to achieve, by use of careful selectivity and critical assessment of the literature, an expression of the country and an appreciation of its nature and national aspirations, to guide the reader towards an understanding of its importance. The keynote of the series is to provide, in a uniform format, an interpretation of each country that will express its culture, its place in the world, and the qualities and background that make it unique. The views expressed in individual volumes, however, are not necessarily those of the publisher.

## VOLUMES IN THE SERIES

1 *Yugoslavia*, Rev. Ed., John J. Horton
2 *Lebanon*, Rev. Ed., C. H. Bleaney
3 *Lesotho*, Rev. Ed., Deborah Johnston
4 *Zimbabwe*, Rev. Ed., Deborah Potts
5 *Saudi Arabia*, Rev. Ed., Frank A. Clements
6 *Russia/USSR*, Second Ed., Lesley Pitman
7 *South Africa*, Rev. Ed., Geoffrey V. Davis
8 *Malawi*, Rev. Ed., Samuel Decalo
9 *Guatemala*, Rev. Ed., Ralph Lee Woodward, Jr.
10 *Pakistan*, David Taylor
11 *Uganda*, Rev. Ed., Balam Nyeko
12 *Malaysia*, Ian Brown and Rajeswary Ampalavanar
13 *France*, Rev. Ed., Frances Chambers
14 *Panama*, Eleanor DeSelms Langstaff
15 *Hungary*, Thomas Kabdebo
16 *USA*, Sheila R. Herstein and Naomi Robbins
17 *Greece*, Richard Clogg and Mary Jo Clogg
18 *New Zealand*, R. F. Grover
19 *Algeria*, Rev. Ed., Richard I. Lawless
20 *Sri Lanka*, Vijaya Samaraweera
21 *Belize*, Second Ed., Peggy Wright and Brian E. Coutts
23 *Luxembourg*, Rev. Ed., Jul Christophory and Emile Thoma
24 *Swaziland*, Rev. Ed., Balam Nyeko
25 *Kenya*, Rev. Ed., Dalvan Coger
26 *India*, Rev. Ed., Ian Derbyshire
27 *Turkey*, Merel Güçlü
28 *Cyprus*, Rev. Ed., P. M. Kitromilides and M. L. Evriviades
29 *Oman*, Rev. Ed., Frank A. Clements
30 *Italy*, Lucio Sponza and Diego Zancani
31 *Finland*, Rev. Ed., J. E. O. Screen
32 *Poland*, Rev. Ed., George Sanford and Adriana Gozdecka-Sanford
33 *Tunisia*, Allan M. Findlay, Anne M. Findlay and Richard I. Lawless
34 *Scotland*, Eric G. Grant
35 *China*, New Ed., Charles W. Hayford
36 *Qatar*, P. T. H. Unwin

# Contents

# Contents

# Introduction

**Historical survey**

The Grand Duchy of Luxembourg is a small sovereign state in the heart of Europe, tucked away between Belgium, France and Germany. With a population of around 430,000 and an area of 999 square miles, it is the smallest of the fifteen member states of the European Union. Long before the country existed as a political unit its territory was one of the historic crossroads of Europe and had been marked by Celtic, Roman and Frankish settlements, traditions and influences. Today Luxembourg comprises an independent national entity which has not only succeeded in preserving its particular characteristics through the vicissitudes of an eventful history, but has also managed to develop and consolidate a sense of national identity within its multinational community. It has become a prosperous and highly industrialized country with a powerful steel industry and a thriving banking sector.

Its history goes back to the year 963 when Count Sigefroi of the Ardennes, a descendant of Charlemagne, acquired a ruined Roman fort in exchange for possessions elsewhere and had a castle built on the rock known as the 'Bock'. This 'Lucilinburhuc' (a Saxon name meaning little fortress) was later to grow into the stronghold of the House of Luxembourg, a formidable fortress famed as the 'Gibraltar of the north' and a highly prized target for any expansionist power.

At the end of the Middle Ages the Luxembourg dynasty gave four emperors to Germany, four kings to Bohemia and one king to Hungary. The illustrious names of Henry VII, John the Blind (the most popular national hero), Wenceslas, Charles IV and Sigismund evoke a period when Luxembourg played an important role on the international stage.

In 1354 Charles IV, Holy Roman Emperor and Count of Luxembourg, made the country into a duchy, but a century later Burgundian troops captured Luxembourg. The next 400 years saw Luxembourg being dominated by various foreign powers, a situation which brought little more than dependence and poverty. The fortress of Luxembourg became the centre of many hard sieges and bloody battles, being devastated on more than twenty occasions by the Spanish, French, Austrians and Prussians. In 1659 the Treaty of the Pyrenees resulted in the first partition of Luxembourg: a large part of the south, the area round Thionville, had to be ceded to France.

In 1815, after the Napoleonic wars, the Congress of Vienna settled the duchy's modern destiny. Luxembourg was given to William I, King of Holland as a personal possession. It lost its eastern territories, the area round Bitburg and Prüm, to Prussia, but was granted the status of grand duchy. A Prussian garrison was stationed in the fortress. The personal union between Luxembourg and the Netherlands was to last until 1890.

Luxembourg became truly independent in 1839, but at the cost of a third amputation: part of its western territory was given to Belgium to become the Province du Luxembourg. In 1842 Luxembourg became a member of the German Customs Union. The Treaty of London, 1867, reaffirmed the territorial integrity of the Grand Duchy and proclaimed it perpetually neutral. The fortress was dismantled and the Prussian garrison withdrew.

With the death of William III of Orange in 1890, the succession fell to the last agnate of the House of Nassau, Adolph, as the female line of Orange was debarred from inheriting. The House of Nassau has remained on the throne ever since. On 28 September 1919 a referendum established that an overwhelming majority of the people wished to retain the monarchical form of government. At the same time the Grand Duchy withdrew from the Customs Union with Germany, entering into a similar union with Belgium in 1922.

In 1944, after traumatic experiences during the Second World War, Luxembourg became a founder of the Benelux Customs Union, which linked it economically with the Netherlands and Belgium and which formed the core of the European Economic Community. The present Grand Duke John of Luxembourg succeeded to the throne in November 1964, when his mother, the Grand Duchess Charlotte, abdicated after a reign of forty-five years.

## Natural resources

From the geological point of view Luxembourg is divided into two distinct areas. The northern part, an extension of the Belgian Ardennes, forms a level plateau from 1,300 to 1,600 feet in altitude, consisting of uneven schistose terrain and dating back to the Devonian period. In the south, the Gutland (good land) offers more fertile soils and richer pastures of more recent geological origin. It is chiefly composed of Triassic sand and limestone with a narrow strip of ironstone deposits in the southwest. The average altitude is approximately 750 feet. A third of the country's area is made up of forest and woodland.

Except for limited reserves of iron ore, Luxembourg possesses no workable mineral resources. Lately, however, the hydrological resources of the country have been harnessed by the construction of dams on three rivers: the Sûre, the Our and the Moselle. Vineyards along the River Moselle produce a good white wine.

## Administration

Administratively the Grand Duchy of Luxembourg is divided into three districts (Luxembourg, Diekirch and Grevenmacher), twelve cantons (Capellen, Esch, Luxembourg, Mersch, Clervaux, Diekirch, Redange, Vianden, Wiltz, Echternach, Grevenmacher and Remich) and 118 communes. Since 1989, the Chamber of Deputies has comprised sixty seats and since 1979 Luxembourg has been represented by six seats in the European Parliament.

There were traditionally four main political parties: the Christian-Socialists (with twenty-one seats in the 1994 election); the Socialist Labour Party (with seventeen seats); the Democrats (twelve seats); and the Communist Party (five seats in 1945, one in 1989, and none in 1994). While the Communist Party lost its last seat, new parties reinforced their representation, for example Déi Gréng (the Greens or Ecological Party) and the ADR (Aktiounskomittee fir Demokratie an Rentegerechtegkeet – Action Committee for Democracy and Fair Pensions).

## Economy

Modern Luxembourg is a 'gift of iron' as Egypt was said to be a gift of the Nile. However, although Luxembourg possessed a large quantity of iron deposits on the extreme southern border of the country, the high phosphorus content made it unsuitable for steel making. It was an invention by the English engineer, Gilchrist Thomas, in 1877, which made it possible to dephosphorize pig-iron so that the iron ore could be exploited profitably. Not only did this process allow the development of a large-scale steel industry in the country, but one of its products, Thomas slag, proved to be an ideal fertilizer for the very poor soils of the northern Ardennes. Since the end of the 19th century Luxembourg has thus rapidly developed an industrial economy which has had to recruit large numbers of foreign workers. Today the percentage of

Introduction

foreign workers is sixty per cent in the steel industry and eighty-five per cent in the building trade. Foreign residents already account for over thirty per cent of the population, which constitutes the highest proportion of foreigners in any EU country. During the 1960s Luxembourg attempted to reverse its disproportionate dependence on steel and to diversify its production of finished goods. New industries were introduced, particularly US-based companies producing tyres, plastics and synthetic fibres. Good Year was the first American company to settle in Colmar-Berg and to boost employment in the Ettelbruck area. In 1959 the Government set up the Board of Economic Development to attract foreign companies, with the result that by 1966 Dupont had established operations in Contern, Monsanto was in Echternach and General Motors was in Bascharage. Later foreign investors include TDK, Guardian and Kronospan.

**Transport and communications**

Luxembourg Findel Airport, though small in international terms, is home to an aviation industry, which links the Grand Duchy directly with most of the important cities of Europe, North America, Africa and Russia. Two Luxembourg airlines operate from Findel: the national carrier, Luxair, which runs scheduled passenger services to major European cities and holiday flights to the most attractive resorts; and Cargolux, which operates cargo routes to destinations all over the globe. As early as 1955, Loftleidir (known today as Icelandair) inaugurated highly competitive flights from Luxembourg to New York via Iceland.

Luxembourg Railways (CFL) reach all areas of the country with electric trains and provides international services leading to Brussels, Liège-Maastricht-Amsterdam, Treves-Coblence, Paris, Strasbourg and Basle. Luxembourg is eager to participate in future TGV (train à grande vitesse – high-speed train) networks and will soon contribute financially to establish rapid connections with French TGV east routes and attempt to join up with the Belgian express service near Liège.

The road network, too, is in excellent conditions all over the country. Free motorways are part of the transcontinental network and link Luxembourg directly to the capitals of all its neighbouring countries.

The canalization of the Moselle in the 1960s proved to be very important, since it linked the landlocked country to the dense network of waterways covering Northern Europe. The port of Mertert which opened in 1966 is the point of access to this network. Since the early 1990s Luxembourg has also displayed a maritime flag on the world's oceans.

## Financial sector

Over the past thirty years the number of banks in the Grand Duchy has grown from 15 to more than 220. Today Luxembourg is rated as the seventh largest financial centre in the world. Its main areas of business are: European market activities, assets management or private banking, and financial engineering. Some thirty of the world's fifty leading banks are represented in Luxembourg.

The Luxembourg Monetary Institute, the IML, an independent supervisory body, was set up by the government to safeguard the quality of banking services and the smooth running of operations. It will shortly be transformed into a fully-fledged central bank to meet the requirements for European Monetary Union as laid down by the Maastricht Treaty. Besides the more than 220 banks, Luxembourg is host to about 7,000 domiciled holding companies and some 900 investment funds. It also functions as a centre for eurobonds in ecus and bond issues in Luxembourg francs. More and more insurance and re-insurance companies settle in the city and diversify the business operations. A severe law against the 'laundering' of drug money was passed in 1992.

The financial centre is focusing its efforts on the development of quality of service and on the professional expertise of its staff. The Luxembourg Bankers' Association established its own training centre in 1991, the Luxembourg Institute for Training in Banking (IFBL).

An international bond clearing house, CEDEL, was founded in 1970 and the number of Stock Exchange listings has grown from 664 in 1970 to around 10,000 in 1995.

## Media

An ambition of Luxembourg is to become the leading European audiovisual platform. Radio-Télé-Luxembourg (RTL), which was founded in 1931, built up its reputation as a multilingual broadcasting company and has become one of the most successful commercial stations in Europe. In 1954 the company expanded its activities into television and was renamed CLT (Compagnie luxembourgeoise de télévision – Luxembourg television company). Today, since it began its first satellite broadcasts on Astra in 1988, the company operates more than twenty television and radio stations in eight different European countries. It has also become involved in film productions, rights acquisition and press activities, growing into one of the foremost multimedia groups in Europe. Although the group employs some 2,800 people Europe-wide, its headquarters remain based in Luxembourg.

Introduction

Another pillar of the Luxembourg media centre is the Société Européenne de Satellites (European Satellite Society) (SES), the private operating company of the Astra Satellite System. SES is committed to introducing digital transmission technology and offering new enhanced audiovisual services by using digital compression. By mid-1994, Astra was delivering programmes to more than 53 million homes.

## Education

In 1881 compulsory primary school attendance was introduced in Luxembourg and so universal literacy in standard German dates from this decade. Secondary education began with the arrival of the Jesuits in 1603, who founded a college near the cathedral, which was later to become the 'Athénée de Luxembourg' (Luxembourg Athenaeum), a stronghold of Latin and Greek teaching.

At the turn of the 20th century other 'lycées' (secondary schools) were set up for boys and girls in Luxembourg city. A first year of post-secondary or tertiary university teaching had been provided since the mid-19th century at the 'Athénée' and later on at the 'Lycée de Garçons' (Boys' Secondary School) under the label, 'Cours Supérieurs' (advanced course). This was later renamed 'Cours Universitaires' (university course) and established in special premises at Limpertsberg. Today the 'Cours Universitaires' takes about 600 students a year through the equivalent of a first-year undergraduate course. Around 3,500 to 4,000 students go to universities in Belgium, France, Germany or Switzerland in order to conclude their university studies.

In Luxembourg only two institutes claim university standards for post-secondary education: the 'Institut Supérieur d'Etudes Péda-gogiques' (Advanced Institute of Educational Studies) (ISERP), a three-year teacher-training college at Walferdange, and the 'Institut Supérieur de Technologie' (Advanced Institute of Technology) (IST), a three-year course for future development and industrial engineers.

Three public research centres (CRP – Centres de recherche publics) complete the university programme offered within Luxembourg, one in connection with the Centre Universitaire, the second with the Technical Institute and the third one with the Ministry of Health.

## Religion

The latest figures show that ninety-five per cent of all native Luxembourgers are Catholic, but that only fifteen to eighteen per cent actually practise their beliefs. In 1970 Protestants represented three per cent of native Luxembourgers and Jews, two per cent.

## The press

Luxembourg's press is dominated by the Catholic newspaper, *Luxemburger Wort* (Luxembourg Word), founded in March 1848 and presently circulating 80,000 copies. The second most popular newspaper is the socialist daily, *Tageblatt* (Daily Sheet), founded in 1913, with a current circulation figure of about 28,000. These two leading dailies are followed by the *Journal* of the Democratic Party (8,000 copies), the *Zeitung vum Letzeburger Vollek* (Paper of the Luxembourg People) of the Communist Party (4,000 copies) and the Luxembourg edition of the French-language daily, *Le Républicain Lorrain*, printed in Metz (France) with a circulation of about 18,000 copies.

## Luxembourg's role in Europe

A small country surrounded by powerful neighbours, Luxembourg places its faith in a united Europe as the best guarantee of its independence and the preservation of its distinct identity. In 1921 Luxembourg formed an economic union with Belgium, and in 1948 it joined the various political, economic and military organizations of Europe and the world. In 1944 the Benelux customs union was established with Belgium and the Netherlands, creating what turned out to be a blueprint for the European Community in the early 1950s when France, Germany and Italy joined the Benelux nations to form the European Coal and Steel Community and subsequently the Economic Community. In 1952 the city offered its facilities to the European Coal and Steel Community and has subsequently welcomed the establishment of other European institutions there.

In the 1960s the Kirchberg plateau, which is separated from the centre of Luxembourg city by the Grand-Duchess Charlotte Bridge, and towers over the Alzette Valley and the suburb of Pfaffenthal, slowly developed into a European district, playing host to a variety of European Community institutions which spread on either side of the motorway leading to the airport and on into Germany. Today, about 8,000 European civil servants work around this area. According to the decisions taken at the European Councils of Edinburgh (1992) and Brussels (1993) the following institutions are definitively based in Luxembourg: the European Court of Justice and Court of First Instance, the European Investment Bank (EIB), the European Court of Auditors, the Statistical Office (Eurostat), the Publications Office, the General Secretariat of the European Parliament and the Translation Office of the Union. Moreover, the regular sessions of the Council of Ministers take place in Luxembourg during the months of April, June and October.

## Introduction

Since January 1995, Luxembourg's former prime minister, Jacques Santer, has been president of the European Commission. Another former Luxembourg prime minister, Gaston Thorn, was president of the Commission from 1981 to 1985. Luxembourg's major asset in Europe is its multicultural, trilingual society, which is a living testimony to successful integration in a peaceful democratic melting pot.

## The language situation

At first sight Luxembourg's linguistic situation seems to lack any coherence. However, this initial diffuse impression quickly vanishes if the situation is envisaged as the result of the country's long historical evolution at the dividing-point of two distinct languages and cultures. The ancient country of Luxembourg embraced both German-speaking and French-speaking territory (although this is no longer the case for the area covered by the present Grand Duchy). Two types of shaping forces have determined Luxembourg's linguistic situation: geographic and ethnic factors; and changing political components.

If, under Count Sigefroi, German influences still determined Luxembourg's orientation, this situation changed after 1196 with Countess Ermesinde, when French culture clearly predominated at court. Alliances and princely marriages corroborated these French links and created strong francophile traditions which endured into the 20th century.

In the choice of languages the attitudes of most Luxembourgers are based on extralinguistic motivations, which very often proceed from complicated political, psychological and sociological factors. The foreign observer will notice in Luxembourg a curious juxtaposition or even a 'superposition' of three different idioms, which each fulfil a need and are used according to a scale of values. In everyday life, within families and at every level of society, a single tongue is used, mostly for verbal communication: Luxembourgish (Lëtzebuergesch).

Luxembourgish is usually classified among the West Germanic languages as a West Middle German dialect called Moselle Franconian (Moselfränkisch). Its historical development took place within the 'west-mitteldeutscher Raum' (West Middle German area) or the Rhenian Fan (Rheinischer Fächer) in the areas of Trier and Coblence. It originated with the bold venture of the Salian Franks (North Sea Franks) and the Ripuarians (Rhenish Franks) who began settling in the Luxembourg region during the 3rd century AD. The linguistic symbiosis between the West Franks and the Romans in northern Gaul after the Frankish conquests resulted in the creation of Luxembourgish.

However, in written communication Luxembourgish could never replace the use of German or French. German is the language currently used in newspapers, eager to reach the greatest possible number of readers, but cultural articles or private and official announcements are written in French. A francophonic newspaper, *Le Républicain Lorrain,* published in Metz, issues a special edition for the Grand Duchy in French, which has a wide circulation.

French is the language of Luxembourg's courts: legal pleas, proceedings and sentences are pronounced, drawn up and printed in French. In parliament most of the debates are held in Luxembourgish, but parliamentary documents and draft laws as well as their published texts are in French. However, texts destined for wider public circulation are bilingual or in German only. As a rule French is used as far as possible, and German whenever it is indispensable for the less educated members of the public to understand. In church, German is the primary language. But over recent years the use of Luxembourgish has been steadily gaining ground, especially for sermons and announcements. Administrators very often use German and French in a parallel way.

In primary schools and in the lower classes of lycées, German tends to be the language of instruction in science subjects. Its place is being gradually taken over by French in the middle and upper age-range classes. Luxembourgish is not normally used for teaching purposes, rather for informal conversation only. On the other hand, German would not be spoken in public, unless for the purpose of addressing a German guest.

## Luxembourg law and the language situation

Legislation governing the use of language in Luxembourg has undergone a slow evolution since the mid-19th century. According to article twenty-four of the royal decree of 3 October 1841, notaries must use the language chosen by the signing parties. Article twenty-nine of the Luxembourg Constitution says, 'The use of the French and German languages is optional. Their use must not be restricted'. However, a revision of 1948 changed the text to read 'the use of language in the field of administration and justice will be ruled by law'. Finally, the following law was passed on 24 February 1984 and brought legal recognition for Lëtzebuergesch (Luxembourgish) after almost 200 years of uncodified and informal usage as the spoken and written language common to all Luxembourgers, as their daily means of expression and communication. Its decisive clauses run as follows:

# Introduction

Article 1: The national language of the Luxembourgers shall be the Luxembourg language.

Article 2: The legislative language
Laws and bye-laws shall be written in French. If legal instruments and regulations are accompanied by a translation, then only the French version shall be considered as authentic.
Should bye-laws, other than those mentioned in the foregoing paragraph, be issued by governmental bodies, local authorities or public establishments in a language other than French, then only the language used by this establishment shall be authentic.
The present article does not depart from the rules applicable to international conventions.

Article 3: For administrative matters, including litigation, and for judicial matters, either French, German or Luxembourgish may be used without prejudice to the specific provisions pertaining to certain matters.

Article 4: Administrative petitions
If a petition is written in Luxembourgish, French or German, administrative bodies should *as far as possible* answer it in the language used by the petitioner.

To sum up, the Luxembourger is monolingual by birth and only speaks Lëtzebuergesch; it is education which makes him bi- or trilingual. French and German are official languages, but Luxembourgish is the backbone, the stronghold and the sentimental refuge of the national soul.

## The bibliography

Bibliography in Luxembourg is in a particularly difficult situation because of the lack of any serious tradition or structure. Often existing by mere chance, and limited in terms of the periods and subjects covered, bibliographies are mostly reduced to a poor existence in periodicals, newspapers and commemorative publications.
A gap of forty-four years exists between Martin Blum's work, *Bibliographie luxembourgeoise* (q.v.), which may be considered as a retrospective national bibliography, and the current national bibliography, edited by the National Library, which starts from 10 September 1944.
In no field, except for Luxembourg history, do we find an abstract journal which offers a continuous survey of the subject. In the domain of critical bibliographies only two works can be cited here. The first is Tony Kellen's *Die luxemburgische Geschichtsschreibung. Ein Rückblick*

*und ein Ausblick. Zugleich ein bibliographischer Führer für die luxemburgische Geschichte und ihre Hilfswissenschaften* (Luxembourg historiography. Retrospective and Prospects. A parallel bibliographical guide to Luxembourg history and its auxiliary sciences) (Luxembourg: Soupert, 1933-37. 2 vols.). However, its annotations are often highly subjective and sometimes make little sense. The other is Gilbert Trausch's 'Structures et problèmes agraires du passé. XV Orientation bibliographique' (Agricultural structures and problems of the past. XV Bibliographical guide), *Hémecht*, vol. 24, no. 2 (1972), p. 225-41.

As to the overall choice of titles listed in this bibliography, we have to point out that the very existence of the Luxembourg state and its geographic situation, political history, complex natural/official language situation, and economic independence/dependence, have made it difficult to respect well-defined criteria. As a rule we retained all the essential book titles in English for each field and recorded some up-to-date periodical articles when there was a lack of more detailed material; for the national publications we mainly relied on official or state-sponsored works and on works which contain reference sources and critical apparatus. Moreover we attempted to strike a sound balance between English-, French- and German-language publications. We need not stress the fact that there are not always equivalent publications for all the subjects, that we could not do justice to all areas and that very little material has been published in some fields. It stands to reason that there is greater detail about certain historical periods and events which proved to be decisive in the history of the nation.

Luxembourg's scientific book production meets with major inland marketing difficulties. Further, very few specialized foreign libraries buy scientific literature from Luxembourg. Basically Luxembourg lacks a strictly organized publishing and sales network: the biggest publishing houses are only willing to publish material if substantial profits can be expected; many books are published by the authors themselves; the few market openings and distribution channels which are available are hardly used; people beyond the national borders are unaware of the country's book production; French and German booksellers' bibliographies take no notice of Luxembourg titles; the annual national bibliography only reaches the biggest foreign libraries; and the imprint of most publications is inadequate.

All the titles in this bibliography are available at the National Library in Luxembourg and can be ordered through the interlibrary loan system. In Germany the following libraries run a special Luxemburgensia collection department: Stadtbibliothek, Trier; Stadt- und Universitäts-bibliothek, Cologne; and Bayerische Staatsbibliothek, Munich. American readers will find excellent documentation centres on Luxembourg at St Thomas University Library in Saint Paul (Minnesota) and at the Mary Couts Burnett Library (Texas Christian University in Fort Worth, Texas). British readers should turn to the British Library in London or to Sheffield University Library (Department of Germanic Studies).

## Acknowledgments

Our grateful thanks are due to Roland Engeldinger who began researching material on Luxembourg published in the 1980s and early 1990s during his probation period at the National Library and subsequently assembled the useful preliminary material for this revised edition of our Luxembourg bibliography. Special appreciation is due to Annemie Wever-Rodenbourg who has been particularly helpful in word-processing the final manuscript. We also acknowledge the spontaneous last-minute assistance of Gisèle Hubsch, Marion Rockenbrod and Claudine Thoma whose help was decisive for the completion of the manuscript by the publisher's deadline.

# List of Addresses

The following list provides the addresses of the most important publishers, editors and printing presses in Luxembourg.

Aciéries Réunies de Burbach-Eich-Dudelange (ARBED)
L-2930 Luxembourg

Action Familiale et Populaire (AFP)
3, rue du Curé, L-1368 Luxembourg

Actioun Lëtzebuergesch 'Eis Sprooch'
b.p. 98, L-2010 Luxembourg

Administration des Contributions
L-2982 Luxembourg

Administration du Cadastre et de la Topographie
b.p. 1761, L-1017 Luxembourg

Amnesty International Luxembourg
b.p. 1914, L-1019 Luxembourg

Archevêche de Luxembourg
b.p. 419, L-2014 Luxembourg

Archives Nationales
b.p. 6, L-2010 Luxembourg

APESS (Association des Professeurs de l'Enseignement Secondaire et Supérieur) (Editions)
17, rue Muller-Frommes, L-9261 Diekirch, Luxembourg

## List of Addresses

Banque et Caisse d'Epargne de l'Etat
L-2954 Luxembourg

Banque Européenne d'investissement
L-2950 Luxembourg

Banque Générale du Luxembourg
L-2951 Luxembourg

Banque Internationale à Luxembourg
L-2953 Luxembourg

Bibliothèque Nationale
37, bd F.-D. Roosevelt, L-2450 Luxembourg

Bourse de Luxembourg
b.p. 165, L-2011 Luxembourg

Caisse Centrale Raiffeisen
b.p. 111, L-2011 Luxembourg

Centrale Paysanne
L-2980 Luxembourg

Centre Alexandre-Wiltheim
162a, avenue de la Faïencerie, L-1511 Luxembourg

Centre Chrétien d'Education des Adultes
5, avenue Marie-Thérèse, L-2132 Luxembourg

Centre Culturel de Differdange
69, rue Prinzenberg, L-4650 Niederkorn, Luxembourg

Centre Information Jeunes
76, bd de la Pétrusse, L-2320 Luxembourg

Centre Luxembourgeois de Documentation et d'Etudes Médiévales
   (CLUDEM)
162a, avenue de la Faïencerie, L-1511 Luxembourg

Centre Universitaire de Luxembourg
162a, avenue de la Faïencerie, L-1511 Luxembourg

Chambre de Commerce
L-2981 Luxembourg

Chambre des Députés
19, rue du Marché-aux-Herbes, L-1728 Luxembourg

Chambre des Employés Privés
13, rue de Bragance, L-1255 Luxembourg

Chambre des Métiers
b.p. 1604, L-1016 Luxembourg

Chambre du Travail
b.p. 1263, L-1012 Luxembourg

Commission des Communautés Européennes
L-2920 Luxembourg

Conseil d'Etat
5, rue Sigefroi, L-2536 Luxembourg

Conseil Economique et Social
b.p. 1306, L-1013 Luxembourg

Cour de Justice des Communautés Européennes
L-2925 Luxembourg

Crédit Européen
L-2965 Luxembourg

Croix-Rouge Luxembourgeoise
b.p. 404, L-2010 Luxembourg

Editions Emile Borschette
21, Fielserstrooss, L-7640 Christnach, Luxembourg

Editions Guy Binsfeld
14, place du Parc, L-2313 Luxembourg

Editions Jean Probst
11, bd Joseph II, L-1840 Luxembourg

Editions John Schmit
44, rue du Kiem, L-8328 Luxembourg

**List of Addresses**

Editions 'Op der Lay'
2, op der Lay, L-9650 Esch-sur-Sûre, Luxembourg

Editions Phi
32, rue Principale, L-6665 Herborn, Luxembourg

Editions Promoculture
14, rue Duchscher, L-1424 Luxembourg

Editions Schortgen
43, rue Marie Müller-Tesch, L-4250 Esch-sur-Alzette, Luxembourg

Editpress
b.p. 147, L-4002 Esch-sur-Alzette, Luxembourg

Entreprise des Postes et Télécommunications
L-2020 Luxembourg

Euroeditor – Editions internationales Nouvelle Europe
b.p. 212, L-2012 Luxembourg

Extension de l'Université Libre de Bruxelles
4, rue Barblé, L-1210 Luxembourg

Fédération des Artisans du Grand-Duché de Luxembourg
2, Circuit de la Foire Internationale, L-1528 Luxembourg

Fédération des Industriels Luxembourgeois
b.p. 1304, L-1013 Luxembourg

Fiduciaire Générale de Luxembourg
21, rue Glesener, L-1011 Luxembourg

Galerie Editions Kutter
17, rue des Bains, L-1212 Luxembourg

Galerie Simoncini
20bis, rue Louvigny, L-1946 Luxembourg

Imprimerie Joseph Beffort
b.p. 507, L-2015 Luxembourg

Imprimerie Victor Buck (Imprimerie de la Cour)
b.p. 1341, L-1013 Luxembourg

Imprimerie Centrale
b.p. 2477, L-1024 Luxembourg

Imprimerie Coopérative Ouvrière de Presse et d'Edition (Copé)
b.p. 2106, L-1021 Luxembourg

Imprimerie Fr. Faber
b.p. 88, L-7501 Mersch, Luxembourg

Imprimerie Graphic Press
17-19, rue du Commerce, L-8220 Mamer, Luxembourg

Imprimerie Kremer-Müller & Cie
b.p. 286, L4003 Esch-sur-Alzette, Luxembourg

Imprimerie Pierre Linden
3, rue Père Raphaël, L-2413 Luxembourg

Imprimerie Print-Service s.à.r.l.
64, rue Baudouin, L-1218 Luxembourg

Imprimerie Saint-Paul S.A.
2, rue Christophe Plantin, L-2339 Luxembourg

Imprimerie P. Worré-Mertens succ. Marco Walisch
7, rue Robert Stumper, L-2557 Luxembourg

Inspection du Travail et des Mines
b.p. 27, L-2010 Luxembourg

Institut Grand-Ducal – Section de Linguistique, de Folklore et de
    Toponymie
2a, rue Kalchesbrëck, L-1852 Luxembourg

Institut Grand-Ducal – Section des Arts et Lettres
2b, bd Grande-Duchesse Charlotte, L-1330 Luxembourg

Institut Grand-Ducal – Section des Sciences Médicales
6, rue des Eglantiers, L-1457 Luxembourg

Institut Grand-Ducal – Section des Sciences Naturelles, Physiques et
    Mathématiques
21, rue Large, L-1917 Luxembourg

## List of Addresses

Institut Grand-Ducal – Section des Sciences Politiques et Morales
b.p. 1503, L-1015 Luxembourg

Institut Grand-Ducal – Section Historique
5, rue Large, L-1917 Luxembourg

Institut Monétaire Luxembourgeois
L-2983 Luxembourg

Institut Universitaire International
161a, avenue de la Faïencerie, L-1511 Luxembourg

Institut Viti-Vinicole de l'Etat
b.p. 15, L-5501 Remich, Luxembourg

Kredietbank S.A. Luxembourgeoise
L-2955 Luxembourg

Lëtzebuerger Land (Editions)
b.p. 2083, L-1020 Luxembourg

Messageries Paul Kraus
11, rue Christophe Plantin, L-2339 Luxembourg

Ministère d'Etat. Présidence du Gouvernement
L-2910 Luxembourg

Ministère de l'Agriculture, de la Viticulture et du Développement
Rural
L-2913 Luxembourg

Ministère de l'Aménagement du Térritoire
L-2946 Luxembourg

Ministère de l'Economie
L-2914 Luxembourg

Ministère de l'Education Nationale et de la Formation Professionnelle
L-2926 Luxembourg

Ministère de l'Education Physique et des Sports
L-2916 Luxembourg

Ministère de l'Energie
L-2449 Luxembourg

Ministère de l'Intérieur
L-2933 Luxembourg

Ministère de la Culture
L-2912 Luxembourg

Ministère de la Famille
L-2919 Luxembourg

Ministère de la Fonction Publique et de la Réforme Administrative
L-2420 Luxembourg

Ministère de la Force Publique
L-2915 Luxembourg

Ministère de la Jeunesse
L-2915 Luxembourg

Ministère de la Justice
L-2934 Luxembourg

Ministère de la Promotion Féminine
L-2919 Luxembourg

Ministère de la Santé
L-2320 Luxembourg

Ministère de la Sécurité Sociale
L-2936 Luxembourg

Ministère des Affaires Etrangères, du Commerce Extérieur et de la
   Coopération
L-2911 Luxembourg

Ministère des Classes Moyennes et du Tourisme
L-2937 Luxembourg

Ministère des Communications
L-2945 Luxembourg

**List of Addresses**

Ministère des Finances
L-2931 Luxembourg

Ministère des Transports
L-2938 Luxembourg

Ministère des Travaux Publics
L-2940 Luxembourg

Ministère du Logement
L-2942 Luxembourg

Ministère du Travail et de l'Emploi
L-2939 Luxembourg

Mouvement Ecologique
b.p. 827, L-2018 Luxembourg

Musée National d'Histoire et d'Art
Marché-aux-Poissons, L-2345 Luxembourg

Musée National d'Histoire Naturelle
7, rue de la Boucherie, L-1247 Luxembourg

Natura – Ligue Luxembourgeoise pour la Protection de la nature et de
    l'environnement
b.p. 91, L-2010 Luxembourg

Office des Publications Officielles des Communautés Européennes
L-2985 Luxembourg

Office National du Tourisme
b.p. 1001, L-1010 Luxembourg

Op der Lay (Editions)
2, op der Lay, L-9650 Esch-sur-Sûre, Luxembourg

Parlement Européen
L-2929 Luxembourg

Parti Chrétien Social
b.p. 826, L-2018 Luxembourg

Parti Communiste Luxembourgeois
b.p. 1463, L-1014 Luxembourg

Parti déi Greng Alternative (GAP)
13, rue du Rost, L-2447 Luxembourg

Parti Démocratique
46, Grand-rue, L-1660 Luxembourg

Parti Ouvrier Socialiste Luxembourgeois
rue de Crécy, L-1364 Luxembourg

Promoculture s.à.r.l.
14, rue Duchscher, L-1424 Luxembourg

Publications Mosellanes (Editions)
64, route d'Esch, L-1470 Luxembourg

Rappel (Editions du)
b.p. 1424, L-1014 Luxembourg

Sécurité Routière
b.p. 29, L-8005 Bertrange, Luxembourg

Service Central de la Statistique et des Etudes Economiques (STATEC)
b.p. 304, L-2013 Luxembourg

Service Central de Législation
43, bd F.-D. Roosevelt, L-2450 Luxembourg

Service Central des Imprimes de l'Etat
b.p. 1302, L-1013 Luxembourg

Service Géologique du Luxembourg
43, bd Grande-Duchesse Charlotte, L-1331 Luxembourg

Service Information et Presse
43, bd F.-D. Roosevelt, L-2450 Luxembourg

Service National de la Jeunesse
b.p. 707, L-2017 Luxembourg

Services Techniques de l'Agriculture
16, route d'Esch, L-1470 Luxembourg

**List of Addresses**

SESAM asbl
12, allée des Tilleuls, L-8508 Rédange-sur-Attert, Luxembourg

Société Nationale des Chemins de Fer Luxembourgeois
b.p. 1803, L-1018 Luxembourg

Syndicat 'Education et Science' dans l'OGB-L
19, rue d'Epernay, L-1490 Luxembourg

Syndicat National des Enseignants
b.p. 2437, L-1024 Luxembourg

UNIAO
10, rue Auguste Laval, L-1922 Luxembourg

Union Grand-Duc Adolphe
2, rue Sosthène Weis, L-2722 Luxembourg

Union Luxembourgeoise des Consommateurs
55, rue des Bruyères, L-1274 Luxembourg/Howald

# The Country and Its People

## General

1 **Luxembourg.** (Luxembourg.)
P. Margue, G. Als, F. Hoffmann, J. Molitor, J. M. Gehring, H. Klees.
Le Puy, France: Edition Christine Bonneton, 1984. 399p.

One of the best overall studies of Luxembourg, this volume's five chapters ('History and Art', 'Ethnology', 'Linguistics and Literature', 'Natural Environment' and 'Economy'), deal with most aspects of this small country. With its illustrations, tables, charts and explanations provided by the foremost expert in each field, the book portrays an accurate image of Luxembourg.

2 **Das ist Luxemburg.** (This is Luxembourg.)
Carlo Hemmer, Emile Krier, Michel Raus, Fons Theis, Gilbert Trausch, Nic Weber, Pierre Werner, Léon Zeches. Stuttgart, FRG: Seewald Verlag, 1983. 243p.

Eight leading Luxembourg authors worked on this competent, non-fiction publication about the Grand Duchy, which addresses those seeking information before visiting Luxembourg. Most aspects of the country are dealt with in the different contributions, which include: a report on Luxembourg cultural life; analyses of the economic importance of the country's steel industry and banking centre; and a study concerning the media landscape of Luxembourg.

3 **Le Luxembourg dans tous ses états.** (Luxembourg in all its moods.)
Claude Gengler. La Garenne-Coombes, France: Editions de l'Espace Européen, 1991. 246p. (Géographies en Liberté).

Gengler aims to show the characteristic advantages but also the challenges facing one of the smallest European countries. The book deals with Luxembourg's history, political life, natural and physical conditions, demography, culture and economy. Addressing students and teachers as well as the interested general reader, the text is abundantly illustrated with maps, recent statistics and humorous drawings.

1

4  **Luxembourg.**
Manfred Veit.   Heroldsberg, FRG: Glock und Lutz, 1979. xvi + 336p.
3 maps. (Kultur der Nationen. Geistige Länderkunde, Bd. 36).

This thorough and detailed study is concerned with the historical, social, political, intellectual, linguistic and economic geography of the Grand Duchy, as seen through the eyes of a German national. Based on statistical evidence, it provides thousands of facts and deals with hundreds of persons from various walks of cultural life. Critics have highlighted both factual inaccuracies and debatable judgements due to biased sources of information. However, all in all, the volume represents an interesting attempt at synthesis and classification.

5  **Luxembourg: livre du Centenaire.** (Luxembourg centenary book.)
Luxembourg: Imprimerie Saint-Paul, 1949. 2nd ed. 673p. maps. bibliog.

This record book represents an ambitious attempt by the Luxembourg government to celebrate the Grand Duchy's centenary of independence in 1939. However, while it was being printed, war broke out, so it only appeared in a first edition in 1948. A series of authoritative articles on basic aspects of Luxembourg's identity and role set out to establish the country's personality and its national mission as an independent people, as well as celebrating its past achievements in the fields of law, politics, education, sciences, literature and the arts. Two articles deal with the emigration of Luxembourgers. The work as a whole illustrates the national consciousness and independent will of a small country.

6  **Le peuple luxembourgeois: essai de psychologie.** (The Luxembourg people: a tentative psychology.)
Nicolas Ries.   Diekirch, Luxembourg: Schroell, 1920. 294p.

This is the first, and so far the only, systematic attempt to inquire into the deeper psychological components of the Luxembourg national character. Specific chapters are devoted to the ethnography and history of Luxembourgers, and their contemporary living, housing and educational conditions. The main chapters delineate the linguistic dualism of the country which the author believes is responsible for a deep psychological dichotomy in the national character. Final sections deal with social and religious factors and stress the ideals of justice, democracy and patriotism. Although many of the theses are controversial and debatable, the book is written in elegant French and remains the basic reference book and starting-point for more scientific modern investigations.

7  **Portrait of the Luxembourger.**
Jul Christophory.   In: *Les Luxembourgeois par eux-mêmes.* (The Luxembourgers as seen by themselves.)   Luxembourg: Imprimerie Bourg-Bourger, 1978, p. 313-28.

Christophory first presents a rough character sketch of the typical Luxembourger, who derives some of his basic attitudes from the psychological structure of the Ardennes peasant: a hard worker with a reserved temperament and a practical and utilitarian turn of mind, who values roots, conformity and permanence. He goes on to inquire into the patriotism of the Luxembourgers, and into the anatomy of their society, and its student world.

8 **Die Entwicklung des Luxemburger Nationalgefühls von 1780 etwa bis heute.** (The evolution of Luxembourg patriotism from 1780 to the present.)
Nicolas Margue. *Ons Hémecht*, vol. 43, no. 3 (1937), p. 188-204.

Margue opens by sketching the situation at the end of the *ancien régime* and the peasant war against the Napoleonic armies to demonstrate that some kind of national feeling survived all the vicissitudes of foreign occupation. However, he goes on to show that the real turning-point came after the First World War, in April 1919, when a demonstration by the population showed that Luxembourg wanted neither to become a big Belgian province nor a small French *département*. A growing concern, awareness and cultivation of national characteristics and culture developed during the 1920s-1930s.

9 **Luxembourgeois, qui êtes-vous? Echos et chuchotements.**
(Luxembourgers, who are you? Echoes and whispers.)
Jul Christophory. Luxembourg: Éditions Guy Binsfeld, 1984. 202p.

Abundant quotations from popular and scholarly publications attempt to define as closely as possible the reality, way of thinking, opinions, and way of life, of the Luxembourg people. Rejecting the classical definitions, Jul Christophory presents a more refined portrait of the Luxembourg people. In view of the population's numerous contacts with foreigners, he examines which aspects of the Luxembourg people retain typical Luxembourg characteristics. Apt caricatures illustrate the main points.

10 **D'Lëtzebuerger. Profils luxembourgeois – Luxemburger Profile – Luxembourg profiles.**
Marc Theis, Gilbert Trausch. Luxembourg: Hannover, 1993. unpaginated.

This luxurious album portrays a hundred better or lesser known Luxembourg people from every walk of life and sets them in their natural context. The high-quality pictures taken by the internationally reputed Luxembourg photographer, Marc Theis, who lives in Germany, are introduced by a refined and discerning analysis of the distinctive character features that define the 'Luxembourger'.

11 **Du sentiment national des luxembourgeois.** (On the national feeling of the Luxembourgers.)
Luxembourg: Imprimerie Saint-Paul, 1984. 272p.

Originally published as a special issue of the cultural magazine, *Nos Cahiers* (Our Folios), in 1984, this publication devotes attention to different aspects of Luxembourg identity and patriotic feeling. A dozen proficient contributions by well-known authors like Pierre Grégoire, Christian Calmes, Gilbert Trausch and Fernand Hoffmann among others, illuminate various facets of this subject. Finally, the volume is completed by a select bibliography by Carlo Hury.

12 **Réflexions autour de l'identité.** (Reflections on identity.)
Jul Christophory, Georges Als, Claude Javeau et al. *Les Cahiers Luxembourgeois*, 1988. Special issue. 166p.

This special issue introduces the revival of *Les Cahiers Luxembourgeois* (Luxembourg Notebooks), one of the best literary magazines, which was founded in 1923 and had disappeared in the mid-1960s. It presents the contributions to an international colloquium organized by the 'Centre d'Etudes de la société luxembourgeoise' (Centre for the Study of Luxembourg Society) at the Cercle Municipal (Municipal Society). Jul Christophory weaves an ironic tapestry around the labels and connotations of the 'genuine Luxembourger', while other contributors deal with aspects of demography, arts, language and education. Some more humorous contributions deal with the role of pubs and the importance of gossip-mongering in a national context.

13   **Merian: Das Monatsheft der Städte und Landschaften, Jg. 17, 1964, Heft 7: Luxemburg.** (Merian: Monthly of Towns and Landscapes, year 17, 1964, issue 7: Luxembourg.)
Hamburg, FRG: Hoffmann und Campe, 1964. 99p.

Sixteen literary contributions, various anecdotes and tales, many black-and-white and colour photographs and reproductions of paintings by Joseph Kutter, the well-known expressionist painter, manage to capture and communicate the particular atmosphere of Luxembourg's countryside and the character of its inhabitants.

14   **The Grand Duchy of Luxembourg. A miniature democratic state of many charms against a feudal background.**
Maynard Owen Williams.   *National Geographic*, Nov. 1924, p. 501-28.

Owen Williams's report on Luxembourg and its cultural life, local customs, landscapes and way of life represents the interesting point of view of a foreigner visiting the Grand Duchy in 1924. Briefly retracing the young state's history, the author describes his tour of the country.

15   **Luxembourg, survivor of invasions.**
Sydney Clark.   *National Geographic*, June 1948, p. 791-810.

Published three years after the end of the Second World War, this sympathetic post-war examination of the Grand Duchy is illustrated by photographs from Maynard Owen Williams who had published a contribution on Luxembourg twenty-four years earlier (q.v.). The author is full of admiration for a population which manages, repeatedly, to reconstruct its country after foreign invasions and wars in a most efficient way.

16   **Luxembourg, the quiet fortress.**
Robert Leslie Conly.   *National Geographic*, July 1970, no. 7, p. 69-97.

Well illustrated with colour photographs, this volume offers many interesting details on economics and tourism.

# Pictorial albums

17  **Luxembourg – Mémorial de l'Histoire. Dokumente zur Geschichte.**
(Luxembourg – A memorial of history. Evidence of the past.)
Guy May.  Luxembourg: Imprimerie Centrale, 1983. 140p.

May's richly illustrated, trilingual (French, German and English) album contains sixty reproductions of fascinating documents from twelve centuries of Luxembourg history. These documents, many of which are published here for the first time, were taken from the archive collections of Luxembourg and other European cities. The introductory study, 'A Historical Moment in the State Archives', was written by Paul Spang, who was director of the State Archives in 1983.

18  **100 Joer Lëtzebuerger Dynastie. Collections et Souvenirs de la Maison Grand-Ducale.** (Centenary of the Luxembourg dynasty. Collections and souvenirs of the Grand Ducal family house.)
Edited by Jean-Claude Muller.  Luxembourg: Imprimerie Buck, 1990. 223p.

This is the official catalogue of an exhibition, containing collections and souvenirs of the Nassau house, which was held at the National Museum (30 November 1990 – 6 January 1991) to mark the centenary of the Luxembourg dynasty. Besides contributions from notable Luxembourg historians, the brochure contains photographs of the most representative objects (jewellery, arms, silver- and goldware) of those on display.

19  **Luxemburg – seine Dynastie.** (Luxembourg – its dynasty.)
François Mersch.  Luxembourg: Editions François Mersch, 1981-82. 2 vols.

Includes a huge number of photographs and documents dating from 1889 onwards, the year in which Adolph, Duke of Nassau, became the sovereign of the Grand Duchy of Luxembourg. Unfortunately the illustrations are not presented in chronological order.

20  **The Luxembourg Grand Ducal Family.**
Luxembourg: Information and Press Service, Ministry of State, 1993. 112p.

Published by the government's information and press service and available free of charge, this small picture album provides the reader with a short survey of the constitutional aspects concerning the grand ducal family. In addition, it presents each of the family members and records some of their state visits abroad as well as significant commemorations and inaugurations of monuments.

21  **Luxembourg. Das Fürstenhaus. La famille royale.** (Luxembourg. The royal family.)
Reginald Davis.  Speyer, FRG: Klambt-Verlag, 1989. 95p.

One of the world's most distinguished photographers of royalty, Reginald Davis presents more than a hundred magnificent colour photographs accompanied by well-written text, which show how Luxembourg's ruling dynasty is guaranteed to last well beyond the 20th century.

22 **Hochzeit im Hause Luxemburg.** (Royal marriage in Luxembourg.)
Luxembourg: Imprimerie Saint-Paul, 1981. 143p.

This album, which is interlarded with numerous colour photographs, presents the reader with details of the wedding between Prince Henri, hereditary grand duke of Luxembourg, and Maria Teresa Mestre, a Swiss lady of Cuban origins, which took place in February 1981. The album also retraces their former lives and provides some information on the Luxembourg dynasty.

23 **Henri & Maria Teresa: Das erste Jahr des Prinzenpaars in Bildern.**
(Henri & Maria Teresa: the first year of the royal couple in pictures.)
Raymond Reuter. Luxembourg: Luxnews, 1981.

Short comments and more than eighty colour photographs illustrate the lives of the hereditary grand duke Henri and his future wife, Maria Teresa, from 7 November 1980, when Grand Duke Jean announced their engagement, up to the birth of their first son in November 1981.

24 **150 Joer onofhängeg – 25 Joer Grand-Duc Jean, Chef vun eisem Land.** (150 years of independence – Grand Duke Jean, head of our country for 25 years.)
Luxembourg: Imprimerie Saint-Paul, 1989. 314p.

Published in 1989, when Luxembourg celebrated 150 years of independence as set up by the Treaty of London (1839) and, at the same time, 25 years since the accession to the throne of Grand Duke Jean. Besides a lot of photographs of the 1989 and 1939 celebrations, this commemorative volume records the texts of speeches and messages given by the Grand Duke and other important Luxembourg personalities as well as some historical flashbacks since the establishment of the Luxembourg nation.

25 **The Grand Duchy: Le Grand-Duché: Das Grossherzogtum.**
Peter Sherwood, photographs by Benno Gross. Luxembourg: Cargo International Airlines, 1979.

This original volume of photographs, accompanied by a lively text, was specially commissioned by Cargolux to celebrate the introduction of their first Boeing 747-200 freighter. The text runs in three parallel columns: English, French and German. This stimulating souvenir book manages to capture the atmosphere of daily life in the Grand Duchy.

26 **Le Grand-Duché de Luxembourg à la Belle Epoque.** (The Grand Duchy of Luxembourg during the *belle époque*.)
François Mersch. Luxembourg: François Mersch, 1978-81. 3 vols.

Pages 9-132 of the first volume reproduce the famous picture album of Charles Bernhoeft, who was born in Pfaffenthal (a suburb of Luxembourg) in 1859, and published high-quality photographs of the town and country of Luxembourg. The remaining pages summarize individual towns and villages in alphabetical order, with postcard views and family pictures capturing the old-world charm of picturesque scenes and significant events. In 1980 and 1981, two other volumes were issued which covered more or less the same historical period, that is to say from 1848 to 1916. Volume II includes an alphabetical picture album of most of the towns and villages of

Luxembourg and is followed by a summary of the economic history of Luxembourg from 1815 to 1915, by Paul Weber. Volume III, on the other hand, opens with a report on the famous revolutionary year of 1848 and is followed by more photographs of most of Luxembourg's villages and towns.

27   **Le Luxembourg pittoresque: das romantische Luxemburg.**
(Picturesque and romantic Luxembourg.)
Michel Engels, Mathias Huss.   Luxembourg: M. Huss, 1901.
Reprinted, Luxembourg: Edouard Kutter, 1973. 82p.

An excellent choice of colour drawings and sketches, accompanied by parallel French and German commentaries, illustrate the natural beauty of the country. Since the publication of N. Liez's drawings in 1834, and those of J. B. Fresez in 1857 (qq.v.), no analogous art had been published and Engels set out to replace these books. This interesting album will appeal both to art-minded people and to historians.

28   **Album pittoresque du Grand-Duché de Luxembourg.** (Picturesque album of the Grand Duchy of Luxembourg.)
Jean-Baptiste Fresez.   Luxembourg: V. Hoffman, 1857. 30p.
Reprinted, Luxembourg: Edouard Kutter, 1968. unpaginated.

Dedicated to Prince Henry of the Netherlands, this volume is the work of the professor of drawing at the Athénée Royal Grand-Ducal de Luxembourg, and consists of thirty splendid drawings of beautiful Luxembourg scenery, accompanied by expert historical commentary in French.

29   **Voyage pittoresque à travers le Grand-Duché de Luxembourg.**
(Colourful trip across the Grand Duchy of Luxembourg.)
Nicolas Liez.   Luxembourg: N. Reuter/Victor Hoffman, 1834.
Reprinted, Luxembourg: Edouard Kutter, 1968.

In 1832 Liez was recruited by the lithographer, Reuter, to collaborate in the production of this splendid album. The work won him wide acclaim and he was subsequently engaged as an engraver by the director of the Faïencerie Boch (porcelain factory at Septfontaines), who allowed him to undertake further study in Paris. In 1851 he opened his own workshop in the rue du Piquet in Luxembourg. This high-quality album presents forty-six drawings and lithographic prints by Liez and occasional collaborators like J.-B. Fresez, F. Clément and J.-P. Schmit.

30   **Vues pittoresques de Luxembourg: dessins et aquarelles, 1775-1851.**
(Romantic views of Luxembourg: sketches and water-colours.)
Joseph M. W. Turner, preface by Timothy Clifford.   Luxembourg:
Edouard Kutter, 1977.

Reproduces for the first time pencil drawings, water-colours and gouaches made on, or resulting from, sketching tours that the English painter, Turner, made to the areas of the Meuse and the Moselle. What is known of Turner's visits to the town and country of Luxembourg comes from itineraries, sketch-maps and annotations in Turner Bequest sketch-books. He visited Luxembourg for the first time in 1825 and again in 1834. His earlier pencil studies seem to have served as a basis for later water-colours. In a preface to the volume, Timothy Clifford celebrates the particular quality and emotion of Turner's Luxembourg series, admiring his technique of creating memorable and visionary statements, and concluding: 'The beauty of the Luxembourg countryside and of the town with its fortress, public buildings and spires, perched on a plateau with steep cliffs overhanging a winding river, was magically captured and distilled by this remarkable series of drawings'. The pencil drawings in the album come from the British Museum collections, with two belonging to the Tate Gallery.

31  **Images du Luxembourg: Bilder aus Luxemburg.** (Pictures from Luxembourg.)
Introduction and captions by Carlo Hemmer, photographs by Marcel Schroeder, English translation by Franz Reuter, R. Warren-Davis.
Luxembourg: Imprimerie Bourg-Bourger, 1972. 103p.

This interesting high-quality album contains an introduction and captions in French, German and English. It portrays Luxembourg's local people, architecture and landscapes.

32  **Aspects du Luxembourg.** (Aspects of Luxembourg.)
Carlo Hemmer, Marcel Schroeder.   Luxembourg: Imprimerie Bourg-Bourger, 1958. 280p.

Presents a splendid picture and souvenir book that is supported by a perceptive and lucid commentary. The main focuses are on the natural environment, some sociological aspects, economic and intellectual life, youth culture and history. Some interesting pages relate the thoughts of some important foreign personalities on aspects of Luxembourg and its people. These famous visitors include Decimus Magnus Ausonius, Francesco Petrarca, Jean Racine, Johann Wolfgang von Goethe, Georg Friedrich Wilhelm Hegel, Victor Hugo, Jules Michelet, Maurice Barrès, Winston Churchill, André Gide and Perle Mesta.

33  **Voyage pittoresque au Luxembourg.** (Picturesque trip in Luxembourg.)
Edited by Pol Tousch.   Ottweiler, FRG: Ottweiler Druckerei, 1981.

The experienced collector, Pol Tousch, presents the reader with twenty lithographic prints from public and private collections. The album not only includes prints depicting picturesque sites, but also information on Luxembourg's everyday rural life during the 19th century.

34  **Le Luxembourg.** (Luxembourg.)
Preface by Victor Hugo, text by Raymond Schaack.   Paris: Romains Pagès Editions, 1991. 128p. (Intime Europe).

Superb photographs by Marcel Schroeder and others, and a witty and elegant commentary by Raymond Schaack, invite the reader along on a highly original and thoroughly enjoyable trip to some idyllic places in the Grand Duchy.

35  **Luxembourg. Bilder und Geschichte.** (Luxembourg. Images and history.)
Photography by Yousef A. P. Hakimi, text by Dr Heinz Monz.   Trier, FRG: YAPH Atelier und Verlag für Photographie, 1995. 144p.

An Iranian photographer living in Trier and a German national united their talents to publish a highly atmospheric picture-book on the town and people of Luxembourg. The commentaries and captions are provided in German, English and French.

36  **Belgium and Luxembourg in pictures.**
E. W. Egan.   New York: Sterlin, 1970. 64p. (Visual Geography Series).

Describes in a popular and interesting way the histories, peoples, governments and economies of these two relatively small European countries which form a wedge between the larger countries of France and Germany. The territory of Belgium is roughly the size of the state of Maryland, whereas Luxembourg covers an area the size of the English county of Derbyshire or of the American state of Rhode Island. Each page is illustrated by one or more splendid photographs.

37  **Luxembourg.**
Emilie U. Lepthien.   Chicago: Children's Press, 1989. 126p.

This delightful album is part of the series, 'Enchantment of the World', which addresses children all over the world. It is a well-illustrated and concise introduction to the land and people of Luxembourg.

38  **Luxemburgo Sevilla '92 Souvenirs.** (Luxembourg Seville '92 Souvenirs.)
Luxembourg: Editions Guy Binsfeld, 1992. 87p.

This souvenir book of the seventh universal exhibition of Seville, from April to October 1992, includes numerous colour photographs of the Luxembourg pavilion and of all the important people that visited it. It also contains pictures of the whole area (215 hectares) of alluvial land on which 110 countries invited people to discover their pavilions. Among these illustrations, the reader will also find contributions in three languages (French-English-Spanish) which review the day of the Grand Duchy in Seville (13 May 1992) and the atmosphere at this international fair, as well as reports of cultural life in Luxembourg and the composition of the Luxembourg pavilion.

39  **Luxembourg capitale à la Belle Epoque.** (Luxembourg city during the *belle époque*.)
Victor Eischen, Henri Kugener.   Luxembourg: Imprimerie Saint-Paul, 1988. 244p.

This luxurious publication is full of picture-postcard views of the heart of the city as well as some of the suburbs of the town such as Grund, Clausen, Pfaffenthal or the district of Limpertsberg. The overall photographic review is interesting for the Luxembourger, who wants to discover the alterations that have been made since the beginning of the century, as well as for the large number of visitors to the capital of the Grand Duchy.

40  **Luxembourg capitale.** (The capital of Luxembourg.)
    Alain Soldeville, Michel Raus.   Luxembourg: Imprimerie Saint-Paul,
    1990. 125p.

This picture album includes approximately 100 colour photographs of the many
different aspects that characterize Luxembourg city, the capital of the Grand Duchy.
Apart from a short introduction which runs in three parallel languages (German,
French and English), the publication does not include any other written text.

41  **Luxembourg City.**
    Photography by Imedia, Vic Fischbach, Jacques Nicolay, text by
    Josiane Kartheiser.   Luxembourg: Editions Guy Binsfeld, 1994. 134p.

Luxembourg, with its more than a thousand years of history, is a capital which has
much to offer its visitors. It is therefore not surprising that the main part of this picture
album concerns tourism. However, other aspects which contribute to the variety of the
city are also depicted in colour photographs, together with short commentaries: the
role of foreign immigrants and the leisure and recreation opportunities, for example. A
final section adds a brief, historical survey of the city of Luxembourg.

42  **Bettembourg à la Belle Epoque.** (Bettembourg during the *belle
    époque.*)
    Victor Eischen, Henri Dondelinger.   Luxembourg: Imprimerie
    Saint-Paul, 1992. 98p.

This album retraces the history of the town of Bettembourg (15 km south of
Luxembourg). Apart from short notes on the numerous photographs, an alphabetical
list of the inhabitants of Bettembourg in 1905-06 is the only written text of this book.

43  **Differdange.**
    Esch-sur-Alzette, Luxembourg: Imprimerie Kremer-Müller, 1982. 124p.

This multilingual picture-book was issued for the seventy-fifth anniversary of the town
of Differdange (1907-82). It presents the town and southern municipality in both past
and present times and deals mainly with the iron-mining industry, which greatly
contributed to the development of the town. Culture, sport and the environment are
further important aspects dealt with in this album.

44  **Differdange à la Belle Epoque.** (Differdange during the *belle époque.*)
    Victor Eischen, Erny Hilgert.   Luxembourg: Imprimerie Saint-Paul,
    1984. 110p.

Differdange is one of the iron-mining towns of Luxembourg that contributed to the
development and prosperity of the Grand Duchy during the 20th century. This picture
album, which is full of postcards, attempts to render the atmosphere of that town in
the early 1900s.

45   **Differdange 1914-1939.**
Victor Eischen, Erny Hilgert.   Luxembourg: Imprimerie Saint-Paul,
1991. 122p.
This beautiful multilingual photograph album of the southern iron-mining town of
Differdange illustrates the streets and life of this municipality from the beginning of
the First World War to the beginning of the Second World War.

46   **Fotografesch.** (Esch in photographs.)
Text by Jeannot Clement.   Virton, Belgium: Imprimerie Michel Frères,
1995. 227p.
This book on Esch (Esch-sur-Alzette), the second biggest town in Luxembourg,
includes short trilingual (French, German and English) summaries on the town, its
history and its development, alongside numerous black-and-white photographs.

47   **Jeux de Lumières – Lichtspiele Ösling.** (Light effects Oesling.)
Raymond Clement.   Luxembourg: Editions Guy Binsfeld, 1994. 209p.
Comprises wonderful colour photographs of the countryside in the northern part of the
country: the Oesling, a region located between the French and Belgian Ardennes and
the German Eifel. The illustrations are sometimes annotated with alternating brief
French-, German- and English-language commentaries.

48   **Cliärwer Bilderbouch.** (Picture-book of Clervaux.)
Luxembourg: Imprimerie Print-Service, 1981. 237p.
For the 125th anniversary of the Clervaux brass band, this commemorative picture
album presents numerous black-and-white photographs of the municipality. These
pictures illustrate Clervaux as it was a century ago and bear testimony to the rich
cultural life of the region.

# Geography

## General

49 **Le Luxembourg: un espace ouvert de l'Europe rhénane.**
(Luxembourg: an open land in Rhenish Europe.)
Jean-Marie Gehring. *Mosella* (Metz), vol. 7, nos. 1-2 (Jan.-June
1977), p. 1-135. maps.
Gehring sees Luxembourg as a small state without borders, which forms part of a
larger European and international economy. Luxembourg was formerly known only as
a centre of an iron and steel industry, but it has succeeded in becoming a meeting
place for many European nations and an important tourist centre.

50 **Pays-Bas Belgique Luxembourg.** (Netherlands Belgium Luxembourg.)
Jean-Claude Boyer. Paris: Masson, 1994. 255p.
In order to provide reliable information on the Benelux countries and to avoid the
usual clichés, Jean-Claude Boyer examines the origins of these small countries and
emphasizes their sociocultural specificity. He sees the Benelux organization as a test-
case which was established before any of the European Community institutions and
which is still in existence despite the absence of any supranational power and its
rather minor impact on the daily lives of its member citizens. The fourth part of the
book, concerning Luxembourg, begins with a short, historical survey of the country,
then reviews its international role and economy before analysing some of its regions
in greater detail.

51 **Benelux: an economic geography of Belgium, the Netherlands and
Luxembourg.**
Raymond Charles Riley, Gregory John Ashworth. London: Chatto &
Windus, 1975. 256p. maps. bibliog.
Represents a good attempt to trace the evolution of the economies of the three
Benelux countries. Sections are devoted to social geography, agriculture, energy
production, manufacturing, tourism, banking, finance, transport, the activities of the

major ports and international trade. By virtue of its systematic treatment, the work is of value to all those interested in the economic geography of advanced countries.

52 **Probleme von Grenzregionen: das Beispiel Saar-Lor-Lux Raum. Beiträge zum Forschungsschwerpunkt der Philosophischen Fakultät der Universität des Saarlandes.** (Problems of bordering areas: the example of the Saar-Lor-Lux area. Contributions to the focal research work of the Faculty of Philosophy of the Saarland University.) Wolfgang Brücher, Peter Robert Franke. Saarbrücken, FRG: Saarbrücker Druckerei, 1987. 144p.

The Saar-Lor-Lux area, where the borders of three countries (Luxembourg, France and Germany) meet, has, for a millennium, experienced influences from both the east and west. The University of Saarbrücken deemed research into the problems of this border region, in both the past and present, and the formulation of well-founded future planning, important enough for them to organize lectures on the subject. This publication, which results from those lectures, includes information on the area's problems.

53 **Climatologie du Grand-Duché de Luxembourg.** (Climatology of the Grand Duchy of Luxembourg.) Robert Faber. Luxembourg: Musée d'Histoire Naturelle, Société des Naturalistes Luxembourgeois, 1971. 48p. maps.

Provides diagrams and charts showing the average and extreme positions of main meteorological factors for periods of twenty, thirty and sixty years, including the new 'normal period' (1931-60) proposed by the World Meteorological Organisation. Faber has drawn on the forty most reliable stations to produce his scale of climatological values. Two German (Trier and Schneifelforsthaus), and one Luxembourg station (Clemency) are used as reference locations.

54 **Temps et climat au Grand-Duché de Luxembourg.** (Weather and climate in the Grand Duchy of Luxembourg.) Eugène Lahr. Luxembourg: Ministère de l'Agriculture, Administration des Services Agricoles, Service Météorologique et Hydrographique, 1964. 289p. maps.

Synthesizes all meteorological observations from 1838 to 1960 and attempts to show how average weather patterns develop in the country. The text is accompanied by fifty tables and thirty figures.

# Regional

55 **Bref aperçu de la Ville de Luxembourg.** (A brief survey of the city of
   Luxembourg.)
   Service Information et Presse du Gouvernement.   Luxembourg:
   Imprimerie Centrale, 1993. 64p.

After a short, historical summary of the city and fortress of Luxembourg, this useful
brochure presents, together with short notes, photographs of the capital's most
significant buildings, such as the Notre Dame cathedral, the town hall, the national
museum and the European buildings at Kirchberg.

56 **Ebauche d'une étude historico-culturelle de la Vallée de la Pétrusse
   à Luxembourg.** (Rough draft of a historical-cultural study of the
   Petrusse valley in Luxembourg.)
   Gaston Zangerlé.   MA thesis, Université de Sciences Humaines,
   Strasbourg, France, 1981. 142p.

In his ethnological thesis, the author aims to provide the reader with an introductory
insight into the cultural richness of the 2.3 km-long Petrusse valley that passes along
the fortress remains of Luxembourg city.

57 **Liewen am Eisleck, la vie des hommes dans la région ardennaise.**
   (Life in the Oesling. The lives of people in the Ardennes region.)
   Ministère d'Etat, Ministère des Affaires Culturelles, Centre national de
   l'audiovisuel.   Luxembourg: Imprimerie Centrale, 1989.

This commemorative volume, issued during 1989, Luxembourg's 150th year of
independence, allows the reader a reliable and original insight into life in the northern
part of the Grand Duchy. The publication is characterized by the authenticity of the
interview extracts it reproduces and it aims to afford the reader a better understanding
of the living conditions of people from the Oesling.

58 **Een Döerf geeschter, haut ... a moër? D'Entwécklung vun eisen
   Deerfer unhand vun enger Kuurzbeschreiwung.** (A village.
   Yesterday, today ... and tomorrow? The development of our villages
   through a short description.)
   Marco Schank.   Esch-Sauer, Luxembourg: Op der Lay, 1992. 103p.

Schank describes the development of Luxembourg villages by making a case-study of
his home village, Eschdorf, in the Oesling (35 km north of Luxembourg). With the
help of historical chronicles, newspaper articles, recent studies, personal statements,
but above all black-and-white photographs, the author evokes the atmosphere of
Luxembourg villages. He also raises the problem of the spoliation of the country's
rural landscapes and asks for structural village development programmes.

59   **Lac de la Haute-Sûre. Stausee an der Ober-Sauer.** (Lake of the
     Upper Sûre.)
     Luxembourg: Imprimerie Saint-Paul, 1981. 218p.

Today the Upper-Sûre district is one of the best-known regions of Luxembourg. It is
now a popular holiday resort, which has been regularly attracting visitors from all over
Europe since the construction of the Esch/Sûre barrage (1955-59) was completed.
However, popularity as a tourist destination has not always been the case for a region
that was profoundly damaged by the Battle of the Bulge in 1944/45. This booklet does
not claim to represent an exhaustive study of the region. Instead, it simply illustrates,
in four languages (German, French, Dutch and English), the manifold features and
aspects of the district, thereby encouraging a deeper understanding of the Upper Sûre.

60   **Clervaux et son abbaye.** (Clervaux and its abbey.)
     Clervaux, Luxembourg: Editions Abbaye St-Maurice et St-Maur, 1930.
     76p.

Neither a tourist guide nor a history book, this volume simply presents a concise
portrait of the northern town of Clervaux and its region, which touches on the place's
history and also briefly describes its most interesting monuments. It is illustrated with
eighty contemporary photo engravings.

61   **La Moselle: son passé, son avenir.** (The Moselle: its past and future.)
     Edited by Martin Gerges.   Luxembourg: Imprimerie Bourg-Bourger,
     1958. 340p.

This book was published on the occasion of the 1958 wine festival in the small
Moselle village of Schwebsingen. Along with comments from Luxembourgers, this
book contains contributions from well-known French and German personalities who
have added their points of view on the cultural and economic role of the Moselle. The
articles range from studies of prehistoric settlements in the Moselle to the problems of
canalization, the fauna of the valley, the representation of vine and grape in national
art, Moselle gastronomy, legends, linguistics, paintings, fishing, hiking, vineyards,
bridges and navigation.

62   **La Mosella: édition, introduction et commentaire.** (*Mosella*:
     an edition, introduction and commentary.)
     Decimus Magnus Ausonius, edited and introduced by Charles Marie
     Ternes.   Paris: Presses Universitaires de France, 1972. 100p. map.
     bibliog. (Erasme: Collection de Textes Latins Commentés, 28).

Ausonius, the author of the *Mosella*, was probably born in Bordeaux in 310 AD. In the
summer of 369 the Roman Emperor Valentinian took Ausonius, the preceptor of
Gratianus and a learned rhetorician, with him on his campaign against the Alemannish
tribes beyond the Rhine. In order to relate this project to the Romans, Ausonius wrote
his *Mosella*, which is largely a work of Roman imperial propaganda. Although
Ausonius mostly celebrates the German banks of the River Moselle, Luxembourgers
take pride in this early Roman testimony to the paradise-like beauties of their national
river.

63  **Kleinräumige Versorgungsbeziehungen und zentrale Orte unterster Stufe an der Luxemburger Mosel.** (Small area supply relations and central places of the lowest level in the Luxembourg Moselle.)
Guy Schmit.  Cologne, FRG: MVR-Druck, 1984. 183p.

After determining the limits of the area in question (the eastern Moselle region of Luxembourg) and describing its geographical and socio-ecological structures, Schmit attempts to analyse, in highly technical language, the relations of supply that come into existence through demands for goods and services in this eastern part of the Grand Duchy.

64  **Muselchronik 1966-1991.** (Chronicle of the Moselle 1966-91.)
Stadtbredimus, Luxembourg: Vinsmoselle, 1992. 239p. bibliog.

This chronicle is in fact a geographical work on the eastern Moselle region which deals with its people and their way of life, its small market towns (bourgs) and straggling villages (bourgades), its wine and its climate. Numerous colourful photographs, as well as twenty-five drawings by A. Houtsch, illustrate a text which describes twenty-five villages situated along the Moselle River.

65  **Echternach: Geschichte einer Stadt.** (Echternach: the history of a town.)
Paul Spang.  Esch-sur-Alzette, Luxembourg: Editpress, 1983. 125p.

Full of illustrations, this luxurious publication introduces the history of the city and abbey of Echternach.

66  **Liewen am Minett, la vie des hommes dans la région du Bassier Minier.** (Life in the 'Minett' [mining region]: the lives of people in the Mining Basin.)
Ministère des Affaires Culturelles.  Luxembourg: Imprimerie Beffort, 1986.

Describing the lives and activities of the men and women of the Luxembourg iron-mining region, this picture album illustrates their environment, their houses and villages and their everyday life. The photographs are published together with written statements from hundreds of people, recorded over several years. This book is a realistic survey of a region which made a major contribution to the industrial development of the country.

67  **Liewen an der Gemeng Käerjhéng.** (Life in the municipality of Käerjhéng.)
Bascharage, FRG: Administration communale, 1993. 149p. + 2 audio cassettes.

Published at the same time as a photography exhibition on Käerjhéng, the first section of the volume consists of a description, in Luxembourgish, of everyday life in each of the three villages of the municipality (Hautcharage, Bascharage and Linger), while the second part contains photographs. German and French summaries of the text, in two parallel columns, conclude the work.

68   **Villages autour du Titelberg. Rodange – Lamadeleine – Fond-de-Gras.** (Villages around the Titelberg. Rodange – Lamadeleine – Fond-de-Gras.)
     Norbert Damé, Jean-Michel Klopp.   Luxembourg: Imprimerie Saint-Paul, 1980.

The authors draw a vivid portrait of the three villages around the Titelberg, a southern region of the Grand Duchy. Mostly a black-and-white picture album, the publication is interlarded with short comments, and a few longer descriptions of this mining region.


# Maps and atlases

69   **Atlas du Luxembourg.** (Atlas of Luxembourg.)
     Ministère de l'Education Nationale.   Luxembourg: Imprimerie Saint-Paul, 1971- .

This atlas has been published in instalments, the first one appearing in 1971. The individual maps reflect changes and developments in Luxembourg since the Second World War. This is the first scientifically and statistically accurate geographic survey of Luxembourg. It has been produced by a Luxembourg team of experts in collaboration with the Institute of Geography from the University of Nottingham, under the direction of K. C. Edwards. The publication is organized in six sections as follows: historic surveys; territorial conditions; administrative divisions; demographic aspects; economic activities; and social services. Each map is accompanied by annotations and source references.

70   **Luxemburg in Karte und Luftbild. Le Luxembourg en cartes et photos aériennes.** (Luxembourg maps and aerial photographs.)
     Guy Schmit, Bernd Wiese.   Luxembourg: Editions Guy Schmit und Bernd Wiese, 1981. 168p.

Clearly illustrated with scientific precision, this atlas conveys detailed insights into the geographical, geological and historical phenomena and connections of the Grand Duchy. First-rate photographs and maps make this volume a popular working tool and interesting collector's object.

71   **Carte du Cabinet des Pays-Bas autrichiens levée à l'initiative du comte de Ferraris: Grand-Duché de Luxembourg.** (Map of the Chancery of the Austrian Netherlands drawn on the initiative of the Count of Ferraris: Grand Duchy of Luxembourg.)
     Joseph de Ferraris.   Brussels: Pro Civitate, 1970. 3 vols. (Collection 'Histoire'. Série in 4°. No. 4).

Based partly on an earlier map drawn by Charles de Lorraine, Governor General of the Austrian Netherlands in Brussels, this is the first topographical map of Belgium. It was drawn during the years 1771-78 and this present edition includes the 'Historical, chronological and economic memoirs', and a few pages of historical, geographic, economic, social and military commentary. The map traces the administrative and judicial divisions, and indicates such features as: gallows, forests, heaths, toponyms, battlefields, parish churches, residential areas, rivers, roads and lanes, vegetation and cultures, ores and industries.

72 **Les cartes géographiques du duché de Luxembourg éditées au XVIe, XVIIe et XVIIIe siècles: catalogue descriptif et illustré.** (The geographical maps of the duchy of Luxembourg published in the 16th, 17th and 18th centuries: descriptive and illustrated catalogue.)
Emile van der Vekene.    Luxembourg: Imprimerie Saint-Paul, 1975. 301p. bibliog.

Emile van der Vekene presents very detailed and thorough descriptions of these historical maps, each of which is reproduced in the volume and accompanied by exact location references. Biographical indexes and secondary literature references are also included.

73 **Les plans de la ville et forteresse de Luxembourg édités de 1581 à 1867: catalogue descriptif et illustré.** (The plans of the town and fortress of Luxembourg, published from 1581 to 1867: descriptive and illustrated catalogue.)
Emile van der Vekene.    Luxembourg: Imprimerie Saint-Paul, 1976. 251p.

The town of Luxembourg's configuration changed many times throughout its history. This album comprises an inventory of the plans published up to 1867, the year in which the fortress was dismantled and Luxembourg became an open town. This well-documented work offers the collector and cartographer much information on a hundred different private collections. The author demonstrates that the fortress of Luxembourg was like any other before the second half of the 16th century, when the Spanish rulers started to develop their system of fortifications, an undertaking which was finally crowned by the efforts of the illustrious French military engineer, Vauban, in the late 17th century.

74 **Cosmographies: Théâtres du Monde & Atlas.** (Cosmographies: World Theatres & Atlases.)
Bibliothèque Nationale Luxembourg.    Luxembourg: Imprimerie Kremer-Müller, 1984. 261p.

This is a complete inventory of all the ancient atlases and topographical books treasured at the National Library. The 254 documents are often illustrated and have been compiled in this unique publication by Emile van der Vekene, curator of the Rare Collections Department of the National Library.

75   **Grand-Duché de Luxembourg: carte topographique et touristique,
     échelle 1:100,000.** (Grand Duchy of Luxembourg: topographical and
     tourist map, scale 1:100,000.)
     Luxembourg: Administration du Cadastre et de la Topographie, 1980.

Drawn in 1970 by the French National Geographic Institute with the help of the
Luxembourg Registry and Topographical Office, this official map of the country was
subsequently revised in 1980.

# Geology

76 **Beiträge zur Geologie von Luxemburg.** (Contributions to the geology
of Luxembourg.)
Michel Lucius.   Luxembourg: Luxemburger Landesaufnahmedienst,
1941. 330p. maps. (Veröffentlichungen des Luxemburger Geologischen
Landesaufnahmedienst, 3).

Deals with the development of the northern fringe of the Oesling in the Triassic
period, and also with the development of geological research in Luxembourg.

77 **Beiträge zur Geologie von Luxemburg.** (Contributions to the geology
of Luxembourg.)
Michel Lucius.   Luxembourg: Service Géologique de Luxembourg,
1955. 2nd rev. ed. 415p.

This volume includes both studies of the geology of Luxembourg and a bibliography
of publications. It deals with the development of Luxembourg's Mesozoic
sedimentation fields and their relationship to Hercynic construction elements and the
age of the Oesling peneplain.

78 **Die Geologie Luxemburgs in ihren Beziehungen zu den
benachbarten Gebieten.** (The geology of Luxembourg and its
relationship with neighbouring regions.)
Michel Lucius.   Luxembourg: Ministère des Travaux Publics, Service
de la Carte Géologique de Luxembourg, 1937. 176p. maps. bibliog.
(Publications du Service de la Carte Géologique de Luxembourg, 1).

Describes and analyses the carbon and lower strata of new red sandstone of the
Ardennes region.

79 **Coral reefs in the past, present and future.**
Edited by Bernard Lathuilière and Jörn Geister. Luxembourg: Service
Géologique, 1994. 272p. (Publications du Service Géologique du
Luxembourg).

Presents the published proceedings of the Second European Regional Meeting of the
International Society for Reef Studies held in Luxembourg at the Centre Universitaire,
6-8 September 1994. Coral reefs can be traced back through several hundred million
years of earth history: they are one of our present-day ecosystems, and very
susceptible to environmental stress. 370 million years ago, when Luxembourg was
inundated by the Early Devonian sea, beautiful coral communities flourished here. In
the Middle Jurassic epoch, some 170 million years ago, many of Europe's most highly
developed coral reefs thrived not far from the southern coastline of the former
Ardennes island, which is known today as the Rhenish Massif. At Rumelange, some
of these reefs are well preserved and reefs of the past can only be studied through the
reefs of the present. The Jurassic reefs of Luxembourg and Lorraine also allow
speculation about the 'reefs of the future'.

80 **Auf Fossiliensuche in Luxemburg, Entstehung und Beschreibung
einer bemerkenswerten Privatsammlung.** (Looking for fossils in
Luxembourg. The origin and description of a remarkable private
collection.)
Jean-Claude Streitz. Luxembourg: Imprimerie Saint-Paul, 1983. 191p.

This marvellous picture-book presents to the reader the most beautiful fossils
discovered in the southern part of Luxembourg. The photographs for this volume are
taken from the collection of Etienne Streitz, the author's father. The publication is a
useful contribution to the scientific exploration of Luxembourg archaeology.

81 **Ardennes, Luxembourg.** (Ardennes, Luxembourg.)
Gérard Waterlot, Alphonse Beugnies, Jacques Bintz, Armand Hary,
Adolphe Muller. Paris: Masson, 1973. 206p. (Guides Géologiques
Régionaux).

This guide is devoted to the primary Ardennes, a fragment of the Hercynian chain, but
also to its Triassic and Jurassic borderline forming the northeast border of the Paris
basin. The first part concerns primary grounds, presents a general stratigraphic survey
and indicates thirteen itineraries. The second part deals with the Jurassic Ardennes
ground bordering the primary massif in the south and indicates three itineraries of
excursions. Part three describes the Devonian, Triassic and Jurassic grounds of
Luxembourg and also gives a series of geological itineraries. The final part presents
several photographic plates of fossils. There is no complete bibliography, but some
basic reference works are indicated.

82 **Livre à la mémoire du docteur Michel Lucius.** (A volume dedicated
to the memory of Doctor Michel Lucius.)
Jacques Bintz. Luxembourg: Ministère des Travaux Publics, Service
Géologique, 1964. 358p. maps. (Publications du Service Géologique de
Luxembourg, vol. 14).

Michel Lucius (died 1961) was Luxembourg's greatest geologist. He rendered his
country a great service through his geological charts and maps, and enjoyed an
international reputation. Fifteen national and international geological experts
contributed to this commemorative volume. The three contributions in English are the
following: J.-P. Bakker and Th. W. M. Levelt's 'Plantation theories and fossil
weathering types in Europe'; P. D. Jungerius's, 'The soils of eastern Nigeria'; and R. C.
Mitchell-Thome's, 'The sediments of the Cape Verde Archipelago'. A Luxembourg
contribution by Jacques Bintz deals with the geology and mining structure in the area of
the Vianden pump storage station, the Our River pumping station which uses a reservoir
in the hills above the valley to generate cheap off-peak electricity.

# Tourism and Travel

83 **Histoire sommaire du tourisme luxembourgeois.** (Summary survey of Luxembourg tourism.)
Roland Pinnel.   Luxembourg: Ministère d'Etat; Ministère des classes moyennes et du tourisme, 1989. 128p.

In 1989, on the occasion of the 150th anniversary of Luxembourg's independence, Roland Pinnel, the director of the Luxembourg City Tourist Office, published this well-documented study of the evolution of tourism in the country and town of Luxembourg. He articulates his didactic analysis in seven chapters ranging from the origins of this relatively modern phenomenon of social mobility to the later orientation towards a planned, economic tourism policy. In general, the author tackles his vast subject in a chronological way, but he simultaneously follows certain thematic developments from a social, economic or merely statistical point of view. Numerous photographs, posters and diagrams complete this pedagogical guidebook for the interested reader.

84 **Le tourisme au Grand-Duché de Luxembourg: Histoire, politique et publicité touristiques des origines à 1952.** (Tourism in the Grand Duchy of Luxembourg: tourist history, politics and publicity from the beginnings to 1952.)
Roland Lacaf.   Luxembourg: Université Internationale des Sciences Comparées, 1972. 330p. bibliog. (Etudes Economiques Luxembourgeoises).

This well-documented study is divided into four parts. Part I provides definitions and explains general concepts in tourism. Part II records the situation of tourism in Luxembourg before the First World War. Part III shows how, in the interwar years, tourism became a national industry. Part IV illustrates tourist activities during the years of occupation and reconstruction. The post-war reconstruction was completed in about 1952, the same year in which the International Institute for Scientific Research in Tourism was founded; from that year onwards official statistics are available on Luxembourg tourism. This study sets out to analyse what kind of tourist policy and publicity best suits Luxembourg.

85 **L'évolution du tourisme dans la région industrielle Saar-Lor-Lux: une nouvelle chance pour une région en crise?** (The tourist evolution in the Saar-Lor-Lux industrial region: a new chance for a region in crisis?)
Robert Steffes. Luxembourg: R. Steffes, 1995. 141p.

Since the 1970s, the industrial part of the Saar-Lor-Lux region has had to deal with the consequences of successive steel crises, while tourism, on the other hand, has experienced significant development over several decades. The archaeological sites, the religious architecture, the fortresses and the steel plants, for example, are all features the tourist manager of the region wants to highlight. In his final dissertation for his degree in teaching (Lycée Michel Rodange, Luxembourg), Robert Steffes set out to discover, amongst other things, whether tourism plays an important part in the region and whether it could be a real regional development factor.

86 **Come along to Luxembourg.**
L. E. Leipold. Minneapolis, Minnesota: Dewison, 1973. 182p.

This guidebook provides a useful initiation to Luxembourg, and deals with the country's history, geography and tourism.

87 **Small boat to Luxembourg.**
Roger Pilkington. London: Macmillan; New York: St. Martin's Press, 1967. 230p.

Making good use of tales and legends, Pilkington presents a personal account of Belgium, France and the Moselle River in Luxembourg from Schengen to Wasserbillig.

88 **Attic in Luxembourg.**
Beryl Miles. London: Murray, 1956. 263p.

A popular investigation into the farm and village life, as well as the social and political features of Luxembourg. Highly subjective, this tourist account weaves history and legend into a charming tableau.

89 **Itinéraire du Luxembourg germanique, ou voyage historique et pittoresque dans le Grand-Duché: nouvelle édition illustrée.**
(Itinerary through German Luxembourg, or historical and picturesque travel in the Grand Duchy: new illustrated edition.)
L'Evêque de la Basse-Mouturie. Luxembourg: Krippler-Müller, 1980. 500p. (Etudes Historiques, Culturelles et Littéraires du Grand-Duché de Luxembourg. Série A: Histoire Générale et Locale, No. 9).

Several years after the Belgian revolution of 1830, a self-appointed Belgian chevalier explored that part of the ancient duchy of Luxembourg which remained independent after the 1839 Treaty of London. He showed great archaeological and folkloristic curiosity, but his historical and etymological speculations are often mere fantasy. The book is introduced by the learned and witty essay which the historian, Jules Vannérus, wrote for the *Cahiers Luxembourgeois* in 1929. The forty sepia drawings of landscapes, buildings and archaeological finds which illustrate the book are said to have been produced by one of the author's sons, either Jules or Emile. Emile van der Vekene wrote the preface.

90 **Grand-Duché de Luxembourg: le Guide.** (The Grand Duchy of
Luxembourg: the Guide.)
Tournai, Belgium: Casterman, 1995. 239p.

This newly published guide, a coproduction of Casterman and the Imprimerie Saint-
Paul printing press, wholly meets the aspirations of the contemporary traveller who
wants to combine leisure time with sightseeing. It details the complete Luxembourg
cultural and tourist spectrum, providing, for example, brief portraits of famous people,
original aspects of Luxembourg history, and information on routes and biking trails,
monuments and addresses, etc. The various contributions are all written by specialists
and so this guide can claim a rare label of quality in both form and content.

91 **Le Grand-Duché de Luxembourg.** (The Grand Duchy of
Luxembourg.)
Peter Smets.    Tielt, Belgium: Lannoo, 1995. 192p.

Smets provides an instructive guide which lists, very clearly, the assets of the Grand
Duchy, region by region. A pertinent introduction which highlights the main villages,
castles and green belts is followed by practical information on automobile touring
routes and hiking and biking tracks.

92 **Luxemburg: Entdeckungsfahrten zu den Burgen, Schlössern,
Kirchen und Städten des Grossherzogtums.** (Luxembourg:
discovering the forts, castles, churches and cities of the Grand Duchy.)
Cologne, FRG: DuMont Buchverlag, 1983. 214p.

Well informed and splendidly illustrated, this volume is an arts guide to the cultural
and architectural heritage of Luxembourg. Numerous practical tips are included on
interesting places to see and routes.

93 **Grand Duchy of Luxembourg. Holiday Guide.**
Brussels: Guide Cosyn, 1983. 144p.

One of the oldest in English, this guide contains historical and technical accounts of
the fortress and feudal castles of Luxembourg, by Jemmy Koltz, the honorary director
of the City Tourist Office. Laid out in a somewhat old-fashioned style, the volume
includes numerous black-and-white photographs.

94 **Grand Duchy of Luxembourg. Tourist guide.**
Luxembourg: Editions Guy Binsfeld, 1994. 190p.

This useful tourist guide, which is also available in French, German and Dutch
editions, offers a wealth of comprehensive and up-to-date information on the Grand
Duchy of Luxembourg as an ideal destination for an excursion or holiday. Following
an alphabetical section, which provides practical general information about the
country and its inhabitants and its history, language, culture and art, the principal part
of the guide, with its colour illustrations and useful maps, details the most interesting
towns, villages and areas of countryside, region by region. Finally, an appendix
presents an abundance of addresses, telephone numbers and opening times for the
complete range of institutes and venues available to the foreign visitor.

95    **Luxembourg: deutsch-nederlands-français.** (Luxembourg: German-
      Dutch-French.)
      Luxembourg: Editions Guy Binsfeld, 1984. 160p.

Another tourist guide produced by the Luxembourg publisher, Guy Binsfeld, this
volume not only includes practical information, but also deals with some more
obscure aspects of the country, such as landscapes, monuments and churches. The
numerous photographs are interspersed with descriptions that run in three parallel
columns: German, Dutch and French.

96    **Belgium and Luxembourg.**
      John Tomes, maps and plans by John Flower.    London: A. & C.
      Black; New York: VW Norton, 1993. 8th ed. 449p. (Blue Guide).

Of the forty-four suggested routes in this volume, four concern the Grand Duchy of
Luxembourg. A short description and historical introduction to the country is followed
by details of the suggested tours, including information on splendid historic towns,
fine art collections and beautiful landscapes. Updated with a great deal of recent data
and containing town plans, this Blue Guide is indeed an indispensable travel
companion.

97    **We go to Belgium and Luxembourg.**
      Mary Dunn.   London: Harrap, 1952. 192p.

Describes a journey through Belgium and Luxembourg as seen through the eyes of the
author's young daughter, Jane, and her contemporary, Michael. They toured the two
countries in a motor car and visited all the principal towns. The volume provides a
vivid and enjoyable blend of information and entertainment.

98    **Belgium and Luxembourg.**
      Nina Nelson.   London; Sydney: Batsford, 1975. 194p. map.

An experienced travel-guide writer explores and celebrates Belgium, the Ruritanian
charm of Luxembourg city, and the places most worth visiting in the rest of the Grand
Duchy (p. 155-94). She sets the two countries in their rich historical and cultural
setting and includes a stimulating chapter on food and drink. Nelson presents a
delightfully unconventional, discriminating and highly perceptive introduction.

99    **Belgium and Luxembourg, 1978-1979.**
      Eugene Fodor.   London: Hodder & Stoughton; New York: D. McKay,
      1987. 275p. maps.

For Fodor's editors Luxembourg remains one of the last miniature countries of
romantic fiction. Alongside the mighty steel foundries and modern farms, they insist, a
mediaeval atmosphere permeates the town. This volume represents a typical
romanticized approach to the Luxembourg scene. Detailed and reliable information on
the sights and practical facilities is combined with quite a personal assessment of
hotels and restaurants.

100 **Anekdotische Reise durch Luxemburg.** (Anecdotal trip through
Luxembourg.)
Carlo Hemmer. Luxembourg: Imprimerie Joseph Beffort, 1981. 146p.

In eight chapters, Carlo Hemmer, founder of the renowned Luxembourg weekly,
*d'Letzebuerger Land* (The country of Luxembourg), offers the reader an interesting
and informative description of Luxembourg villages. He reports on their customs and
traditions and manages to present the reader with an authentic view of Luxembourg
local ways of life.

101 **L'Ardennes mystérieuse.** (The mysterious Ardennes.)
Paul de Saint-Hilaire. Brussels: Rossel, 1976. 191p. (Nouveaux
Guides de Belgique, 10).

Covers the extraordinary and unexpected, exotic and occult aspects of the Belgo-
Luxembourg Ardennes – the haunt of Knights Templars and druids, the land of
sleeping stones, gold-diggers, gods, heroes and political refugees.

102 **Das alte Luxemburg heute: Burgen-Schlösser-Kirchen-Friedhöfe-
Dörfer.** (The old Luxembourg today: castles-churches-cemeteries-
villages.)
Robert Krantz, Norbert Quintus. Fleurus, Belgium: Bietlot Frères,
1984. 271p.

The two authors present a well-illustrated, useful pocket guide which lists the
historically valuable monuments of the Middle Ages and the modern age. It selects the
key facts about Luxembourg's important building heritage rather than representing a
complete historical art guide.

103 **Taschenführer durch die Burgen und Schlösser in Luxemburg.**
(Pocket guide to the castles of Luxembourg.)
Roger Bour. Luxembourg: Imprimerie Saint-Paul, 1990. 3rd ed.
2 vols.

The first volume of this pocket guide deals with thirty of Luxembourg's most important
castles. Besides providing the location of the buildings and tips for the visitor, the
author offers a historical summary of each building. The second volume covers castles
which are perhaps less attractive to tourists, but which nevertheless played an important
part in Luxembourg's development. Also contained in the second volume are three
appendices: the first includes plans of the castles, most of which are actually dealt with
in the first volume; the second comprises sixty-two shields (escutcheons) and a short
foray through Luxembourg heraldry; while the third contains forty-nine sections from a
topographic map to help the reader find the castles more easily.

104 **Luxemburg: Burgen und Schlösser. Châteaux et châteaux-forts.
Burchten en kastelen.** (Luxembourg: castles and fortified castles.)
Evy Friedrich. Luxembourg: Editions Guy Binsfeld, 1984. 64p.

In this four-language (German, French, English and Dutch) publication, Friedrich
describes 100 castles, 30 of which are fortified, while providing supplementary
explanations on forts and defensive walls. The text is accompanied by numerous
colourful photographs.

105  **40 randonnées cyclistes. Radwanderwege.** (Forty cycling routes.)
Ministère du Tourisme, Ministère des Sports.   Stavelot, Belgium:
Chauveheid, 1995. 24p. 40 maps.

These forty cycling routes are presented in alphabetical order of the towns and
villages in which they begin. Descriptions of the main tours always include extra
suggestions so that the reader can choose from among 189 possibilities. The range of
routes allows for 111 of the 118 Luxembourg municipalities to be crossed and each
route is described in detail.

106  **Wandern in Luxemburg. 50 ausgewählte Wanderungen im
Grossherzogtum.** (Hiking in Luxembourg. Fifty selected hiking trails
in the Grand Duchy.)
Evy Friedrich.   Luxembourg: Editions Guy Binsfeld, 1983-84. 2 vols.

Within the two volumes of this useful guide are listed 100 hiking trails through
Luxembourg. Also provided are route plans and information about the sights along the
routes.

107  **Besinnlich-kritisches Luxemburger Wanderbuch.** (A thoughtful and
critical walking companion to Luxembourg.)
Carlo Hemmer.   Luxembourg: Imprimerie Bourg-Bourger, 1974.
224p.

Hemmer's meditative book contains a series of interesting cultural observations he
made while on numerous hiking or cycling tours around the country. A reliable
guidebook to many hidden natural and artistic treasures, it is enhanced by engravings,
woodcuts and drawings from the Romantic period. The photographs are by Marcel
Schroeder.

108  **Le petit futé. City guide Luxembourg 1995.** (The little smart
companion city guide Luxembourg 1995.)
Paul Mathieu, Daniel Mathieu.   Brussels: Neocity, 1995. 256p.

Provides up-to-date information on where to find specific publications on, for example,
the position of women in Luxembourg, or which of the city's bakeries are open on
Sundays. The 256 pages of this city guide include a wealth of useful information on
the capital as well as tips on walking routes and hotel-restaurants all over the country.

109  **A brief survey of the City of Luxembourg.**
Luxembourg: Government Information and Press Service, 1993. 64p.

The best English-language introduction to the city and fortress of Luxembourg, this
volume includes concise descriptions of all the architectural sights and historic
monuments, accompanied by superb illustrations and an essential bibliography.

110  **Luxembourg: la forteresse.** (Luxembourg: the fortress.)
Paul Rousseau.   Luxembourg: Editions Guy Binsfeld, 1984. 64p.

Rousseau's picture album provides a historical and architectural description of the
fortress of Luxembourg, capital of the Grand Duchy, in four languages (French,
German, English and Dutch).

111 **Stadt und Festung Luxemburg von A bis Z.** (City and fortress of
Luxembourg from A to Z.)
Roger Bour. Luxembourg: Imprimerie Saint-Paul, 1992. 293p.

In many parts of the city of Luxembourg, it can be seen that Luxembourg had been a
fortress for a long time. Roger Bour aims to guide both tourists and local people in the
direction of the city's monuments, buildings and fortified parts while providing them
with brief and practical information. His resulting reference book, which has been
newly edited and updated in the light of the latest historical knowledge, and which
contains 107 illustrations, plans and maps (all drawn by the author himself), easily
meets this target.

112 **"1000 ans en 100 minutes": un circuit culturel dans le temps et
dans l'espace, du Conseil de l'Europe.** ('1000 years in 100 minutes':
a cultural tour in time and space by the European Council.)
Edited by Service des Sites et Monuments Nationaux. Luxembourg:
Imprimerie Saint-Paul, 1995. 96p.

This useful guide includes a cultural tour of the historic city of Luxembourg, which
was registered in 1994 by UNESCO as a world heritage site. The sites described have
been chosen for their historical and architectural interest.

113 **Oesling. Les Ardennes luxembourgeoises.** (Oesling. The
Luxembourg Ardennes.)
Adrien Ries. Luxembourg: Editions Guy Binsfeld, 1984. 64p.

The Luxembourg Ardennes are 'the Oesling' for Luxembourgers, the north of the
Grand Duchy for geographers and the site of the Battle of the Bulge for historians.
Adrien Ries suggests three different tours (by car, by bicycle and on foot) through the
area, in four different languages (French, German, English and Dutch). The volume is
illustrated with many colour photographs of the region.

114 **Vianden. Cité médiévale.** (Vianden. Mediaeval city.)
Jean Milmeister. Luxembourg: Editions Guy Binsfeld, 1984. 64p.

This picture album gives the reader a good impression (in French, German, English
and Dutch) of the mediaeval city of Vianden. The great French poet, Victor Hugo,
used to visit Vianden in the 1860s, during his years of exile, to draw and to write
poetry. The house he used to stay in was turned into a museum in 1935.

115 **Le Sud du Grand Duché de Luxembourg.** (The south of the Grand
Duchy of Luxembourg.)
Esch-sur-Alzette, Luxembourg: Entente du Sud, 1994. 36p.

Since the discovery of iron ore in 1838, the southern region (Minette) of Luxembourg
has experienced a long period of growth. Including a brief inventory of the area's
attractions, this brochure mainly addresses the visitor to Luxembourg who is keen on
finding out information about a region that is not so obviously attractive to the tourist.

116   **Industriekultur in Esch: eine stadtgeschichtliche Wanderung durch die Luxemburger Minettmetropole.** (Industrial culture in Esch: a historical city walk through the Luxembourg mining metropolis.)
Denis Scuto.   Esch-sur-Alzette, Luxembourg: Imprimerie Polyprint, 1993. 115p.

Describes a 17-km walk which takes in 29 industrial sites in Esch-sur-Alzette. The guide contains a chronology of the urban history as well as a general overview of the industrial museums and monuments of the second town of the Grand Duchy.

117   **Luxemburgisches in Lothringen, Ardennen und Eifel. Ein kulturhistorischer Streifzug durch die Burgen und Schlösser altluxemburgischer Grenzlande.** (Luxembourg relics in the Lorraine, the Ardennes and the Eifel: exploring history and culture through the castles of the old-Luxembourg border area.)
Roger Bour.   Esch-sur-Alzette, Luxembourg: Editpress, 1986. 435p.

A useful and entertaining historical guide to this region, which includes maps drawn by the author.

118   **Landschaft ohne Grenzen Eifel-Ardennen: Geschichte, Kultur, Radtouren, Wanderungen.** (The Eifel-Ardennes: a landscape without frontiers: history, culture, cycle tours and hikes.)
Cologne, FRG: J. P. Bachem Verlag, 1993. 350p.

Thirty-seven authors from Luxembourg, Belgium and the Netherlands contributed to this volume which aims to promote the development of environmentally friendly tourism in this region, which stretches across parts of Luxembourg, Belgium, France and Germany. The topics covered include history, culture, nature conservation, religious life and agriculture, and the cycling and hiking tours have been designed to have a minimal impact on the region's environment. The French edition is entitled: *Entre schiste et genêt. Rencontre en Ardennes-Eifel* (Between shale and gorse. Meetings in the Ardennes and the Eifel).

# Flora and Fauna

119 **Biotopenkartierung der Agrarfläche Luxemburgs. Pilotstudie in 11 Gemeinden des Westens Luxemburg.** (The charting of biotopes in the agricultural area of Luxembourg. A pilot study in eleven western municipalities of Luxembourg.)
Marc Meyer, Fernand Schoos. Luxembourg: Musée d'histoire naturelle, Jeunes et environnement, 1983. 104p. 11 maps.

Provides the reader with fundamental information on the ecological structure of a part of Luxembourg's agricultural area. Such a study naturally includes new approaches to nature conservation whose influence, the authors believe, is still rather weak.

120 **Bibliographisches Handbuch der Luxemburger Ornithologie.** (Bibliographical handbook of Luxembourg ornithology.)
René Assa. Luxembourg: Selbstverlag des Verfassers, 1980-81. 2 vols.

Lists articles concerning ornithology in Luxembourg. The works are arranged by three different methods: chronological, alphabetical, and, most usefully, according to scientific classification.

121 **Synopsis der Avifauna Luxemburgs.** (Synopsis of Luxembourg birds.)
René Assa. Luxembourg: Selbstverlag des Verfassers, 1978. 108p.

The main part of this work updates the ongoing species list of Luxembourg birds while the appendix includes details of two research projects, one undertaken in a nature reserve in the Biver municipality and the other in the wider region.

122 **Atlas der Brutvögel Luxemburgs.** (Atlas of breeding birds in
Luxembourg.)
Lëtzebuerger Natur-a Vulleschutzliga a.s.b.l. Esch-sur-Alzette,
Luxembourg: Imprimerie Kremer-Müller, 1987. 336p.

Published by the voluntary Luxembourg Nature and Birds' Protection League, this
atlas represents the most comprehensive recent work on the subject of breeding birds.
The authors spent about six years sifting through all the data to produce the maps and
texts in the book. Moreover, they included in this trilingual (French, German and
English) atlas as much additional information as possible on such local phenomena as
breeding biology, phenology, migration, ringing and population density.

123 **Vögel Luxemburgs: Bilderatlas der heimischen Vogelwelt.** (The
birds of Luxembourg: a picture atlas of native birds.)
Luxemburger Landesverband für Vogelkunde und Vogelschutz.
Bern, Switzerland: Hallwag, 1979. 5th ed. 89p. bibliog.

Aimed at both schoolchildren and the general reader, this well-illustrated guidebook
set out to familiarize the reader with the most current varieties of birds and their
natural habitats. A list of Luxembourg's breeding birds, advice on how to feed and
protect birds and an index of German, French, Latin and Luxembourgish names make
this volume an indispensable handbook for every amateur ornithologist and ecologist.

124 **Die häufigsten Vögel, Fledermäuse, Amphibien Luxemburgs.** (The
most common birds, bats and amphibians of Luxembourg.)
Ligue Luxembourgeoise pour l'Etude et la Protection des Oiseaux.
Luxembourg: Usborne Publishing Limited, 1982. 96p.

The aim behind this colour pocket guide is, above all, to promote a better knowledge
of Luxembourg's birds. More than 200 bird illustrations are compiled together with
short notes which include each bird's exact name, size and typology.

125 **Arbres remarquables du Grand-Duché de Luxembourg.**
(Remarkable trees of the Grand Duchy of Luxembourg.)
Administration des Eaux et Forêts. Luxembourg: Imprimerie
Saint-Paul, 1981. 166p.

Luxembourg has an inestimable treasure of trees, avenues and parks. This colourful
brochure, which covers more than sixty types of tree, analyses them in detail.

# Prehistory and Archaeology

126 **Vor- und Frühgeschichte Luxemburgs.** (Luxembourg's prehistory
and early history.)
Gérard Thill. Luxembourg: Imprimerie Bourg-Bourger, 1977. 2nd ed.
118p. bibliog. (Manuel d'Histoire Luxembourgeoise en Quatre
Volumes à l'Usage des Classes de l'Enseignement Secondaire au
Grand-Duché de Luxembourg, Vol. 1).
Characterized by excellent layout, concise text and superb illustrations, this volume
describes Luxembourg's history prior to the foundation of Luxembourg by Sigefroi in
963 AD.

127 **Contributions à la préhistoire du Grand-Duché de Luxembourg.**
(Contributions to the prehistory of the Grand Duchy of Luxembourg.)
Marcel Lamesch. Luxembourg: Joseph Beffort, 1975. 98p. bibliog.
In this offprint the author provides a description of Palaeolithic quartzite tools found
throughout Luxembourg, and presents his latest prehistoric finds made on the plateau
of the Marscherwald. Fourteen photographic plates and many drawings produced by
the author illustrate these studies. This material was published originally in
*Publications de la Section Historique de l'Institut g.-d. de Luxembourg*, vol. 89
(1975), no. 127.

128 **Documents préhistoriques du territoire luxembourgeois: le milieu
naturel: l'homme et son oeuvre, Fasc. I.** (Papers on Luxembourg in
prehistoric times: the natural environment; man and his work, Part 1.)
Marcel Heuertz. Luxembourg: Musée d'Histoire Naturelle et Société
des Naturalistes Luxembourgeois, 1969. 295p.
The aim of this study is to present a first collation of artefacts from Luxembourg
territory and to stimulate further research. It analyses the geological and geographical
bases of Luxembourg's prehistory, and the ancient flora and fauna of the area. It also
presents Palaeolithic surface finds and the layers, strata and deposits of Oetrange,

Berdorf, Pétange and the valley of the River Ernz noire. Of the reproductions of surface collections, the most impressive artefacts are from Merscherwald and Titelberg.

129   **Vor- und frühgeschichtliche Burgwälle des Grossherzogtums Luxemburg.** (Castle mounds from the prehistory and early history of the Grand Duchy of Luxembourg.)
Reinhard Schindler, Karl-Heinz Koch.   Trier, FRG: Verlag Rheinisches Landesmuseum, 1977. 61p. maps. bibliog. (Trierer Grabungen und Forschungen, Vol. 13, 1).

The surveying of castle mounds, recorded in this volume, was undertaken in collaboration with the Luxembourg Land Registry Office and the State Museum from 1972-76. Scientifically precise descriptions and plans of about thirty-four different sites are accompanied by photographs by the authors and Marcel Schroeder.

130   **Répertoire archéologique du Grand-Duché de Luxembourg.**
(Archaeological catalogue of the Grand Duchy of Luxembourg.)
Charles Marie Ternes.   Brussels: Centre National de Recherches Archéologiques en Belgique, 1970. 2 vols. 6 maps. bibliog.

This catalogue is subdivided geographically and presents the objects found in each locality. Keyed to present-day Luxembourg territory, it covers the period from the Palaeolithic to the Merovingian epoch. It mentions 150,000 indexed objects and reproduces a series of drawings by Luxembourg's first great archaeologist, Alexandre Wiltheim.

131   **Itinéraires archéologiques à travers le Grand-Duché de Luxembourg, I: Mamer, Goeblange, Bill, Mersch, Steinsel.**
(Archaeological itineraries across the Grand Duchy of Luxembourg, I: Mamer, Goeblange, Bill, Mersch, Steinsel.)
Fernand Faber, Louis Schlim.   Luxembourg: Centre Alexandre-Wiltheim, 1977. 55p. maps. (Itinéraires Archéologiques à travers le Grand-Duché de Luxembourg).

This is the first volume of a series of small guides intended to familiarize the larger public with the most interesting sites and finds of Luxembourg's rich archaeological past. For each site, the reader is instructed on how to get there; how to locate the ruins; what there is to see at the site or in the museum; and how to learn more about what he has seen. The information is keyed to reference maps, and the text is in French and German.

132   **Itinéraires archéologiques à travers le Grand-Duché de Luxembourg, II: Diekirch, Ferschweiler.** (Archaeological itineraries through the Grand Duchy of Luxembourg, II: Diekirch, Ferschweiler.)
Fernand Faber, Jos Herr, Paul Jost.   Luxembourg: Centre Alexandre-Wiltheim, 1978. 80p. maps.

The second volume of this set of practical handbooks moves from Luxembourg city to Diekirch and then to the plateau of Ferschweiler by the German border and the River Sûre. It is a valuable pocket guide for the amateur, with the format being the same as for the first volume.

133 **Aux sources de l'archéologie luxembourgeoise, I.** (The sources of
Luxembourg archaeology, I.)
Charles Marie Ternes. Luxembourg: Centre Alexandre-Wiltheim,
1978. 145p. bibliog. (Série 'Documentation', Fasc. I).

Reprints twenty-three articles which appeared in the Luxembourg press in 1968 and
1969. The author wanted to draw wider public attention to archaeological papers
originating from the 16th century onwards, which form the basis of archaeological
investigation in Luxembourg. He summarizes the main points made by these
predecessors and reviews their theories in the light of present knowledge. This volume
is part of a general programme of scientific popularization launched by the
archaeological and historical study section of the Centre Alexandre-Wiltheim.

134 **Carte archéologique du Grand-Duché de Luxembourg.**
(Archaeological map of the Grand Duchy of Luxembourg.)
Musée d'Histoire et d'Art. Luxembourg: Marché aux Poissons,
1975- .

This series of maps includes the following sheets: Feuille 17: *Junglinster* by Nicolas
Folmer. 1975. 58p.; Feuille 18: *Betzdorf* by Nicolas Folmer and Johny Zimmer. 1974.
47p.; Feuille 26: *Mondorf-les-Bains* by Nicolas Folmer, Jeannot Metzler and Georges
Hess. 1977. 79p.; Feuille 27: *Remich* by Nicolas Folmer, Jeannot Metzler and Georges
Hess. 1977. 47p.; Feuille 30: *Remerschen* by Nicolas Folmer, Gérard Thill and
Georges Hess. 1979. 43p. Every map indicates place names, prehistoric sites, tumuli,
road systems, sanctuaries and monuments, and traces of the iron industry. The
accompanying text provides, in each case, technical and historical explanations about
the communes and areas covered by the particular map.

135 **Das Treverische Oppidum auf dem Titelberg: zur Kontinuität
zwischen der spätkeltischen und der frührömischen Zeit in
Nord-Gallien.** (The Treverian oppidum on the Titelberg: the
continuity between the Late Celtic and the Early Roman period in
Northern Gaul.)
Jeannot Metzler. Luxembourg: Musée national d'histoire et d'art,
1995. 368p. (Dossiers d'Archéologie du Musée d'Histoire et d'Art; 2).

This work was presented in June 1995 as a PhD thesis for the Faculty of Philosophy at
the Johann-Wolfgang Goethe University in Frankfurt, Germany. It describes and sets
in context the important archaeological findings on the Titelberg made by the author in
1985 and from earlier excavations. The Titelberg is situated near the village of
Lamdelaine in the southeastern area of Luxembourg, alongside the French border. It is
one of the most important archaeological sites in Luxembourg, famous for its Early
Roman metal finds and Late Celtic and Gallic ceramics and coins.

136 **Le Grand-Duché de Luxembourg à l'époque romaine.** (The Grand
Duchy during the Roman period.)
Charles Marie Ternes. Luxembourg: Centre Alexandre-Wiltheim,
1991. 302p.

By treating such different matters as the economic structures, cultural life, religion
and the Roman history of Luxembourg city, Ternes's main aim is to interest a larger

public in what happened in the area between the Rhine and the Meuse during Roman times. Moreover, he wants to promote cultural tourism in the country, on the part of both Luxembourg people and foreign visitors, by raising their interest in local sites, objects and monuments.

137 **Die Römer an Rhein und Mosel: Geschichte und Kultur.** (The Romans on the Rhine and the Moselle: history and culture.)
Charles Marie Ternes.    Stuttgart, FRG: Reclam, 1975. 351p.

This is a translation of the original French edition, whose title, *La vie quotidienne en Rhénanie romaine, Ier-IVe siècle* (Everyday life in the Roman Rhineland, 100 AD-400 AD) (Paris: Hachette, 1972. 339p.) describes the scope of this book more clearly. Ternes, a Luxembourg professor of Roman history and literature, relies on archaeology and philology to reconstruct the complex politics and economics of a region that was only superficially controlled by the Romans.

138 **Das römische Luxemburg.** (Roman Luxembourg.)
Charles Marie Ternes.    Küssnacht-Zürich, Switzerland: Raggi, 1973. 195p. maps.

The preface admits that the book's title is something of a contradiction, because during the Roman occupation Luxembourg belonged to the Civitas of the Trevires and to the province, Belgica. The name Luxembourg only originated in the 9th and 10th century. This book is based on the pioneering work of the founder of Luxembourg archaeology, Alexandre Wiltheim, *Luxemburgum Romanum*, which was written between 1630 and 1682 and left unfinished (about 1,000 pages). It was published only in 1842, by Auguste Neyen. Important chapters in Ternes's book explain the basic features of the pre-Roman settlement, the Roman roadwork, and Roman housing and farming, religious cults, burial and commerce. A final chapter deals with the *Mosella* song of the Gallo-Roman poet, Ausonius. This work is instructive not only for Luxembourg readers; it also shows the contribution of a small country to the archaeological research into Europe's common past.

139 **Pfarrer Georges Kayser. Auf den Spuren der Vergangenheit.** (Parson Georges Kayser. On the tracks of the past.)
Jacques Bonifas, Georges Kayser, G. Thill et al.    Luxembourg: Imprimerie Saint-Paul, 1989. 328p.

The Syndicat d'initiative of Nospelt (west of Luxembourg city) issued this fitting tribute to the priest, Georges Kayser, who died in 1988. He uncovered many archaeological finds in the Nospelt region and this publication includes his own manuscripts, a description of the excavation work he undertook together with his collaborator, Jacques Bonifas, and, finally, a compilation of the contributions about these finds that have already been published in various Luxembourg newspapers and periodicals.

140 **25 Jahre Raschpëtzer-Forschung.** (Twenty-five years of 'Raschpëtzer' research work.)
Nicolas Kohl, Georges Faber.    Walferdange, Luxembourg: Syndicat d'Initiative et de Tourisme, 1990. 383p.

In 1965, the first excavation work began at Raschpëtzer, an archaeological site near Walferdange (close to Luxembourg city). Twenty-one years later, the excavators dug up a 35m-deep shaft and discovered a sewerage system. It was the first time that, in addition to the numerous Gallo-Roman finds above ground, explorers had found an underground water pipe that was used by the Romans to pump spring water. This commemorative volume was published to celebrate twenty-five years since the beginning of this research work and it retraces the various stages which led up to the final breakthrough in 1986. The fourth and last part of this well-illustrated volume includes valuable contributions from many of the people who were involved in the project at the time.

# History

## General

141  **Histoire du Luxembourg.** (History of Luxembourg.)
Gilbert Trausch.   Paris: Hatier, 1992. 256p.

This brilliant historical survey is part of the series, 'Nations d'Europe' (directed by
Serge Berstein and Pierre Milza). It addresses both the general reader and the
university student who needs precise facts presented in the context of a long-term
European perspective. It concludes with an essay, entitled 'Le difficile art d'être petit'
(The difficult art of being small), which is insistent about the particular problems a
prosperous, small country has to face in the modern world.

142  **Histoire du Grand-Duché de Luxembourg.** (History of the Grand
Duchy of Luxembourg.)
Christian Calmes, Danielle Bossaert.   Luxembourg: Imprimerie Saint-
Paul, 1994. 549p.

How was it possible that a completely artificially-created state, moreover one which
was the poorest of the ten Belgian provinces, became a real political community, a
country possessing all the attributes of a nation and which even became one of the
founder members of the European Community? This is only one of the questions the
Luxembourg historians, Christian Calmes and Danielle Bossaert, attempt to answer by
analysing Luxembourg history from the Congress of Vienna (1815) to the present day.
They deal with the multiple forces that influenced this region throughout many
troublesome years and offer the reader a chronological presentation of the eventful
years from 1815 to 1950. The first part of the book explains the background to the
problems, while the second section attempts to summarize the facts in a vast synthesis.

143 **Le Luxembourg: émergence d'une Nation.** (Luxembourg: the rise of a Nation.)
Gilbert Trausch, with the collaboration of Guy May and Jean-Claude Muller, illustrations by Marcel Schroeder. Antwerp, Belgium: Fonds Mercator, 1989. 382p.

Published on the occasion of the 150th anniversary of Luxembourg's independence, this luxurious album is characterized by splendid iconography, magnificent full-page illustrations and masterly layout. This brilliant survey demonstrates the way in which the state of Luxembourg was slowly developing after the Congress of Vienna (1815) and how the vicissitudes of the 20th century melted this people into a nation.

144 **The making of a nation: from 1815 to the present day.**
Christian Calmes. Luxembourg: Imprimerie Saint-Paul, 1989. 527p.

The creation of Luxembourg was imposed from outside, at the Congress of Vienna in 1814/15. Calmes therefore analyses, in a chronological way, how this artificial structure was able to stand the test of time and become an independent country, despite successive European crises that endangered its existence. This volume, which is available in French, German and English editions, highlights the fact that the nascent Luxembourg did not experience any revolt and that the Luxembourg people did not consciously cooperate in the setting-up of this state.

145 **Du particularisme à la nation: Vom Sonderbewusstsein zur Nation.**
(From the awareness of a particular identity to the nation.)
Gilbert Trausch. Luxembourg: Imprimerie Saint-Paul, 1988. 436p.

This collection of studies in three languages (French, German and English) deals with some of the main historical problems of the European microcosm, Luxembourg. These contributions, originally published individually abroad, begin with the period of the end of the *ancien régime* (1788) and end with the Second World War. The first part of the research deals with the French Revolution (1789), the annexation to France (1795-1814) as well as with Belgian independence in 1830. These years, during which Luxembourg caught up with the modern world, are fundamental to its history. The second part of these studies begins with independence and partition in 1839 and ends at the Second World War. The volume shows how the independence of Luxembourg was at first so fragile that it was jeopardized every time Europe experienced another crisis.

146 **De l'état à la nation 1839-1989. 150 joer onofhängeg. Catalogue de l'exposition du 19 avril-20 août, prolongée jusqu'au 1er octobre 1989.** (From the state to the nation 1839-1989. 150 years of independence. Catalogue of the exhibition held from 19 April to 20 August, extended until 1 October 1989.)
Luxembourg: Imprimerie Saint-Paul, 1989. 223p.

The impressive exhibition which celebrated the 150 years of Luxembourg's existence was of course documented by a catalogue. Despite the fact that it includes a historical retrospective from prehistoric times to the present day, the aim of the publication was not to provide a complete survey of Luxembourg history. Rather, the organizers of the exhibition wanted to highlight the most important historical events that helped to build a Luxembourg nation. The five chronological chapters consist of various contributions from historians, economists and scholars. Full of illustrations and documents, this rich guide is available in French and German editions and deserves to be part of every Luxembourg home library.

147 **The Grand Duchy of Luxembourg. The Evolution of Nationhood.**
James Newcomer. Christnach, Luxembourg: Emile Borschette, 1995. 320p.

Dr. James Newcomer is Vice-Chancellor Emeritus of Texas Christian University, Fort Worth, Texas. He went to Luxembourg during the liberation of the Grand Duchy, in September 1944, as an officer of the Third American Army. Since then he has visited Luxembourg many times, enchanted as he was by the mentality of the population and the characteristics of the country and its history. In 1984 he published the first version of his book with the University Press of America. With the assistance of Dr. A. M. Pate, Honorary Consul of Luxembourg for Texas, New Mexico and Arizona, he founded the Pate-Newcomer Collection at his home university library. Today, this collection of well over 3,000 significant books on Luxembourg and Lëtzebuergesch (the Luxembourg language) are at the disposal of all interested people in a special room in the Library of the Texas Christian University. Newcomer's study of Luxembourg history, which is marked by a generous sympathy for Luxembourg people and an enlightened optimism for the country's future, is a homage of friendship and a testimonial to the solid foundation of the American-Luxembourg relationship.

148 **Le Luxembourg et l'étranger: présences et contacts. Luxemburg und das Ausland: Begegnungen und Beziehungen.** (Luxembourg's relations with foreign countries: meetings and contacts.)
Jean-Claude Muller, Frank Wilhelm. Luxembourg: SESAM, 1987. 279p.

This volume of essays was published to celebrate the seventy-fifth birthday of Professor Tony Bourg, who is known in Luxembourg for his research work on French writers who stayed in the Grand Duchy. The various contributions are mainly concerned with cultural, political, economic, social and religious exchanges and impressions, from the 16th century to the present. The last contribution summarizes Bourg's life and work in the form of a detailed bio-bibliography.

149 **Au fil de l'histoire.** (The currents of history.)
Albert Calmes, Christian Calmes. Luxembourg: Imprimerie Saint-Paul, 1968-77. 4 vols.

A collection of articles comprising four volumes. Volume I contains sixty-two articles in which Albert Calmes deals with major events of national history, ranging from the French siege in 1794 to the foundation of Luxembourg railways in 1858. He sketches the daily lives of Luxembourg's ancestors, illustrating their economic hardship and showing the different ways of life of all the countrymen who went abroad. He also deals with the Luxembourg generals in the Belgian army as well as the emigrants who went to the Congo, Indonesia or Guatemala. Volume II includes sixty-eight articles, published between 1949 and 1962, concerning 19th-century history. Many outstanding personalities and important economic or industrial features are discussed. Volume III, written jointly by Albert and his son, Christian, covers significant people and events from 19th-century economic life. A special chapter in this volume is devoted to the link between history and literature and *De Renert* (The tale of the fox), by Michel

Rodange, the great animal epic poem which epitomizes the history and character of the Luxembourger. Volume IV, by Christian Calmes, deals with four main topics: the Eyschen-Servais controversy about the constitution of 1868; the school law of 1912; the mining law of 1913; and the peace efforts of Paul Eyschen.

150  **Im Banne der Grenzlandgeschichte.** (Under the spell of the border area history.)
     Edouard Molitor.   Luxembourg: Imprimerie Saint-Paul, Volume 1: 1981, 203p. Volume 2: 1983, 221p.

The whole of Luxembourg is in fact a border area, but the people living right on the borders with the three surrounding countries often had a more heightened experience of historical developments. Molitor describes the events people had to face in the small border villages in the canton of Grevenmacher (on the German border). His book is not a work of historical research, nor an autobiography, but rather an attempt to render something of the atmosphere which existed for the people living in these border areas, for example, during the Second World War.

151  **Tatsachen aus der Geschichte des Luxemburger Landes. Ikonographie: Antoine May, Marcel Schroeder, Nicolas Müller.** (Facts from the history of Luxembourg. Iconography: Antoine May, Marcel Schroeder, Nicolas Müller.)
     Pierre-Jean Müller.   Luxembourg: 'De Frendeskrees', 1968. 4th ed. 547p.

A fascinating chronological history of Luxembourg, containing a plethora of facts and comments. Coverage ends in December 1967, and the work includes an index of persons and places.

152  **Histoire du Grand-Duché de Luxembourg.** (History of the Grand Duchy of Luxembourg.)
     Paul Weber.   Brussels: Office de Publicité, 1961. 4th ed. 132p. map.

Aimed at the general reader, this volume provides a short-cut through Luxembourg's eventful history.

153  **History of the Grand Duchy of Luxembourg.**
     Arthur Herchen, Nicolas Margue, Joseph Meyers, translated by A. H. Cooper-Prichard.   Luxembourg: P. Linden, 1950. 299p. maps. bibliog.

A eulogistic survey of a small country's tumultuous history: 'this patient home-loving stalwart little nation, small by the extent of land it covers but whose place in history is wholly out of proportion, shining in movement, interesting in its infinite variety, and full of matter of reflections in the philosophy which always must be the background of historical study' (preface). The book contains a contribution by the translator, entitled 'Illustrations from contemporary history'. The work considers Luxembourg's role in the evolution of European civilization, especially in the context of the larger and more important countries which surround her.

154   **1.000 jähriges Luxemburg. Woher? – Wohin? Ein Beitrag zum besseren Verständnis der Geschichte des Luxemburger Landes.** (Millenary Luxembourg: whence and whereto? A contribution to a better comprehension of the history of the country of Luxembourg.) Jean Kill.   Luxembourg: COPE, 1963. 254p.

Presents a communist interpretation of the history of the country, similar to that expounded for many years by the Luxembourg Communist Party.

155   **Terre commune: histoire des pays de Benelux, microcosme de l'Europe.** (Common territory: history of the Benelux countries, a microcosm of Europe.) Henri Bernard.   Brussels: Brepols, 1961. 699p. maps. (Destin de l'Europe, 2).

Bernard sets out to show that, through common vicissitudes, the three Benelux countries (Belgium, the Netherlands and Luxembourg) are one; they prefigure the shape of a future united Europe as a confederation of sovereign states. The economic example is as striking as the political one: already Benelux represents the fourth economic power in the world.

156   **Kulturgeschichte des Luxemburger Landes.** (Cultural history of the country of Luxembourg.) Nicolas van Werveke.   Luxembourg: Soupert, 1923-26. 3 vols.

Represents a vast cultural survey of the most significant facts and features of Luxembourg's cultural past, which serves as a basic reference work. Volume 1 covers the period from prehistoric times to the days of serfs and witch-trials. Volume 2 is mainly devoted to the mediaeval past of the town of Luxembourg, with interesting essays on jurisdiction and the corporations of tradesmen and craftsmen. Volume 3 concludes with a study of towns and citizens, and then focuses on the church and clergy.

157   **Überlegungen zu einigen Aspekten der Geschichte Luxemburgs.** (Reflections on some aspects of Luxembourg history.) Pierre Hamer.   Luxembourg: Imprimerie Saint-Paul, 1986. 160p.

An unusual book which highlights and analyses particular aspects of Luxembourg's history, from the 18th century to the present. The coverage includes some little known events such as the student uprising of 1750. Hamer also makes some predictions regarding Luxembourg's future.

158   **Die geschichtlichen Verbindungen zwischen Luxemburg und Trier.** (The historical connections between Luxembourg and Trier.) J. P. Koltz.   Trier, FRG: Kreisverwaltung Trier-Saarburg, 1983. 81p.

In the yearbook of Trier-Saarburg, two German cities close to the Luxembourg border, J. P. Koltz published, between 1981 and 1983, three contributions on the historical connections between Luxembourg and Trier: from 963 up to 1815 (part I of the 1981 yearbook, p. 150-63); from 1815 up to the Second World War (part II of the 1982 yearbook, p. 311-41); and in recent history (part III of the 1983 yearbook, p. 340-67). The 1983 yearbook also includes an interview on the connections between Luxembourg and Trier with former prime minister, Pierre Werner.

159   **Le Grand-Duché de Luxembourg historique et pittoresque.** (The
      historical and picturesque Grand Duchy of Luxembourg.)
      Jean-Pierre Glaesener.   Esch-sur-Alzette, Luxembourg: Schortgen,
      1985. 454p.

J.-P. Glaesener, a doctor who lived in the 19th century, was also known for his local
historical research. However, this work considers the whole of Luxembourg. He took
his information from the publications of the 'Institut Royal Grand-Ducal' (called the
Institut Grand-Ducal today) which he then attempted to condense, in order to make it
accessible to the reader. Divided into three parts, it provides details on Luxembourg's
history (from prehistoric times up to the 19th century) as well as technical data on the
climate and geology. A description of the 'most interesting spots of the country'
concludes this highly personal survey.

160   **La formation territoriale du pays de Luxembourg depuis les
      origines jusqu'au milieu du XVe siècle. Exposition documentaire
      organisée par les Archives de l'Etat, septembre-octobre 1963;
      catalogue.** (The territorial formation of Luxembourg from its origins to
      the middle of the 15th century.)
      Joseph Goedert.   Luxembourg: Archives de l'Etat, 1963. 178p. map.

This is the official catalogue of a documentary exhibition organized by the
Luxembourg State Archives to mark the millennium of the capital and country of
Luxembourg. It comments on about 370 various documents which originate from
Merovingian times up to the period of the Burgundians. The different periods are
presented in a masterful and lively way by the curator of the State Archives.

161   **Le Luxembourg en Lotharingie. Luxemburg im lotharingischen
      Raum. Mélanges Paul Margue.** (Luxembourg in the Lotharingian era.
      Commemorative volume for Paul Margue.)
      Luxembourg: Imprimerie Saint-Paul, 1993. 775p.

For the seventieth birthday of Paul Margue, his friends published this commemorative
volume containing various essays such as 'The cycling race Nancy-Luxembourg in
1913' and 'The relations of Luxembourg with France and Germany' by Gilbert
Trausch, or '1940-1990: half a century of financial development in Luxembourg' by
Pierre Werner, as well as more than forty historical contributions on the Middle Ages.
The introduction is composed of a short biography of the historian alongside a
chronological bibliography of his publications.

# Middle Ages

162   **Luxembourg in the Middle Ages.**
      John Allyne Gade.   Leiden, Netherlands: Brill, 1951. 238p.

Engagingly written and well documented, this volume provides a general account of
Luxembourg's leading figures of the Middle Ages, from Roman times to the 15th century.

163 **Luxemburg in Mittelalter und Neuzeit, 10. bis 18. Jahrhundert.**
(Luxembourg in the Middle Ages and modern times, from the 10th to
the 18th century.)
Paul Margue.   Luxembourg: Editions Bourg-Bourger, 1974. 160p.
maps. bibliog. (Manuel d'Histoire Luxembourgeoise en Quatre
Volumes, à l'Usage des Classes de l'Enseignement Secondaire au
Grand-Duché de Luxembourg, Vol. 2).

This useful guide is divided into five chapters. Chapter I deals with Luxembourg in the
High Middle Ages (950-1247); chapter II analyses the social system during the feudal
period; chapter III begins with Ermesinde's successors and covers the late Middle
Ages (1247-1443); chapter IV follows Luxembourg into early modern times up to the
Treaty of the Pyrenees (1659); and finally, chapter V looks at Luxembourg in the
shadow of French imperialism (1659-1715). The volume provides concise information,
drawn from chronicles, documents, genealogical tables, maps, poets' and historians'
comments and impressions.

164 **Die Beziehungen des Hauses Luxemburg zu Frankreich in den
Jahren 1247-1346.** (The relationship of the House of Luxembourg
with France in the years 1247-1346.)
Carl D. Dietmar.   Cologne, FRG: Hundt Druck GmbH, 1983. 245p.

Henry VII was the first emperor of the House of Luxembourg who acceded to the
German throne in spite of his Romance background and education. Dietmar attempts
to analyse how far the House of Luxembourg, which was located at the periphery of
the empire, used its close connections with the French royal dynasty in order to
strengthen its own territorial and dynastic position.

165 **Luxembourg dans les grandes chroniques de France.** (Luxembourg
in the great chronicles of France.)
Joseph Petit.   Luxembourg: Imprimerie Saint-Paul, 1982. 255p.

This study takes a fresh perspective on the relations between France and Luxembourg,
an essential theme for anyone who wants to understand Luxembourg and its history.
Petit's fundamental analysis also makes the reader reflect on the very existence of
Luxembourg. How could it maintain or even reconstruct itself after certain crises?
What constitutes its basic identity? This analysis will inform the reader about Henry
VII, John the Blind and, above all, Charles IV, who is treated in greater detail.

166 **Les villes au pays de Luxembourg, 1196-1383.** (Towns in the country
of Luxembourg, 1196-1383.)
Camille-J. Joset.   Brussels: Vermaut; Louvain, Belgium: Bibliothèque
de l'Université, 1940. 235p. map. (Université de Louvain. Recueil de
Travaux d'Histoire et de Philologie. 3me série, 5me fasc.).

Examines the development of the small feudal country of Luxembourg into a
mediaeval principality. The different chapters deal with subjects including privileged
localities and various types of franchises. A rich bibliography and onomastic tables
are included.

167    **Ermesinde, 1196-1247, fondatrice du Pays de Luxembourg.**
       (Ermesinde, 1196-1247, founder of the country of Luxembourg.)
       Camille-J. Joset.    Arlon, Belgium: Les Amis de Clairefontaine, 1947.
       78p.
This small tome was published by a philosophy professor at the University of Namur
on the seventh centenary of Ermesinde's death. A popular legend says that Ermesinde
founded the abbey of Clairefontaine after seeing a vision of the Virgin among a flock
of white sheep. The seven chapters deal with various stages in Ermesinde's life, from
being a disinherited orphan to becoming a territorial princess.

168    **Ermesinde et l'affranchissement de la ville de Luxembourg. Etudes
       sur la femme, le pouvoir et la ville au XIIIe siècle.** (Ermesinde and
       the granting of the city of Luxembourg's charter. Studies on women,
       power and the city in the 13th century.)
       Michel Margue.    Luxembourg: Publications du CLUDEM, 1994. 327p.
In 1994 the city of Luxembourg celebrated the 750th anniversary of the granting of its
charter    by    Countess    Ermesinde.    To    mark    the    occasion    the    Luxembourg
Documentation and Mediaeval Studies Centre organized a series of lectures about
Ermesinde and her time which are published in this volume. The publication
highlights the role of women in politics in the 13th century and provides an overall
view of the city in the Middle Ages. Some maps and genealogical tables, a biography
of Ermesinde, an annotated new edition of the 'affranchisement' letter of 1244 as well
as studies concerning the seals of Luxembourg and Ermesinde are included. Together
with the wealth of previously unpublished documentary photographs reproduced in the
volume, all these documents throw new light on the evolution of the country of
Luxembourg in the late Middle Ages.

169    **Kaiser Heinrich VII: Dantes Kaiser.** (Emperor Henry VII: Dante's
       emperor.)
       Friedrich Schneider.    Hildesheim, FRG: Olms, 1973. Reprint of 1943
       ed. 300p. bibliog.
Examines the career and personality of Henry VII, Holy Roman Emperor, 1312-13
(originally Count of Luxembourg). He was oblivious to criticism and devoted his whole
life to the restoration of Holy Roman imperial power. Dante was much impressed by
Henry's characteristics and achievements, and this was reflected in his writings.

170    **Kaiser Heinrichs Romfahrt. Die Bilderchronik von Kaiser Heinrich
       VII und Kurfürst Balduin von Luxemburg, 1308-1313.** (Emperor
       Henry's journey to Rome. The pictorial chronicle of Emperor Henry
       VII and the Elector Baldwin of Luxembourg, 1308-13.)
       Franz-Joseph Heyen.    Boppard, FRG: Boldt, 1965. 156p.
In 1310 King Henry VII, also Count of Luxembourg, went to Italy with his brother
Baldwin, Archbishop of Trier, to restore imperial power in a land torn between the
Guelfs and the Ghibellines, city-state wars, and the interference of the French king,
the Pope and the King of Naples. In 1312 Henry was crowned emperor, but he died in
1313 near Siena. This marvellous pictorial chronicle, illustrating the journey's
account, originated in Trier in about 1340.

171  **Jean l'Aveugle, comte de Luxembourg, roi de Bohême.** (John the Blind, Count of Luxembourg, King of Bohemia.)
Raymond Cazelles.  Bourges, France: Tardy, 1947. 292p. bibliog.
John the Blind is without doubt the most popular figure in Luxembourg's history. He perished heroically at the battle of Crécy in 1346 when he helped Philip VI fight the English invader, Edward III. Cazelles finds that the Luxembourg people, for whom John died, are largely unaware of the details of his astonishing life, which are studied in this volume. In 1946 John's remains were solemnly brought back to Luxembourg, and interred in the crypt of the cathedral.

172  **Philip the Bold: the formation of the Burgundian state.**
Richard Vaughan.  London; New York: Longman, 1979. 278p. maps. bibliog.
A detailed survey of the emergence of a Burgundian state under Philip the Bold's leadership in the years 1384 to 1404, the crucial acquisition of Flanders and of the way in which Philip's government functioned. The Burgundian dukes became involved in the affairs of what is now Belgium and Luxembourg as a consequence of the marriage, in 1384, of Philip the Bold, grandfather of Philip the Good, to the heiress of the Count of Flanders who was the niece of Wenzel I of Luxembourg. Thus they acquired Flanders (1384), Namur (1429), Brabant, Limburg (1430), Hainault, Holland and Zealand (1433). Under the rule of Philip the Good, Luxembourg came under Burgundian dominion (1443), a situation which continued until the death of Philip the Fair in 1506.

173  **Kaiser Karl IV. Eine mediävale Kulturpotenz aus dem Hause Luxemburg.** (Emperor Charles IV: a powerful mediaeval cultural personality from the House of Luxembourg.)
Pierre Grégoire.  Luxembourg: Imprimerie Saint-Paul, 1984. 212p.
Grégoire analyses in great detail the life of Holy Roman Emperor Charles IV (1316-78), oldest son of King John from the House of Luxembourg and one of the most important rulers of the late Middle Ages. From 1346 to 1353 Charles IV was Count of Luxembourg, until he left the country to be ruled by his half brother, Wenceslaw I, in 1353.

174  **Carolus Quartus Romanorum Imperator et Boemie Rex.** (Charles IV, [Holy] Roman Emperor and King of Bohemia.)
Alexej Pludek.  Prague: Orbis Press Agency, 1978. 74p.
This is a marvellous, trilingual (English-German-French) picture-book which traces the life of Charles IV (1316-78).

175  **Kaiser Karl IV: Staatsmann und Mäzen.** (Emperor Charles IV: statesman and patron.)
Edited by Ferdinand Seibt.  Munich, FRG: Prestel, 1978. 496p. 21 maps. bibliog.
Published in connection with the exhibitions dedicated to Charles IV in Cologne and Nuremberg in 1978 and 1979, this is a glorious collection of fifty important contributions in words, pictures, tables, maps and charts. The contributions consider

several topics, including: the king and the emperor; the basic features of his European policy; Charles as ruler; the ruler and his court; and the emperor and art.

176 **Kaiser Karl IV: ein Kaiser in Europa, 1346-1378.** (Charles IV: an emperor in Europe, 1346-78.)
Ferdinand Seibt. Munich, FRG: Süddeutscher Verlag, 1978. 488p. 2 maps. bibliog.

Seibt sets out to give an overall picture of Charles IV, a representative of the House of Luxembourg, and Holy Roman Emperor during the 14th century. Charles' main idea was to replace the Holy Roman Empire with a German-Slavic empire centred in Bohemia, with Prague as capital. During his rule the House of Luxembourg extended from the North Sea and the mouth of the Schelde to the eastern Carpathians. The author sheds new light on the dynastic power policy and peace efforts of the emperor, who had great designs in Europe but shamefully neglected his native Luxembourg.

177 **Karl IV: Sein Leben und seine staatsmännische Leistung.** (Charles IV: the life and achievement of a great statesman.)
Jiří Spěváček. Prague: Academia; Vienna: Böhlau, 1978. 208p.

Spěváček examines the social forces, mediaeval institutions, ideological trends and events which formed Charles IV's personality, and shows how he manipulated events to his own ends. In addition, he traces the limits of Charles' social and ideological actions, and delineates his tragic shortcomings. Chapter III focuses on the situation in Luxembourg, but the book's overall perspective is European.

178 **Karl IV und die Kultur und Kunst seiner Zeit.** (Charles IV and the culture and art of his time.)
Karel Stejskal, photographs by Karel Neubert. Hanau, FRG: Dausien, 1978. 240p.

Considers Charles IV's many journeys through France, Germany, Italy, Luxembourg, Belgium, Austria, Hungary, and Lithuania, with particular reference to the great artists of the time: Mathias of Arras, Peter Parler, Master Theodoricus and Petrarca. Translated from the Czech, this album contains splendid colour reproductions.

179 **L'abbaye Saint-Willibrord d'Echternach au XIV siècle. Aspects économiques et sociaux.** (The Saint-Willibrord abbey of Echternach in the 14th century: economic and social aspects.)
Henri Trauffler. MA thesis, Université de Paris-Sorbonne (Paris IV), 1980-81. 122p.

Examines the political and socio-economic framework within which the Abbey of Echternach operated at this time and discusses, for example, its feudal rights, its development, its local importance, its relationship with the bourgeoisie and its structure.

180 **Recherches sur la noblesse du Duché de Luxembourg au XVe siècle.** (Investigations into the nobility of the Duchy of Luxembourg in the 15th century.)
Michel Margue. MA thesis, Université des Sciences Humaines, Strasbourg, France, 1981-82. 189p.

Over the last twenty-five years, although a lot has been written on the nobility of the neighbouring countries of Luxembourg, studies of the duchy of Luxembourg itself, which also belonged to the countries of ancient Lotharingia, are few. This is in fact the first attempt to inventorize and classify the duchy's noble families. Margue studied each of the thirty families under analysis according to geographical, economic, political and social criteria. Since this synthesis was undertaken to allow further analysis of the nobility group it therefore goes on to deal with some specific aspects of the nobility's inter-familial relations in the 15th century.

# 16th and 17th centuries

181 **Zeittafel zur Geschichte der Luxemburger Pfarreien von 1500-1800.** (Chronological tables on the history of Luxembourg parishes, 1500-1800.)
Arthur Schon. Esch-sur-Alzette, Luxembourg: Kremer-Müller, 1954-57. 5 vols.

Contains an informative introduction which is followed by chronological notes on local parish life in the old duchy of Luxembourg, based on the archives of the ancient provincial council and the public notary's record files of the pre-1789 period. The main emphasis is on the territory which now forms the Grand Duchy. This multi-volume work is a unique treasure-house of legal, constitutional, social and cultural history.

182 **Index des noms de lieux figurant dans les tables chronologiques d'Arthur Schon.** (Index of place names mentioned in the chronological tables of Arthur Schon.)
Antoine May. Luxembourg: Imprimerie Saint-Paul, 1962. 103p.
(Publications Nationales du Ministère des Arts et des Sciences).

Arthur Schon's *Zeittafel zur Geschichte der Luxemburger Pfarreien von 1500-1800* (see preceding entry) covers three centuries of national history. Unfortunately, the author died before completing the indexes, which are indispensable research tools for a work of this nature. May fills this gap by presenting an alphabetical table of the places mentioned in the *Zeittafel*. See also the following entry.

183   **Index des noms de personnes figurant dans les tables chronologiques d'Arthur Schon.** (Index of persons mentioned in the chronological tables of Arthur Schon.)
Antoine May.   Esch-sur-Alzette, Luxembourg: Imprimerie Coopérative Luxembourgeoise, 1977. 246p. (Publications Nationales du Ministère des Arts et des Sciences).

This volume is a personal name index to Schon's work, prepared by May to complement his place name index (see preceding entry). A subject index remains to be compiled in order to allow optimum use of Schon's chronological tables.

184   **La répression de la sorcellerie dans le Duché de Luxembourg aux 16 et 17ième siècles.** (The repression of witchcraft in the Duchy of Luxembourg in the 16th and 17th century.)
Marie-Sylvie Dupont-Bouchat.   PhD thesis, Université catholique, Louvain, Belgium, 1977. 306p.

Examines the problem of sorcery in the context of Western Christian civilization, with particular reference to the Duchy of Luxembourg of the 16th and 17th centuries. Moreover, the author attempts to explain why sorcery has always evoked such powerful feelings of fear and fascination.

185   **Vauban à Luxembourg, place forte de l'Europe (1684-1697).** (Vauban in Luxembourg, strong-hold of Europe [1684-97].)
Jacques Dollar.   Luxembourg: Imprimerie Centrale, 1983. 127p.

Vauban was one of the most reputed military engineers, who made Luxembourg into the 'Gibraltar of the north' after the city was taken by the troops of Louis XIV in 1684. In order to discover more about Vauban's personality, some of his writings are cited in this historical study by Jacques Dollar. The numerous photographs and drawings that Vauban produced after the capture of Luxembourg illustrate the military architecture of the 17th century.

186   **Logements militaires dans la Forteresse de Luxembourg (1639-1794). Epoques espagnole, française et autrichienne.** (Military lodgings in the fortress of Luxembourg [1639-1794]. Spanish, French and Austrian period.)
Alphonse Sprunck.   Luxembourg: Imprimerie Saint-Paul, 1977. 240p.

Sprunck attempts to describe the relations between the military authorities of the fortress and the civil authorities of the city and province. During that period, the 'bourgeois' were under the reign of foreign sovereigns that only considered the possession of Luxembourg important because of the strategic situation of its capital. The author also analyses the relations between those 'bourgeois' and the soldiers.

187   **Vom Schweden – bis zum 'Kloeppel'-Kriege.** (From the war of Sweden – to the war of bludgeons.)
Pierre Grégoire.   Luxembourg: Imprimerie Saint-Paul, 1982. 305p.

This book forms part of Grégoire's studies on the history of thought in Luxembourg. It retraces the country's vicissitudes under Spanish and Austrian rulers from 1600 to 1800.

# 18th century

188 **Le Luxembourg sous l'Ancien Régime: 17e, 18e siècles et début du
19e siècle.** (Luxembourg under the *ancien régime*: 17th, 18th and early
19th centuries.)
Gilbert Trausch.  Luxembourg: Imprimerie Bourg-Bourger, 1977.
176p. maps. bibliog. (Manuel d'Histoire Luxembourgeoise en Quatre
Volumes, à l'Usage des Classes de l'Enseignement Secondaire au
Grand-Duché de Luxembourg, Vol. 3).
Part I deals with the era of great reforms of 1750-1830, and the personalities and
events of the time, while part II analyses the *ancien régime* in all its significant
aspects. The author particularly emphasizes the importance of agricultural and mining
traditions, which helped make Luxembourg one of the major steel manufacturers of
the 20th century. The running commentary is interspersed with extracts from historical
texts and excellent illustrations.

189 **Etudes sur la vie économique et sociale dans le Luxembourg au 18e
siècle: les classes rurales.** (Studies on the economic and social life of
Luxembourg during the 18th century: the rural classes.)
Alphonse Sprunck.  Luxembourg: Editions du Centre, 1956-63.
2 vols.
Sprunck, the foremost historian of the 18th-century Duchy of Luxembourg, examines
the social and economic problems that preoccupied the states of the duchy in this
period. His analysis ranges far beyond the present territory of the Grand Duchy and
stresses the disastrous economic situation in Luxembourg after the Spanish War of
Succession, when, in 1714, Emperor Charles VI became Duke of Luxembourg. In the
second volume Sprunck investigates the life of the rural classes, but centres his
interest on the social problems at the time of Maria-Theresa and Joseph II.

190 **Du roi Charles II d'Espagne à l'empereur Charles VI: première
partie.** (From King Charles II of Spain to Emperor Charles VI: first
part.)
Alphonse Sprunck.  *Publications de la Section Historique de l'Institut
g.-d. de Luxembourg*, vol. 78 (1960), p. 1-344.
This study covers the period between the invasion of the Duchy by Louis XIV in 1684
and the consolidation of the Austrian régime by 1737, the end of Charles VI's rule.
This period saw the Duchy being invaded and occupied by the armies of Louis XIV
and his ally, Maximilian II Emmanuel, later on by those of Marlborough, and finally
laid waste by Prussian armies. Sprunck analyses: the machinations of the Chambre
Royale de Metz which wanted to acquire a large part of the province of Luxembourg;
the relationship of the Grand Duchy with Prussia from 1706 to 1717; and the
territorial friction with France about the Rodemack region and the Moselle Valley.

191 **La forteresse et le Duché de Luxembourg sous le régime autrichien d'après la correspondance des gouverneurs et des commandants: première partie.** (The fortress and the Duchy of Luxembourg under Austrian rule, according to the correspondence of the governors and commanders: first part.)
Alphonse Sprunck. *Publications de la Section Historique de l'Institut g.-d. de Luxembourg*, vol. 86 (1966), p. 113-368.

In 1726, the government of Vienna had already started reinforcing Luxembourg's fortifications, but this study covers the years 1730-67, and is based on documents drawn from the Luxembourg, Belgian and Austrian government archives. Until May 1756 the military commanders were also civil governors with wide-ranging powers.

192 **Le Duché de Luxembourg pendant la Guerre de Succession d'Autriche de 1744-1748.** (The Duchy of Luxembourg during the War of Austrian Succession, 1744-48.)
Alphonse Sprunck.   Luxembourg: Buck, 1945. 168p.

The Ryswick treaty of 1697 restored Luxembourg to Spain, but the Spanish War of Succession brought it under the rule of the Austrian Habsburgs. The Austrian régime (1715-94), often considered a golden age by Luxembourg historians, actually brought only minor material advantages, as the rulers considered the country merely as foreign land acquired by chance negotiations. At the same time, the people were short of money and food because they had to provision the troops stationed in the country.

193 **Le Duché de Luxembourg et la révolution brabançonne: première partie.** (The Duchy of Luxembourg and the Brabant revolution: first part.)
Alphonse Sprunck. *Publications de la Section Historique de l'Institut g.-d. de Luxembourg*, vol. 73 (1953), p. 7-155.

This study covers the period from March 1786 to the return of the French imperial troops in December 1790. It is based mainly on information provided by the two periodicals of the time, François-Xavier de Feller's *Journal Historique et Littéraire* and Henri-Ignace Brosius' *Journal Philosophique et Chrétien*. Discontent arose above all over the administrative and judicial reorganization which was considered draconian. Sprunck attributes the relative calmness of the Luxembourgers to the absence of a national bishop who could have organized the resistance of clergy and laity.

194 **Le dénombrement thérésien (1766-1771).** (The Theresian census [1766-71].)
Guy Lemaire.   BA thesis, Université catholique, Louvain, Belgium, 1965. 2 vols. 492p.

At the end of the *ancien régime*, the Duchy of Luxembourg was the first Austrian-Dutch province to get a complete and detailed cadastral survey. This thesis therefore examines the economic and social context, i.e. the circumstances that preceded the census, while also attempting to deal with its consequences. Among other questions, Lemaire asks who took the initiative to order such a census and how can the form it took be explained.

195 **Joseph II: an imperial reformer for the Austrian Netherlands.**
Walter W. Davis. The Hague, Netherlands: Nijhoff, 1974. 338p. map.
bibliog.

A biographical study of the Holy Roman Emperor Joseph II, who reigned from 1765
to 1790, which pays particular attention to his religious, economic and political
reforms of the Austrian Netherlands, which included Luxembourg. He aimed to
achieve religious toleration, the restriction of papal prerogatives and administrative
centralization.

196 **Luxembourg and her neighbours: a record of the political fortunes
of the present Grand Duchy from the eve of the French Revolution
to the Great War, with a preliminary sketch of events from 963 to
1780.**
Ruth Putnam. New York; London: Putnam, 1918. 484p. maps.

Putnam presents a well-documented and detailed political history. The troublesome
period in which the report was written makes it all the more interesting. An appendix
provides the texts of the principal treaties and conventions affecting Luxembourg from
1441 to 1867.

197 **La prise de Luxembourg par l'armée républicaine.** (The capture of
Luxembourg by the Republican army.)
Jacques Dollar. Luxembourg: Imprimerie Centrale, 1984. 289p.

When in 1794-95 the French Republican armies seized the city of Luxembourg, the
Grand Duchy did not exist as an independent state, but was an Austrian-Dutch
province given up by the Spanish in favour of the Habsburg dynasty in 1714. This
aspect of Luxembourg's history had been mainly studied by German authors and
published in the German language, so Jacques Dollar decided to publish a book in
French. The resulting volume does not merely recount military facts, but also
represents a testimony to the life of the troops warring against Austria and Prussia.

198 **Histoire du Département des Forêts (le Duché de Luxembourg de
1795 à 1814) d'après les Archives du Gouvernement grand-ducal et
des documents français inédits. Tome 1.** (History of the Department
of Forests [the Duchy of Luxembourg, 1795-1814] according to Grand
Ducal Government Archives and unpublished French documents.
Volume 1.)
Alfred Lefort. Paris: Picard; Brussels: Schepens; Luxembourg:
Imprimerie Worré-Mertens, 1905. 350p. bibliog.

Concentrating on the period from 1794 to 1798, this volume surveys the states of the
Duchy of Luxembourg and particularly the county of Chiny (formerly part of the
Luxembourg duchy in the present Belgian Province of Luxembourg since the time of
Countess Ermesinde) in 1794. It deals with their administrative, judicial and financial
organization, religious persecution and emigrants. Other chapters are devoted to the
French garrison, poor law administration, education, the arts, the press and national
holidays. The book has a distinctly Francophile slant.

199 **Napoléon et le Luxembourg.** (Napoleon and Luxembourg.)
Jacques Dollar. Luxembourg: Imprimerie Saint-Paul, 1979. 415p.

Napoleon visited the town of Luxembourg on 9 October 1804. To celebrate the 175th anniversary of this event, Jacques Dollar gathered a wide range of documents from private and public archives to illustrate the atmosphere of the French occupation of Luxembourg from 1795 to 1815. The author provides the numbers and names of all the *grognards*, i.e. the soldiers and officers who served under the French banner and were decorated with the Médaille de Sainte-Hélène or other honours. A special Cercle Culturel Napoléon was founded in Luxembourg in 1968 to revive the memory of that period and bring together the emperor's admirers.

200 **La conscription militaire au Département des Forêts. Premier volume: de 1798 à 1808 ou de la levée primitive de l'an VII à la levée extraordinaire. Deuxième Volume: de 1809 à 1814 ou de la levée de 1810 à la fin du régime français.** (Military conscription in the Department of Forests. First volume: 1798 to 1808, or the first levy of the year VII to the extraordinary levy. Second volume: 1809 to 1814 or from the levy of 1810 to the end of the French administration.)
François Decker. Luxembourg: Imprimerie Saint-Paul, 1980. 2 vols.

From 1798 to 1814, 14,176 Luxembourgers were drafted into the Napoleonic armies and 9,089 died on the battlefields. In a minute and painstaking analysis, Decker examines the various requisitions, levies and conscriptions, screening all the documents, statistics and historical reports.

201 **Lettres de soldats luxembourgeois au service de la France, 1798-1814, conservées aux Archives de l'Etat.** (Letters from Luxembourg soldiers in the service of France, 1798-1814, preserved in the State Archives.)
François Decker. Luxembourg: Mersch, 1971. 384p.

Presents 142 original letters from Luxembourg recruits who were enrolled into the service of France, discovered by Decker at the State Archives. It is worthwhile to note that seventeen others were published by Charles Schaack in volumes 57 and 58 of the *Publications de la Section Historique de l'Institut g.-d. de Luxembourg* in 1909 and 1910 under the title: '1792-1815: les Luxembourgeois, soldats de la France' (1792-1815: the Luxembourgers, soldiers of France). This documentary evidence from eyewitnesses who travelled throughout Europe in Napoleon's armies is interesting in many respects. It provides information about their national feeling, their social, political and religious attitudes, the state of the Luxembourgish language in that period, and their family situation back home. Eighty pages of illustrations conclude this volume. Unfortunately, Decker translated the Luxembourgish letters into German and so destroyed their documentary value and folkloristic charm.

202 **La démystification du 'Klöppelkrich'.** (The demystification of the war of bludgeons.)
Jacques Dollar. Luxembourg: Imprimerie Saint-Paul, 1981. 414p.

Gilbert Trausch first applied objective analysis to the 'Klöppelkrich' (war of bludgeons) in his 1967 essay, 'La répression des soulèvements paysans de 1798 dans le Département des Forêts' (q.v.). Jacques Dollar sets out to demystify, further, the so-called war of bludgeons. Through detailed study of contemporary documents he aims to recount, dispassionately, what really happened in 1798, when a number of Luxembourg peasants rose against the French régime on being drafted into the Napoleonic armies, armed only with farm tools, clubs and sticks.

203 **Klöppelkrieg. Die Bauernrevolte gegen die Franzosen in Luxemburg und in der Eifel.** (The war of bludgeons. The peasants' revolts against the French in Luxembourg and the Eifel.)
Pol Tousch.   Luxembourg: Pol Tousch, 1982. 256p.
(Ardennenchronik, 2).
Pol Tousch based this volume about the legendary Klöppelkrieg (war of bludgeons) on previously unknown facts which he discovered during his research. The details he presents help the reader gain a better understanding of the peasants who lived towards the end of the 18th century, when the revolt against French conscription broke out (1798).

204 **La répression des soulèvements paysans de 1798 dans le Département des Forêts.** (The repression of the 1798 peasants' rising in the Département des Forêts.)
Gilbert Trausch.   *Publications de la Section Historique de l'Institut g.-d. de Luxembourg*, vol. 82 (1967), p. 7-245. 2 maps.
Few episodes in Luxembourg's history have struck the popular imagination as much as the war of bludgeons which grew into a national legend fostered by the biased accounts of two historian-priests, Jean Engling and Wilhelm Zorn. Trausch's essay represents the first attempt to analyse facts in an objective way and to cast aside folkloristic hero-worship.

# 19th century

205 **Quelque part entre Vienne et Londres ... Le Grand-Duché de Luxembourg de 1815 à 1867.** (Somewhere between Vienna and London ... The Grand Duchy of Luxembourg from 1815 to 1867.)
Edouard M. Kayser.   Luxembourg: Imprimerie Saint-Paul, 1990. 109p.
Kayser's intention is not to present new information, but to re-familiarize readers with the major period of Luxembourg's history from when the 1815 Treaty of Vienna created the country legally to 1839, when it came into real existence, albeit reduced in size. Luxembourg's independence was endangered again in 1867, when both the French and Prussian powers had designs on the area. This volume presents a summary which is enriched with footnotes, maps, portraits and landscapes.

206 **Naissance et débuts du Grand-Duché, 1814-1830: le Grand-Duché de Luxembourg dans le royaume des Pays-Bas.** (Birth and beginnings of the Grand Duchy, 1814-30: the Grand Duchy of Luxembourg in the kingdom of the Netherlands.)
Albert Calmes. Brussels: Edition Universelle, 1971. 2nd ed. 570p. (Histoire Contemporaine du Grand-Duché de Luxembourg, Vol. 1).

This volume is the result of an ambitious attempt to produce an overall synthesis of over one hundred years of Luxembourg history. The work was started by Albert Calmes (university lecturer and later diplomat) and continued by his son, Christian (lawyer and later General Secretary of the EEC in Brussels). Only a few chronological gaps remain to be filled.

207 **Das Grossherzogtum Luxemburg unter Wilhelm I, 1815-1840.** (The Grand Duchy of Luxembourg under William I, 1815-40.)
Prosper Muellendorff. Luxembourg: Buck, 1921. 370p.

Muellendorff's work was the first consistent study of Luxembourg in the early 19th century after the end of French imperial dominion. The 1815 Vienna Congress made the old Dukedom of Luxembourg into the Grand Duchy of Luxembourg, and decided that it should be given to the King of the Netherlands, William I of Orange-Nassau, 'to be possessed in perpetuity and personal title by him and his legitimate successors'. However, instead of recognizing the autonomy and political individuality of the Grand Duchy, King William made the country into the eighteenth province of the Kingdom of the Netherlands, an action which gave rise to much discontent among the Luxembourgers. The situation was only to change under the congenial William II, who inaugurated a new era and was extremely popular with the Luxembourgers.

208 **Le Grand-Duché de Luxembourg dans la Révolution belge, 1830-1839.** (The Grand Duchy of Luxembourg in the Belgian revolution, 1830-39.)
Albert Calmes. Luxembourg: Imprimerie Saint-Paul, 1939. 423p. (Histoire Contemporaine du Grand-Duché de Luxembourg, Vol. 2).

Deals with the period from the beginning of the Belgian revolution in August 1830 to its final resolution by the Treaty of London on 19 April 1839. The treaty finalized the partition of the Grand Duchy, thereby setting the course for the development of modern Luxembourg.

209 **Luxembourgeois de 1830.** (Luxembourg people of 1830.)
Louis Lefebvre. Arlon, Belgium: G. Everling, 1980. 160p. (Le Vieil Arlon).

In the Belgian revolution of 1830, some Luxembourgers decided to help their neighbours in their struggle against the Dutch reign, in so doing helping to liberate themselves as well. Their disappointment was therefore great when part of Luxembourg was accorded to Belgium in 1839 after the latter's independence in 1830. Although this volume includes some previously unpublished testimonies, it is basically a synthesis of known facts as taken from public documents.

210 **Am Wege zur Unabhängigkeit Luxemburgs.** (Luxembourg on its way to independence.)
Auguste Collart. Luxembourg: Linden, 1938. 448p.

In 1939 Luxembourg commemorated the first centenary of its independence. Collart sets out to study the evolution of its struggle for independence and to evoke the atmosphere of 1840-67 by relating anecdotes and details, rather than great events. Following a first chapter dealing with the background, the second analyses various preliminaries (the Belgian revolution, for example) during the reign of William I. The final chapter covers William II, Prince Henry of the Netherlands as the Lieutenant-King, and William III up to the Conference of London in 1867, which finally ratified independence. The book is enhanced with numerous pictures and extracts from documents and newspapers.

211 **Le Luxembourg à l'époque contemporaine: du partage de 1839 à nos jours.** (Contemporary Luxembourg from the partition of 1839 to the present.)
Gilbert Trausch. Luxembourg: Imprimerie Bourg-Bourger, 1975. 232p. bibliog. (Manuel d'Histoire Luxembourgeoise en Quatre Volumes, à l'Usage des Classes de l'Enseignement Secondaire au Grand-Duché de Luxembourg, Vol. 4).

The period following the critical years of 1867-72 has remained largely unexplored by Luxembourg's historians. Trausch sets out to fill this gap and to tackle some of the more delicate problems of the 20th century; without neglecting the political dimension, he also stresses the parallel social and economic features. The survey is divided into three parts: Part I proceeds from the last partition of the country in 1839 to the First World War; Part II tackles the inter-war years; and Part III attempts to portray the present-day social and political reality, and the latest liberal-socialist government under Prime Minister Gaston Thorn (1974-79). The volume is characterized by outstanding documentary and pictorial presentation.

212 **La restauration de Guillaume Ier, roi des Pays-Bas (L'ère Hassenpflug), 1839-1840.** (The restoration of William I, King of the Netherlands: the era of Hassenpflug, 1839-40.)
Albert Calmes. Luxembourg: Imprimerie Saint-Paul, 1947. 424p. (Histoire Contemporaine du Grand-Duché de Luxembourg, Vol. 3).

Presents a concentrated study of the historically decisive and troubled eighteen months in Luxembourg's history from 19 April 1839 (i.e. the Treaty of London when the Grand Duchy was partitioned), to 7 October 1840 when William I, King of the Netherlands and Grand Duke of Luxembourg, abdicated.

213 **La création d'un Etat, 1841-1847.** (The creation of a state, 1841-47.)
Albert Calmes. Luxembourg: Imprimerie Saint-Paul, 1954. 473p. (Histoire Contemporaine du Grand-Duché de Luxembourg, Vol. 4).

William I was succeeded to the throne upon abdication by his son, William II, whose reign is described in this volume up to the dawn of the revolutionary year of 1848. William II, whose reign was marked by great church-state tensions, granted Luxembourg its first constitution on 12 October 1841.

214   **La révolution de 1848 au Luxembourg.** (The revolution of 1848 in
      Luxembourg.)
      Albert Calmes.   Luxembourg: Imprimerie Saint-Paul, 1957. 301p.
      (Histoire Contemporaine du Grand-Duché de Luxembourg, Vol. 5).

Deals with the revolutionary period from 25 February 1848, when Luxembourg first
learned of the Paris uprising, to 17 March 1849, when William II died.

215   **1867, l'affaire du Luxembourg.** (The 'Luxembourg affair' of 1867.)
      Christian Calmes.   Luxembourg: Imprimerie Saint-Paul, 1967. 557p.
      (Histoire Contemporaine du Grand-Duché de Luxembourg, Vol. 7).

Luxembourg came to the forefront of international politics in 1867, when Napoleon III
became set on annexing the country. Prussia equivocated at this prospect, but Austria-
Hungary and Russia were sufficiently concerned to organize an international
conference on the issue in London. That meeting, held from 7-11 May 1867, agreed to
guarantee Luxembourg's neutrality and therefore made Prussia forgo her right to
garrison the Luxembourg fortress.

216   **British foreign policy and the coming of the Franco-Prussian war.**
      Richard Millman.   Oxford: Clarendon Press, 1965. 238p. bibliog.

The dissolution of the Germanic Confederation in 1867 allowed Napoleon III to claim
the Grand Duchy of Luxembourg as compensation. Meanwhile, William III, King of
the Netherlands, was ready to sell Luxembourg to France, because this territory
belonged to him only through personal union. Bismarck promised not to stand in the
way of this deal, as long as it was engineered so as not to arouse German national
feeling. However, the French mismanaged the affair, the news leaked out, and the
arrangements broke down. The period of acute crisis that followed was closed by a
compromise in the form of a treaty signed after the international conference held in
London from 7-11 May 1867. The treaty of London (9 September 1867) guaranteed
Luxembourg's neutrality and independence. Millman analyses Britain's attitude
during these difficult moments in the precarious existence of a small country.
Luxembourg is dealt with on pages 46-109.

217   **Le Luxembourg dans la guerre de 1870.** (Luxembourg in the war of
      1870.)
      Christian Calmes.   Luxembourg: Imprimerie Saint-Paul, 1970. 673p.
      (Histoire Contemporaine du Grand-Duché de Luxembourg, Vol. 8).

Examines the threat to Luxembourg's newly-acquired independence posed by the
Franco-Prussian War of 1870. The country managed to preserve its status, and its civic
spirit was actually strengthened during this testing time.

# 20th century

218 **Le Luxembourg indépendant: essai d'histoire politique contemporaine et de droit international public.** (Independent Luxembourg: an essay on contemporary political history and international public law.)
Pierre Majerus. Luxembourg: Joseph Beffort, 1945. 222p.

Examines the evolution of the international status of the Grand Duchy of Luxembourg. The first two parts of this volume, written before the Second World War, analyse the juridical documents concerning Luxembourg's independence (Conventions de La Haye of 1899 and 1907) and the impact of the First World War on Luxembourg's international status. Part three contrasts the brutal invasion of the Nazi régime and Luxembourg's victorious resistance, which proved that the Luxembourg people were able to assert a newly-awakened feeling of identity and solidarity.

219 **Thron und Dynastie: Aufsätze aus drei Jahrzehnten.** (Throne and dynasty: essays from three decades.)
Jean Schoos. Luxembourg: Imprimerie Saint-Paul, 1978. 338p.

This superbly illustrated souvenir album was compiled and published to pay tribute to the Grand Duke and Grand Duchess of Luxembourg on the occasion of their silver wedding celebration. It is a collection of articles by the author, who is Professor of History at Bonn University, on the most significant events in the dynastic and family life of Luxembourg's monarchs.

220 **Sturm um Luxemburgs Thron 1907-1920.** (Storm about the Luxembourg throne 1907-20.)
Auguste Collart. Luxembourg: Imprimerie Saint-Paul, 1991. 399p.

This is the facsimile reprint of a publication that was first issued by Auguste Collart, who was a member of the government during the troublesome period of 1918-19, in 1959 (Luxembourg: Bourg-Bourger, 1959. 347p.). He reviews the consequences of the Congress of Vienna (1815), then discusses the successions to the throne from William III (1849-90) to Duke Adolphe of Nassau (1890-1905) and William IV (1905-12). Furthermore he describes the difficulties of Grand Duchess Marie-Adélaïde (1912-19) and the successful reign of Princess Charlotte (1919-64). The work is enlivened by Collart's own personal recollections and his inclusion of numerous anecdotes.

221 **Le Luxembourg au centre de l'annexionnisme belge, 1914-1919.** (Luxembourg in the centre of Belgian annexationism, 1914-19.)
Christian Calmes. Luxembourg: Imprimerie Saint-Paul, 1976. 537p.
(Histoire Contemporaine du Grand-Duché de Luxembourg, Vol. 10).

During the First World War and shortly after, Belgium tried to bring Luxembourg under its sovereignty; Belgian politicians were prepared to consider both dynastic union and outright annexation as their means. The latter option was nearly used after the Armistice, and only direct French intervention prevented a Belgian invasion of Luxembourg.

222 **L'étrange référendum du 28 septembre 1919.** (The strange referendum of 28 September 1919.)
Christian Calmes. Luxembourg: Imprimerie Saint-Paul, 1979. 541p.
(Histoire Contemporaine du Grand-Duché de Luxembourg, Vol. 11).
The year 1919 was politically very turbulent for Luxembourg. Republican feeling was running high, with many in favour of abolishing the dynasty and establishing a republic modelled on the new German one. However, the referendum of 28 September determined that the dynasty would be retained and stronger economic ties with France would be sought.

223 **Aspekte der belgischen Sicherheitspolitik nach dem ersten Weltkrieg: das französisch-belgische Militärabkommen und die Luxemburg Frage?** (Aspects of Belgian security policy after the First World War: the Franco-Belgian military pact of 1920 and the Luxembourg question.)
Birgit Galler. PhD thesis, University of Bern, Switzerland, Faculty of Philosophy and History, 1978. 332p.
In this thesis, Luxembourg, which has always been a declared interest of its neighbouring countries, is only an indirect subject. After the First World War and the conclusion of the Franco-Belgian military pact of 1920, the question of the Grand Duchy was raised again. Galler asks herself in what conditions this pact was finally concluded while explaining the importance of Luxembourg for the two protagonist countries.

224 **Im Dienste: Erinnerungen aus verworrener Zeit.** (Serving my country: recollections from a troubled period.)
Nikolaus Welter. Luxembourg: Sankt-Paulus-Druckerei, 1925. 231p.
From July to August 1918 elections were held in Luxembourg to form a Constituent Assembly, whose purpose was to create a democratic constitution. A government of national union was formed under Emile Reuter to defend Luxembourg's independence after the Armistice. However, national union only lasted for three months and Reuter was faced with a grave crisis between November 1918 and January 1919; the ambitious personal policy of Grand Duchess Marie-Adélaïde had aroused political passions and her deposition was proposed. Written by one of the ministers and defenders of Marie-Adélaïde, this volume recalls some of the key moments of those tumultuous days, when a revolutionary committee intended to turn the Grand Duchy into a republic and when, on 9 January 1919, the Grand Duchess decided to abdicate in favour of her sister, Princess Charlotte.

225 **Sous le signe de la grande grève de mars 1921. Les années sans pareilles du mouvement ouvrier luxembourgeois.** (Under the banner of the general strike of March 1921. The unparalleled years of the Luxembourg labour movement.)
Denis Scuto. Luxembourg: Editpress, 1990. 464p.
After the First World War, Luxembourg experienced some socio-political problems which forced the government to react. At the end of 1918, they announced the creation of factory councils (conseils d'usine) which were intended to calm the situation down.

Scuto analyses the hesitations of the authorities, but above all, he describes all those involved (strikers, soldiers, bosses) in the strike that took place three years later and which was strongly linked with the existence of these factory councils. Although this subject has often been treated, Scuto manages to put new life into the world of the workers at a crucial moment in their history. He remains impartial even if his sympathies for the labour movement cannot be denied. The book ends with condensed biographical notes on the protagonists of this troublesome period.

226 **Aspects des rélations de la Belgique, du Grand-Duché de Luxembourg et des Pays-Bas avec l'Italie: 1925-1940.** (Aspects of the relations of Belgium, the Grand Duchy of Luxembourg and the Netherlands with Italy: 1925-40.)
Under the direction of Michel Dumoulin, Jacques Willequet. Istituto italiano di cultura, Brussels; Comité belge de l'Istituto per la Storia de Risorgimento italiano, Brussels, 1983. 374p.

Among the papers presented at this inter-university seminar which attempted to foster a better understanding of the ideological, cultural and diplomatic relations of Belgium, Luxembourg and the Netherlands with Italy, the reader will find two contributions concerning the Grand Duchy: the first is written by the European parliamentarian, Ben Fayot, and entitled 'The Luxembourg socialists and fascist Italy', whereas the second is a general view, a conclusion which analyses the attitudes of these three small northwestern democracies towards Italy.

227 **Ils ont dit NON au fascisme. Rejet de la loi muselière par le référendum de 1937.** (They said NO to Fascism. Rejection of the 'muzzle law' by the referendum of 1937.)
Henri Koch-Kent. Luxembourg: H. Koch-Kent, 1982. 109p.

In May 1935, Prime Minister Joseph Bech presented a bill to ban the Luxembourg Communist Party. Its content was largely adopted by Parliament, but public opposition and the referendum that followed in June 1937 finally stopped the law (70,371 people were in favour of the law, and 72,300 were against). In his usual colourful style, Koch-Kent describes his view of this fight against the 'muzzle law'.

228 **Bombenangriffe auf Luxemburg in zwei Weltkriegen.** (Bomb attacks on Luxembourg in two world wars.)
E. T. Melchers. Luxembourg: Imprimerie Saint-Paul, 1984. 504p.

In eight chapters, Melchers provides a general overview of aviation in the years preceding the two world wars, before analysing the bomb attacks on Luxembourg and their consequences. Each of the two world conflicts is treated in four chapters which follow a chronological order and are accompanied by numerous photographs, posters, broadsheets, maps and documents of the period. Melchers also wrote *Les deux libérations du Luxembourg, 1944-1945* (The two liberations of Luxembourg, 1944-45) (Luxembourg: Editions du Centre, 1958. 264p.), followed by a revised and augmented German edition, entitled *Luxemburg, Befreiung und Ardennen Offensive 1944-1945* (Luxembourg, liberation and the Ardennes offensive 1944-45) (Luxembourg: Editions du Centre, 1984. 556p.).

229 **Kriegsschauplatz Luxemburg, August 1914-Mai 1940.**
(Luxembourg, military theatre, August 1914-May 1940.)
Emile-Théodore Melchers. Luxembourg: Sankt-Paulus-Druckerei,
1991. 5th rev. ed. 657p. 17 maps.

On 1 August 1914 hostilities broke out between Germany and Russia, and that same
day a German detachment occupied the Luxembourg railway station at Troisvierges.
The next day German troops occupied the town and entire country of Luxembourg.
The author, a military specialist, analyses succeeding military developments in detail.
There are chapters devoted to: the famous Maginot Line in the south of the country;
the Siegfried Line; espionage rings in neutral Luxembourg; the German invasion of 10
May 1940 and the French entry in the south, and the early German occupation.

230 **Vu et entendu. (Seen and heard.) 1912-1940. Vol. II: Années d'exil.
(Years of exile.) 1940-1945.**
Henri Koch-Kent. Luxembourg: Imprimerie Hermann, 1983-86.
2 vols.

These two volumes, written during a period of six years, represent the personal
recollections and interpretations of Henri Koch-Kent (born in 1906). In his first
volume, which covers the years from 1912 to 1940, the author, who became president
of the general students' organization in 1933, deals with different events concerning
the Grand Duchy, such as the accession of Marie Adélaïde to the throne, the
repercussions of the Spanish Civil War (1936-39), and the discussion about the
controversial 'muzzle law' (loi muselière) which was finally rejected by a referendum
of 1937. As a war correspondent and independent journalist in London during the
Second World War, Koch-Kent sharply criticizes the Luxembourg government which
was exiled in London at this time. He reproaches the official authorities for their
improvisations and negligence, but above all for their lack of moral solidarity and
financial support of their fellow people who were experiencing difficulties during the
years of occupation.

231 **Henri Koch-Kent raconte ... remémore, relève, rectifie.** (Henri
Koch-Kent reports ... recalls, emphasizes, rectifies.)
Henri Koch-Kent. Luxembourg: Imprimerie Centrale, 1993. 326p.

In 1993, at the age of eighty-seven, the reputed and controversial Luxembourg author,
Henri Koch-Kent, reviewed certain events that have changed Europe since the
beginning of the 20th century. By presenting the facts as personal testimonies and
backing them up with documents from the time, Koch-Kent reconstructs the situation
in which Luxembourg found itself before the First World War. Besides publishing
articles that are almost forgotten today, the author deals with problems ranging from
the Armistice of 1918 to the invasion of Luxembourg by German troops in May 1940.

232 **Der antifaschistische Widerstand in Luxemburg 1933-1944.** (The
anti-Fascist resistance in Luxembourg 1933-44.)
Henri Wehenkel. Luxembourg: COPE, 1985. 399p.

Wehenkel's well-illustrated book sets out to highlight the way the Luxembourg
population united to resist a common enemy: Hitler and Fascism. It is interesting to
note that Henri Wehenkel, who is still a member of the Communist Party of
Luxembourg, opens with Hitler's seizure of power in 1933 and not with the

subsequent invasion of Luxembourg by German troops. In a second section, he describes the publications of the 'illegal' press of the time (from Communist Party material to resistance group documents). At the end of the volume is included a detailed but understandably non-exhaustive list of the members of resistance groups as revealed by testimonies or German search lists.

233   **Hitlertum in Luxemburg, 1933-1944.** (Hitlerism in Luxembourg, 1933-44.)
Henri Koch-Kent, Jean Hames, Francis Steffen.   Luxembourg: Imprimerie Hermann, 1972. 2nd ed. 47p. (Beiträge zur Zeitgeschichte, 1).

Contains three exposés made at the national congress of the Luxembourg Association of Nazi Victims, concerning those who had been forced into the German armies. They criticize the attitude of the Luxembourg government in exile (in Canada and England) towards Luxembourg deserters, war prisoners and others who resisted the occupying forces. All the reports are personal testimonies: the relevant official reports are either missing or inaccessible.

# Second World War

234   **Im Vorfeld der Maginot-Linie 1939-1940.** (On the glacis of the Maginot Line 1939-40.)
Fernand Lorang.   Esch-sur-Alzette, Luxembourg: Editions Schortgen, 1994. 2nd ed. 296p.

The author, who was a teacher in Rumelange, Luxembourg, provides an account of this small mining and border village which was situated on the glacis of important military operations during the invasion of Luxembourg by German troops in 1940. Originally published in 1975, the volume describes the rotten atmosphere that spread in the once peaceful village due to action on the Maginot Line.

235   **Das Kriegsgeschehen an der Dreiländerecke 1939-1940.** (The events of the war in the three countries borderland 1939-40.)
Norbert Etringer.   Luxembourg: Imprimerie Saint-Paul, 1983. 117p.

Etringer's extended new edition of his 'Village in no-man's-land', published in 1960, includes seventy-two photographs, illustrations and reports on the Luxembourg-French-German border area that witnessed a period at the beginning of the Second World War known as the 'drôle de guerre'.

236 **Radioscopie de la littérature luxembourgeoise sur la 2e Guerre Mondiale.** (Radioscopy of Luxembourg literature on the Second World War.)
Jul Christophory.   Luxembourg: RTL Editions, 1987. 300p.

250 monographs are listed in chronological order and briefly annotated. General and specific survey tables, indexes and synopses of yearly publication figures and languages in use, for example, facilitate research from thematic, literary and linguistic points of view. An indispensable companion for the general reader, the volume illustrates the lasting effect that the Second World War still exerts on the Luxembourg population.

237 **Geschichte Luxemburgs im Zweiten Weltkrieg.** (History of Luxembourg in the Second World War.)
Paul Weber.   Luxembourg: Victor Buck, 1948. 158p.

Represents a pioneering attempt to provide a first-hand account of the war in Luxembourg, using various original documents, especially those from the War Crimes Office in Luxembourg. It is an interesting documentary and personal record of the invasion, the organization of the civil administration, terror and propaganda, and the liberation.

238 **Luxemburg zwischen Selbstbehauptung und nationaler Selbstaufgabe. Die deutsche Besatzungspolitik und die Volksdeutsche Bewegung 1940-1945.** (Luxembourg between self-assertion and national surrender. German occupation policy and 'Volksdeutsche Bewegung' [Nazi movement] 1940-45.)
Paul Dostert.   Luxembourg: Imprimerie Saint-Paul, 1985. 267p.

Dostert presented this work in order to obtain his PhD from the Albert Ludwig University in Freiburg, Germany. He aims to provide a general survey of German occupation policy during the Second World War. Although there exists a great number of publications on this subject, it had only been treated in partial aspects. The subject of Luxembourg's contact with the Nazis and the activities of the 'Volksdeutsche Bewegung' (the Nazi movement which aimed to convert the Luxembourg population to the theories of National Socialism) had never been dealt with before. The author sets out to find out for what reasons and on what levels the decisions of the German occupying power were taken. In order to understand the resistance of the Luxembourg nation, Dostert provides an introduction to Luxembourg and its relationship with the neighbouring countries.

239 **Luxemburg unter dem Hakenkreuz.** (Luxembourg under the swastika.)
Victor Delcourt.   Christnach, Luxembourg: Editions Emile Borschette, 1988. 299p.

Delcourt describes his memories of what he and his family endured during the 1940-45 war years. The text's coverage opens with the early morning of 10 May 1940 when Hitler's troops crossed the frontiers of the Grand Duchy to attack France. The last chapter, entitled 'The liberation', records a discussion between the author and his father concerning their experiences from 1940 to 1945 on the one hand, and, on the other, posing questions that have still not been satisfactorily answered today, such as: how it was possible for a whole nation to support one of the most terrible dictators history has ever known.

240 **1940-1944: Luxemburg im Zweiten Weltkrieg: ein Kriegstagebuch.**
(1940-44: Luxembourg in the Second World War: a wartime diary.)
Franz Delvaux. Christnach, Luxembourg: Editions Emile Borschette,
1989. 378p.

Presents a highly personal record of both significant and commonplace war incidents
interspersed with literary and philosophical reflections and classical quotations.

241 **10 mai 1940 en Luxembourg: témoignages et documents.** (10 May
1940 in Luxembourg: witness reports and documents.)
Henri Koch-Kent. Mersch, Luxembourg: Faber, 1971. 336p. bibliog.

In the early morning of 10 May 1940, Hitler's armies crossed Luxembourg's frontiers
to attack France. Koch-Kent examined a remarkable number of German and Allied
documents in order to clarify a multitude of questions concerning the situation in
Luxembourg and France on 10 May 1940 and the reasons the whole operation went so
smoothly. Several Allied press articles alleged, for example, that German
collaborators existed among the Luxembourg population. Koch-Kent sets out to clear
the reputation of Luxembourg's popular resistance and to overturn erroneous
interpretations and malevolent rumours surrounding the situation in the border areas
of Esch, Differdange and Rodange.

242 **The German administration in Luxembourg, 1940-1942: towards a
'de facto' annexation.**
W. A. Fletcher. *Historical Journal*, vol. 13 (1970), p. 533-44.

Describes the administrative situation in Luxembourg following the German invasion
of 10 May 1940. The main figure of that period was the gauleiter, Gustav Simon, who
had been named Chef der Zivilverwaltung (Head of the Civil Service) in Luxembourg,
an office derived from German military administrative practices. He undertook the
radical reconstruction (Aufbauwerk) of Luxembourg's administration through issuing
thousands of ordinances promoting the Gleichschaltung (harmonization) process. In
August 1942 German citizenship was extended to the areas of Alsace, Lorraine and
Luxembourg, and forced military conscription of those born between 1920 and 1924
was proclaimed. In spite of a general protest strike, this conscription caused the death
of 4,000 Luxembourg youths out of a contingent of 11,000.

243 **L'exode des Luxembourgeois sur les routes de France en mai 1940.**
(The exodus of the Luxembourg people on French roads in May 1940.)
Jacques Dollar. Luxembourg: Imprimerie Centrale, 1990. 415p.

The German invasion of the Grand Duchy on 10 May 1940 led to an exodus of nearly
50,000 people. Dollar relates this dramatic time for the Luxembourgers who took the
road to Southern France. The study is based both on authentic documents, partially
reproduced in the volume, and on eyewitness reports from former refugees.

244 **Le gouvernement luxembourgeois en exil.** (The Luxembourg
government in exile.)
Georges Heisbourg. Luxembourg: Imprimerie Saint-Paul, 1986-91.
4 vols.

Heisbourg, who has held important posts as ambassador and general secretary of the
Western European Union, examines the years the Luxembourg government spent in
exile from 10 May 1940 to the liberation of the country in September 1944. While
concluding with a tribute to the government in exile, Heisbourg hopes that these
volumes will contribute to a better understanding of this short but essential period of
recent Luxembourg history. The wide-ranging project is mainly based on the public
archives of the Benelux countries, France, Great Britain, the former Federal Republic
of Germany and the United States. The aim of the work was not to be exhaustive, and
for further information on this period other publications should be read such as *La
Grand-Duchesse et son gouvernement pendant la Deuxième Guerre mondiale* (The
Grand Duchess and her government during the Second World War) by E. Haag and
E. Krier (Luxembourg: RTL-Edition, 1987. 309p.). Heisbourg includes, at the end of
each volume, an appendix containing the speeches of the Grand Duchess and her
government members.

245 **Sie boten Trotz: Luxemburger im Freiheitskampf, 1939-1945.**
(They withstood: Luxembourgers in the fight for freedom, 1939-45.)
Henri Koch-Kent. Luxembourg: Imprimerie Hermann, 1974. 412p.
bibliog. 2 maps.

During the Second World War Koch-Kent was a foreign correspondent in London. His
close knowledge of background events enabled him to write a fascinating account of
the armed resistance of the Luxembourgers after 10 May 1940, although he was not
allowed to consult one of the main sources of documentation, namely the acts of the
Luxembourg government in exile. He describes the many and various methods of
resistance, the intelligence network, and the different theatres of operation in France,
Belgium, Spain and Great Britain. Individual reports highlight acts of bravery,
fortunate and unfortunate accidents, communications shortcomings, and personal and
organizational failures and difficulties.

246 **La résistance du peuple luxembourgeois.** (The resistance of the
Luxembourg people.)
Gino Candidi, Georgette Bisdorff. Luxembourg: Editions du
'Rappel', 1977. 239p.

Provides an account of Luxembourg's resistance against the Nazi occupying forces
from 1940 to 1945.

247 **La Résistance au Grand-Duché de Luxembourg (1940-1945).
Sociologie, idéologies et programmes.** (The resistance in the Grand
Duchy of Luxembourg [1940-45]. Sociology, ideologies and
programmes.)
Lucien Blau. MA thesis, Université de Metz, France, 1983-84. 136p.

The Luxembourg resistance movement of the Second World War is often presented as
a harmonious and homogeneous organization. Blau aims to delve deeper than simple

factual accounts of history by defining the individual member of the resistance before analysing the resistance movement itself. His thesis is mainly targeted towards assessing how uniform or divided was the political opinion of the resistance.

248  **Josy Goerres et les PI-MEN dans la résistance.** (Josy Goerres and the PI-MEN in the resistance.)

Jacques Dollar.  Luxembourg: Imprimerie Saint-Paul, 1986. 317p.

This reproduction of authentic documents taken from the private collection of Josy Goerres, founder and president of the 'Formation des Patriotes Indépendants Luxembourgeois' (PI-MEN) (Luxembourg Independent Patriots' Group), is the author's grateful tribute to his fellow citizen.

249  **L'épopée des sans-uniforme.** (The epic adventure of those who wore no uniform.)

Union des Mouvements de Résistance Luxembourgeois.

Luxembourg: Union, 1979. 119p.

Dedicated to all those who took part in the resistance in order to safeguard their own liberty and the independence of their country, this brochure marks the thirty-fifth anniversary of the Union of Luxembourg Resistance Movements' founding on 23 March 1944. An appendix containing extracts from documents supports the French and Luxembourgish text.

250  **Luxemburger als Freiwild.** (Luxembourgers as fair game.)

Henri Koch-Kent, André Hohengarten.  Luxembourg: Imprimerie Hermann, 1972. 2nd ed. 40p. (Beiträge zur Zeitgeschichte, No. 2).

Deals with the German Wanted Person's file, which was issued by the Reich Criminal Police Office in Berlin on 1 October 1943. This file comprises 976 pages, each containing about 55 names of wanted persons. The authors managed to locate and identify about 50,000 Luxembourgers after month-long efforts. This publication was intended to stimulate further investigations in that direction.

251  **Luxemburg im SD-Spiegel: ein Bericht vom 12. Juli 1940.**

(Luxembourg in the mirror of the Nazi Security Service: a report of 12 July 1940.)

Henri Koch-Kent, André Hohengarten.  Luxembourg: Imprimerie Hermann, 1973. 48p. (Beiträge zur Zeitgeschichte, No. 3).

The Nazi Security Service headquarters were based in Luxembourg at the Villa Sternberg on Boulevard Grande-Duchesse Charlotte. This report of 12 July 1940 is one of the first general reports on the situation in Luxembourg, two months after the invasion of 10 May. It covers: the general situation, the administrative measures taken, the economy, politics, rumours and enemies. The final pages contain some important correspondence between the German Nazi headquarters and Luxembourg authorities, such as the General Secretary of the government, Albert Wehrer.

252  **Freiwëllegekompanie 1940-45.** (Volunteers' Company 1940-45.)
Louis Jacoby, René Trauffler.   Luxembourg: Imprimerie Saint-Paul,
1980-86. 2 vols.

The first of these two volumes by Jacoby and Trauffler was published for the fortieth anniversary of the forced dissolution of the Volunteers' Company (4 December 1940). 378 soldiers were forced to leave Luxembourg for Weimar, Germany and in August 1940 this company was actually absorbed into the German 'Schutzpolizei' (Municipal Police) and disappeared. The second volume, published six years later (1986), is the result of a joint effort of old members of that Luxembourg contingent. Opening with a description of the organization's foundation in 1881, further chapters present various testimonies and an outline of Luxembourg's military history. This interesting documentary report is concluded by an excellent epilogue by Marcel Engel.

253  **Wie es im zweiten Weltkrieg (1939-1945) zur Zwangsrekrutierung Luxemburger Staatsbürger zum Nazi-Heer kam.** (How Luxembourg citizens were conscripted by force into the Nazi army during the Second World War, 1939-45.)
André Hohengarten.   Luxembourg: Fédération des Victimes du Nazisme Enrôlés de Force, 1975. 31p.

Hohengarten analyses the decisions behind the Nazi administration's forcible conscription of Luxembourg citizens into the German army. The Luxembourg Volunteers' Company was pressed into German combat units, and youngsters aged from seventeen to twenty-seven were forcibly recruited for the Labour Services of the Reich. On 30 August 1942 compulsory military service was introduced in Luxembourg for those born between 1920 and 1927. Out of the 15,409 persons concerned, 2,848 were killed in battle.

254  **Waffenträger wider Willen.** (Weapon carriers against their wills.)
Marcel Staar.   Luxembourg: Imprimerie Saint-Paul, 1987. 401p.

Staar, who was aged fourteen in 1940, presents his impressions of the Second World War. His intention is to illustrate the psychology of young Luxembourg people during this war. He describes how the love of his home, heightened by homesickness, took on a new significance. Illustrated with some black-and-white pictures, the account begins in 1943, when the German occupying power recruited air force assistants in Luxembourg. This measure made it possible, later on, for the Germans to assign about 100,000 air soldiers to their ground troops.

255  **Enrôlé de force, déserteur de la Wehrmacht.** (Forced conscript, deserter from the Wehrmacht.)
Aimé Knepper.   Luxembourg: COPE, 1985. 2nd ed. 169p.

The author, Aimé Knepper, who was still a student in 1940, worked for the 'Reichsarbeitsdienst' (a youth workers' association) in Oriental Prussia and Lettonia from October 1942 to April 1943. He was then conscripted to the Wehrmacht until November 1943 when he deserted and went into hiding with various Luxembourg families before leaving for France. It was not Knepper's intention to write a tribute to himself, but even if the circumstances are often specific and personal, one should not forget that thousands of people from Luxembourg, Alsace and Lorraine experienced similar adventures. The author attempted to narrate as faithfully as possible the events he remembered or had written down at the time.

256 **Les réfractaires dans les bunkers.** (The rebel soldiers in the bunkers.) Aimé Knepper. Luxembourg: Imprimerie Saint-Paul, 1988. new ed. 206p.

The resistance movement in Luxembourg set up underground refuges in order to protect the Luxembourg rebel defaulters and deserters from compulsory German military service. These hidings, or bunkers, were located outside the villages. Of the 11,168 young people enlisted by the Nazis, 3,510 tried to escape, 2,400 were hidden by the Luxembourg resistance and 1,100 took refuge in France. Lacking written documentation about these underground hiding places, the author, himself a rebel, took the material for his book from the oral testimonies of more than 300 people.

257 **RAD (Reichsarbeitsdienst) Gembitz-Deutschwalde 1944.** (Labour service of the Reich Gembitz-Deutschwalde 1944.) Amicale Gembitz-Deutschwalde. Luxembourg: Imprimerie Saint-Paul, 1993. 234p.

Relates the short stay (July-November 1944) of some Luxembourg forced conscripts at the camps of Gembitz (Gebice) and Deutschwalde (Mondliborzyce) in Poland. In addition to numerous photographs and documents, the volume includes information about the association formed by the former Luxembourg prisoners of these two camps.

258 **Die geopferte Generation: die Geschichte der Luxemburger Jugend während des zweiten Weltkrieges.** (The sacrificed generation: the history of Luxembourg's youth during the Second World War.) Francis Steffen. Luxembourg: Föderation der Luxemburger zwangsrekrutierten Naziopfer, 1977. 2nd ed. 316p.

By describing individual but representative lives, the author attempts to provide the younger generation with an insight into the various institutions, events and features of the Nazi period in Luxembourg.

259 **Vom Halbmond zum Ziegenkopf. Die Geschichte der Luxemburger Häftlinge in Lublin 1942-1945.** (From halfmoon to the goat's head. The history of the Luxembourg prisoners in Lublin 1942-45.) André Hohengarten. Luxembourg: Verlag der Sankt-Paulus-Druckerei, 1991. 594p. bibliog.

The reprisals taken by the Nazi occupying forces after the general strike of 1942 were very severe. Hohengarten writes about the common destiny of a group of Luxembourg people who were captured after these troubles. Their long ordeal comprised various stages: the drumhead court martial; the SS special camp of Hinzert; followed by the difficult journey to Lublin where the Nazis had built up a special area for carrying out experiments relating to their racial policy. The Luxembourg prisoners were finally sent to the Birkenhof camp in Dabrowica before being released to their deported families or to their homes with the obligation to enrol in the German army. The text is based mainly on eyewitness reports as very few written documents exist.

260    **Hinzert. Das SS-Sonderlager im Hunsrück 1939-1945.** (Hinzert. The
       SS special camp in the Hunsrück 1939-45.)
       Marcel Engel, André Hohengarten.   Luxembourg: Imprimerie
       Saint-Paul, 1983. 632p.

The site of the Nazi camp of Hinzert in the Hunsrück has become a place of martyrs
and a symbol of horror for the Luxembourg people. This publication provides
authoritative documentation on the camp and is divided into five main chapters which
deal with subjects including the German occupation, the Gestapo terror, the SS special
camp and life in the camp. Throughout the book the reader will notice a constant
striving for objectivity and clarity.

261    **Hinzert – kein richtiges KZ? Ein Beispiel unter 2000.** (Hinzert – not
       a real concentration camp? An example among 2000.)
       Eberhard Klopp.    Trier, FRG: Editions Tréves, 1983. 141p.

During the Second World War, Hinzert was a small concentration camp where most of
the members of the Luxembourg resistance were imprisoned. Many died there. This
publication represents a compendium of all the known material on the camp and
includes photographs and documentary evidence.

262    **Student in Hinzert und Natzweiler.** (Student at Hinzert and
       Natzweiler.)
       Metty Barbel.    Luxembourg: Imprimerie Centrale, 1992. 192p.

After the death of Metty Barbel, his daughter and the LPPD (Ligue luxembourgeoise
des prisonniers et déportés politiques – Luxembourg League of Prisoners and
Deported Persons) decided to publish his memoirs. Born in 1923, he was arrested by
the Gestapo in 1942 when he was a student and member of the Luxembourg resistance
organization, LPL (Ligue Patriotique Luxembourgeoise – Luxembourg Patriotic
League). Transferred to the concentration camps of Hinzert and Natzweiler, he
escaped in November 1944 and remained in hiding with the help of French resisters
until the liberation of the Alsace. He finally returned to Luxembourg in December
1944. With its many drawings and photographs, the book sets out to inform younger
generations about that dramatic period.

263    **Bergen-Belsen: Drei Beiträge zur Geschichte des Lagers.**
       (Bergen-Belsen: three contributions to the history of the camp.)
       Pierre Petit.    Luxembourg: private edition, 1988. 76p.

Petit, who was a prisoner at the concentration camp of Bergen-Belsen, provides a
critical account of the 'horror camp' which was finally liberated in April 1945 by
British troops. The first contribution (1970) is an overall review of the history of the
camp while the second part (1970), entitled 'The armistice' of Bergen-Belsen,
criticizes the armistice that seemed not to have been concluded to liberate the 60,000
people but rather to avoid a catastrophe among the surrounding population, who were
alarmed by the ever-increasing escapes of the prisoners. In the more recent (1985) and
last part of this publication, the author questions the choice of the accused as well as
the form of the war criminals' trial which took place in Lüneburg, Germany in
September 1945.

264    **KZ Buchenwald 1937-1945. Das SS-Konzentrations – Lager bei Weimar in Thüringen.** (Buchenwald concentration camp 1937-45. The SS camp at Weimar in Thüringen.)
Amicale de Buchenwald.    Luxembourg: Imprimerie Saint-Paul, 1985. 237p.

For the fortieth anniversary of the liberation from German occupation, 240 former Luxembourg prisoners of the Buchenwald, Thüringen camp compiled this publication which not only has historical value, but also represents a tribute to the 24 Luxembourgers who did not return home from this camp. This book is less an academic work than a testimony to the inhuman conditions that prevailed in the Nazi concentration camps.

265    **Lëtzebuerger zu Mauthausen.** (Luxembourgers at Mauthausen.)
Amicale de Mauthausen.    Luxembourg: Imprimerie Centrale, 1970. 426p.

Mauthausen is today a peaceful settlement of 7,500 inhabitants, situated 29 km from Linz in Austria. Here the Wienergraben quarry was for seven years the site of one of the most hateful dramas of the Second World War, the systematic extermination of about 111,000 people. The highest number of registered prisoners held there at any one time was 140,000, to which we must add about 70,000 unregistered people. Among them were 145 Luxembourgers, of whom 46 lost their lives at Mauthausen or the neighbouring camps. This book consists of moving testimonies from former prisoners.

266    **Tambow, 1943-1945. Les prisonniers de guerre de Tambow, enrôlés de force.** (Tambov, 1943-45: the forced conscripts as prisoners of war.)
Association of Former Tambov War Camp Prisoners.    Luxembourg: Imprimerie Hermann, 1963. 179p.

More than a thousand young Luxembourgers were held as prisoners of war in Soviet camps, 217 of whom died in the camps of Tambov or Kirsanov, USSR, or in the course of repatriation. This commemorative brochure records the experiences of some of those who survived.

267    **Die Umsiedlung in Luxemburg 1942-1945.** (Resettlement in Luxembourg 1942-45.)
Marie-Madeleine Schiltges.    Luxembourg: Imprimerie Saint-Paul, 1988. 203p.

Schiltges provides a chronological overview of the resettlement of Luxembourg families that the occupying force began to implement against all those who resisted Nazi rule. This eyewitness report addresses younger readers above all, but it also represents a tribute to the families who were lucky enough to remain in the Grand Duchy and who sent packages to those who were deported. The author, who was herself deported at the age of thirteen, describes events and relates the stories of other survivors who were deported to camps located in Silesia, the Sudetenland and the Hunsrück region.

268 **Als Luxemburg entvölkert werden sollte: Geschichte und Geschichten der Umsiedlung.** (When Luxembourg was to be depopulated: the history and accounts of resettlement.)
Evy Friedrich. Luxembourg: Editions Krippler-Müller, 1989. 159p.

Surveys the deportation of thousands of Luxembourgers to the German Reich during the Second World War. Friedrich devotes attention to each of the different places of encampment, and contrasts the wartime pictures with photographs he took on a visit to the camps twenty-five years later. He relates significant events, anecdotes and family destinies, and includes a list of all those who were deported. This moving account is based on original documents, first-hand eyewitness reports and photographs.

269 **Lëtzebuerg 44/45. Fotodokumenter iwwer d'Joër vun der Liberatioun.** (Luxembourg 44/45. Photo documents of the liberation year.)
Luxembourg: Imprimerie Victor Buck, 1984. 159p.

This volume on Luxembourg's liberation from Nazi occupation includes more than 300 photographs which document the country's final hours of oppression, the temporary liberation of September 1944 and the permanent one of 1945, and the mood of the following days and weeks.

270 **Schumanns Eck. 1944-1945 Liberation Memorial.** (Schumann's corner. 1944-45 Liberation Memorial.)
Luxembourg: Imprimerie Rapidpress, 1994. 195p.

To commemorate the fiftieth anniversary of the liberation of Luxembourg, the Liberation Memorial Association decided to construct a monument at the strategic crossroads of 'Schumanns Eck' (near the martyr town of Wiltz). It is meant to remind the passers-by of the desperate and murderous fights that occurred between American troops and the German occupying force. This volume provides a detailed account of these violent struggles, and documents them for future generations.

271 **La voie de la Liberté au Grand-Duché de Luxembourg 1944-84.** (The Road to Liberty in the Grand Duchy of Luxembourg 1944-84.)
Comité Luxembourgeois de la Voie de la Liberté. Luxembourg: Imprimerie Saint-Paul, 1984. 255p.

Published for the fortieth anniversary of the liberation of Luxembourg by American troops, this volume comprises the contributions of different personalities such as the prime minister of Luxembourg. Well illustrated, it is, as the former President of the United States, Ronald Reagan writes in the preface, 'a fitting tribute indeed to those who trod that road in defense of liberty'.

272 **Wéi wann et eréischt haut geschitt wier ...** (As if it had happened but today ...)
Contributions to the *Luxemburger Wort* supplement. Luxembourg: Imprimerie Saint-Paul, 1993. 362p.

During the year 1942 Luxembourg staged a general strike as a protest against the Nazi decision to enrol young Luxembourgers into the Wehrmacht (German army). To celebrate the fiftieth anniversary of that strike, which was severely punished by the Germans, the decision was taken to publish a book containing more than fifty contributions on this subject (by well-known Luxembourg historians such as Paul Dostert and G. Heisbourg). Aptly illustrated and well documented, this publication is a compilation of contributions to a supplement of the Luxembourg daily, *Luxemburger Wort* (28 August 1992) and reports issued during the commemorative celebration.

273 **Die Ardennen-Offensive.** (The offensive of the Ardennes.)
William K. Goolrick, Ogden Tanner. Amsterdam: Time-Life, 1981. 208p.

A captivating description of the Battle of the Ardennes in the winter of 1944/45, popularly called the Battle of the Bulge. This German counterattack against thinly held American lines in the Belgian and Luxembourg sectors incurred heavy Allied casualties. The two authors, who served in the American navy during the war, report, among other events, on the German encirclement of the hilly region of the Eifel in which 7,000 American soldiers surrendered, and on the bloody fighting for the junction of Bastogne. Backed up by abundant photographic material, the publication draws an impressive picture of these dramatic events.

274 **Luxemburg in der Ardennenoffensive, 1944/45.** (Luxembourg in the Ardennes offensive, 1944-45.)
Joseph Maertz. Luxembourg: Sankt-Paulus-Druckerei, 1969. 5th rev. expanded ed. 505p. 32 maps. bibliog.

Maertz's work has become a bestseller in Luxembourg; it describes the German Ardennes offensive, which destroyed about half of Luxembourg's territory, from the point of view of the Ardennes peasants who lived through it. This book offers a panoramic view of military operations from 10 September 1944 (the date of Luxembourg's first temporary liberation) to 16 December (when German divisions reinvaded the country).

275 **Battles lost and won: great campaigns of World War II.**
Hanson W. Baldwin. New York; Evanston, Illinois; London: Harper & Row, 1966. 532p. maps.

The military editor and analyst of the *New York Times* evaluates eleven crucial battles of the Second World War. The author writes: 'Each was an entity, many a turning-point, upon some the scales of history rested'. The Battle of the Bulge, 'a case history in intelligence', which took place from December 1944 to January 1945 in northern Luxembourg and the Belgian Ardennes, forms the subject of chapter ten. Written for both the general reader and the expert, this book combines the emotional and dramatic intensity of great events with knowledge and insight.

276 **The Battle of the Bulge in Luxembourg: the southern Flank December 1944-January 1945.**
Roland Gaul. Atglen, Pennsylvania: Schiffer Publishing Ltd, 1995. 2 vols.

On the fiftieth anniversary of the Allied invasion of Normandy, Roland Gaul, the curator and founder of the Diekirch Historical Museum in Luxembourg, published two volumes covering the events of the Battle of the Bulge that involved the northern part of the Grand Duchy. The Battle of the Bulge is the popular name for the German offensive of the Ardennes in the winter of 1944/45. It is so called because, having penetrated the American front in the Belgian Ardennes, German forces drove deep into Belgium, creating a dent, or 'bulge', in the Allied lines. The first volume describes events from the German position, whereas volume two records the American point of view as well as accounts from local civilians and participants.

277  **50 Jahre später: Spuren der Ardennenoffensive 1944.** (Fifty years
later: traces of the Battle of the Bulge 1944.)
Joseph Emonts-Pohl, Hermann-Josef Schüren.   Eupen, Belgium:
G.E.V., 1994. 158p.

Today, the tanks that stand in villages where the Battle of the Bulge took place in the winter of 1944/45 act as tourist attractions and symbolize war. The intention behind the portrayal of these tanks in the photographs included in this volume is to warn against ever letting such dark events occur again.

278  **Die Ardennen-Schlacht 1944-1945 in Luxemburg.** (The Battle of the
Bulge of 1944-45 in Luxembourg.)
Jean Milmeister.   Luxembourg: Imprimerie Saint-Paul, 1994. 1,015p.

In the winter of 1944/45, three American armies fought for six weeks against nearly a million German soldiers in the Ardennes, during the famous Battle of the Bulge. Milmeister, who has studied the Second World War for many years, describes the Ardennes operations. He provides a short overview of the German offensive, the American counter-offensive and the crossing of the border rivers, to aid a better understanding of the details of events which have to be seen as a whole. Jean Milmeister records eyewitness accounts from people who were involved (soldiers, nurses and civilians) and analyses questions concerning the causes of this war that have not yet been solved satisfactorily. An interesting appendix includes a detailed bibliography as well as a synopsis of this final turning-point in the Second World War.

279  **Ardennen 1944/45.** (Ardennes 1944/45.)
Cercle d'études sur la Bataille des Ardennes.   Luxembourg:
Imprimerie Saint-Paul, 1983. 168p.

This commemorative volume was published to accompany the inauguration of the American soldiers' monument in Clervaux (north of Luxembourg city). It includes interesting contributions concerning the Battle of the Bulge which began in December 1944 with the sudden final attack of the German army.

280  **Bataille des Ardennes. Itinéraires du souvenir.** (Battle of the Bulge.
Memory routes.)
Brussels: Editions de la Longue Vue, 1994. 153p.

The Battle of the Bulge (December 1944-January 1945) was one of the most bloody conflicts of the Second World War. This pocket guide illustrates and describes, in four languages (French, English, Dutch and German), more than 100 monuments in Belgium and the Grand Duchy of Luxembourg. A detailed map of the area, an introduction to the battle and a directory of all the monuments dedicated to this offensive in Europe, complete the volume.

281   **The Ardennes: Battle of the Bulge.**
Hugh M. Cole.   Washington, DC: Office of the Chief of Military
History, Department of the Army, 1965. 720p.  14  maps. bibliog.
(United States Army in World War II: the European Theater of
Operations, Vol. 8).

The German counter-offensive in the Luxembourg and Belgian Ardennes, named 'The
Offensive of Rundstedt' or 'The Ardennes Offensive', but popularly known in the
United States as the Battle of the Bulge, began on 16 December 1944. This work is
based on personal memoirs of, and interviews with, American and German participants
in the battle. The author of this analytical work writes: 'It has been alleged by survivors
of the German High Command that this operation was intended to re-establish the
military prestige of the Third Reich, carry its people through the gruelling sixth winter
of war and win a favourable bargaining position for a suitable and acceptable peace. Or
was it to take the initiative for its own sake without a viable strategic objective in view?'

282   **1944/45: Schicksale zwischen Sauer und Our. Soldaten und
Zivilpersonen erzählen.** (1944/45: Destinies between the Sauer and
the Our. Stories of soldiers and civilians.)
Roland Gaul.   Luxembourg: Imprimerie Saint-Paul, 1986-87. 2 vols.

The host of photographs contained in these two volumes perfectly illustrate the aim of
the publication: to establish the facts of the 1944-45 Battle of the Bulge on the basis of
civil and military statements while remaining impartial and avoiding personal
comments. As Gaul limited the story of this famous battle to Diekirch (a city in the
north of Luxembourg) and its surrounding areas, he made a minutely detailed study of
all the information he was given. The first volume treats the German point of view
(the author had contacts with German veterans and researched in the military archives
at Freiburg im Breisgau), whereas the second volume, which highlighted the points of
view of the American soliders and the Luxembourg civilians, helps to provide a better
overall picture.

283   **Lëtzebuerg 1944-45. Ein dokumentarischer Bildband über
Befreiung und Ardennenoffensive.** (A documentary book of pictures
about the liberation and the Ardennes offensive.)
Roland Gaul, Fred Karen, Frank Rockenbrod.   Luxembourg:
Imprimerie Saint-Paul, 1994. 272p.

Photographs sometimes express the cruelty of war more effectively than the written
word. With the aid of original and unique photographic material, the three authors
therefore attempted to produce an objective contribution on the Battle of the Bulge.
The wealth of previously unpublished German and American accounts they include
strengthens the impact of the volume. The publication is divided into four chapters, on
the liberation, the offensive, the counterblow, and after the offensive.

284   **G.I. Tom Myers' War Memoirs.**
Tom Myers, Marcel Scheidweiler.   Luxembourg: Imprimerie
Saint-Paul, 1991. 207p.

Tom Myers was an American soldier who fought in the Battle of the Bulge at the end
of the Second World War. This book was compiled on the basis of his reports and

letters and written from the point of view of a soldier who was captured by the Germans. In 1983, Tom Myer returned to Weiler (Luxembourg), where he had stayed on 16 December 1944, to inaugurate a monument in the honour of the American soldiers and a square bearing his name. This English edition was preceded by a slightly different German edition of the same title, *G.I. Tom Myers' Kriegserinnerungen* (Luxembourg: Sankt-Paulus-Druckerei, 1988. 119p.).

285 **Les deux libérations du Luxembourg, 1944-1945.** (The two
liberations of Luxembourg, 1944-45.)
Emile-Théodore Melchers. Luxembourg: Editions du Centre, 1958.
264p. 21 maps.
Written by a military specialist, this is the standard volume on the double American liberation of the Grand Duchy from Nazi occupation during the Second World War. The five chapters deal with: the first liberation of September 1944 by two American divisions; the genesis of the Ardennes attack; the daily succession of events during the Battle of the Bulge; the liberation campaign fought around Bastogne from 22 December 1944 to 18 January 1945; and the second and final liberation of Luxembourg from 18 January to 2 March 1945.

286 **Patton, the commander.**
H. Essame. London: Batsford, 1974. 288p. maps.
As a field commander, George Patton proved himself an equal to Manstein or Rommel. Major-General H. Essame, a Brigade Commander throughout the northwest European campaign, draws a perceptive portrait of this American general who contributed so much to the liberation of Luxembourg. Patton is buried in the American Cemetery of Hamm in Luxembourg, along with the men of the Third Army who fought and died in the Ardennes. His great deeds are commemorated every year in a special Remembrance Day, organized by the town of Ettelbruck, the gate-town of the Luxembourg Ardennes.

287 **Histoire de la 'Luxembourg Battery'.** (History of the 'Luxembourg
Battery'.)
Jacques Dollar, Robert Kayser. Luxembourg: Imprimerie Centrale,
1982. 196p.
Deals with the story of the 'Luxembourg battery' that was made up of men who managed to escape serving in the German army and reach Great Britain between 1940 and 1944. By deserting the German *Wehrmacht* they risked the highest punishment. One of the members of that 'battery', Robert Kayser, kept a field diary which allowed the authors to reconstitute the main facts concerning its formation and activities as part of the Belgian brigade, Piron.

288 **Longtemps j'aurai mémoire: documents et témoignages sur les Juifs du Grand-Duché de Luxembourg durant la Seconde Guerre mondiale.** (Long shall I remember: documents and witnesses' reports on the Jews of the Grand Duchy of Luxembourg in the Second World War.)
Paul Cerf. Luxembourg: Editions du 'Lëtzebuerger Land', 1974. 227p. bibliog.

During the Second World War 628 Luxembourg Jews died in the process of deportation. Thirty years after the end of the conflict the son of a deported family testifies to this cruel period and describes the fate of the Jewish community of Luxembourg. Telling documents and eyewitness reports illustrate the liquidation methods used by the Nazi bureaucracy. Cerf provides lists of: the numerous anti-Jewish decrees; the names of people who were deported; and important Jewish firms that were sequestered.

289 **Dégagez-moi cette racaille.** (Take away that scum.)
Paul Cerf. Luxembourg: Imprimerie Saint-Paul, 1995. 111p.

This publication, which contains a foreword by Serge Klarsfeld, deals with the epic of a Jewish family that had to escape to France after the Nazis occupied Luxembourg. Cerf places the odyssey of his family – a tragedy multiplied thousands of times during 1940-45 – in its wider historical context.

290 **Wéi et deemols wor.** (How things went in those days.)
Nicolas Kremer. Pétange, Luxembourg: Imprimerie Heintz, 1987. 407p.

Kremer gathered his experiences and autobiographical memories of the Second World War in order 'to give the following generations a vivid and true image of the poverty and oppression but also the bravery of that time'. Entirely written in Luxembourgish, this well-illustrated document is divided into five parts. Parts I and II describe the atmosphere in pre-war Differdange, south of Luxembourg, while the following two chapters document the problems Differdange experienced because of German occupation during the Second World War. The final section attempts to compare present times with the situation in the Second World War using the author's personal archives.

291 **Das Postwesen in Luxemburg während der deutschen Besetzung im 2. Weltkrieg 10.5.1940-10.9.1944.** (The postal system in Luxembourg during the German occupation in the Second World War 10.5.1940-10.9.1944.)
Marcel Staar. Luxembourg: Imprimerie Saint-Paul, 1983. 251p.

Staar's systematic and detailed research into the Luxembourg postal system during the German occupation from 1940 to 1944 is above all a historical monograph about the postal organization, but it also contains much detail that will interest both the Luxembourg and the German philatelist.

292 **Der Schienenstrang war ihr Zeuge.** (The railway track was their witness.)
Willy Konzem. Luxembourg: Imprimerie Watgen, 1989. 199p.

As a railwayman during the Second World War, Willy Konzem is a unique witness, and this makes his account stand out from the wealth of other publications on the conflict. Highly detailed and containing numerous black-and-white photographs, these memoirs were previously published in instalments in the weekly, *Lëtzebuerger Sondesblad.*

293 **Tränen. Eltern weinten um ihre Söhne.** (Tears. Parents cried for their sons.)
Armand Blau, translated by Liette Derrmann-Loutsch. Luxembourg: Imprimerie Saint-Paul, 1995. 219p.

On 1 July 1945, the American Graves Registration Command took over the task of developing and caring for Hamm Cemetery (a suburb east of Luxembourg city) and thirty-six other United States Temporary Military Cemeteries of the Second World War in Europe. Armand Blau attempts to retrace the history of Hamm Cemetery in this illustrated, German-English publication. The majority of the 8,411 American soldiers who are buried there served in the United States Third Army. The author appended a long list (p. 110-219) of selected burials which include the interred soldier's name, rank, unit and decoration.

294 **Aus dunkler Zeit.** (From a dark period.)
Nicolas Kremer. Pétange, Luxembourg: Imprimerie Heintz, 1993. 348p.

Before describing the individual ordeals of people pursued by the Nazi occupiers (for example, the dramatic story of A. Oppenheimer who lost his whole family in concentration camps, only managing to escape by chance), the local historian, Kremer, attempts to analyse the period preceding the Second World War and explain how it was possible for Hitler to come to power. Well illustrated and interlarded with contemporary documents, this is a brief but incisive chronicle of the years before and during the war which aids a better understanding of the period.

295 **Biller aus dem Krich.** (Pictures of the war.)
Norbert Quintus, Fernand Heischling, Georges Holzmacher. Luxembourg: Imprimerie Saint-Paul, 1985. unpaginated.

380 photographs and numerous documents make of this picture album a unique testimony to the dramatic period Luxembourg experienced from 1939 to 1946. The huge propaganda efforts made by the Nazi occupants to win the Luxembourg population over to their devastating ideology are detailed here in chronological order.

296 **Von der Zauberflöte zum Standgericht. Naziplakate in Luxemburg 1940-1944.** (From the magic flute to the court martial. Nazi posters in Luxembourg 1940-44.)
Paul Spang. Luxembourg: Imprimerie Saint-Paul, 1982. 467p.

During the occupation of Luxembourg from 1940 to 1944, the Nazi occupants used all kinds of psychological war methods in their propaganda. With the reproduction of 678

posters (78 in colour), numerous documents and drawings, the author has compiled a
very revealing work. In his introduction, Spang explains the various purposes behind
each of these posters.

297  **Le Monument national de la Solidarité luxembourgeoise pendant
la Deuxième Guerre mondiale.** (The National Monument to
Luxembourg Solidarity during the Second World War.)
Joseph Petit.   Luxembourg: Imprimerie Saint-Paul, 1972. 127p.
On 10 October 1971 the population of Luxembourg paid their respects to their war
victims by erecting a new and architecturally impressive monument in the very centre
of the city, on the 'cannon's hill' (*um Kanounenhiwel*) near the viaduct. This booklet
documents the commemoration and illustrates the artistic merit of the monument.

298  **Am Dauschen iwer d'Strooss vun Eisen ...: Bettemburg im
Zweiten Weltkrieg.** (While rumbling over the railway ...:
Bettembourg during the Second World War.)
Fernand Lorang.   Luxembourg: Imprimerie Saint-Paul, 1989-92.
2 vols.
The railway town of Bettembourg (in southern Luxembourg) suffered artillery fire in
May 1940 and bomb attacks during the Second World War. The first part of this
historical and literary work, which covers the period from the outbreak of hostilities to
the introduction of conscription in August 1942, was published to commemorate
Luxembourg's 150th year of independence. The second volume was issued in 1992
and deals with the general strike of 1942 up to the liberation of the town in September
1944.

299  **Düdelingen im 2. Weltkrieg.** (Dudelange during the Second World
War.)
Erny Thiel.   Dudelange, Luxembourg: Stadtverwaltung und
Kulturkommission, 1994. 132p.
The aim behind this work is to provide an accurate account of the military situation in
Dudelange (a town at the French border) before, during and after its invasion by
German troops in 1940. Erny Thiel, a former colonel-lieutenant, manages to provide
an objective chronicle of that dramatic period. His work is made even more conclusive
by the aptly chosen photographs and the informative documents contained in the
appendix. The author demonstrates that Dudelange became strategically important
because of its geographical location.

300  **Die Stadt Luxemburg unter der Naziherrschaft 1940-1945: Führer
für einen alternativen Stadtrundgang.** (The city of Luxembourg
under Nazi rule 1940-45: a guide for an alternative city tour.)
André Hohengarten.   Itzig, Luxembourg: A. Hohengarten, 1995.
231p.
The author suggests a trip through the heart of the city and some of the most
picturesque corners of the capital of the Grand Duchy. The alternative nature of this
guide is in the way it presents streets, houses and buildings, monuments and
memorials in the context of the dramatic events they witnessed between 1940 and

1945 as well as some of the Nazi offices that were to be found in the town at the time. Every site Hohengarten describes is specified by number so that it can easily be found on the city map which is included in the book.

301  **Pétange 1940-1944-1994.** (Pétange 1940-1944-1994.)
Luxembourg: Imprimerie Kieffer, 1995. 192p.

In 1994 it was fifty years since Pétange (a town in southern Luxembourg) had been liberated from Nazi occupation by American troops. To celebrate this anniversary, the local tourist association decided to publish a commemorative volume. Numerous photographs and documents alternate with different historical contributions and make this volume a lively and interesting account.

302  **Stroossen: seng Krichsaffer 1940-1945.** (Strassen and its war victims 1940-45.)
Roger Gallion.   Luxembourg: Imprimerie Saint-Paul, 1992. 622p. bibliog.

To commemorate the fiftieth anniversary of the introduction of forced conscription into the German armed forces of Luxembourg young men who were born between 1920 and 1927, Gallion issued this rigorous analysis of the consequences of the war for a small, peripheral Luxembourg town called Strassen. Entirely written in Luxembourgish and well documented, it describes, among other things, the long ordeal of twenty-four war victims from Strassen.

# The post-war years

303  **De l'épuration au Grand-Duché de Luxembourg après la Seconde Guerre mondiale.** (Purging the Grand Duchy of Luxembourg after the Second World War.)
Paul Cerf.   Luxembourg: Imprimerie Saint-Paul, 1980. 262p.

Three weeks after the liberation of Luxembourg by Allied forces, at the end of September 1944, about 700 Nazi supporters and associates were arrested in Luxembourg; this number was to increase to 5,101 by 7 July 1945. In the end more than 10,000 files had to be checked of which 3,000 were classified without any sanction being taken. A parallel administrative purge was also undertaken, involving a further 20,000 files. The results of these investigations were as follows: 12 death sentences were pronounced; 220 collaborators were sentenced to forced labour; 1,500 received prison sentences; 650 were assigned to solitary confinement; and about 1,200 lost their Luxembourg citizenship. Cerf analyses what motivated so many men and women to work against their country, and to betray, or report on, their fellow countrymen. He also stresses the shortcomings and irregularities of the war crimes investigations.

304 **Halte à la falsification de l'histoire. Le Procès Gomand (1945-1947): 114 témoins contre le gouvernement luxembourgeois en exil.** (Stop the falsification of history. The Gomand trial [1945-47]: 114 witnesses against the Luxembourg government in exile.)
Henri Koch-Kent. Luxembourg: Imprimerie Hermann, 1988. 152p.

Koch-Kent questions the attitude of the Luxembourg government in exile in London, where he lived as a foreign war correspondent. He reports on the Gomand trial, dealing with the Luxembourg law student who publicly attacked the three Luxembourg ministers – Dupong, Bodson and Bech – in 1945, after managing to reach London. Supporting his account with many oral eyewitness reports, Koch-Kent refuses to acknowledge historians who only take into consideration the existing written documents.

305 **L'abolition de la neutralité luxembourgeoise au lendemain de la seconde guerre mondiale.** (The abolition of Luxembourg neutrality after the Second World War.)
Ben Hadj Abdallah Said. PhD thesis, Université de Paris-Sorbonne (Paris IV), 1981. 125p.

Attempts to explain the reasons behind the abolition of Luxembourg's neutrality at the end of the Second World War. The author therefore analyses Luxembourg's former neutral status which had been granted by the Great Powers in the 1867 Treaty of London.

306 **Le Luxembourg et son armée. Le service obligatoire à Luxembourg de 1945-1967.** (Luxembourg and its army. Compulsory service in Luxembourg from 1945-67.)
Paul Cerf. Luxembourg: RTL Edition, 1984. 216p.

Despite having been accorded a neutral status when the country's territorial integrity was reaffirmed by the Great Powers in 1867, Luxembourg was still to suffer occupation twice in less than twenty-five years. Luxembourg's government therefore decided to establish an army based on compulsory service (1944-67). Cerf provides a history of these years, without neglecting the human aspects, so that his account ranges from Luxembourg's international alliances to the influence of the resulting large army on a small country and everyday life in the army. The volume includes studies of Luxembourg politicians and goes well beyond the narrow, national Luxembourg context in both its content and approach.

307 **L'armée luxembourgeoise d'après-guerre. Structures-Fonctions-Fonctionnement.** (The Luxembourg army after the war. Structures-Functions-Working.)
Jacques Leider. Luxembourg: Imprimerie Saint-Paul, 1993. 255p.

Leider's work concentrates on the immediate post-war years (mainly from 1945 to 1947) when, after having been liberated by the Allied powers, Luxembourg decided to introduce compulsory national service in order to be able to fulfil its NATO obligations. The author describes the creation and evolution of the country's military politics and of the army itself up to the beginning of the 1950s. Through the three parts of his book ('Structures', 'Functions' and 'Working'), he also deals with the problem of time constraints: the conscription of recruits had to be done at the same time as the training of the officer corps.

308  **'Eis Garde': Die Geschichte der Grossherzoglichen Garde (1945-1966) im Rahmen der luxemburgischen Pflichtarmee.** ('Our guard': The history of the guard of the Grand Duchy in the context of the compulsory army 1945-66.)
Willy Bourg, André Muller.   Luxembourg: Imprimerie Saint-Paul, 1990. 467p. bibliog.

The two authors were both members of *Eis Garde*, a special unit of the Luxembourg army which was dissolved in February 1966. The irregular, unsystematic and highly contested development of the Luxembourg army forms the background to the eventful history of the guard. With reliable documentation at hand, Bourg and Muller provide an objective explanation of what it really stood for and its role in guarding the Grand-Ducal palace and enhancing military parades. In order to present a detailed study, the authors combed through the entire military archives. The last part of the book contains numerous photographs of this unit, which enjoyed considerable prestige in the 1950s and 1960s, and a useful appendix provides an alphabetical list of the guard's members, each of which is accompanied by its page reference.

309  **Krieg im Land der Morgenstille. Der Luxemburger Einsatz in Korea.** (War in the land of the morning silence. The Luxembourg mission in Korea.)
Armand Blau.   Luxembourg: Imprimerie Saint-Paul, 1993. 195p.

Provides an account of Luxembourg's participation (eighty-five persons) in the Korean war. Well illustrated and interlarded with documents (including letters and reports), the volume also contains numerous citations from soldiers who report on their adventures. Blau also includes a description of the international circumstances before and during the war and information on everyday life in Korea.

310  **Le Luxembourg et la guerre de Corée (25 juin 1950–27 juillet 1953).** (Luxembourg and the Korean war, 25 June 1950–27 July 1953.)
Fernand Kartheiser.   Lille, France: Atelier National de reprod. des thèses, 1992. 614p.

Kartheiser is the first author to study the position of Luxembourg in the Korean war, that confrontation between the two Super Powers at one of the most critical periods of the Cold War. Therefore, his main aim is to provide information about Luxembourg's participation in this war, which occurred only six years after the end of the Second World War when Luxembourg gave up its neutrality. Kartheiser examines questions such as how the Allied powers viewed Luxembourg's role in the conflict and the identity of the eighty-five Luxembourg soldiers who enrolled with the Belgian battalion. The largest part of this volume, however, is taken up with an investigation into the constitution of the troops and their integration in the international forces under the UN banner.

# Regions and cities

311  **Les Cahiers luxembourgeois. Revue libre des Lettres, des Sciences et des Arts.** (Luxembourg Notebooks. Independent Review of Letters, Sciences and Arts.)
Luxembourg: Raymon Mehlen, 1923-64.

For over forty years the *Cahiers Luxembourgeois* best represented Luxembourg cultural life. From time to time this literary periodical published monographs on certain regions and towns of interest, written by experts in the field. They include: *Paysages et choses de chez nous* (Landscapes and objects from home), 1923/1924, nos. 6-7; *Harmonies ardennaises* (Harmonious Ardennes), 1929, no. 1; *Echternach*, 1930, nos. 1-2; *Vianden et la vallée de l'Our* (Vianden and the Our Valley), 1931, nos. 1-3, 1935, nos. 1-2; *L'ancien Hôtel de Ville et actuel Palais grand-ducal* (The former town hall and present Grand Ducal Palace), 1936, nos. 1-2; *Monographie de l'Hôtel de Gouvernement* (Monograph of the Government Hall), 1937, nos. 1-2; *Larochette*, 1938, nos. 1-2; *Bourscheid*, 1939, nos. 1-2; *Notre Moselle*, 1940, nos. 1-4; *Mondorf Thermal* (The Mondorf Spa), 1946, nos. 5-6; *Notre bassin minier* (Our iron ore basin), 1947, nos. 10-11; *Luxembourg 1900*, 1948, no. 4; *Mersch*, 1949, no. 1; *Dudelange*, 1951, no. 6; *Differdange*, 1957, no. 3; *Echternach*, 1958, no. 6; and *Le visage de Luxembourg* (The face of Luxembourg), 1964, nos. 5-6.

312  **Six villes, une Europe.** (Six cities, one Europe.)
Georges Sion.   Brussels: Union des Capitales de la Communauté Européenne, 1968. 358p.

Draws interesting parallels between six capital cities of Europe: Amsterdam, Bonn, Brussels, Luxembourg, Paris and Rome. The volume represents a personal effort of coordination and synthesis which highlights the common features of six strongly individual national centres of European life.

313  **La ville de Luxembourg.** (The city of Luxembourg.)
Directed by Gilbert Trausch.   Antwerp, Belgium: Fonds Mercator, Paribas, 1994. 463p.

The city of Luxembourg has played an exceptional role in the country's history. Indeed, the Luxembourg historian, Gilbert Trausch, explains in his foreword that without the existence of the city of Luxembourg, there would be no Luxembourg. This impressive volume on a city whose identity has been influenced by many and varied cultures, gathers together thirty-five chapters by thirty different authors. The capital's history is viewed from three perspectives: its international development and specific problems; its position as a tourist attraction; and, finally, its role in international politics – until 1867, when it was declared neutral and the fortress was dismantled, the city (more so than the country) had been a bone of contention between European powers.

314 **Baugeschichte der Stadt und Festung Luxemburg mit besonderer Berücksichtigung der kriegsgeschichtlichen Ereignisse.** (The history of the construction of the city and fortress of Luxembourg.)
Jean-Pierre Koltz. Luxembourg: Imprimerie Saint-Paul, 1946-72.
3 vols. maps. bibliog.

Koltz's work is a complete and very detailed account of the different stages of Luxembourg city's urban development, containing much information on religious houses and orders, industry, trade, transport and trade in paintings. Numerous biographies are included, along with genealogical data, and a special emphasis is placed on war-time events.

315 **Chronik der Stadt Luxemburg, 963-1443.** (Chronicle of the town of Luxembourg, 963-1443.)
François Lascombes, illustrated by Antoine May. Luxembourg: Sankt-Paulus-Druckerei, 1968. 402p. bibliog.

The distinctions between the town of Luxembourg and the country have often been hazy. This first part of a chronicle of the town of Luxembourg studies its history from 963-1443 and presents a fascinating combination of everyday events in the town and contemporary international background.

316 **Chronik der Stadt Luxemburg, 1444-1684.** (Chronicle of the town of Luxembourg, 1444-1684.)
François Lascombes. Luxembourg: Sankt-Paulus-Druckerei, 1976. 867p.

This second volume of the chronicle of the town of Luxembourg continues the town's history from 1444 to 1684, a period when the Duchy of Luxembourg was ruled by dukes of Burgundy from their capital in Brussels and by the Spanish Netherlands up to the capture of the fortress by the troops of Louis XIV. It is a detailed account of daily life in a fortified city.

317 **Luxembourg, tausend Jahre: kulturgeschichtliche Entwicklung der Stadt von 963-1963.** (Luxembourg, a thousand years: cultural and historical development of the town, 963-1963.)
Jean-Pierre Erpelding. Luxembourg: Sankt-Paulus-Druckerei, 1963. 151p.

Erpelding's intellectual survey of the cultural history of Luxembourg town describes both its everyday life and its higher social, moral and spiritual activity in a wider European and Western context. The fine pen-and-ink drawings and photographic material make this commemorative album a lasting artistic souvenir of the millennium celebrations of 1963. The line-drawings are by Roger Bertemes, Frantz Kinnen, Félix Mersch and Jang Thill.

318 **Geschichte der Stadt und Festung Luxembourg, seit ihrer ersten Entstehung bis auf unsere Tage: Luxembourg, 1850.** (History of the town and fortress of Luxembourg from the beginnings to the present day.)
Friedrich Wilhelm Engelhardt. Luxembourg: Krippler-Müller, 1979. 276p. map.

This work is the first systematic account of the development of Luxembourg's fortress, and the various monuments and military events linked to it. It is an indispensable basic work for the general reader.

319 **Luxembourg: forteresse et Belle Epoque.** (Luxembourg: fortress and the *belle époque*.)
François Mersch, Jean-Pierre Koltz. Luxembourg: François Mersch, 1976. 304p.

Mersch and Koltz's historical album covers the period from 1859 to 1914.

320 **Luxembourg: Belle Epoque, guerre et paix.** (Luxembourg: *belle époque*, war and peace.)
François Mersch. Luxembourg: François Mersch, 1978. 404p.

A companion to Mersch and Koltz's earlier volume (see previous entry), this publication studies the years from 1859 to 1939, the coverage expanded to deal with the First World War and the interwar years.

321 **Logements militaires à Luxembourg pendant la période de 1794 à 1814; aperçu historique sur les rues et maisons de la Ville Haute.**
(Military lodgings in Luxembourg from 1794 to 1814; historical survey of the streets and houses of the upper town.)
Alphonse Rupprecht, edited by Carlo Hury. Luxembourg: Krippler-Müller, 1979. 468p. map. bibliog. (Etudes Historiques, Culturelles et Littéraires du Grand-Duché de Luxembourg. Série A: Histoire Générale et Locale, Vol. 8).

Based on a record which listed the number of houses of both the upper town and the suburbs of Grund and Pfaffenthal, prepared by Nicolas Couturier for the period from 1794 to 1814. Rupprecht researched this source and was able to establish the genealogy of most of the owners and tenants and he describes the history of the houses and streets. He also studied: the cults of the saints; processions; armorials; inn-signs and ornaments; civil and religious feasts; markets and fairs; auctions; and foundation deeds. The book is illustrated with drawings of the town made in 1802 by Martin Boitard and a plan by Paul Wurth-Majerus. A systematic subject bibliography and an index of people and places is included.

322 **Luxemburg: von der Festung zur offenen Stadt.** (Luxembourg: from
the fortress to the open city.)
Jos Pauly, Paul Spang. Luxembourg: Imprimerie Bourg-Bourger,
1982. 131p.
This volume juxtaposes photographs of the modern-day city of Luxembourg with
illustrations of the fortress model drawn up by French soldiers under Emperor
Napoleon between 1802 and 1805. It opens with a study of everyday life in
Luxembourg during Napoleon's reign (1795-1815). Pauly and Spang also make a plea
for a halt to the destruction of Luxembourg's cultural and human heritage.

323 **Bilder aus der ehemaligen Bundesfestung Luxembourg; Images de
Luxembourg, ancienne forteresse de la Confédération germanique.**
(Pictures of the former fortress of the German confederation:
Luxembourg.)
Michel Engels, French translation by Marcel Lamesch. Luxembourg:
Krippler-Müller, 1979. 38p.
This album of twenty-five fine pencil drawings shows different aspects of the fortress
throughout its 900 years of existence.

324 **Luxembourg et Vauban, 1684-1984: tricentenaire de la prise et de
l'occupation de Luxembourg par les troupes de Louis XIV.**
(Luxembourg and Vauban, 1684-1984: tricentennial of the capture and
occupation of Luxembourg by the troops of Louis XIV.)
Service culturel de la Ville de Luxembourg. Luxembourg:
Imprimerie Joseph Beffort, 1984. 91p.
This book does not merely catalogue the objects on display at the 'Luxembourg et
Vauban' exhibition, held in Luxembourg in 1984 to commemorate the capture and
occupation of Luxembourg by the troops of Louis XIV 300 years earlier, in 1684. Its
different contributions rather attempt to honour Vauban, one of Louis XIV's generals
and the inventor of the modern system of military fortification, whose task it was to
reshape the fortress. The work sets out to render the atmosphere of the years under
French occupation (1684-97) and to illustrate the lives of the men who made
Luxembourg into one of the strongest fortresses in Europe. French rule over
Luxembourg came to an end in 1697 with the treaty of Ryswick, which forced Louis
to give up most of his conquests in the Netherlands.

325 **Vieilles demeures nobiliaires et bourgeoises de la ville de Luxembourg: une promenade historique, archéologique et généalogique à travers les vieux quartiers de la ville.** (Old houses and mansions of the nobility and townsmen of Luxembourg city: a historical, archaeological and genealogical trip through the old town districts.)
Jean Harpes. Luxembourg: Editions du Centre, 1959. 251p. (Etudes Historiques, Culturelles et Littéraires du Grand-Duché de Luxembourg, Série A: Histoire Générale et Locale, Vol. 2).

Harpes's volume is a detailed inventory of the outstanding historically significant houses and mansions in various upper-town districts, whose styles reflect different stages of the town's development and the genealogy of their owners. Well designed and systematically ordered, the book is illustrated with remarkable photographs by Batty Fischer and Bernard Wolff.

326 **Luxembourg: album de souvenirs.** (Luxembourg: souvenir album.)
Batty Fischer. Luxembourg: Edouard Kutter, 1966. unpaginated.

One of the best picture albums of Luxembourg town, covering the period 1890-1933, this volume offers insights into the daily lives of the inhabitants.

327 **Luxembourg millennial city: official guide of Luxembourg city.**
Maurice Cosyn, Jean-Pierre Koltz. Brussels: Guides Cosyn, 1974. 5th ed. 55p. maps.

Well written and documented, this booklet contains concise notes on Luxembourg's past, its main sights and its future European prospects. The guide also offers detailed descriptions of walks for tourists, in and around the city.

328 **Luxembourg: Promenade à travers le coeur historique de la capitale. Rundgang durch das historische Herz der Hauptstadt.**
(Luxembourg: a walk through the historical heart of the capital city.)
Guy Pauly, Roland Pinnel, Norbert Quintus, Marc Angel, Heng Bruch. Luxembourg: Syndicat d'Initiative et de Tourisme Ville de Luxembourg, 1995. unpaginated.

This useful, illustrated guidebook provides information about sixty interesting monuments, houses and sights aimed at the tourist who wishes to discover the 1,000-year-old town on foot.

329 **Am Dierfchen: Monographie d'un quartier disparu de la Vieille Ville de Luxembourg.** (Am Dierfechen: Monograph of a vanished district of the old city of Luxembourg.)
Tony Wehenkel-Guillier. Luxembourg: Les Amis de l'histoire, 1995. 272p.

The Dierfchen was a small grouping of six or seven houses, which in the 16th and 17th centuries huddled against the foot of the second wall of the fortress of Luxembourg. Contemporary documents call it the small village, 'Dierfchen' in

Luxembourgish. It is situated at the intersection of today's Grand'rue, the rue du Nord and the Côte d'Eich and has retained a unique mediaeval atmosphere through its inner court-yard (flanked by a restaurant, tavern and small underground theatre, le Théâtre du Centaure). The author, a well-known engineer and former government minister (1964 and 1968), successfully restored some of these houses, one of which was the birth-place of his wife.

330 **Lëtzebuerg am Zäitvergläich.** (Luxembourg in the wheel of time.)
Jean-Pierre Fiedler, François Buny, Paul Rousseau. Esch-sur-Alzette, Luxembourg: Editions Schortgen, 1994-95. 2 vols.

Includes a wealth of photographs of the heart of Luxembourg city and its suburbs, with pictures of the main streets and squares as they were in the past and as they are now. Thus the reader can see the profound changes that Luxembourg city has experienced in less than a century.

331 **Eis Gëlle Fra. 1923-1940-1984.** (Our Golden Lady. 1923-1940-1984.)
Edited by Gast Gengler, Guy May, Aloyse Raths, Lex Roth.
Luxembourg: Commission gouvernementale pour la reconstruction du Monument du Souvenir, 1985. 80p.

The 'Monument du Souvenir', known as 'Gëlle Fra', was erected in 1923 in Constitution Square to honour the valiant deaths of Luxembourg soldiers in the French army during the First World War. The Nazi occupiers destroyed this monument on 21 October 1940 and so it was turned into a symbol of freedom and partly rebuilt in 1958 to include the commemoration of the victims of the Second World War. It was only in 1985 that the monument was restored to its original state with the 'Golden Lady' on top.

332 **Liebes, altes Hollerich.** (Dear old Hollerich.)
Norbert Etringer. Christnach, Luxembourg: Editions Emile Borschette, 1989. 172p.

With numerous photographs accompanied by short notes, Etringer portrays how Hollerich, a southern suburb of the city of Luxembourg, looked a century ago. Unfortunately the lively village of the past has lost most of its character after being split by a motorway section.

333 **Echternach, notre ville: le livre d'or du centenaire.** (Echternach, our town: the golden centenary book.)
Echternach, Luxembourg: Société d'Embellissement et de Tourisme, 1977. 282p. maps.

Remarkable both for its technical layout and artistic illustration, the main contributions in this volume deal with historical aspects of tourism and culture. In the summer of 1977 alone Echternach received 77,000 foreign visitors. The international Echternach music festival, which began in the 1970s and is held in July each year, has attracted some of the most renowned artists in the world.

334 **Das Andere Esch-An der Alzette: ein Gang durch seine Geschichte.**
(The other Esch on the Alzette: a walk through its history.)
Joseph Flies.   Luxembourg: Imprimerie Saint-Paul, 1979. 1,302p.

Presents a monumental local chronicle of Luxembourg's second biggest town, Esch-sur-Alzette, the metropolis of steel and iron production in the south of the country, on the French border. Entertainingly written and well illustrated, it surveys many different aspects of community life from prehistoric times up to 1978. As a clergyman and former deacon of Esch, Flies' emphasis is on the social, cultural and religious dimensions of the community's experience, rather than on the town's industrial and economic dimensions.

335 **Livre du Cinquantenaire de la Ville d'Esch-sur-Alzette, 1906-1956.**
(Book of the fiftieth anniversary of the proclamation of the town of Esch-sur-Alzette, 1906-56.)
Esch-sur-Alzette, Luxembourg: Imprimerie Coopérative luxembourgeoise, 1956. 402p.

This luxuriously illustrated book was published on the occasion of the fiftieth anniversary of the proclamation of the town of Esch-sur-Alzette. Besides photographs it also contains colour reproductions of selected paintings by local artists like Rabinger and Mousset and other fellow painters like Klopp and Kinnen.

336 **Esch-sur-Alzette: du village à la ville industrielle.** (Esch-sur-Alzette: from the village to the industrial city.)
Ville d'Esch-sur-Alzette.   Esch-sur-Alzette, Luxembourg: Imprimerie Kremer-Müller, 1989. 104p.

Esch-sur-Alzette is Luxembourg's second town and has about 24,000 inhabitants. The city organized an exhibition for the 150th anniversary of the independence of Luxembourg that was held in October and November 1989. This catalogue of the exhibition contains documents, photographs and paintings relating to the industrial revolution which was so important in this part of Luxembourg famous for its iron industry which was established in the mid-19th century.

337 **Düdelinger Chronik.** (Chronicle of Dudelange.)
Léon Koerperich, Robert Krantz, Jean-Pierre Conrardy.   Esch-sur-Alzette, Luxembourg: Editpress, 1980-82. 2 vols.

Both of these volumes recount the history of Dudelange (a town near the French border) and are well organized and unique reference books which provide an overall view of the numerous cultural and historical events that occurred there. Whereas the first volume retraces the events that marked Dudelange and its inhabitants from 798 to 1907 (the year in which the village became a town), the second volume, which deals with the period from 1908 to 1981, continues with a description of the small village's evolution into a modern industrial town.

338 **Dudelange. Passé et présent d'une ville industrielle.** (Dudelange.
Past and present of an industrial town.)
Jean-Pierre Conrardy, Robert Krantz. Dudelange, Luxembourg:
Administration communale, 1991. 2 vols.

Dudelange is a typical example of an agricultural small-market town which, under the influence of its important iron industry, developed very quickly into an industrial site. Both volumes contain a lot of previously unpublished documents and memorable facts. The first volume covers the general development of Dudelange since the beginning of the industrial era, while the second deals specifically with the history of the iron industry.

339 **Festivités du centenaire de la commune de Rumelange 1891-1991.**
(Festivities of the centenary of the municipality of Rumelange
1891-1991.)
Commission pour l'Information Publique de la Ville de Rumelange.
Esch-sur-Alzette, Luxembourg: Polyprint, 1992. 355p.

The development of Rumelange is closely linked with the discovery of iron ore that changed the future evolution of the whole country. Until 1891 Rumelange had belonged to the municipality of Kayl but, with the signature of a decree by Grand Duke Adolphe in that year, Rumelange became a distinct municipality. This volume, which was published to celebrate the centenary of this event, illustrates the history of the southern municipality by means of photographs and the text of a keynote speech by the historian, Gilbert Trausch.

340 **Péiténg. Aus der Geschichte einer Ortschaft.** (Pétange. The history
of a town.)
Administration communale Pétange. Luxembourg: Imprimerie
Saint-Paul, 1982. 249p.

Published to commemorate the 700th anniversary of the town of Pétange which is located in the southern mining region of Luxembourg, this work recounts the long history and development of Pétange in three different, well-illustrated parts which deal with: early history; the years from 1281 to 1800; and finally the period from 1800 onwards.

341 **Mit der Bannmühle durch die Jahrhunderte.** (The soke mill through
the centuries.)
Jules Kauffmann. Luxembourg: Imprimerie Polyprint S.A., 1993.
140p.

Kauffmann discusses the soke mill of Kayl (a town located to the southeast of Luxembourg city), a kind of mill which was under special jurisdiction during feudal times. The feudal subjects not only had to mill their grain there (or risk severe punishment) but they also had to leave a part of their crop to the lord. This duty began in about the 9th century and was only abolished with the beginning of the French Revolution. Kauffmann structures the findings of his research in three chronological sections and includes photographs, drawings and documents. Even though the mill stopped operating in 1937, it is still an important meeting-point in Kayl for different associations such as the voluntary firemen, the civil defence and the association for elderly people.

342   **Eng Gemeng an hir Geschicht. Bieles, Eileréng, Suessem, Zolwer.**
(A municipality and its history. Belvaux, Ehlerange, Sanem, Soleuvre.)
Edited by the municipality of Sanem in cooperation with les Amis de
l'Histoire.   Pétange, Luxembourg: Imprimerie Heintz, 1993. 311p.

Published by les Amis de l'Histoire de Sanem (Friends of History of Sanem), this
volume continues the work of numerous local studies that preceded it and attempts to
describe and explain the history of the municipality from the Stone Age to the present.
The various authors do not neglect the particular evolution of each of the four villages
which compose the municipality: Belvaux, Ehlerange, Sanem and Soleuvre. They also
deal with related subjects such as fossils, traces of Roman history and the significance
of names and places.

343   **1200 Joër Buurg Zolwer.** (1,200 years of the Zolver castle.)
Anicet Hoffmann, Jean Reitz, Fred Sünnen, Jean Thinnes, Tano
Tornambe, Camille Wagner.   Soleuvre, Luxembourg: Syndicat
d'initiative, 1993. 319p.

The 25th anniversary of the Syndicat d'initiative (Tourist office) as well as the 1,200
years of the castle of Zolver (20 km southwest of Luxembourg) were celebrated with
the publication of this volume. Various historical contributions, interlarded with
photographs, documents and sketches, deal with the history of the village and its
surroundings from the origins of Luxembourg castles (illustrated by the example of
the first wooden fortified castle built at the 'Zolverknapp', the hill above the village)
to the forced enrolment of its youth during the Second World War.

344   **Ardennen – chronik.** (Chronicle of the Ardennes.)
Pol Tousch.   Luxembourg: Typolith, 1981. 287p.

Tousch's chronicle presents a selection of historical details on the court of Liefringen
(a place of regional jurisdiction in feudal times) and the parish of Dünrodt as well as
on the neighbouring towns of Boeven, Kaundorf, Nothum, Esch-sur-Sûre and Wiltz.
He also includes local details on the Battle of the Bulge.

345   **Les mairies du canton de Clervaux sous le régime français
(1795-1814).** (The municipalities of the Clervaux canton under the
French government, 1795-1814.)
Joseph Goedert.   Clervaux, Luxembourg: De Cliärrwer Kanton, 1989.
112p.

Goedert analyses how the north of Luxembourg, which had been isolated for centuries
until the year 1795 when the events of the French Revolution came to shake this
deeply traditional society, was gradually transformed under French rule. Moreover he
describes the conditions in which the French administrative policy was carried out and
on what level the local administration, the personalities, priests and inhabitants of
these northern villages contributed to the management of local affairs. Goedert
attempts to analyse how far this foreign influence transformed traditional attitudes. His
inquiry is based exclusively on documents from the State Archives of Luxembourg.

346 **Chronik der Stadt Vianden vom Jahre 1815-1925.** (Chronicle of the town of Vianden, 1825-1925.)
Theodor Bassing.   Vianden, Luxembourg: Veiner Geschichtsfrënn, 1974. 149p. bibliog.
This is a new edition of Bassing's *Geschichtsbilder aus der Heimat. Chronik der Stadt Vianden vom Jahre 1815-1925* (Historical pictures from the home country. Chronicle of the town of Vianden from 1815 to 1925) published in 1926. It has been revised by the author's son, Pierre Bassing, and Jean Milmeister.

347 **Chronik der Stadt Vianden, 1926-1950.** (Chronicle of the town of Vianden, 1926-50.)
Jean Milmeister.   Vianden, Luxembourg: Veiner Geschichtsfrënn, 1976. 191p.
Milmeister's volume is a continuation of, and companion to, Bassing's book on Vianden (see preceding item).

348 **Harmonie Grand-Ducale Municipale Wiltz: Livre d'or 1794-1994.** (Grand Ducal and Municipal Brass and Reed Band of Wiltz: Golden book 1794-1994.)
Luxembourg: Imprimerie Saint-Paul, 1994. 821p.
This volume was published to celebrate the bicentenary (1794-1994) of the Grand Ducal and Municipal Brass and Reed Band of Wiltz (situated about 60 km to the north of Luxembourg city). The authors emphasize the close links between history and music and the town of Wiltz and divide the publication into three sections, which provide: a chronicle of the band; a detailed essay on the history of the town and its inhabitants; and an exhaustive bibliography of literature on Wiltz, compiled by Emile Thoma.

349 **Wéltzer Leggt a Wéltzer Geschichten.** (People and stories of Wiltz.)
Will Schumacher.   Esch-sur-Alzette, Luxembourg: Editions Schortgen, 1993. 705p.
The local events of 1885 to 1940 – published in the *Ardenner Zeitung* (Journal of the Ardennes) – are the basic elements of the twenty-three contributions in this publication. Eight of these papers had already been published in the daily, *Luxemburger Wort*, in 1990 and 1991, but they were revised for inclusion in this volume. The contributions deal with the castle, the town's situation during the two world wars, the leather factories and other aspects of the social and economic life of the town.

350 **Wolz. Porträt einer Stadt = portret van een stad = Porträt einer Stadt.** (Wiltz: portrait of a town.)
Luxembourg: Editions Guy Binsfeld, 1987. 95p.
This magnificent book of photographs, published on the occasion of the 100th anniversary of Wiltz's tourist office, not only recounts the history of the 'capital of the Ardennes' but also represents a snapshot of life there today.

351 **D'Gemeng Elwen. D'Liäwen an d'Lékt am Louf van der Zékt.** (The municipality of Troisvierges [Ulflingen]. The life and times of its population.)
Fanfare Troisvierges. Luxembourg: Imprimerie Print-Service, 1989. 428p.

Published to commemorate the centenary of the foundation of the brass band of the municipality of Elwen (Troisvierges/Ulflingen), this volume reproduces hundreds of photographs which illustrate the social life of the area and the destruction wrought by the Second World War. It also contains contributions on subjects such as geology and archaeology.

352 **Wanseler Haiserbuch.** (The book of Winseler houses.)
Georges Keipes. Luxembourg: Imprimerie Print-Service, 1990. 436p.

Keipes made this inventory of more than 350 names and titles of houses and families together with family dates, and followed their development through the centuries. This illustrated study was drawn up for the municipality of Winseler (north of Luxembourg city). An appendix provides the family registers of the different villages that constitute the municipality.

353 **Bauschelt, Baschelt a Syr vu gëschter bis haut, 1939-1989.**
(Boulaide, Bauschleiden and Surré, past and present, 1939-89.)
Fanfare Concordia Gemeng Bauschelt. Luxembourg: Les éditions 33 66 99, 1989. 748p.

The fiftieth anniversary of the brass band of Boulaide (north of Luxembourg city, near the Upper Sûre lake) provided the occasion to publish a commemorative volume on the municipality which includes the villages of Boulaide, Baschleiden and Surré. The authors attempted to present a vivid and all-embracing picture and carefully researched the history of the area from the Middle Ages up to the present.

354 **25 Joer Al Dikkrich: 1968-1993.** (Twenty-five years Old Diekirch: 1968-93.)
Amis du Vieux Diekirch. Luxembourg: Imprimerie Reka, 1993. 164p.

For the 25th anniversary of the association, 'Amis du Vieux Diekirch' (Friends of Old Diekirch, a town located 35 km to the north of Luxembourg city), this commemorative volume was issued. It retraces the history of Diekirch and of the old district of St-Laurent in particular. This vivid account includes numerous photographs and colour plates.

355 **Diekirch. Hier et aujourd'hui.** (Diekirch. Past and present.)
Jos Herr. Luxembourg: Imprimerie Saint-Paul, 1980. 401p.

The author, Jos Herr, former mayor and historian of the town of Diekirch, collected a wealth of photographic material for this album. Thanks to his notes and explanations, this volume is a useful historical work that sketches the main stages of the locality's history. An appendix includes a genealogical table of the families of Diekirch which dates back to the year 1800.

356 **Ettelbruck portrait.** (Ettelbruck portrait.)
Administration communale. Ettelbruck, Luxembourg: Imprimerie
d'Ettelbruck, 1993. 151p.

Ettelbruck's economic and religious links with the abbey of Echternach date back to
the 10th century. However, the purpose of this picture album is not to provide a
detailed account of local history. Rather, the texts in German, French and English and
numerous photographs are intended to awaken an increased interest in the city and
region.

357 **Ettelbruck 1780-1980. 200 Jahre Marktgeschehen.** (Ettelbruck
1780-1980. 200 years of market life.)
Edited by Will Dondelinger, Maria Ludwig, Arthur Muller, Jos
Trauffler. Ettelbruck, Luxembourg: Administration communale,
1980. 189p.

This volume was published on the 200th anniversary of the Empress Maria-Theresia's
death. After 1778 she allowed the people of Ettelbruck to hold their market every
month rather than once a year. With the aid of numerous reproduced documents and
photographs, the authors provide a history of this long-running event.

358 **d'Geschicht vu Miersch.** (The history of Mersch.)
Roger Hilbert, René Fisch. Mersch, Luxembourg: Imprimerie Faber,
1992-94. 2 vols.

These two volumes recount the history of Mersch, a town located 16 km to the north
of Luxembourg (city). The first volume deals with the time from Antiquity to the
French Revolution, while the second volume opens with the arrival of French
Revolutionary troops and ends at the present day. These two luxurious reference
volumes provide a brief, popular and non-exhaustive outline of Mersch's history.

359 **De Kanton Miersch.** (The canton of Mersch.)
Mersch, Luxembourg: Imprimerie Faber, 1989. 228p.

Mersch is one of the twelve cantons of the Grand Duchy, and forms part of the district
of Luxembourg. Published to celebrate the Grand Duchy's 150 years of independence,
this volume provides the reader with historical and other information as well as colour
illustrations of each of the eleven municipalities composing the canton of Mersch.

360 **Die Wegkreuze des Kantons Mersch.** (The roadside crosses of the
canton of Mersch.)
Joseph Hirsch. Luxembourg: Imprimerie Saint-Paul, 1992. 435p.

Hirsch presents the findings of his detailed investigation of 144 roadside crosses in the
canton of Mersch (16 km north of Luxembourg city), and includes rich photographic
material.

361 **Echternacher Studien: études epternaciennes.** (Studies on Echternach.)
Jean Schroeder, Joseph Kohnen, Pierre Kauthen, Paul Spang.
Luxembourg: Imprimerie Saint-Paul, 1979. 111p.

Deals with Echternach's linguistic history, its dancing procession, and the history of the abbey library. It is reprinted from *Hémecht*, no. 1, 1979.

362 **Das totgesagte Echternach (1944-45).** (Echternach the village declared dead.)
Paul Spang. Luxembourg: Imprimerie Saint-Paul, 1985. 143p.

In September 1944, when major parts of Luxembourg had been liberated, Echternach, a town near the German border, was still occupied by Nazi forces. A great number of photographs, annotated by Paul Spang, illustrate the level of devastation suffered by Echternach during the winter of 1944-45.

363 **Beaufort im Wandel der Zeiten.** (Beaufort throughout the ages.)
Beaufort, Luxembourg: Gemeindeverwaltung, 1993. 2 vols.

These two well-produced volumes include thirty-seven contributions from renowned Luxembourg and foreign authors concerning the history, geography, commerce and culture of the municipality of Beaufort (east of Luxembourg city).

364 **Waldbëlleg 1989.** (Waldbillig 1989.)
Chorale St Cécile Waldbillig. Luxembourg: Imprimerie Kremer-Müller, 1989. 218p.

Recounts the history of Waldbillig (a municipality in the eastern part of Luxembourg) and presents the programme of the 1989 festivities and group photographs from the past. This publication resulted from five commemorations: the 750th anniversary of the parish of Waldbillig; the 250th anniversary of the construction of the church of Waldbillig; the 150th anniversary of the independence of Luxembourg; the centenary of the Chorale St. Cécile of Waldbillig; and the 25th anniversary of the accession to the throne of Grand Duke Jean.

365 **Wasserbillig im 19. und 20. Jahrhundert.** (Wasserbillig in the 19th and 20th century.)
François Mathieu. Luxembourg: Imprimerie Saint-Paul, 1977. 464p.

Wasserbillig is a town in the east of Luxembourg on the German border at the confluence of the Sûre and the Moselle River. Mathieu presents the local and regional events of the last two centuries together with numerous dates, facts, descriptions and anecdotes concerning the lowest town (150m above sea level) of the Grand Duchy. An appendix contains photographs of Wasserbillig, past and present.

366 **Chronik der Gemeinde Wellenstein. Der Hof und die Meierei Remich.** (Chronicle of the municipality of Wellenstein. The manor and bailiffdom of Remich.)
Joseph Schumacher. Luxembourg: Les publications mosellanes de Schwebsange, 1988-90. 2 vols.

This volume is a work of historical research on the author's home village of Wellenstein, which is located near the French-German-Luxembourg triangle (Dreiländereck). Schumacher included the manor of Remich (the main eastern region of the country until 1795) in his study in order to explain the historical background more satisfactorily. After a short introduction on the situation of the area today by the former Prime Minister, Jacques Santer, the author provides a general study of the region up to 1815. The work is well illustrated and an extensive index of places and persons is to be found at the end of the second volume.

367 **Chronik der 'Stadt' und Gemeinde Bad Mondorf.** (Chronicle of the 'city' and municipality of Mondorf.)
Lé Tanson. Luxembourg: Imprimerie Saint-Paul, 1981. 414p. bibliog.

This commemorative volume was issued to celebrate the 700 years of Mondorf's existence, the municipality located near the French border, southeast of Luxembourg city. The author has provided a chronological account of Mondorf's eventful past.

368 **Vun déi Säit der Syr: aus der Schoul geschwat (1936-1945).** (From the other side of the Syre: telling tales out of school, 1936-45.)
Milly Thill. Luxembourg: Imprimerie Saint-Paul, 1990. 351p.

Thill recounts fifty-one authentic stories of the small village of Olingen in the Syre Valley (between Luxembourg city and the Moselle River) before and during the Second World War. Written in Luxembourgish and divided into two parts (from 1936-40 and 1940-45), the author presents her childhood memories and succeeds in conveying the typical village atmosphere of those days.

369 **Duelem: eis Kirch.** (Dalheim: our church.)
Victor Loos. Luxembourg: Imprimerie Kremer-Müller, 1993. 312p.

Published to celebrate the 250th anniversary of the church of Dalheim (a village located about 15 km to the east of Luxembourg city), this sumptuous history of the church is based on three years of research by the author and his family.

370 **Walferdinger Familienchronik 1650-1900.** (The chronicle of the families of Walferdange 1650-1900.)
Jos Bour. Luxembourg: Imprimerie Saint-Paul, 1990. 255p.

Bour presents the findings of his research into families who live or have lived in Walferdange (near Luxembourg city) over three centuries.

371 **150 Joer Por Walfer 1843-1993.** (150 years of the parish of
Walferdange 1843-1993.)
Luxembourg: Imprimerie Saint-Paul, 1993. 189p.

To celebrate the 150th anniversary of the parish of Walferdange (1843-1993) which
was founded by a decree of Grand Duke Guillaume II, this commemorative volume
was published. Numerous photographs accompanied by short notes illustrate parish
life.

372 **Bartréng Union-Fanfare Bertrange 1910-1985.** (Bertrange Union –
Brass Band of Bertrange 1910-85.)
Edited by Luss Gérard. Luxembourg: Imprimerie Saint-Paul, 1985.
422p.

To commemorate its seventy-fifth anniversary, the Brass Band of Bertrange (6 km to
the west of Luxembourg city) published this volume which deals with topics such as
the municipality's territory and development and the educational situation since 1843.
It contains a statistical and geographical appendix.

# Auxiliary sciences

373 **Urkunden-und Quellenbuch zur Geschichte der
altluxemburgischen Territorien bis zur burgundischen Zeit.** (Book
of documents and sources on the history of ancient Luxembourg
territories up to the Burgundian epoch.)
Camille Wampach. Luxembourg: Sankt-Paulus-Druckerei, 1935-55.
11 vols. bibliog.

Represents the complete source material for the history of the territories of the middle
Moselle and the middle Meuse. For each document there are data about the original,
copies thereof, and notes on reference passages (loci) in which the documents are
copied in full or in part. Critical annotations and explanations are provided in
footnotes.

374 **Les inscriptions antiques du Luxembourg.** (Ancient inscriptions in
Luxembourg.)
Charles Marie Ternes. *Hémecht*, vol. 17, no. 3/4 (1965), p. 267-478.
map. bibliog.

This work is based on a manuscript written by Paul Medinger before the war, which
Joseph Meyers (historian and chief editor of *Hémecht* for many years) had planned to
publish, when his early death prevented him from doing so. Ternes undertook to
produce this catalogue of inscriptions which does not claim to be exhaustive, but
presents the author's comments, the parallel Medinger manuscript and photographs.

375 **Studien zur Toponymie und Geschichte der Gemeinde Differdingen.** (Studies concerning the toponymy and history of the municipality of Differdange.)
Nicolas Kodisch. Luxembourg: Imprimerie Saint-Paul, 1978-81. 2 vols.

These two volumes list the toponyms of the southern municipality of Differdange. Each place, which is characterized by old customs, is briefly described. Unfortunately, the author, Nicolas Kodisch (1917-76), died two years before the publication of the first volume and so his manuscript had to be edited by other people who did, however, respect the author's style.

376 **Les médailles dans l'histoire du pays de Luxembourg.** (Medals in the history of Luxembourg.)
Raymond Weiller. Louvain, Belgium: Institut Supérieur d'Archéologie et d'Histoire de l'Art, 1979. 392p. (Publications d'Histoire de l'Art et d'Archéologie de l'Université Catholique de Louvain, 19. Numismatica Lovaniensis, 4).

About 2,000 medals and various emblems and badges are classified and described in 392 pages of text and 160 pages of photographic plates. The items are grouped by subject, and an index of the artists, manufacturing houses, editing and intermediary houses which issue the medals is included. The work is based on the collections of the Medal Cabinet of the Luxembourg Museum of History and Art; Weiller, the curator of this Cabinet, is an internationally renowned expert.

377 **Les monnaies luxembourgeoises.** (Luxembourg coins.)
Raymond Weiller. Louvain, Belgium: Institut Supérieur d'Archéologie et d'Histoire de l'Art, 1977. 311p. bibliog. (Publications d'Histoire de l'Art et d'Archéologie de l'Université Catholique de Louvain, IX. Numismatica Lovaniensis, 2).

Weiller's authoritative survey includes forty photographic plates at the end. It opens with an almost exhaustive catalogue of Luxembourg coins; attributions and datings are provided in a special chapter. Weiller also deals with: imitations and forging; non-Luxembourg coins; coins no longer in circulation; and numeration systems.

378 **La circulation monétaire et les trouvailles numismatiques du moyen âge et des temps modernes au pays de Luxembourg.**
(Monetary circulation and numismatic finds of the Middle Ages and modern times in the country of Luxembourg.)
Raymond Weiller. Luxembourg: Ministère des Arts et des Sciences, 1975. 576p. map. bibliog. (Publications Nationales du Ministère des Arts et des Sciences).

This volume records all the known numismatic finds made on present-day Luxembourg territory, but it also includes certain treasures originating from the ancient Luxembourg territories of Saint-Vith and Konzem, which are now stored in Luxembourg. Weiller includes: a summary bibliography (p. 69-70); a chart of the rulers of the county, duchy, then Grand Duchy of Luxembourg (p. 71-73); an index of origins (p. 545-60); an index of treasures (p. 561-64); an index of gold coins (p. 565-66); and an index of mints (p. 567-72).

379   **Les monnayages étrangers des princes luxembourgeois.** (Foreign coinings of Luxembourg princes.)
Raymond Weiller.   Luxembourg: Editpress, 1982. 311p.

This catalogue includes the foreign coins of more than twenty-four public collections and two private collections. Such a work relies above all on its illustrations while additional information is given on each coin such as the place where it is kept. The study begins with a chronological list of the princes and prelates who came from the House or the country of Luxembourg and who had the power to coin money.

380   **La circulation monétaire et les trouvailles numismatiques du moyen âge et des temps modernes au pays de Luxembourg.**
(Monetary circulation and numismatic finds of the Middle Ages and modern times in the country of Luxembourg.)
Raymond Weiller.   Wetteren, Belgium: Imprimerie Cultura, 1989. 269p.

Since the publication of his first volume in 1975, *La circulation monétaire et les trouvailles numismatiques du moyen âge et des temps modernes au pays de Luxembourg* (q.v.), the author did not make many new finds. The analysis of monetary discoveries of the Middle Ages and modern times in Luxembourg and its surrounding regions is therefore the main interest of the book. The study also confirms the modest monetary traffic in these regions before the 12th century.

381   **Les monnaies gauloises du Titelberg.** (Gallic coins from the Titelberg.)
Lucien Reding.   Luxembourg: Ministère des Arts et des Sciences, 1972. 347p. maps.

Reding's descriptive catalogue details the 2,494 Gallic coins which have been found so far at Titelberg, a hill close to the town of Pétange. Twenty-five photographic plates complete this very thorough and well-designed volume.

382 **Armorial du Pays de Luxembourg contenant la description des armes des princes de la maison de Luxembourg, de tous les souverains d'autres maisons ayant régné sur ce pays, des gouverneurs ayant exercé le pouvoir en leur nom, ainsi que celles des familles nobles, bourgeoises ou paysannes, pour autant qu'elles ont pu être retrouvées.** (Armorial of the Country of Luxembourg containing descriptions of the arms of the princes from the House of Luxembourg, of all the sovereigns from other houses which ruled this country, of governors having exercised power on their behalf, and of the noble, bourgeois or peasant families, in so far as they could be reconstructed.)
Jean-Claude Loutsch.    Luxembourg: Ministère des Arts et des Sciences, 1974. 869p. (Publications Nationales du Ministère des Arts et des Sciences).

This descriptive catalogue includes drawings of each coat of arms by the author, a heraldic dictionary (p. 17-20) and heraldic tables (p. 841-69). It is the only reference work of value in this field.

383 **La noblesse au Grand-Duché de Luxembourg.** (Nobility in the Grand Duchy of Luxembourg.)
Jean-Robert Schleich de Bossé.    Luxembourg: Editions du Centre, 1954-59. 2 vols.

Only about thirty noble families are still settled in Luxembourg or own property in the Grand Duchy. Most of them were driven to Germany or Austria during one of the country's many occupations or during the French Revolution. There remains only one fully indigenous family, that of the Comtes de Marchant et d'Ansembourg.

384 **Les emblèmes nationaux du Grand-Duché de Luxembourg.** (The national emblems of the Grand Duchy of Luxembourg.)
Annotated and illustrated by Jean Henzig.    Luxembourg: Service Information et Presse, 1972. 15p.

On 18 May 1972 the Chamber of Deputies adopted the draft of a bill which defined the composition of the state's coat of arms, the national flag, and the colours of the river fleet and aircraft. This booklet records the text of the public report presented by the rapporteur, Colette Flesch, expounding the origins of the Luxembourg coat of arms and the national and military flag. It also contains reproductions of interesting heraldic documentation and emblem clichés by Jean Henzig.

385 **Orden und Ehrenzeichen.** (Medals and badges of honour.)
Jean Schoos.    Luxembourg: Imprimerie Saint-Paul, 1990. 423p.

In publishing his research, Schoos intended to provide a reference work that could also become a handbook for Luxembourg's administrative and diplomatic service. Divided into four sections, the introduction includes a condensed historical analysis of the evolution of orders from the crusades to modern times. The second section deals with the history of Luxembourg and the Nassau order, while the main part is a reference section on today's Luxembourg order and decorations. Finally, Schoos provides a list of sources.

386    **Armorial communal du Grand-Duché de Luxembourg.** (Municipal
       armorial bearings from the Grand Duchy of Luxembourg.)
       Dr Jean-Clause Loutsch (director), Nicolas Lemogne, Marcel Lenertz.
       Luxembourg: J. A. Fisch, 1989. 329p.

This luxurious publication usefully collects in one volume all the armorial bearings of
the Grand Duke, of the state of Luxembourg as well as of the Luxembourg cities and
municipalities. As the author consulted the original drawings of the arms and worked
together with members of the State Heraldic Commission, the documentation has an
official cachet.

# Biographies

387 **Biographie luxembourgeoise: histoire des hommes distingués originaires de ce pays.** (Luxembourg biography: history of distinguished men originating in this country.)
Auguste Neyen.   Hildesheim, FRG; New York: Olms, 1972-73. 3 vols.
Neyen's three volumes are central to Luxembourg's national biography. Dynasties and important families are dealt with in collective articles. Often unreliable in its subjective approach, some of the choices of personalities for inclusion are questionable. The publication is a reprint of the original edition (Luxembourg: P. Bruck; Jean Joris, 1869-77. 3 vols.).

388 **Biographie nationale du Pays de Luxembourg depuis ses origines jusqu'à nos jours.** (A national biography of the country of Luxembourg from its origins to the present day.)
Introduction by Jules Mersch.   Luxembourg: Imprimerie Victor Buck, 1947-75. 11 vols. bibliog.
The author only mentioned personalities who had been dead for twenty years or more; most of the persons listed belong to the 19th-century upper-middle classes. The contributions were written by several authors and constitute real family monographs with wide-ranging genealogy. The bibliographical coverage is uneven, but detailed personal indexes are included in each volume.

389 **Porträt-Gallerie hervorragender Persönlichkeiten aus der Geschichte des Luxemburger Landes von ihren Anfängen bis zur Neuzeit, mit biographischen Notizen.** (A portrait gallery of distinguished personalities in the history of Luxembourg from its origins to modern times, with biographical sketches.)
Karl Arendt.   Luxembourg: Huss, 1904-10. Reprinted, Luxembourg: Edouard Kutter, 1972. 514p.
Reprints Arendt's original 1904-10 volume with the addition of a name index. Arendt presents pictures and photographs of distinguished personalities. A rather personal

# Biographies

selection, which included only deceased persons, the work is chronologically ordered with summary bibliographical notes.

390 **Collection de portraits luxembourgeois.** (Collection of Luxembourg portraits.)
Katrin C. Martin. Luxembourg: Editions 'La Meuse', 1954. 227p.

This collection is a humorous, but somewhat rhapsodic and epic presentation of about sixty official personalities and outstanding, or simply popular, people from Luxembourg's public life.

391 **Charlotte de Luxembourg.** (Charlotte of Luxembourg.)
Pol Weitz. Luxembourg: Imprimerie Saint-Paul, 1988. 128p.
(Biographies Luxembourgeoises; 1).

Published in the 'Luxembourg Biographies' series (available in French and German), this useful volume retraces the life of the well-liked and respected Grand Duchess Charlotte (1896-1985) who acceded to the throne as a young girl after the troubles of 1918/1919 and the forced abdication of her sister, Marie-Adelaïde. The Luxembourg population became very attached to her over the years, until she abdicated in favour of her son, Grand Duke Jean, in 1964. Interlarded with photographs and quotes, the publication is a vivid portrait of an illustrious personality.

392 **Charlotte: Portrait d'une Grande Dame/Porträt einer grossen Dame.** (Charlotte: Portrait of a great lady.)
Raymond Reuter. Rome: Fratelli Spada, 1982. 248p.

Raymond Reuter's French-German publication is a colourful and detailed description of the life of the Grand Duchess Charlotte who acceded to the throne in 1919 after the forced abdication of her sister, Marie-Adelaïde, who was not recognized by any of the neighbouring countries. (Marie-Adelaïde had been suspected of collaborating with the German invaders in the First World War.) Grand Duchess Charlotte's welcome by President J. F. Kennedy in April 1963 shows the evolution the Grand Duchy experienced during her reign.

393 **Monument Grand-Duchesse Charlotte 29 Abrëll 1990.** (Grand Duchesse Charlotte Monument 29 April 1990.)
Luxembourg: Regéierungskommissioun fi d'Monument, 1990. 104p.

This brochure was published for the inauguration of the bronze statue of the Grand Duchess Charlotte, a national monument erected at the Place de Clairefontaine in the Government district. 75,000 copies, donated by the 'Oeuvre nationale de secours Grand-Duchesse Charlotte' (Grand Duchess Charlotte National Charitable Fund), were distributed free of charge to the attending crowd and the population of Luxembourg. Besides providing a chronological outline of her life and a transcript of her famous London message broadcast by the BBC on 5 September 1940, the book reports on how it was decided what kind of monument should be erected. This is followed by a short fact file on the French sculptor, Jean Cardot, who created the statue. An interesting bio-bibliography by Emile Thoma concludes this interesting homage in text and pictures to the life of the venerated 'Grande Dame'.

394 **Emmanuel Servais: Autobiographie.** (Emmanuel Servais: Autobiography.)
Emmanuel Servais, preface by Christian Calmes. Luxembourg: Léon Buck, 1895. 120p. Reprinted with a preface, Luxembourg: Fondation Servais, 1990. 210p. (Publications de la Fondation Servais).

Servais, who was, among other things, consecutively member of the German parliament (1848/49), member of the Luxembourg Simons government (1853-57), prime minister (1867-74), president of the State Council (1874-87), and mayor of Luxembourg city (1875-90) was one of the rare Luxembourgers who wrote his autobiography (1879). This 1990 edition of his work is preceded by a rather detailed introduction by the Luxembourg historian, Christian Calmes, who criticizes some of the gaps he found in Servais' work (for example, his role in the German parliament), but who concludes that a statesman should be judged by his actions and not by his writings even if they represent, as Calmes puts it, 'a valuable contribution to Luxembourg history'. It should not be forgotten that Servais governed the country during the most difficult years of its existence (1866-72), when its recently acquired independence was threatened from all sides.

395 **Joseph Bech, un homme dans son siècle: cinquante années d'histoire luxembourgeoise, 1914-1964.** (Joseph Bech, a man of his century: fifty years of Luxembourg history, 1914-64.)
Gilbert Trausch. Luxembourg: Imprimerie Saint-Paul, 1978. 257p.

The career of the statesman, Joseph Bech (d. 1975), was exceptional in every respect; his fifty years of political activity (June 1914-May 1964) included thirty-eight years in government, fifteen years as president of the government, thirty-three years as foreign secretary, and thirteen years in Parliament. Relying on private family papers and foreign archival sources, Trausch depicts a winning patriarchal personality who dominated Luxembourg's political life during the first half of the 20th century.

396 **Pierre Werner: une carrière politique.** (Pierre Werner: a political career.)
Robert Frank. Luxembourg: Imprimerie Saint-Paul, 1988. 103p.
(Biographies Luxembourgeoises; 2).

Available in French and German, this volume retraces the life and work of Pierre Werner, who influenced Luxembourg's political life for thirty years. A member of the Christian Social Party, he was minister of finance from 1953 to 1974 and prime minister from 1959 to 1974, and 1979 to 1984. From his early years Pierre Werner was a convinced European and an ardent supporter of economic and monetary union. In 1970 he chaired a group of financial experts whose job it was to suggest new financial policies to lead towards this union. The resulting Werner Plan, which called for closer economic and monetary links and the EMS (European Monetary System), was specifically designed to limit currency fluctuations among member states and was launched on 5 December 1978.

397 **Itinéraires luxembourgeois et européens. Evolutions et Souvenirs 1945-1985.** (Luxembourg and European itineraries. Evolutions and Souvenirs 1945-85.)
Pierre Werner. Luxembourg: Imprimerie Saint-Paul, 1992.
2nd rev. ed. 2 vols.

Werner retraces his extraordinary political career that began in 1945 with administrative functions and ended in 1985 as prime minister. In describing his own experiences in Luxembourg politics, he aims to explain the country's evolution from the situation it knew in 1945 to its present state. Werner illustrates the diversity of a Luxembourg politician's work which might involve local problems one day and decision-making at European level the next. In many parts of the book, particularly at the end, Werner expounds his basic creed: his belief in the greatness of the political job.

398 **Présence de Pierre Frieden.** (Presence of Pierre Frieden.)
Rosemarie Kieffer, in collaboration with Madeleine Frieden-Kinnen.
Luxembourg: Imprimerie Saint-Paul, 1995. 256p.

Illustrates Frieden's eventful career up to his premature death in 1959: he was successively an educator, writer, librarian and politician. The eleven chapters of this biography retrace those different stages and conclude with a transcription of one of the speeches he made as prime minister and member of the Christian Social Party in 1958.

399 **Le portrait dans l'histoire du Pays de Luxembourg.** (The portrait in the history of the country of Luxembourg.)
Raymond Weiller. Luxembourg: Imprimerie Saint-Paul, 1979-83.
2 vols.

The print room of the Luxembourg Museum of History and Art has never yet exhibited its collection of engraved portraits. To fill this gap the author presents reproductions of the Museum's portraits of personalities from the *ancien régime*. Most of the people represented are sovereigns, governors and generals who played an important role in the history of the country. In the second half of the 16th century the simple portrait was replaced by more imposing ones which depicted the monarch in a martial or theatrical pose, and exhibited the insignia of his power. In the baroque period, this prestige-representation became the dominant style. The second volume includes more engraved portraits of figures from the *ancien régime*, but also contains portraits from the 19th century.

400 **Vie et carrière de Pierre Dupong.** (Life and career of Pierre Dupong.)
Pierre Grégoire. Luxembourg: Imprimerie Saint-Paul, 1985. 102p.

Entering the Bech government in 1926, Pierre Dupong became prime minister in 1937 and remained in office until his death in 1953. He experienced the dramatic period of the Second World War in exile in London, together with three of his ministers, where they reshaped the Party of the Right into the Christian Social Party in 1944/45. This biography was written by his party colleague, Pierre Grégoire, a former minister from 1959 to 1967. With the aid of documents and a lot of photographs of portraits, visits and commemorations, the author presents Pierre Dupong in two different contributions, one in French and the other in German.

401   **Robert Schuman, ein Porträt.** (Robert Schuman: a portrait.)
Lutz Hermann.   Freudenstadt, FRG: Lutzeger, 1968. 70p.
(Persönlichkeiten der Europäischen Integration, 3).

Robert Schuman (1886-1963) was born in a Luxembourg suburb, but because his
father's French homeland, the Lorraine, had been annexed by Germany in 1871, his
nationality was German until he recovered French nationality after the First World
War in 1918. From 1919 onwards he was therefore able to enter French politics and to
sit in the Assemblée Nationale (National Assembly) in Paris. Schuman was
successively the French finance minister (1946, 1947), premier (1947-48) and foreign
minister (1948-53). In this latter role he did much to promote European unity; the
Schuman Plan of 1950 resulted in the 1951 formation of the European Coal and Steel
Community, which was the nucleus of the present-day European Union. This
biography also includes many anecdotes about Schuman's political colleagues,
companions and contemporaries.

402   **Die Tudors in Rosport. Dokumentation über das Leben und die
Verdienste der Gebrüder Tudor für ihre Heimatortschaft Rosport.**
(The Tudors in Rosport. Documentation on the life and contributions
of the Tudor Brothers to their native place Rosport.)
Aloyse Steinmetz.   Luxembourg: Rapidpress, 1981. 68p.

This commemorative brochure provides an account of the life and achievements of the
Tudors, a family of Welsh origin whose home village was Rosport (a village in the
eastern part of Luxembourg known for its sparkling mineral water). Henri Tudor was
the inventor of the first portable lead battery while his brother was the mayor of the
municipality of Rosport from 1888 to 1924. Madeleine Tudor-Pescatore was known
for her commitment to many charitable organizations.

403   **Emile Mayrisch et la politique du patronat européen, 1926-1933.**
(Emile Mayrisch and the politics of the European employers, 1926-33.)
Jacques de Launay.   Brussels: De Meyère, 1965. 84p. (Collection
'Portraits', no. 9).

In 1911 Mayrisch negotiated the merger of the three existing steel plants, Burbach,
Eich and Dudelange, which became the Aciéries Réunies de Burbach-Eich-Dudelange
(ARBED) (United Steelworks of Burbach-Eich-Dudelange). Mayrisch became its
technical managing director, and placed Luxembourg's steel industry in the forefront
of the world market. In 1976 he became president of the International Steel Entente
which groups together German, Belgian, French, Luxembourg and Saar producers. His
policy consisted of adjusting production levels to meet demand and keeping prices
stable. Launay sketches a vivid picture of European 'cartelization' and projects in
Asia and Africa. Mayrisch can in some ways be seen as a forerunner of the European
Economic Union.

404   **Carlo Hemmer: sa vie son oeuvre.** (Carlo Hemmer: his life, his
work.)
Lex Jacoby.   Luxembourg: Imprimerie Saint-Paul, 1991. 297p.

Carlo Hemmer, a multi-talented Luxembourg personality, died in October 1988 in
Ettelbruck. After his doctoral studies in economics at Paris and Leipzig, he held many
important posts in government and industry and with the European Communities in

## Biographies

Brussels. From 1962 to 1977 he was the director of the Luxembourg Chamber of Commerce, and subsequently he was president of the Luxembourg Stock Exchange (1978-85). In 1954 he founded the liberal weekly, *d'Lëtzebuerger Land* (The Country of Luxembourg) (q.v.). Hemmer was also a great lover of nature and the fine arts. He devoted his leisure time to cultural hiking tours and youth-hostel activities, publishing various guides on the best hiking tracks in the Luxembourg countryside. A circle of friends, under the leadership of the writer, Lex Jacoby, devoted this volume to his memory. An extensive bibliography by Hugues Schaffner (1,600 titles) and the uncompleted text of the second volume of his 'Luxemburger Wanderbuch' (Luxembourg hiking book) conclude this commemorative compilation.

405 **René Engelmann 1880-1915: Leben – Werk – Zeit.** (René Engelmann 1880-1915: his life, work and times.)
Compiled by Cornel Meder with the assistance of Claude Meintz.
Esch-sur-Alzette, Luxembourg: Imprimerie Kremer-Müller, 1990.
431p. (Publications de la Fondation Servais).

René Engelmann (1880-1915) was a Luxembourg poet who committed suicide at the age of thirty-five years and whose work has somewhat fallen into oblivion. The exhibition that took place in 1990 to commemorate the seventy-fifth anniversary of his death also saw the publication of this biography. Cornel Meder set out to present a vivid account of an interesting personality, and to try to understand Engelmann's life within a particular social context. The volume is divided into two parts: the first section includes chronicles, texts, letters and a bibliography, all complementary to the exhibition; the second part, on the other hand, contains documents displayed at the exhibition as well as many black-and-white photographs.

406 **Siggy vu Lëtzebuerg 1888-1961.** (Siggy of Luxembourg 1888-1961.)
Luxembourg: Comité Siggy, 1987. 60p.

This handy brochure retraces the life of Lucien Koenig (1888-1961), a well-known Luxembourg patriot who got the nick-name of Siggy of Luxembourg after the first count of Luxembourg Sigefroi, who bought the Castellum Lucilinburhuc in 963. Interlarded with numerous photographs, the reader discovers, among other things, that Siggy composed the hymn, 'U Lëtzebuerg' (Lëtzebuerg de Lëtzebuerger), which means 'Luxembourg to the Luxembourg people' in 1909 and that, one year later, he was one of the founders of the 'Lëtzebuerger Nationalunio'n' (Luxembourg national union) which set out to arouse national feeling among the Luxembourg population.

407 **Karl Voss. Zum 16. Mai 1982.** (Karl Voss. For the 16 May 1982.)
Compiled by Marie-Thérèse Kariger.   London: The World of Books Limited, 1982. 144p.

For the seventy-fifth birthday of Dr Karl Voss (1907- ), the first director of the European school in Luxembourg (1960-71) and director of the Thomas Mann library, Luxembourg Goethe Institute (1971-75), his friends published this commemorative volume.

408 **Joseph Kutter.**
Ingeborg Kuhn-Regnier. Luxembourg: Imprimerie Saint-Paul, 1990.
103p. (Luxemburger Biographien; 4).
Joseph Kutter (1894-1941), the first Luxembourg artist to become famous abroad, is
surely also the country's first modern artist. With the aid of photographs and black-
and-white reproductions of his best-known paintings, Kuhn-Regnier attempts to reveal
how Kutter lived, what he liked and what hopes he nourished. Although the works of
an artist should usually prevail in studies like these, the author is justified in devoting
attention to Kutter's life because his deep fits of melancholy seem to be reflected in
the expressive nature of his work.

409 **Lily Unden.**
Christiane Schlesser-Knaff. Luxembourg: Imprimerie Saint-Paul,
1991. 261p.
An account of the life of Lily Unden (1908-89) is provided in this publication written
by the niece of the well-known Luxembourg patriot and artist. During the Second
World War, Unden was deported to the concentration camp of Ravensbrück, as she
refused to obey the instructions of the German occupiers.

410 **Albert Simon: Luxemburgs 'Schnellkarikaturist'.** (Albert Simon:
the 'fast caricaturist' of Luxembourg.)
Pol Tousch, Guy Van Hulle. Luxembourg: Imprimerie Coopérative,
1983. 179p.
'Fast caricaturist' is the name given to Albert Simon (1901-56), one of the most
popular caricaturists to contribute to the satirical magazine, *De Guckuk* (Cuckoo).
This volume, which is written by, and about, Albert Simon, also reproduces some of
his best caricatures.

411 **Claus Cito (1882-1965) und seine Zeit.** (Claus Cito 1882-1965 and
his time.)
Lotty Braun-Breck. Luxembourg: Imprimerie Saint-Paul, 1995. 165p.
Claus Cito was the Luxembourg sculptor who created the 'Gëlle Fra' (Golden Lady), a
monument to the Allied soldiers who died in the First World War. The statue soon
became one of the architectural symbols of the capital. The author was able to consult
Claus Cito's personal papers, such as old photographs, extracts from newspapers and
letters, and she retraces a lively biography of a man who had somehow fallen into
oblivion. Braun-Breck also provides information on Cito's friendship with the German
expressionist painter, August Macke, and the eventful history of the 'Gëlle Fra'
monument.

412 **Camille Frieden.**
Luxembourg: Imprimerie Saint-Paul, 1992. 409p.
Camille Frieden is above all a well-known Luxembourg architect, but he was also a
poet, the head of cultural affairs at Radio Luxembourg, a teacher at the Higher
Technological Institute (I.S.T.) and the founder of two architectural magazines,
*Formes Nouvelles* (New Forms) (1953) and *Luxemburger Bau-Forum* (Luxembourg
Building Forum) (1957). This volume not only reports on the lifelong efforts of

someone whose aim was to create new forms of architectural environment, but it also includes some of his poems, autoportraits and drawings. Frieden also introduces a selection of the architects, painters, sculptors and engineers he most respected.

413　**Jean Gaspard de Cicignon, seigneur de Oberwampach.** (Jean Gaspard de Cicignon, seignior of Oberwampach.)
Bob Frommes.　Luxembourg: Published by the author, 1977. 342p. maps. bibliog.

'Major General, Military Engineer, Commander of the Fortress, Governor, General Inspector of Danish Fortifications, Knight of Danebrog, Vauban of the North'. So manifold were the titles of the protagonist of this book, who originated from Oberwampach in Luxembourg and made a great adventurer's career in the 17th-century Danish and Norwegian armies.

414　**Der parteilose Einzelgänger im Blickfeld seiner Zeitgenossen.** (The independent loner viewed by his contemporaries.)
Esch-sur-Alzette, Luxembourg: Editpress, 1990. 432p.

This biography of Henri Koch-Kent, a famous but controversial personality of Luxembourg society, is comprised of contributions from more than twenty of his contemporaries. Born in 1906, he disturbed (and still disturbs) many people, because he keeps fighting for the oppressed and the weak, never hesitating to criticize the officials. In one of his books he severely criticizes the government in exile of 1940-44, years which he also spent in London as a war correspondent. His most noteworthy achievement was his very early realization of the dangers which Hitler's accession to power could constitute for Luxembourg and other nations. An appendix added by Koch-Kent himself includes national and international press articles, reactions to his numerous publications and a list of the 875 Luxembourg people who were condemned by the special court created by the Nazi occupiers.

415　**Jean Schortgen 1880-1918.**
Esch-sur-Alzette, Luxembourg: Imprimerie Coopérative, 1980. 112p.

Provides an account of the life of Jean Schortgen (1880-1918), the first worker-parliamentarian of the Luxembourg Socialist Workers' Party, who died in 1918 after an accident at work.

416　**John Grün.**
Frank Zeimet.　Luxembourg: Imprimerie Saint-Paul, 1989. 101p.
(Biographies Luxembourgeoises; 3).

Born in Mondorf (in the east of Luxembourg) in 1868, John Grün emigrated to America in 1889, as did a lot of Luxembourgers at that time. Once there he became world-famous as the strongest man in the world. Zeimet provides an account of his life and illustrates the volume with many contemporary photographs and documents. An important chapter summarizes the muscular power performance records established by Grün and provides information about Georges Christen who is now performing similar power exercises.

417 **Henri de Brandenbourg.** (Henry of Brandenbourg.)
Pierre Hamer. Luxembourg: Imprimerie Saint-Paul, 1983. 351p.

Henry of Brandenbourg (1665-1738) was the last male descendant of a noble Luxembourg family, who travelled widely around Europe to places such as Brussels, Paris, Genoa and Madrid. Wherever he was, he would get in touch with high-ranking people, until, however, he was imprisoned by Louis XIV at the Bastille, on suspicion of espionage for the Austrians (Luxembourg was at that time ruled by the Habsburgs). Hamer attempts to discover whether Henry was really a spy. While he was in prison for eleven years, there was a lively exchange of letters, travel notes, police reports and poems of his in different languages; all documents that can be found throughout the book. Because of his lack of inhibition, and his free thinking, Hamer's view is that Henry of Brandenbourg announces the century of enlightenment. Seven years later, another research work on Henry of Brandenbourg was published by the same author, *Du nouveau sur Henri de Brandenbourg* (More on Henry of Brandenbourg) (Luxembourg: P. Hamer, 1987), on further details of his life.

418 **Humanisten um Janus Coricius.** (Humanists around Janus Coricius.)
Pierre Grégoire. Luxembourg: Imprimerie Saint-Paul, 1980. 329p.

Janus Coricius (1457-1527) was a 'highly esteemed humanist and Maecenas'. As he was of simple origins, he took the name of his native village: Koerich in Luxembourg. Pierre Grégoire's literary and cultural study familiarizes us with this generous patron of poets and artists.

419 **Elisabeth Dufaing.**
Anne-Marie Leyder. Luxembourg: Imprimerie Saint-Paul, 1980. 372p.

Elisabeth Dufaing (1804-80) founded the order of Franciscan nuns in Luxembourg. This order is well-known in Luxembourg and abroad and its hospitals and schools are living testimony to the charitable activities of this female community. Written by Anne-Marie Leyder, a Franciscan nun herself, this volume recounts the story of the order's beginnings and the life of the founder.

420 **Die zivilen und militärischen Ärzte und Chirurgen in Luxemburg: von den Anfängen bis 1914.** (Civilian and military doctors and surgeons in Luxembourg: from the beginnings to 1914.)
Henri Kugener. Luxembourg: Published by the author, 1995. 768p.

The author set out to establish a biography of those doctors and surgeons who practised in Luxembourg up to the First World War. He deliberately does not distinguish between those foreign practitioners who utilized their talents with occupying armies or in the garrison of the Federal Fortress of Luxembourg from 1815 to 1867 in order to better point out the links between the military and the civilian world, and between Luxembourg and Europe. By references to birth, marriage and death records the author manages to illustrate the mobility of medical practitioners in previous centuries and the special role of supply and exchange played by the central platform of the town of Luxembourg.

# Population

421 **Studien zur Siedlungsgeschichte Luxemburgs.** (Studies on the
history of the settlement of Luxembourg.)
Joseph Meyers. Luxembourg: Krippler-Müller, 1976. 217p. 19
maps. bibliog. (Etudes Historiques, Culturelles et Littéraires du Grand-
Duché de Luxembourg, Série A: Histoire Générale et Locale, Vol. V).

Written in the wake of the significant work by Adolf Bach, *Die Siedlungsnamen des
Taunusgebietes in ihrer Bedeutung für die Besiedlungsgeschichte* (Bonn, Germany,
1927) on the toponyms of the Taunus area, this study only traces very general lines of
development. The three chapters deal with the natural features of the soil,
Luxembourg toponyms and the significance of these names for the history of the
area's settlement.

422 **La démographie du Luxembourg: passé, présent et avenir.** (The
demography of Luxembourg: past, present and future.)
Gérard Calot, Jean-Claude Chesnais. Luxembourg: Service Central
de la Statistique et des Etudes Economiques, 1978. 165p. (Cahiers
Economiques, 56).

Calot was commissioned by the Luxembourg government to carry out this scientific
study at the National Institute of Demographic Studies in Paris. Luxembourg's birth
rate has become the lowest in the world and is plummeting at an alarming rate. Calot
illustrates this catastrophic situation by means of mathematical and statistical graphs,
charts and projections. His final diagnosis is that Luxembourg will probably need four
or five decades to recover.

423　**La natalité et la mortalité au Grand-Duché de Luxembourg: une étude démographique avec initiation méthodologique.** (Natality and mortality in the Grand Duchy of Luxembourg: a demographic study with an introduction to the methods used.)
Gérard Trausch.　Luxembourg: Institut Universitaire International de Luxembourg, 1977. 208p. (Etudes Economiques Luxembourgeoises).

The author is guided by two concerns: to provide the reader with the minimal statistical tools used in general demography; and to apply them to Luxembourg. In a special chapter he also surveys some 19th-century demographic data.

424　**La croissance démographique du Grand-Duché de Luxembourg du début du XIXe siècle à nos jours: les mouvements naturels de la population.** (Demographic growth of the Grand Duchy of Luxembourg from the beginning of the 19th century to the present: natural movements of the population.)
Gérard Trausch.　Luxembourg: Published by the author, 1973. 281p. maps. bibliog.

Trausch's study follows the natural movement of Luxembourg's population. It deals only tangentially with migratory movements, but there is an extensive bibliographical index and an appendix of retrospective and comparative tables.

425　**Die Entwicklung der Bevölkerungsverteilung und der Agrarstruktur im Grossherzogtum Luxemburg seit dem Aufblühen der Eisenindustrie auf der Minetteformation.** (The development of population distribution and the agrarian structure in the Grand Duchy since the beginning of the iron industry.)
Paul Weirich.　Luxembourg: Imprimerie Bourg-Bourger, 1960. 114p. 17 maps. bibliog.

The rise of the steel industry in the second half of the 19th century brought on a spatial shift of the rural population. Using excellent charts and maps, Weirich illustrates the development of population density between 1866 and 1957, the density of the farming population, and the shifting of agricultural acreage in the 1950s. He notes the occupational redirection and spatial regroupment of the population and important changes in the size and structure of agricultural holdings.

426　**Famille et structures sociales au Luxembourg.** (Family and social structures in Luxembourg.)
Françoise Bedos, Mireille Pongy, Yves Toussaint.　Luxembourg: Ministère de la Famille, du Logement Social et de la Solidarité Sociale, 1978. 366p.

This study, carried out at the request of the Luxembourg Ministry of the Family, Housing and Social Solidarity, sets out to analyse Luxembourg's social structure and its dependence on the institution of the family. It examines the transformation of family models, taking into account the overall connection between the processes of industrialization and urbanization and the family.

427 **Geographie der Luxemburger Familiennamen.** (Geography of
Luxembourg surnames.)
Luxembourg: Institut Grand-Ducal, Section de linguistique, de
toponymie et de folklore, 1989. 463p.

This publication is the outcome of work that was begun in the 1930s. It lists
Luxembourg surnames and shows the local or regional distribution of each of them. It
also cites the 500 most frequent Luxembourg surnames, thus providing a good
starting-point for interdisciplinary research (for example, linguistics and socio-
economic history). Finally, 112 maps drawn by Henri Klees illustrate the geographic
concentration of some of these names.

428 **Die Luxemburger und ihre Vornamen.** (The Luxembourg people and
their first names.)
STATEC. Luxembourg: RTL Editions, 1987. 166p.

Four years after their publication of *Die Luxemburger und ihre Familiennamen* (The
Luxembourgers and their surnames) (Luxembourg: STATEC, 1983) the Luxembourg
economics and statistics centre (STATEC) issued this study on the history and origins
of the population's Christian names. This research work has the advantage of
presenting the evolution (from 1886 to 1986) of the whole Luxembourg population
over a period of 100 years (1886-1986). The authors consecutively analysed the
motivation and preferences behind the choices of first names, then made a historical
review of their origins before comparing Luxembourg's legal regulations with those of
other countries. The last part contains statistics, such as a table including the first
names of people alive at 1 January 1987 (in alphabetical order) and the 350 most
frequent first names of men and women throughout decades. Diagrams show how the
preferences for some Christian names changed from period to period.

429 **Habitat et structures sociales au Luxembourg.** (Housing and social
structures in Luxembourg.)
IREP, Grenoble and ARMGEN, Paris. Luxembourg: Ministère de la
Famille, du Logement Social et de la Solidarité Sociale, 1978. 527p.

Aims at describing the everyday reality of Luxembourg family life and certain social
features connected with housing. The study outlines legislation, describes some
communal and employers' policies and analyses the answers to a questionnaire as
given by inhabitants of different parts of the country.

430 **Les Luxembourgeois, un peuple épris de sécurité.** (The
Luxembourgers, a people bent on security.)
André Heiderscheid. Luxembourg: Université Internationale de
Sciences Comparées, 1970. 154p. bibliog. (Etudes Economiques
Luxembourgeoises).

Divided into five chapters, this study deals in turn with natality in Luxembourg and
aspects of the country's social, economic, political and religious life. In every area
Heiderscheid notes a kind of innate reflex in favour of security. This is especially
striking in the field of religion, where the rate of Sunday observance is relatively high,
in spite of an obvious lack of religious fervour. More recent investigations have
revealed a scaling down of this high rate of observance, and so dismissed the apparent
contradiction perceived by Heiderscheid.

# Emigration and Immigration

431 **L'émigration luxembourgeoise.** (Luxembourg emigration.)
Joseph Hess. In: *Le Luxembourg. Livre du centenaire.* (Luxembourg
centenary book.) Luxembourg: Imprimerie Saint-Paul, 1949. 2nd ed.,
p. 593-618.

Before the development of the national steel industry, many Luxembourg labourers
chose to go and earn a living in milder climates and on more productive lands. Hess
distinguishes four successive exoduses: the emigration to Transylvania in the Southern
Carpathian mountains, in response to an appeal from Geza II, King of Hungary, in
1141-61; the colonization of the territories of lower Hungary in the second half of the
18th century (about 1,600 Luxembourg families thus settled in the Hungarian region
of Banat); a continuous stream of individual emigration to the USA between 1850 and
1900; and the infiltration of Luxembourgers into France and Belgium. The author
provides much statistical evidence and quotes many cases of Luxembourgers who
have distinguished themselves in industry, science and public life abroad.

432 **Dann singen wir – Victoria! Luxemburger immigration to
America. 1848-1872: a selective bibliography.**
Mary E. Nilles. Brussels: Center for American Studies, 1979. 49p.

During the mid-19th century thousands of Luxembourgers migrated to America; their
history has yet to be written. The largest Luxembourger settlements were in the
Midwest: about 1,860 colonies were formed in the Chicago, Dubuque, Milwaukee and
St. Paul areas. Through their 'brotherhoods', which were social, religious and political
associations, they preserved their Luxembourg identity: an outstanding example is the
Luxembourger settlement at Rollingstone, Minnesota. This bibliography is a
compilation of various international publications which analyse and provide material
on Luxembourgers' experience in the United States. Its approach is selective, so as to
serve as an incentive for further genealogical, historical and bibliographical study.
Mary Nilles, who is of Luxembourg origin, carried out the research for this
bibliography between 1973 and 1975 while she was Fulbright Professor of English in
Luxembourg at the Cours Universitaire.

433 **Luxemburger in Amerika.** (Luxembourgers in America.)
Roger Krieps. Luxembourg: Imprimerie Bourg-Bourger, 1962. 320p.
7 maps. bibliog.

Although the emigration of Luxembourgers to the United States dates back to the period of the Pilgrim Fathers, this movement only reached its peak in about 1830 when a massive wave of Luxembourgers settled in the Midwest. Krieps investigates how much of their language and traditions these emigrants were able to preserve and cultivate in America. He found that it was only after the Second World War that the American melting-pot really succeeded in submerging ancestral customs and behaviour in the Chicago area, where the majority of Luxembourgers had settled.

434 **Die Luxemburger in der neuen Welt: Beiträge zur Geschichte der Luxemburger.** (The Luxembourgers in the New World: contributions to the history of the Luxembourgers.)
Nicolas Gonner. Dubuque, Iowa: Luxemburger Gazette, 1889. 489p.
map.

Gonner's authoritative study is divided into four parts that deal with: the emigration of Luxembourgers to South and Central America, especially to Brazil, Guatemala and Argentina; the various stages of their emigration towards North America and the employment and lifestyles of Luxembourg settlers in the various states; biographical notes on about 200 Luxembourgers who made outstanding careers in various fields of public life; and practical advice for all emigrants to North and South America. Published over a hundred years ago, Gonner's book set out to draw a well-documented portrait of Luxembourg settlers in this region that would be of benefit to all those Europeans who had only a vague idea about the New World.

435 **Die Luxemburger in der neuen Welt.** (Luxembourgers in the New World.)
Nicolas Gonner, edited by Jean Ensch, Carlo Hury, Jean-Claude Muller with the collaboration of Antoine Gonner and Liliane
Stemper-Brickler. Esch-sur-Alzette, Luxembourg: Editions
Schortgen, 1985. New illustrated edition. 2 vols.

Nicolas Gonner, like thousands of his compatriots, emigrated to the United States during the mid-19th century (1866). From 1872 onwards, he collected information on Luxembourg settlements in the United States. This illustrated publication is still the as yet unrivalled summary of inquiries on the period. The editors split this new edition (Gonner's original book dates from 1889), into two volumes: the first volume is an exact reproduction of the original work, whereas the second volume contains additional information such as biographies of emigrants and an inventory of the archival material relating to the emigration.

436 **Good Earth, Black Soil.**
Frank W. Klein, Suzanne L. Bunkers. Winona, Minnesota: Saint
Mary's College Press, 1981. 179p.

'Good Earth' represents the more distant history of the two authors, who are descendants of the Klein family of Feulen in Luxembourg and who now live in the Sioux County, Iowa, in the heart of America, a flat prairie they refer to as 'Black

Soil'. Historical documents, family photographs and folk-tales support the story of this Luxembourg family which emigrated to America in the second half of the 19th century. Rather than reciting a chronology of names and dates, the authors have combined historical fact with imaginative detail in order to create what might be termed historical fiction.

### 437   Rollingstone. A Luxembourgish village in Minnesota.
Mary E. Nilles.   Luxembourg: Editions Guy Binsfeld, 1983. 223p.

Mary E. Nilles, herself a descendant of the 72,000 Luxembourg emigrants who left their homeland, bound mainly for America, in the 19th century, describes their history on the basis of a unique example: the village of Rollingstone, Minnesota. This town and its community were founded in the mid-1850s by citizens of the Grand Duchy, and over the following decades the place developed into one of America's largest Luxembourg settlements. With its wealth of previously unpublished pictorial material, letters, official documents and newspaper reports, this book provides a vivid description of the long journey undertaken by these Luxembourg emigrant families.

### 438   American Luxembourg Society 1882-1982.
Luxembourg: Imprimerie Saint-Paul, 1991. 258p.

The American Luxembourg Society was founded in 1882 by the Luxembourg emigrants who returned to Luxembourg, but wished to maintain contact with their circle of friends in the United States. Following a general chronological survey the volume deals with certain specific developments, such as changes in statutes, and some particular aspects of the society itself.

### 439   Les Luxembourgeois au Congo et en Extrême-Orient.
(Luxembourgers in the Congo and in the Far East.)
Mathias Thill.   In: *Le Luxembourg. Livre du centenaire.* (Luxembourg centenary book.)   Luxembourg: Gouvernement grand-ducal, 1949. 2nd ed., p. 621-30.

Many Luxembourgers contributed to the development of the Belgian Congo under King Leopold. A 1938 record indicates that 233 Luxembourgers went to those regions in that year. There were also hundreds of Luxembourgers in former Dutch and British colonies and in China.

### 440   Lëtzebuerg de Lëtzebuerger? Le Luxembourg face à l'immigration. (Luxembourg for the Luxembourg people? Luxembourg facing immigration.)
Association de Soutien aux Travailleurs Immigrés (ASTI).
Luxembourg: Editions Guy Binsfeld, 1985. 191p.

Various contributions deal with the phenomenon of immigration to Luxembourg, which has aided the country's economic development since the beginning of its period of industrialization in the latter half of the 19th century. This study is the first attempt to write the history of these people and it asks whether the immigrants were really satisfactorily integrated into their new country, and how much of the local culture and lifestyle they were able to assimilate. These are questions the publication poses. This account also assesses the current situation, making a plea for an all-embracing policy to deal with it, and provides useful and practical information.

441 **Les étrangers et leur insertion à la collectivité luxembourgeoise.**
(The foreigners and their integration into the Luxembourg community.)
Institut Grand-Ducal. Luxembourg: Imprimerie Saint-Paul, 1981.
113p.

Six contributions from historians and social scientists deal with some of the main questions relating to the foreign presence in Luxembourg at the beginning of the 1980s. No other European country is home to such a high percentage of foreign people as the Grand Duchy, where foreign citizens now represent around thirty-three per cent of its population.

442 **Centenario: gli Italiani in Luxemburgo. Centenaire: les Italiens au Luxembourg.** (Centenary: the Italians in Luxembourg.)
Benito Gallo. Luxembourg: Imprimerie Saint-Paul, 1992. 525p.

Benito Gallo, an Italian priest, compiled this volume of photographs to relate one hundred years of Italian settlers who immigrated into Luxembourg at the end of the 19th century and in the 1960s. Composed of six chronological chapters, the book introduces members of the Italian community, from mining and steel workers and businessmen to sportspeople. The volume concludes with an alphabetical list of the main Italian families in Luxembourg, past and present.

# Social Organization and Social Conditions

**443  La peste au pays de Luxembourg: essai historique et médical.** (The plague in the country of Luxembourg: historical and medical essay.)
Jean Harpes.  Luxembourg: P. Linden, 1952. 108p.

The first genuine mention of an epidemic of plague in the country dates back to 1030, but the 17th century saw the greatest misery. During the 1626 epidemic the Provincial Council left the town and held its sessions at Echternach, while the markets were deserted and a famine developed. In 1637 the population of Luxembourg province was decimated by two-thirds, and entire villages disappeared. The Provincial Council, the magistrate of Luxembourg and the representatives of the three estates (nobility, clergy and burghers) officially chose 'Our Lady, Consolatress of the Afflicted', as the Patron Saint of the town of Luxembourg, and in 1677 the Assembly of the three estates proclaimed her patron of the whole country.

**444  Prestations sociales au Grand-Duché de Luxembourg.** (Social security benefits in the Grand Duchy of Luxembourg.)
Robert Schaack.  Luxembourg: Ministère de l'Education Nationale, 1969. 4th ed. 249p.

Examines the legislation on multiple social security schemes, sickness benefits and mutual help provisions that exist in Luxembourg. Schaack includes historical surveys of each benefit scheme.

**445  100 Joër Mutualitéits-Gesetz 1891-1991.** (100 years of Mutual Insurance law.)
Conseil Supérieur de la Mutualité.  Luxembourg: Imprimerie Hengen, 1992. 273p.

By promulgating the first law on mutual benefit societies in 1891, the Luxembourg state officially recognized the friendly societies that can be considered as having triggered off the social movements based on collective solidarity. Although the publication was issued to commemorate the centenary of this first law, it specifically documents the origins and activities of the mutual benefit societies while showing how this law contributed and still contributes to the social security of the inhabitants of the Grand Duchy.

446 **Cinquantenaire de la Caritas luxembourgeoise 1932-1982.** (Fiftieth anniversary of the Luxembourg Caritas 1932-82.)
Luxembourg: Imprimerie Saint-Paul, 1982. 179p.

When Bishop Nommesch founded the church welfare institute, Caritas, in Luxembourg in 1932, he laid the foundations of an organization which began by doing pioneering work and which now has a firm place in the security net of social benefits. This commemorative volume contains numerous contributions that deal with the history of the organization, its current activity and its latest targets for charitable work in Luxembourg.

447 **Vers une société pluriculturelle. Vivre et agir ensemble. Approches sociétale et pastorale.** (Towards a pluralist society. Live and act together. Society and pastoral approach.)
Luxembourg: SESOPI – Centre Intercommunautaire, 1994. 80p.

Over thirty per cent of Luxembourg's population is foreign. The SESOPI (Service Socio-Pastoral Intercommunautaire – Socio-Pastoral Intercommunal Service) pleads for a pluralist society in which Luxembourgers and foreigners should live more closely together and this brochure, published on the occasion of its inauguration, focuses on the various conferences it has held and the challenges it faces. It also considers the role to be played by the church in the phenomenon of migration and analyses the cohabitation of different communities from a historical, political, sociological and pastoral point of view.

448 **Luxemburgs Arbeiterkolonien und billige Wohnungen 1860-1940. '... wo der Arbeiter sich daheimgefühlt und die Schnapskneipe meiden lernt'.** (Luxembourg workers' settlements and cheap housing 1860-1940. '... where the worker feels at home and learns to avoid the pub and spirits'.)
Antoinette Lorang. Luxembourg: Imprimerie Centrale, 1994. 391p.

At the end of the 19th century, the development of the mining industry attracted thousands of workers to the south of Luxembourg, a region that had retained much of its rural character. The stream of immigrants quickly became too large for the existing accommodation structures to cope with and led to a housing shortage. This publication examines the characteristic features of the policy established in Luxembourg to provide low-priced workers' houses and considers the French, Belgian and German models. Lorang examines both public and private initiatives in her final chapter.

449 **Fraen zu Lëtzebuerg.** (Women in Luxembourg.)
Edited by the Municipality of Bettembourg. Luxembourg: Joseph Beffort, 1993. 67p.

These nine contributions on the situation of women in Luxembourg are written almost exclusively by women, except the one by Lucien Lux (mayor of Bettembourg) and the one by Guy Rewenig, a Luxembourg writer. The short essays concern: the relation between women and politics; the situation of women in the Luxembourg labour market; and Portuguese women and their lives in the Grand Duchy. This recent publication goes some way towards filling the gap concerning studies on women in Luxembourg.

450  **Le Luxembourg et ses travailleurs frontaliers.** (Luxembourg and its border workers.)
Claude Gengler.  *Revue Géographique de l'Est*, 1991, no. 1, p. 123-30.
Gengler's short paper describes the evolution of the Luxembourg labour market which is in constant need of more and more foreign workers (more than 50,000 border workers commute every day to Luxembourg – they represent about twenty-five per cent of the labour market) and presents the most striking results of a case-study undertaken in one of the leading Luxembourg banks.

451  **z.B. TOM: Report über den Drogenplatz Luxemburg.** (e.g. TOM: report on the drug scene of Luxembourg.)
Josy Braun, Jacques Drescher, Jürgen Frank, Josiane Kartheiser, Daniel Lammar.  1981. 108p.
Although this description of Luxembourg's drug scene was written in 1981, it is very much of current interest, as the number of drug-related deaths in the Grand Duchy each year has become extremely high. The publication examines the drug consumer's attitude as well as considering critical comments concerning Luxembourg's drugs policy.

452  **Des suicides dans nos prisons à quatre étoiles?** (Suicides in our four star prisons?)
Alphonse Spielmann.  Luxembourg: Imprimerie Centrale, 1982. 86p.
This is one of the rare studies that exists on Luxembourg's prisons and is mainly based on statistics and documents taken from the archives of Luxembourg prisons since 1940. Unfortunately, the total lack of information on the personality of the suicide victims does not allow any analysis of their motivation.

453  **Mémorial 1929-1994.** (Memorial 1929-94.)
Rotary Club Luxembourg.  Luxembourg: Imprimerie Centrale, 1994. 272p.
The Rotary Club numbers 1,200,000 members in about 27,000 clubs in 150 countries. The Luxembourg section was founded in 1929 and the members decided to publish this volume to commemorate its sixty-five years of existence. Besides a short historical overview of Rotary Club Luxembourg, the publication includes more than eighty portraits of the lives and works of deceased members who all played an important role in the country's economic, cultural or political life.

454  **Lëtzebuerger Pompjéesverband 1883-1993.** (Luxembourg Federation of Firemen 1883-1983.)
Fédération Nationale des Corps de Sapeurs-Pompiers du GDL. Luxembourg: Imprimerie Saint-Paul, 1985. 762p.
For its 100th birthday, the Luxembourg Federation of Firemen issued this extensive, well-illustrated volume on its history, which contains short descriptions of all the member-villages in the different cantons of Luxembourg.

# Politics

455 **La vie politique au Grand-Duché de Luxembourg.** (Political life in
the Grand Duchy of Luxembourg.)
Service Information et Presse du Gouvernement. Luxembourg:
Imprimerie Linden, 1995. 88p.

Published by the Information and Press Service of the government, this useful
brochure addresses those seeking salient details, rather than specialist knowledge, on
the political life of Luxembourg. It briefly describes the functions of the parliament,
the government and the State Council. Following a summary of the history and recent
situation of Luxembourg's political parties, the brochure provides brief outlines of the
role of the press and audiovisual media in political life and the activities of the trade
unions, the professional chambers and the Economic and Social Council.

456 **Structures socio-politiques du Luxembourg.** (Socio-political
structures of Luxembourg.)
Michel Delvaux. Luxembourg: Institut Universitaire International de
Luxembourg, 1977. 178p. (Etudes Economiques Luxembourgeoises).

This study is divided into five chapters. Chapter I analyses the sociological situation in
1974, discusses an economic mortgage on Luxembourg's sovereignty and considers
the state's possibilities before outlining some contemporary theories on the state in
general. Chapter II examines important elements relating to social class and asks
whether Luxembourg is a classless society. Chapter III examines the mechanism of
social peace and syndical unification and outlines the functions of professional
chambers and their relationship with the state and the 'Economic and Social Council'.
Chapter IV deals with the sociology of political life, cultural mutations, the
depoliticization and professionalization of politics, and the revolutionary extreme left.
Finally, chapter V analyses the five main parties: the Christian Social People's Party
(CSV), the Luxembourg Socialist Workers' Party (LSAP), the Democratic Party (DP),
the Communist Party (KP) and the Social Democratic Party (SDP).

457 **Histoire de l'idéologie politique dans le Grand Duché de Luxembourg.** (History of political ideology in the Grand Duchy of Luxembourg from 1841 to 1867.)
Victor Molitor. Luxembourg: Imprimerie Worré-Mertens, 1939. 310p.

Written for the centenary celebration of Luxembourg's independence, this book retraces the birth and evolution of the country's political parties, the material wealth of the steel and mining sector, and the first national newspapers.

458 **Ursprung und Leistung einer Partei: Rechtspartei und Christliche-Soziale Volkspartei, 1914-1974.** (The origins and achievements of a political party: Party of the Right and Christian Social People's Party, 1914-74.)
Emile Schaus. Luxembourg: Sankt-Paulus-Druckerei, 1974. 344p. bibliog.

Published on its sixtieth anniversary, this volume traces the development of the Christian Social People's Party (CSV) which has held government responsibility for nearly fifty years. Eyewitness accounts compensate for the lack of documentation available for the years 1940-44, and deal with many previously obscure subjects, like the exiled government in Canada and in London during the Second World War. The volume includes a survey of the politically-orientated or anti-political press and a bibliography on 19th- and 20th-century political history (p. 302-15).

459 **Innovation – Intégration. Festschrift für Pierre Werner. Mélanges pour Pierre Werner.** (Innovation – Integration. Commemorative volume in honour of Pierre Werner.)
Luxembourg: Imprimerie Saint-Paul, 1993. 592p.

This commemorative volume was published to celebrate the eightieth birthday of Pierre Werner, Luxembourg's prime minister from 1959 to 1974 and 1979 to 1984. It compiles more than seventy contributions from Luxembourg and foreign personalities, such as Helmut Kohl, Jacques Santer, Hans Tietmeyer, Javier Pérez de Cuellar and Manfred Wörner. These contributions, which cover many different areas, are divided into six different sections such as 'Luxembourg as an international partner' or 'Europe – our future'.

460 **Sozialismus in Luxemburg: von den Anfängen bis 1940.** (Socialism in Luxembourg: from the beginnings to 1940.)
Ben Fayot. Luxembourg: Centre de Recherches et d'Etudes Socialistes, 1979. 483p.

Fayot's first volume on socialism in Luxembourg studies its development up to 1940 and represents the best study of the evolution of the Socialist Workers' Party (LSAP-POSL) in this period. Although the work was commissioned by the party for its seventy-fifth anniversary, the author is remarkably objective. His first chapters cover the period 1896-1920, and deal with the slow evolution of the idea of the 'Sozialdemokratie' (social democracy) towards the establishment of the Sozialistische Partei Luxemburgs (Socialist Party of Luxembourg). Later chapters examine the connection between Luxembourg's Socialist Party and international socialism and analyse the party's internal organization and local, communal, trade-unionist and youth sections over the years 1924-40.

461 **Sozialismus in Luxemburg: Von 1940 bis zu Beginn der achtziger Jahre.** (Socialism in Luxembourg: from 1940 to the early 1980s.)
Ben Fayot.   Luxembourg: Centre de Recherches et d'Etudes Socialistes, 1989. 371p.

Ben Fayot became President of Luxembourg's Socialist Workers' Party (LSAP-POSL) in 1989. This, his second volume on socialism in Luxembourg begins where the first volume (see previous item) left off, with the invasion of Luxembourg by German troops in May 1940, and ends with the second elections for the European Parliament in 1984. Of particular interest are the ninth chapter, which deals with the socialist politicians in the different municipalities of Luxembourg, and the final chapter, which looks back at the evolution, from 1944-79, of two subdivisions of the organization: the socialist women and the youth section.

462 **75 Jor Lëtzebuerger Sozialismus: aus dem Parteileben Luxemburger Arbeiter und Sozialisten.** (Seventy-five years of Luxembourg socialism.)
Antoine Krier.   Esch-sur-Alzette, Luxembourg: Imprimerie Victor, 1977. 300p.

Krier recounts the founding years of the Luxembourg Socialist Workers' Party (LSAP-POSL). Founded in 1902 as the Luxembourg Social Democratic Party, it adopted its present name after the Second World War and had become the strongest party in Luxembourg by 1964. In 1969 the party split. While the original Socialist Workers' Party went on to form a coalition government with the Liberal Democratic Party in 1974, the newly formed Sozialdemocratesch Partei (Social Democratic Party) only survived for ten years.

463 **Les relations du Parti Socialiste Luxembourgeois avec les Internationales.** (The links between the Luxembourg Socialist Party and the 'Internationales'.)
Germain Hanff.   MA thesis, University of Besançon, France, 1983. 209p.

Examines the links between Luxembourg's Socialist Workers' Party and the Communist International organization. The study is divided into three time periods (1902-14; 1914-21; and 1921-23) and demonstrates that the last period was the crucial one for Luxembourg's Socialist Workers' Party. In the elections of October 1919, the party had suffered considerable losses, and it needed the force of two strong personalities, the union leader, Pierre Krier (1885-1947) and the lawyer, René Blum (1881-1967), to unify the party after the loss of extreme-left members to the Communist Party.

464 **Aus Liebe zur Freiheit: 150 Jahre Liberalismus in Luxemburg.** (For the love of freedom: 150 years of liberalism in Luxembourg.)
Rob Roemen.   Luxembourg: Imprimerie Centrale, 1996. 530p.

Provides a history of liberalism in Luxembourg, the country's oldest political force, from the mid-19th century to the present. Liberal politicians have assumed high office in the past without the support of an effective party structure. A liberal league was founded in 1904, which can be considered as an early forerunner of today's party.

During the 20th century, liberals have been divided on religious, social and economic grounds, and many illiberal attitudes have prevailed. The liberal party became more popular after the Second World War and, thanks to the support of some prominent personalities, they were instrumental in nominating Gaston Thorn as prime minister in the coalition government with the Socialists between 1974 and 1979. They have participated in coalition governments under Prime Minister Pierre Werner from February 1969 to June 1974 and July 1979 to June 1984.

465    **The Luxembourg Liberal Party.**
       Derek Hearl.    In: *Liberal parties in Western Europe.*    Edited by Emil
       J. Kirchner.    Cambridge, England: Cambridge University Press, 1988,
       p. 376-95.
In his twenty-page article, Hearl describes the development of liberalism in Luxembourg as well as the evolution of the Demokratesch Partei (DP) (Liberal Democratic Party), which, according to the author's words, 'only acquired any measure of electoral stability and, hence, real governmental power, in the late 1960s'.

466    **40 Jahre Kommunistische Partei Luxemburgs.** (Forty years of the
       Luxembourg Communist Party.)
       Kommunistische Partei Luxemburg.    Luxembourg: COPE, 1960. 55p.
Founded on 2 January 1921, the Luxembourg Communist Party went through a number of crises up to 1931. The 1934 elections finally gave it a seat in the Chamber of Deputies, yet this electoral mandate was cancelled by the Chamber itself. The end of the Second World War brought a radical change. The 1945 elections gave the communists five seats. In 1959 nine per cent of the electorate voted communist, but in 1979 (beyond the scope of this volume) communist parliamentary representation had dropped to two seats. This work lists all the party publications and various press organs.

467    **Mat ugepaakt, fir dass et virugeet zu Lëtzebuerg. 25. Kongress vun
       der Kommunistescher Partei vu Lëtzebuerg 23. a 24. Abrëll 1988.**
       (Down to business, to make things advance in Luxembourg.
       Twenty-fifth Congress of the Luxembourg Communist Party.
       23-24 April 1988.)
       Luxembourg: COPE, 1988. 300p.
Reproduces the documents and discussions of the twenty-fifth Luxembourg Communist Party Congress held in April 1988.

468    **Les élections législatives, communales et européennes. Recueil de
       Législation. Textes coordonnés et jurisprudence.** (The legislative,
       municipal and European elections. Collection of Legislation.
       Coordinated texts and jurisprudence.)
       Edited by Service central de législation.    Luxembourg: Imprimerie
       Kieffer, 1993. 142p.
Besides extracts from the revised constitution of 1868, this compilation also includes the texts of different laws, information on the number of councillors for each municipality as well as details on the election of the European parliamentarians.

469 Systèmes et comportements électoraux. Analyse et synthèse des scrutins de 1974, 1979 et 1984: étude réalisée pour la Chambre des Députés du Grand-Duché de Luxembourg. (Grand Duchy of Luxembourg. Systems and electoral behaviour. Analysis and synthesis of the 1974, 1979 and 1984 polls: study for the Luxembourg Parliament.)
Centre de recherches et d'information socio-politiques (CRISP), Bruxelles. Luxembourg: Imprimerie Centrale, 1987. 163p.

As a parliamentary democracy with its own representative and pluralistic political system, the Grand Duchy offers its more than 200,000 voting nationals a wide possibility of choices. In considering some social, cultural and economic interrelations, this study does more than merely illustrate election results. The research undertaken by CRISP (Centre de recherches et d'information socio-politiques – Socio-political Research Centre) deals with five different polls since 1974: the parliamentary elections of 1974, 1979 and 1984 as well as the first European elections of 1979 and 1984.

470 La Chambre des Députés: Histoire et Lieux de Travail. (The Chamber of Deputies: history and workplace.)
Nicolas Als, Robert L. Philippart. Luxembourg: Imprimerie Saint-Paul, 1994. 559p.

The Luxembourg Parliament is only composed of one chamber, the current 'Chambre des Députés' (Chamber of Deputies), which brings together sixty parliamentarians. This is the first volume on Luxembourg's parliamentary institution. The research was undertaken by two young historians and deals with the origins and evolution of the country's foremost institution in text and illustrations. Split into three periods (1839-58, 1858-60 and 1860-1991), this detailed study aids towards an understanding of the role and activities of the Chamber of Deputies, and its parliamentarians.

471 Tripartism in Luxembourg: the limits of social concertation.
Mario Hirsch. West European Politics, vol. 9, no. 1 (January 1986), p. 54-66.

Mario Hirsch, a Luxembourg journalist, attempts to demonstrate that the tripartite mechanism, also known as the 'Luxembourg model', shows some defects. Institutionalized in a law of 1977, this tripartite mechanism is the concertation meeting of the government, trade unions and employers' associations which is automatically convened whenever the economic situation of Luxembourg shows serious signs of deterioration.

472 'Wie eine frühreife Frucht': Zur Geschichte des Frauenwahlrechts in Luxemburg. ('Like an early-maturing fruit': the history of votes for women in Luxembourg.)
Renée Wagner. Luxembourg: Rapid Press, 1994. 121p.

In contrast to other European countries, women's suffrage was fully introduced in Luxembourg in 1919 within the framework of universal suffrage and without great disputes. The expression, 'like an early maturing fruit', was used only nine years later by the municipal councillor, Catherine Schleimer-Kill, the founder of 'Action féminine' (Feminine Action) to express the special meaning of the introduction of the women's suffrage. Renée Wagner's work, which is scattered with short portraits of the women who played a role during these years, is one of the rare publications which examines women's history and provides an account of the evolution that led to the introduction of female suffrage. A parliamentarian of the Green Party since 1994, she also analyses the contribution of the political parties and the women's movements which supported the female claim to suffrage, and reflects on the outcome of such sudden political equality.

# Law and Constitution

473  **Fir eng ekologesch Gemengepolitik.** (For an ecological municipal
    policy.)
    Luxembourg: Mouvement écologique, 1987. 76p.
This brochure was issued just before the municipal elections of 1993 by the
'Mouvement écologique' (Ecological Movement), an important pressure group, to
present suggestions for an ecological municipal policy. It is actually a catalogue of
ideas supported by possible plans of action, background information and detailed
resolutions, that were based partly on the work of the German League for
Environment and Nature (Bund für Umwelt und Naturschutz). The proposals deal with
suggestions for securing effective environmental commissions and for energy saving
in the municipalities. In addition they plead against the use of tropical wood in public
buildings.

474  **Guide to foreign legal materials: Belgium, Luxembourg,**
    **Netherlands.**
    Paul Graulich, Paulette Guillitte, Jan F. Glastra van Loon, L. E. van
    Holk.   Dobbs Ferry, New York: Oceana, 1968. 258p.
This work is intended primarily to provide the American common law lawyer with the
relevant material for studying comparative and European law. It is a guide to the use
of Benelux legal material including laws, reports and theory. The Luxembourg section
(p. 91-119) first presents sources on judicial order, then deals with statute law, general
regulations or decrees, publications of legislative acts, secondary sources, customs and
international sources. The section on Luxembourg also analyses the sources of law
since the French Revolution and includes a select bibliography (with a cut-off date of
1965) subdivided into collections of laws and collections of reports.

475 **Histoire du droit dans le Grand-Duché de Luxembourg.** (The
history of law in the Grand Duchy of Luxembourg.)
Nicolas Majerus. Luxembourg: Imprimerie Saint-Paul, 1949. 2 vols.

Majerus's authoritative history of Luxembourg's legal system begins with the
political, social and religious organizations of the Celtic period and ends with the
developments which took place under the Nazi régime.

476 **Introduction à la science du droit: réimpression avec mise à jour
1978.** (Introduction to the science of law: 1978 updated reprint.)
Pierre Pescatore. Luxembourg: Centre Universitaire, 1978. 592p.

This comprehensive textbook was written for first-year law students. It conveys
fundamental juridical concepts, patterns of judicial reasoning and a coherent
framework which would serve as a basis for more specialized studies. The first section
is called 'Encyclopaedia of law', while the second part is entitled 'General theory of
law' and the third is an initiation into the philosophy of law which delineates the
philosophical problems that arise from the judicial order. This fundamental work
includes an appendix of documents on specific Luxembourg laws.

477 **Mélanges de droit luxembourgeois.** (Miscellaneous Luxembourg
laws.)
Léon Metzler. Brussels: Bruylant; Luxembourg: Joseph Beffort,
1949. 402p.

Divided into four chapters, this work examines: the evolution of Luxembourg
commercial law up to the German invasion of 10 May 1940; legislation under Nazi
occupation, 10 May 1940 to 10 September 1944; the revival of Luxembourg
jurisdiction after the liberation of the country; and topical, juridical questions and the
revision of the constitution in 1948.

478 **Documents et textes relatifs aux constitutions et institutions
politiques luxembourgeoises.** (Documents and texts concerning
Luxembourg constitutions and political institutions.)
Jean Thill. Luxembourg: Centre de Documentation Communale,
1973. 2nd ed. 339p.

Thill's textbook is intended for law students, civil servants, employees of the
communal administration and all those interested in constitutional law. The book
reproduces some documents that are not easily accessible such as the internal rules for
the Chamber of Deputies, the statutes of political parties and certain traditional laws.

479 **Das Staatsrecht des Grossherzogtums Luxemburg.** (The public law
of the Grand Duchy of Luxembourg.)
Paul Eyschen. Tübingen, Germany: Mohr, 1910. 231p. (Das
Öffentliche Recht der Gegenwart, 11).

This monograph deals with the constitutional and administrative law in Luxembourg
as it existed at the turn of the 20th century. Although published in 1910, the work is
still of great comparative value for present-day studies, as constitutional and
administrative law has only slowly evolved. After providing information on the Grand

**Law and Constitution**

Duchy's historical and legal background, Eyschen outlines the country's organization
and analyses its juridical system, communes (Luxembourg's division into 118
boroughs), legislation and fiscal situation. A final chapter summarizes the legal
structures of various other areas of social, political and economic life.

480  **Précis d'instruction criminelle en droit luxembourgeois.** (Concise
     handbook of criminal procedure under Luxembourg law.)
     Roger Thiry.  Luxembourg: de Bourcy, 1971. 411p.

Luxembourg's code of criminal procedure is based on the 1808 French code, and has
been adapted to the specific needs of the Grand Duchy. This short treatise is intended
to provide young law students with a practical course book and to present an updated
complement to Luxembourg's published compendium of laws and case-books,
*Pasicrisie luxembourgeoise: recueil trimestriel de la jurisprudence luxembourgeoise*
(Luxembourg: Ministry of Justice). It deals with all stages of criminal investigation
and procedure, judicial competence and organization and grounds for appeal to, and
arbitration by, the superior court.

481  **Diagonales à travers le droit luxembourgeois. Livre jubilaire de la
     Conférence Saint-Yves 1946-1986.** (A glimpse at Luxembourg law.
     Anniversary book of the Saint-Yves Conference 1946-86.)
     Luxembourg: Imprimerie Saint-Paul, 1986. 1,024p.

Contains various contributions from some fifty lawyers, members of the Saint Yves
Conference(a Catholic lawyers' association). This publication, however, reaches the
whole of the lawyer's family and has thus become the meeting-point of specialists
from all professional fields. The different subjects of the contributions are widespread
and range from law and institutions in ancient Greece to the application of community
law in the Grand Duchy of Luxembourg.

482  **Der Staatsrat des Grossherzogtums Luxemburg.** (The State Council
     of the Grand Duchy of Luxembourg.)
     Alex Bonn.  Luxembourg: Imprimerie Centrale, 1984. 148p.

In European democracies people often have a poor knowledge of their state
institutions. According to Alex Bonn this is also the case in Luxembourg and for this
reason he set out to provide further information on the Grand Duchy's council of state,
an institution which was taken from French constitutional law and adapted to
Luxembourg's specific conditions of politics. The author describes the origin and
development of the council and provides details on its characteristics in past, present
and future Luxembourg law.

483  **L'exercice en société des professions libérales en droit belge et
     luxembourgeois.** (The practice of the liberal professions in society,
     under Belgian and Luxembourg law.)
     Christiane Robert.  Brussels: Larcier, 1975. 253p. bibliog.

This inquiry into forms of association within liberal professions was instigated by the
EEC, and forms part of a general comparative study carried out for the Executive
Commission of the EEC. The author established that Belgian and Luxembourg

legislation in this area lags behind the reform movements of other countries. She analyses the possibilities of group-work among lawyers, notaries, architects, doctors, pharmacists and consultant engineers.

484   **Fondements du droit et des sociétés commerciales au Luxembourg.**
(The fundamentals of law and of the commercial companies in Luxembourg.)
Emile Dennewald.   Christnach, Luxembourg: Editions Borschette, 1994. 2nd ed. 199p.

This updated and annotated second edition of a useful work will be of value to anyone who needs to understand the fundamental rules of commercial law, whether they be businessmen, managers, accountants or students. Since the first edition (1988), the legislation concerning commercial companies has known far-reaching modifications. This volume includes a study of commercial transactions and commercial contracts as well as a detailed explanation of transport contracts. The final and largest section of the book concerns the different forms of companies that exist in Luxembourg law, such as limited company, private limited company and cooperative.

485   **Recueil du droit du travail au Grand-Duché de Luxembourg.**
(Collection of labour law in the Grand Duchy of Luxembourg.)
Armand Haas.   Luxembourg: Compagnie fiducière, 1987. 3rd ed. 3 vols.

Haas presents a useful file that collects the Luxembourg laws, edicts and regulations concerning labour organization. The work includes all the resolutions in existence up until 1987 that relate to: the working conditions of the employees; their specific protection within the law as well as the role of the Inspection du Travail et des Mines (Inspectorship of Labour and Mines); the representation of workers in the firms; and, finally, the possible conflicts, litigations and oppositions in the relations between employers and employees.

486   **Le statut des étrangers dans le Grand-Duché de Luxembourg.**
(The legal status of foreigners in the Grand Duchy of Luxembourg.)
Marcel Majerus.   Luxembourg: Imprimerie Saint-Paul, 1980. 353p. bibliog.

Around 125,000 foreigners currently live in Luxembourg at present, a situation which entails certain special dispositions in internal legislation. The main chapters of this authoritative and indispensable survey deal with: conditions of admission and stay; the job situation and protection for the wage-earning classes and liberal professions; social security; the fiscal régime; double taxation privileges and immunities; international organs; status and juridical capacities; and the acquisition of Luxembourg nationality.

487  **De la 'loi Eyschen' à la 'loi Eugène Schaus'. Etude sur le sursis au Grand-Duché.** (From the 'Eyschen law' to the 'Eugène Schaus law'. Study on probation in the Grand Duchy.)
Alphonse Spielmann.  Luxembourg: Imprimerie Centrale, 1980. 224p.

The author tries to point out the practical considerations that arise from the application of the following two laws: the Eyschen (a Luxembourg minister of government) law of May 1892 which concerns simple probation procedures; and the law of June 1973 which was proposed by former justice minister, Eugéne Schaus, a strong supporter of penal reform.

488  **Jeunes: vos droits et devoirs.** (Young people: your rights and obligations.)
Réseau luxembourgeois des centres d'information, de rencontre et d'animation pour jeunes.  Luxembourg: Imprimerie Buck, 1994. 2nd rev. ed. 595p.

One merit of this second, revised edition is that it makes known the fundamental principle of the 1990 United Nations Convention on the Rights of the Child (ratified by Luxembourg in December 1993); the lives and normal development of children should have absolute priority in the preoccupations of society. The eleven chapters which cover young people and parental authority, spare time and work, constitute an important working document for those whose professions relate to children as well as an information source for the young people themselves. An index, numerous addresses and a bibliography enhance the volume's research value.

489  **Die Luxemburger Gemeinden nach den Weistümern, Lehenerklärungen und Prozessen.** (The Luxembourg communes according to the judicial sentences, feudal fees records and lawsuits.)
Nicolas Majerus.  Luxembourg: Sankt-Paulus Druckerei, 1955-63. 7 vols. (Publications Littéraires et Scientifiques du Ministère de l'Education Nationale du Grand-Duché de Luxembourg).

An account of the instructions and directions pronounced by aldermen of Luxembourg before the French Revolution. A previous collection of judicial sentences published in 1868-70 by Mathias Hardt contained only about a quarter of what is known now. These records and lawsuits constitute the juridical basis of communal organization as it existed before 1976, i.e. the specific legislation pertaining to regional and local autonomy. The documents, which are arranged alphabetically, refer to villages and towns on the present territory of the Grand Duchy.

490  **Les Etats des Duché de Luxembourg et Comté de Chiny.** (The states of the Duchy of Luxembourg and the County of Chiny.)
Roger Petit.  In: *Assemblées d'Etats.* (State Assemblies.)  Louvain, Belgium: Nauwelaerts, 1965, p. 87-108.

Up to the end of the 13th century, political representation in Luxembourg was practically the preserve of the nobility; from the 14th century onwards, however, magistrates and clergymen entered the representative assemblies. It was in the middle of the 15th century that the assembly of the three estates (nobility, magistrates and clergymen, and burghers) emerged. The 17th century witnessed the development of the administrative tasks of the assembly and in the 18th century it evolved gradually towards limited representation. Petit surveys the organization, competence and procedures of the assembly and its relationship with the overall authority of the States General of the Netherlands.

491   **L'état luxembourgeois: manuel de droit constitutionnel et de droit administratif.** (The Luxembourg state: handbook of constitutional and administrative law.)
Pierre Majerus.   Luxembourg: Imprimerie Saint-Paul, 1983. 407p. bibliog.

First published in 1948, this basic textbook is an indispensable aid for all lawyers, teachers and civil servants. Frequent revisions make it the best available tool for anyone with an interest in public life. It presents the current text of the Constitution, together with its historical modifications.

492   **The institutions of the Grand Duchy of Luxembourg.**
Pierre Majerus.   Luxembourg: Service Information et Presse, 1995. 80p.

Written by a former ambassador, this is a very competent guidebook on Luxembourg's institutional framework. Precise information is provided under the following headings: 'General'; 'The Grand Duke and the government'; 'The Chamber of Deputies'; 'The Council of State'; 'The Courts of law'; 'Public administration'; and 'The Communes' (relating to the country's division into 118 administrative local authorities). The 121 articles of the Constitution conclude this practical survey.

493   **Le Conseil d'Etat du Grand-Duché de Luxembourg: livre jubilaire publié à l'occasion du centième anniversaire de sa création, 27 novembre 1856-27 novembre 1956.** (The Council of State of the Grand Duchy of Luxembourg: a jubilee book published on the centenary of its creation, 27 November 1856-27 November 1956.)
Luxembourg: Imprimerie Bourg-Bourger, 1957. 623p.

This publication is divided into five sections and includes the following: transcripts of the speeches given at the Council of State's commemorative session; information on the Councils of State and administrative jurisdiction in the countries of the EEC; a political history of the Grand Duchy; studies on public and social law; and a list of all the past and present chairmen and members of the Council of State.

494   **Le contentieux administratif en droit luxembourgeois.**
(Administrative disputes in Luxembourg law.)
Alex Bonn.   Luxembourg: Peiffer, 1966. 229p.

The author states that in the field of administrative law, Luxembourgish studies and publications are rather fragmentary. This work attempts to provide a systematic survey of the facts, institutions and practical problems that arise in this area and to describe the various jurisdictions and their competences.

495 **Nouveau guide pratique des officiers de l'état civil et des
secrétaires communaux.** (New practical guide for civil registry
officers and secretaries of communes.)
Marcel Franck.   Luxembourg: Ministère de l'Intérieur, Centre de
Documentation Communale, 1971. 372p.

Franck's book is of great assistance in the administrative and legislative jungle of civil
registry. The first section (p. 1-92) explains the organization of the official registry
office, and examines its functions from a European perspective. Part II lists all the
forms related to birth, parentage, marriage, divorce, death, adoption and name-giving,
while part III provides a chronological and an alphabetical record of conventions,
laws, decrees, memoranda and instructions concerning civil registry and the rights of
citizenship. Finally, part IV deals with the different stages and modes of acquiring
Luxembourg citizenship (naturalization, option and recovery).

496 **Liberté d'expression ou censure?** (Freedom of speech or
censorship?)
Alphonse Spielmann.   Luxembourg: Imprimerie Centrale, 1982. 322p.

This study sets out to investigate the problem of freedom of speech and censorship in
Luxembourg through the examination of case-studies. Above all, the author aimed to
present the views of some of the relevant authorities concerning this problem at
various moments in history. Based on authentic, mostly unpublished articles, the
publication does not set out to be of too judicial a nature.

# Government and Administration

497 **Annuaire officiel d'administration et de législation 1986.** (Official administrative and legislative yearbook, 1986.)
Luxembourg: Service Central de Législation, 1986. 1,425p.

Contains detailed information on the characteristics, personnel and legislation of Luxembourg's civil service as of autumn 1986. An appendix provides data on topics including: the Council of State, the judicial organization, the Audit Chamber, the Economic and Social Council, the professional chambers and councils, the Constitution, national emblems and official holidays.

498 **Handbuch der Regierungs-und Verwaltungsstellen im Grenzraum Saar-Lor-Lux.** (Repertory of governmental and administrative services in the border region of Saar-Lorraine-Luxembourg.)
Commission Régionale Saar-Lorraine-Luxembourg-Rhénanie/Palatinat. Saarbrücken, FRG: Kommissionsverlag Saarbrücker Druckerei und Verlag, 1979. 166p. maps.

This bilingual, pocket guidebook provides useful data and addresses necessary for official dealings with the public organizations of the Saar, the Lorraine, the Grand Duchy of Luxembourg and the Rhineland-Palatinate.

499 **Code Administratif. Textes coordonnés et jurisprudence.** (Administrative Code. Coordinated texts and jurisprudence.)
Luxembourg: Service Central de Législation, 1994. Variously paginated.

The Central Service of Legislation (Ministry of State) issued this new form of statute-book in 1994. These convenient files replace the old code and its sixteen updated editions, published from 1967 to 1988. Volume 1 concerns institutions, volume 2 deals with some procedures and volume 3 collects the most important legal and statutory texts on public offices.

500 **Kommunal-Gesetzgebung in Luxemburg.** (Communal legislation in Luxembourg.)

Nicolas Eickmann. Esch-sur-Alzette, Luxembourg: Editions Le Phare, 1995. 330p.

In the mid-1950s the mayor of Esch-sur-Alzette and then vice-president of the Chamber of Deputies, Hubert Clement, published a volume entitled *Manuel du Conseiller Communal* (Handbook of the communal councillor) (Esch-sur-Alzette, Luxembourg: Imprimerie Coopérative, 1955. 453p.). He wanted to involve a greater number of interested citizens in the running of their commune. Eickmann has set himself a similar target. By translating into German all the authoritative texts in French that highlight communal legislation in Luxembourg, his aim is to initiate a greater number of politically-interested citizens into the administrative details of local government. His main chapters deal with: the evolution and development of communal legislation; the European charter of communal autonomy; the committee of the regions; the electoral law; the communal law; the different local taxes; education and regional planning; social affairs; secondary residences; communal employees and local unions; and Luxembourg nationality.

501 **The Luxembourg Grand Ducal family.**

Luxembourg: Service Information et Presse, 1994. 112p.

Offers interesting details about His Royal Highness, the Grand Duke Jean, and Her Royal Highness, the Grand Duchess Joséphine-Charlotte, and their family members. Separate chapters also cover grand ducal powers, the order of succession, the regency and the lieutenancy, the prerogatives of the Grand Duke, the official visits of the royal family abroad, visiting heads of States, the centenary of Luxembourg's dynasty and the national monument in memory of H.R.H. Grand Duchess Charlotte.

502 **Le Gouvernement du Grand-Duché de Luxembourg 1995.** (The Government of the Grand Duchy of Luxembourg 1995.)

Luxembourg: Service Information et Presse, 1995. 51p.

Provides full details about the formation and composition of the government which resulted from the legislative elections of 12 June 1994. Besides providing full biographical details about its members, it lists the competences of the ministerial departments and offers a survey table of the distribution of party seats in the Chamber of Deputies since 1945.

503 **La Composition des Gouvernements du Grand-Duché de Luxembourg de 1848 à 1995.** (The Composition of the Governments of the Grand Duchy of Luxembourg, from 1848 to 1995.)

Luxembourg: Service Information et Presse, 1995. 48p.

Presents a full nominal list of all the members of government since 1 August 1848, the effective date of Luxembourg's new constitution. The period from 1831 to 1888 had already been covered by an earlier publication, Pierre Ruppert's *Statistique historique du Grand-Duché de Luxembourg* (Historical statistics of the Grand Duchy of Luxembourg) (Luxembourg: Imprimerie Buck, 1889).

504 **Les garanties étatiques au Grand-Duché de Luxembourg.** (State
guarantees in the Grand Duchy of Luxembourg.)
René Link.   Luxembourg: Editions Guy Binsfeld, 1984. 112p.
Link provides a descriptive, legal and historical study of the financial guarantees
granted by the Luxembourg state.

505 **Code du Fonctionnaire et de l'Employé de l'Etat.** (Statute-book for
the civil servant and the public employee.)
Luxembourg: Confédération Générale de la Fonction Publique, 1994.
Various pagination.
This recently published (1994) statute-book for State agents, civil servants, state
employees and state workers includes all the relevant information concerning their
respective statutes, extracts of relevant laws, arrangements, working hours, possible
promotions and security. The document is published by the main trade union for civil
servants, the General Confederation of the Public Service.

506 **Histoire de l'impôt direct 1842-1992 au Grand-Duché de
Luxembourg.** (The history of direct taxation 1842-1992 in the Grand
Duchy of Luxembourg.)
Administration des contributions.   Luxembourg: Imprimerie
Saint-Paul, 1995. 360p.
Compiled by some of the former and current staff of the tax and excise administration,
this recent publication retraces the history of direct taxation in Luxembourg. It
chronicles the history of this administration and explains its internal organization. The
work begins with the years 1841-42 because it was then, just after the country's
newly-gained independence of 1839, when fiscal sovereignty finally belonged to the
state. The appendix includes an account of the fiscal situation under French
domination (1795-1814) which shows how that reign influenced both the assessment
and the collection of taxes up to the beginning of the Second World War.

507 **Douanes luxembourgeoises. Association des douaniers
luxembourgeois.** (Luxembourg customs. Luxembourg Customs
Officers' Association.)
Gilbert H. Hauffels.   Luxembourg: Imprimerie Saint-Paul, 1980.
735p.
For the sixtieth anniversary of the Luxembourg Customs Officers' Association, one of
its members, Gilbert H. Hauffels, wrote this historical essay on Luxembourg's
customs. He presents a survey on the different periods the Luxembourg region has
known, such as the French reign (1795-1815) or its membership in the German
customs union from 1842 to 1918.

Government and Administration

508 **Livre du centenaire.** (Centenary book.)
Fernand Froehling, Jean-Pierre Muller, Joseph Schoettert, Maurice Schumann, François Thilgen, Henri Wildschutz. Luxembourg: Imprimerie Saint-Paul, 1990. 3 vols.
These three volumes were published to celebrate the centenary of the 'Association de secours mutuels de la Gendarmerie grand-ducale' (Mutual Rescue Benefit Society of the Luxembourg Police). Whereas the first volume retraces the history of the century-old existence of that association, the second and third volumes look back at the history of the mounted police from 963 to 1945. Besides numerous historical documents and photographs, the last two volumes contain an alphabetical list of the members over those years.

509 **'Ons Arméi'. Die Luxemburger Pflichtarmee 1944-1967. Band 1.**
('Our Army'. The Luxembourg compulsory army 1944-67. Volume 1.)
Willy Bourg, André Muller. Luxembourg: Imprimerie Saint-Paul, 1993. 743p.
Compulsory national service was introduced in 1944 when Luxembourg gave up its neutrality. Twenty-three years later, in 1967, when the Parliament decided to abolish compulsory armed service, more than 34,500 Luxembourg recruits had passed through it. In this first volume (the wealth of material led the authors to the decision that other volumes should follow) the two authors, themselves officers with the voluntary fighting units, set out to include as many photographs as possible and to keep the written text as short as possible. Each of the seven chapters include a German, French and English introduction, and illustrate subjects such as sport in the army and the various battalions.

510 **Les insignes de l'armée luxembourgeoise et des Luxembourgeois dans les armées alliées.** (The badges of the Luxembourg army and of the Luxembourg soldiers in the Allied armies.)
Vic Jaeger. Luxembourg: Imprimerie Saint-Paul, 1995. 183p.
Jaeger lists the military badges of: the Luxembourg army, the Luxembourg soldiers who fought with the Allied forces during the Second World War, the Korean War volunteers and those who served in the protection forces of the United Nations. The badges are illustrated and accompanied by a short description and/or a historical summary of their assignments in the Luxembourg army. The publication mainly addresses military collectors who have already visited the complete badge and uniform collections at the National Military History Museum in Diekirch.

511 **Eis Post. Les postes et télécommunications au Luxembourg.** (Our post. The post and telecommunications in Luxembourg.)
Administration des postes et telecommunications. Luxembourg: Imprimerie Saint-Paul, 1992. 311p.
This commemorative volume was published to celebrate the 150th anniversary of Luxembourg's post administration which was founded only three years after the country's independence. Divided into seven periods of time and containing numerous photographs, the various contributions provide an account of the development of postal facilities in the Luxembourg region in the past and present.

# Foreign Relations

## General

512 **Les relations franco-luxembourgeoises de Louis XIV à Robert Schuman: actes du colloque de Luxembourg, 17-19 novembre 1977.** (Franco-Luxembourg relations from Louis XIV to Robert Schuman: acts of Luxembourg colloquy, 17-19 November 1977.) Raymond Poidevin, Gilbert Trausch. Metz, France: Centre de Recherche des Relations Internationales de l'Université de Metz, 1978. 330p. maps. bibliog.

This volume contains: twenty contributions by French and Luxembourg specialists on various geographical, historical, military, economic, literary and artistic aspects of the centuries-old relationship between a large nation and a small state. It includes chapters on: the Luxembourgers under Louis XIV, by Paul Margue; the Luxembourgers and the French Revolution, by Gilbert Trausch; French-Luxembourg relations after World War I, by Gilbert Trausch; Luxembourg in the French novel, by Tony Bourg; the image of France in Luxembourg literature, by Cornel Meder; and light and shadow in three centuries of French-Luxembourg relations: a tentative conclusion, by Gilbert Trausch.

513 **Les Luxembourgeois et la France de Poincaré à Pompidou.** (The Luxembourgers and France from Poincaré to Pompidou.) Jacques Dollar. Luxembourg: Imprimerie Saint-Paul, 1973. 334p.

Provides an account of the history and friendship which unites France and Luxembourg. As well as illustrating historical personalities, events and the official ritual of state visits and receptions, it includes extensive lists of: Luxembourg officers of the military academy of Saint Cyr; Luxembourgers who fought in the service of France; decorated members of friendship clubs; and subscribers to the monument raised at Colombey in memory of General de Gaulle.

514  **France-Luxembourg: extrait du Bulletin de Documentation.**
(France-Luxembourg: offprint from the *Bulletin de Documentation*.)
Marcel Noppeney.  Luxembourg: Service Information et Presse, 1963.
15p.

Traces the common origins of the communities of France and Luxembourg, and the
historical relationships between their ruling houses. Noppeney, who was the senior
Luxembourg Francophile poet and writer, and the founder of the Société des Ecrivains
Luxembourgeois de Langue Française (SELF), discusses the 'linguistic and
sentimental phenomena' of French usage in the Grand Duchy.

515  **Durbuy et le Luxembourg depuis 1331.** (Durbuy and Luxembourg
from 1331 onwards.)
Durbuy, Belgium, 1981. 69p.

This catalogue was issued to accompany an exhibition that celebrated the 650th
anniversary of the act of John of Bohemia – which gave the inhabitants of Durbuy
(today a Belgian town) their enfranchisement rights. It also recalls the historical links
that unite Durbuy with the Grand Duchy of Luxembourg.

516  **L'UEBL. Un mariage sexagénaire en crise.** (The UEBL. A sixty
year's marriage passes through a crisis.)
Norbert von Kunitzki.  Luxembourg: Imprimerie Centrale, 1982. 159p.

In spite of its positive experience of the customs union with Germany since 1842,
Luxembourg had no choice but to relinquish its economic relationship with the German
empire after the latter had violated its neutrality in 1914. The UEBL (Union économique
belgo-luxembourgeoise – Luxembourg-Belgian economic union) treaty was finally
signed in July 1921 and became effective in May 1922. After dealing with the leading
principles of this union and the economic cooperation which is still extant today, von
Kunitzki details some of the problems it has experienced in its long existence.

517  **Luxembourg in the U.S.A.: a state visit. Chronicle and reflections.**
Christian Calmes.  Luxembourg: RTL Edition, 1985. 121p.

Christian Calmes is known for his works on the recent history of Luxembourg (q.v.),
and in this publication he relates the state visit that Grand Duke Jean and Grand
Duchess Joséphine-Charlotte paid to the United States in November 1984. Besides
presenting pictures of the various stages of this visit, the author analyses the
relationship that has existed between the two countries from the past to the present.

518  **Luxemburg – URSS (Russie). Pages de l'histoire 1867-1984.**
(Luxembourg – USSR [Russia]. Pages of history 1867-1984.)
Luxembourg: Archives de l'Etat, 1985. 313p.

Published to celebrate the fiftieth anniversary of the beginning of diplomatic relations
between the USSR and Luxembourg which opened in 1935. Luxembourg had had
diplomatic relations with Russia since 1867 when the latter was one of the guarantors
of Luxembourg's neutrality at the London conference of May 1967. After the first
World War, in common with other countries, Luxembourg took its time to recognize
the new régime. Divided into two parts, this compilation presents speeches,
multilateral agreements, official statements, treaties and telegrams in chronological

order from 1867 to 1912 and from 1935 to 1984. The documents concern political, business, scientific, technical and cultural relations and present the main tendencies, views and developments of that bilateral cooperation.

519 **Die Luxemburger in der Welt. Le tour du monde des Luxembourgeois 1795-1995.** (The Luxembourgers in the world. The world tour of Luxembourgers 1795-1995.)
Edited and annotated by Mars Klein. Luxembourg: Imprimerie Kremer-Müller, 1995. 343p.

This German- and French-language anthology is the first systematic presentation of Luxembourg travel literature, and documents the development of travelling since the 18th century. Each contribution is introduced by a biographical notice on the author while the foreword introduces the philosophy of travelling. The collection includes illustrations of foreign subjects by Luxembourg artists.

# Luxembourg and Europe

520 **Le Luxembourg et l'Europe.** (Luxembourg and Europe.)
Centre d'études et de recherches européennes Robert Schuman. Luxembourg: Imprimerie Centrale, 1994. 315p.

This bibliographical compilation includes about 1,600 titles of books and articles concerning Luxembourg and European integration from 1945 to the present.

521 **Europa Neu. Das Konzept des Präsidenten der EU-Kommission Jacques Santer.** (New Europe. The concept of the EU-Commission President Jacques Santer.)
Klaus Emmerich. Wien, Austria: Wirtschaftsverlag Ueberreuter, 1995. 301p.

Jacques Santer, the former prime minister of Luxembourg and now president of the European Commission (since 1995), will play a decisive role in the evolution of the European Union. The Austrian journalist, Klaus Emmerich, discusses Santer's personal background, and describes what people expect from the EU executive team as regards the future development of European integration.

522 **Le Grand-Duché de Luxembourg et la construction européenne.** (The Grand Duchy of Luxembourg and European construction.)
Vincent Fally. Luxembourg: Editions Saint-Paul, 1992. 2 vols.

Fally analyses the position of various Luxembourg governments regarding the construction of Europe, from the end of the First World War to Luxembourg's presidency of the European Community in 1991, and assesses the country's role in the setting up of the European Union, supporting the text with transcripts of official statements and speeches from Luxembourg authorities.

523 **Vers l'Union Européenne; 35e anniversaire et 40e anniversaire; Union Européenne An 2000.** (Towards European Union; thirty-fifth and fortieth anniversaries; European Union year 2000.)
Mouvement Européen du Luxembourg. Luxembourg: Imprimerie Zierden, 1986. 127p.

Just after the draft project (1983) which made the first post-signature amendments to the treaty of Rome in view of establishing the European Union (which was adopted by the European Parliament in 1984), the Luxembourg European movement (established in 1948) celebrated its thirty-fifth anniversary and the centenary of the birth of Robert Schuman (1886-1963) by publishing this commemorative volume. It includes various contributions from 'convinced Europeans' (including Luxembourg government ministers, managers and parliamentarians) arranged in four different sections: united Europe; the Grand Duchy of Luxembourg in the European Community; the future of the European Parliament; and Europe as seen by Luxembourg artists and writers. The same booklet was republished (Luxembourg: Mouvement européen, 1988. 127p.) to celebrate the fortieth anniversary of the movement and includes further contributions on the consequences of the single market for Luxembourg.

524 **Le marché unique de 1993 et ses répercussions sur le Grand-Duché de Luxembourg.** (The single market of 1993 and its consequences for the Grand Duchy of Luxembourg.)
Institut Grand-Ducal; Section des Sciences Morales et Politiques.
Luxembourg: Imprimerie Centrale, 1989-90. 2 vols.

Published in 1989 and 1990, these eleven contributions, collected in two volumes, have to be seen as a prospective analysis of the possible consequences for Luxembourg once the single European market was set up in 1993. Considerations concerning the possible modifications of Luxembourg legislation and the possible harmonization of the taxation system are only some of the aspects raised by eminent Luxembourg specialists in European affairs.

525 **Le traité de Maastricht. Genèse, Analyse, Commentaires.** (The Maastricht Treaty. Genesis, Analysis, Comments.)
J. Cloos, G. Reinesch, D. Vignes, J. Weyland. Brussels: Etablissements Bruylant, 1994. 2nd ed. 814p.

Never in the history of the European Community has a treaty caused such a stir as that signed in Maastricht in February 1992. The debates which preceded the ratifications in each member country clearly showed that the idea of European integration was less accepted by the public than had been thought before. By providing the reader with a basic knowledge of the Community's past history and the significance of the Maastricht treaty for European construction, this collective work aims to aid a better understanding of the contents of the treaty in order to allow serious and dispassionate discussion. The second part of this large volume is composed of a detailed and complete analysis of the treaty's subject matter. Avoiding any juridical jargon, the authors explain the origins of the different elements of the treaty, the hidden stakes behind the discussions from Luxembourg's point of view and the reasons the final clauses were agreed. Three of the four Luxembourg authors were closely involved in the discussions and the drafting of the first text of the Maastricht treaty and are able to allow the reader an original insight into the negotiations.

526 **Small States in Europe and Dependence.**
Austrian Institute for International Affairs.   Wien, Austria:
Novographic, 1983. 341p. (The Laxenburg Papers).
Deals with the problems and dependent nature of the small states of Europe, including
two case-studies of Luxembourg. The first one, written by the journalist, Mario
Hirsch, analyses the experiences of Luxembourg within the EEC, whereas Charles
Doerner's contribution discusses Luxembourg as an international banking centre and
the dualism of its monetary system.

527 **Unter Europäern. Die andere Kultur.** (Among Europeans. The other
culture.)
Wolfgang Schmitt.   Lebach, FRG: Hempel Verlag, 1991. 274p.
The essays and literary texts of thirty-six authors describe how foreign people live in
Europe with their own culture. Among the contributions are six on experiences in
Luxembourg. The volume provides an authentic insight into a growing multicultural
society and reminds us that Europe is not only a large economic power, but also a
cultural community.

528 **Jean Monnet et le Luxembourg dans la construction de l'Europe.**
(Jean Monnet and Luxembourg in the construction of Europe.)
Jacques Poos, Henri Rieben.   Lausanne, Switzerland: Imprimeries
Réunies, 1989. 134p.
In addition to the transcripts of two speeches, one by Jacques Poos, Luxembourg's
minister of foreign affairs, and the other by Henri Rieben, a professor at the European
Research Centre of Lausanne, entitled, respectively, 'Jean Monnet, the visionary' and
'Jean Monnet, Luxembourg and Europe', the publication contains other interesting
documents. These include a contribution by Emile Mayrisch, Luxembourg's
outstanding steel entrepreneur of the 1920s, as well as original writings from Jean
Monnet.

529 **Robert Schuman, 1886-1986: les racines et l'oeuvre d'un grand
Européen.** (Robert Schuman,1886-1986: the roots and works of a great
European.)
Edited by Comité pour la commémoration du 100e anniversaire de
Robert Schuman.   Luxembourg: Imprimerie Buck, 1986. 120p.
Robert Schuman was born in Luxembourg in 1886 and, by transposing Jean Monnet's
idea of the ECCS (European Community for Coal and Steel) into fact, he is considered
today as the father of Europe. In order to demonstrate its belief in the European idea,
Luxembourg's government organized commemorative ceremonies in 1986 to celebrate
the centenary of Schuman's (1886-1963) birth. Besides an important historical
contribution by the well-known Luxembourg historian, Gilbert Trausch, about the
relationship between Schuman and Luxembourg and the famous Schuman plan and its
consequences for Luxembourg, the second part offers contributions written by, and
about, Robert Schuman.

530    **Robert Schuman, 1886-1986. Les cérémonies commémoratives du 17 juin 1986 à Luxembourg.** (Robert Schuman, 1886-1986. The commemorative ceremonies of 17 June 1986 in Luxembourg.)
Edited by the Comité pour la commémoration du 100e anniversaire de Robert Schuman.    Luxembourg: Imprimerie Buck, 1986. 62p.

This booklet reproduces the speeches given by different personalities, including Jacques Santer, Pierre Werner and Jacques Delors during the academical session of the commemorations for the centenary of Robert Schuman's birth. It also briefly describes and illustrates the Robert Schuman exhibition in the city of Luxembourg and includes a bibliography of works written by, and about, the great European. The brochure complements the volume *Robert Schuman 1886-1986: les racines et l'oeuvre d'un grand Européen* which was also published for the commemorations (see preceding item).

# Economy and Statistics

531   **Sarre-Lorraine-Luxembourg-Trèves/Palatinat Occidental.
      Annuaire statistique 1994.** (Sarre-Lorraine-Luxembourg-
      Treves/Western Palatinate. 1994 Statistical Annual.)
      Luxembourg: Statistisches Landesamt Rheinland Pfalz, STATEC;
      Nancy, France: INSEE Lorraine; Saarbrücken, Germany: Statistisches
      Landesamt Saarland, 1994. 124p.

In 1992 the statistical offices of the Lorraine, Luxembourg, Saarland and
Treves/Western Palatinate published a first trans-border statistical annual. This
almanac aroused such a large interest in the professional world that it was the
beginning of more such publications by the same team. The 1994 edition updates and
completes the original figures, the main areas dealt with being population, schools,
employment, economic development, health, environment and living conditions.

532   **Statistiques historiques 1839-1989.** (Historical statistics 1839-1989.)
      Service Central de la Statistique et des Etudes Economiques
      (STATEC).   Luxembourg: Editpress, 1990. 616p.

This substantial publication was STATEC's contribution to the 150th anniversary
celebrations of Luxembourg's independence. It contains all kinds of statistics
concerning Luxembourg, with every aspect of the country taken into consideration,
including its territory, climate, population, agriculture, industrial sector, service
sector, banks and tourism. The volume concludes with figures relating to subjects
including health, politics, sport and social security.

533   **Histoire de l'économie luxembourgeoise: publiée à l'occasion du centenaire de la Chambre de Commerce.** (History of Luxembourg's economy: published on the occasion of the centenary of the Chamber of Commerce.)
Paul Weber.   Luxembourg: Buck, 1950. 431p.
Weber's significant survey of Luxembourg's economic development since Gallo-Roman times emphasizes the constant features that link feudal, *ancien régime* and modern economic, organization. Later landmarks dealt with in the volume are Luxembourg's admission to the German Zollverein (customs union) (1842); the signing of the UEBL (Union économique belgo-luxembourgeoise – Luxembourg-Belgian economic union) in 1921, and after the Second World War, the Marshall Plan. This volume remains a standard work despite being in need of updating.

534   **L'économie du Grand-Duché de Luxembourg.** (The economy of the Grand Duchy of Luxembourg.)
Carlo Hemmer.   Luxembourg: Joseph Beffort, 1948-53. 2 vols.
Although somewhat out of date now, Hemmer's work is still a valuable documentary source. The first volume deals with: national and social conditions; primary production; extractive industries; agriculture; viticulture; and sylviculture. Volume two examines: secondary production; raw materials; the human factor; equipment; capital; production; marketing; and Luxembourg's steel industry in the context of the European Community for Coal and Steel.

535   **L'évolution économique, financière et sociale du pays 1995; Avis.** (The economic, financial and social evolution of the country 1995; Advisory Note.)
Conseil Economique et Social.   Luxembourg: Service Central des Imprimés de l'Etat, 1995. 96p.
Every year the Economic and Social Council, in accordance with its statutes, issues a notice on the economic, financial and social state of the country. It discusses the challenges that the Grand Duchy will have to meet in the short- and middle-term period and presents the government with general directions on how to prepare the country for the future. In the economic field, the 1995 Advisory Note pleads for a structural policy concentrating on economic diversification, and expresses its concern about the rise of unemployment, seeking consensual solutions to the problem.

536   **Portrait économique du Luxembourg.** (Economic portrait of Luxembourg.)
Service Information et Presse in collaboration with STATEC.
Luxembourg: STATEC, 1995. 168p.
This is the latest general account of the history and development of Luxembourg's economy since 1839. The main chapters deal with population, employment, agriculture, industry, services, social security and public finance.

537   **Le modèle luxembourgeois.** (The Luxembourg model.)
      Jacques F. Poos.   Luxembourg: Imprimeries Réunies, Lausanne,
      1977. 75p.

Jacques F. Poos, Luxembourg's minister of foreign affairs, made this speech at the opening ceremony of the academical year, 1977-78, at the School of High Commercial Studies at the University of Lausanne while he was the minister of financial affairs. It deals with the economic crises which were caused by the first petrol shock of 1971 and the specific problems faced by small nations, and explains the measures taken by the Luxembourg government to counteract the economic deterioration of the 1970s, an initiative that was named the Luxembourg model.

538   **The Luxembourg economic model.**
      Luxembourg: STATEC (Service Central de la Statistique et des Etudes
      Economiques); SEO (Foundation for Economic Research of the
      University of Amsterdam), 1991. 286p.

This report contains a detailed description of 'mod-L', the first comprehensive econometric model of Luxembourg's economy. It can be used for simulation and forecasting purposes. A base-run projection for the period, 1990 to 1993, as well as three shock scenarios are included in the report. The steel industry and banking sector, major sectors in Luxembourg's economy, appear as separate blocks in the model. In addition, there is a very detailed representation of the social security system and of the taxation structure. The model has about 700 equations, of which 150 have been estimated by regression analysis.

539   **La population du Luxembourg. Bilan et analyses statistiques et
      sociographiques par commune.** (The population of Luxembourg.
      Statistical and sociographical balance sheets and analyses of each
      municipality.)
      SESOPI – Service Socio-Pastoral Intercommunautaire.   Luxembourg:
      Imprimerie Saint-Paul, 1995. 336p.

This substantial statistical compilation by the SESOPI (Service Socio-Pastoral Intercommunautaire – Socio-Pastoral Intercommunal Service) creates an economic, demographic and socio-professional portrait of each municipality of the Grand Duchy. The file mainly includes graphics and pie-charts while explanatory text is limited to the minimum.

540   **Population et économie du Luxembourg 1839-1939.** (Population and
      economy of Luxembourg, 1839-1939.)
      Georges Als.   Luxembourg: Banque Générale, 1989. 76p.

Georges Als, former director of the Central Service of Statistics and Economic Studies (STATEC) published this volume on the occasion of the 150th anniversary of Luxembourg's independence. It comprises valuable analysis of subjects including: the ageing Luxembourg population; the economic and demographic transition of the country; and agricultural activity. With the aid of abundant statistics, the author has managed to document the structure of the population and economy of Luxembourg since the 19th century.

541 **Le Luxembourg dans l'Union économique belgo-luxembourgeoise.**
(Luxembourg in the Belgian-Luxembourg economic union.)
Norbert von Kunitzki. Luxembourg: Editions 'd'Lëtzebuerger Land',
1972. 91p.

On 25 July 1921 the longest lasting (and still extant) European economic union was
signed in Brussels by Belgium and Luxembourg. Published on the fiftieth anniversary
of this date, von Kunitzki's account is of the treaty's history and its repercussions on
Luxembourg's economy and the legal status of Luxembourg's currency.

542 **Une expérience d'union économique: bilan de dix années d'union
économique belgo-luxembourgeoise.** (A ten-year experiment of
economic union: appraisal of ten years of economic union between
Belgium and Luxembourg.)
Luc Hommel. Louvain, Belgium: Société d'Etudes Morales, Sociales
et Juridiques, 1933. 216p.

Hommel's volume takes stock of ten years of the Belgian-Luxembourg economic
union. The chapters deal with: the early history of the union, which was concluded in
1921 after three years of negotiations; the content of the treaty itself; its administrative
and juridical mechanisms; its special clauses concerning alcohol, Moselle wines, steel
conflicts, Luxembourg's railways and agriculture, and cultural and tourist exchanges;
statistical evidence illustrating the results of economic development in all fields. The
final chapter concludes that both countries profit from the union. An appendix contains
the text of the convention which was concluded in Brussels on 25 July 1921 and
signed by Henri Jaspar for Belgium and Emile Reuter for Luxembourg.

543 **Das Wirtschaftsbündnis des Grossherzogtums Luxemburg mit
Belgien.** (The economic union of the Grand Duchy of Luxembourg
with Belgium.)
Emil Majerus. Luxembourg: Hausemer, 1928. 117p.

Writing in 1928, Majerus assesses the prospects for Luxembourg's economy within
the Belgian-Luxembourg customs union. Chapter I analyses the contents of the treaty;
chapters II and III deal with industry and agriculture; chapter IV explains the treaty's
so-called financial clause; and chapter V considers the railway problem.

544 **L'économie luxembourgeoise sous le régime de l'Union douanière
belgo-luxembourgeoise: mémoire.** (The Luxembourg economy under
the régime of the Belgo-Luxembourg customs union: a memoir.)
J. Treinen. Luxembourg: Joseph Beffort, 1934. 137p.

Provides an outline of Luxembourg's economic situation after the Second World War.
It includes information on the steel and mining industries, construction workshops,
foundries, commerce, banks, agriculture, viticulture, horticulture, railways and wine
and beer industry as well as the text of the Belgian-Luxembourg customs union
convention.

545 **L'Ardenne et l'Ardennais: l'évolution économique et sociale d'une région.** (The Ardennes and the Ardennes people. The economic and social evolution of a region.)
Giovanni Hoyois. Brussels, Paris: Editions Universitaires; Arlon, Belgium: Conseil Economique et Social, 1949-53. 2 vols. bibliog.

The Ardennes region comprises the Belgian Ardennes, the province of Luxembourg in Belgium, the northeast area of Belgium (the districts of Malmédy, Saint-Vith, Montjoie and Eupen), the Oesling in the Grand Duchy and the French Ardennes. This work deals with the historical evolution of the area's agriculture, stock farming, forests, moorlands, industry, commerce, communications, social régime, demography, housing, customs, mores, beliefs and characteristic features of the population. It includes statistical tables of various kinds from 1840 to 1950. Hoyois collected much of his documentation on the spot, and first-hand witness reports are provided in an appendix.

546 **Die wirtschaftliche Entwicklung des Grossherzogtums Luxemburg innerhalb der Deutschen Zollvereins 1842-1872: ein Beitrag zur Wirtschaftsgeschichte Luxemburgs.** (The economic evolution of the Grand Duchy of Luxembourg within the German Customs Union *Zollverein*, 1842-72: a contribution to the economic history of Luxembourg.)
Josef Oswald. Esch-sur-Alzette, Luxembourg: Kremer und Rettel, 1921. 318p.

This publication continues the work of A. Widung's *Der Anschluss des Grossherzogtums Luxemburg an das Zollsystem Preussens und der ubrigen Staaten des Zollvereins* (The annexation of the Grand Duchy of Luxembourg to the Prussian customs system and those of the other states of the Customs Union) (Luxembourg: G. Soupert, 1912. 167p.). Oswald surveys Luxembourg's economic isolation from 1839 to 1842, its remoteness from the Netherlands and the poor transportation system. Entry into the German customs union greatly benefited Luxembourg.

547 **Der Zollanschluss des Grossherzogtums Luxemburg an Deutschland, 1842-1918.** (The customs union of the Grand Duchy of Luxembourg with Germany, 1842-1918.)
Albert Calmes. Luxembourg: Beffort, 1919. 2 vols.

The first volume examines the run-up to Luxembourg's entry into the German customs union (1839-42), while the second volume deals with its continuation and eventual dissolution after seventy-seven years. Calmes, who was professor at the University of Frankfurt, investigates the political and economic background in a detached and objective way, which is noteworthy since this book was written during the years of the First World War.

548 **Introduction à la Microéconomie.** (Introduction to Micro-economics.)
Gérard Trausch. Luxembourg: Institut Universitaire International, 1980. 359p.

Provides a methodological introduction to micro-economics for first-year students with practical exercises and bibliographical reading suggestions in three languages.

The book is based on lectures presented at the 1979/80 session of Luxembourg Economic Studies organized by the Institut Universitaire International (International University Institute).

549 **La préparation de l'an 2000 au Grand-Duché de Luxembourg.**
(Preparing for the year 2000 in the Grand Duchy of Luxembourg.)
Adrien Ries. Luxembourg: Université Internationale de Sciences
Comparées, 1972. 154p. maps. bibliog. (Etudes Economiques
Luxembourgeoises).

Outlines the basic demographic and regional planning perspectives for the year 2000.
Chapter I provides a general survey of the year 2000 as seen by futurologists, while
chapter II sketches a possible way to prepare for that year in Luxembourg. An
appendix presents the different questionnaires used by Ries in his research.

550 **Luxembourg an 2000: problèmes particuliers.** (Luxembourg in the
year 2000: particular problems.)
Adrien Ries. Luxembourg: Université Internationale de Sciences
Comparées, 1974. 171p. maps. bibliog. (Etudes Economiques
Luxembourgeoises).

This volume continues the work of the preceding entry. It compares the responses of
various groups to two wide-ranging questionnaires on Luxembourg's economic
problems, with a view to the year 2000.

551 **Recueil statistique sur la présence des étrangers au Luxembourg.**
(Statistical compilation of the foreign presence in Luxembourg.)
SESOPI – Centre Intercommunautaire. Luxembourg: Imprimerie
Saint-Paul, 1995. 128p.

Providing people with objective information about the immigration phenomenon is
very important in a period when xenophobic attitudes are unfortunately becoming
more and more popular. This statistical guide, with its graphics, clear maps and short
notes is one of the steps towards a better understanding of the dynamics of
immigration in space and time in a country that is often envied for its harmonious
cohabitation of about thirty per cent foreigners with the Luxembourg population.

552 **Les travailleurs frontaliers travaillant au Luxembourg.** (The border
area commuters working in Luxembourg.)
In: *Vivre en Lorraine et travailler à l'étranger.* (Living in Lorraine and
working abroad.) Nancy, France: INSEE Lorraine (Institut national
des statistiques et des études économiques), 1994. 85p.

Clearly illustrated with tables and charts, this publication paints a social portrait of the
increasing number of border area workers (42,000 in March 1993) who live in
Lorraine, Trier or Arlon but work in Luxembourg.

553    **Précis de la TVA au Luxembourg.** (Abstract of V.A.T. in
       Luxembourg.)
       Jean-Pierre Winandy.   Luxembourg: Imprimerie Saint-Paul, 1995.
       661p.

Winandy describes the system of Value Added Tax (V.A.T.) and the way it is used in
Luxembourg in 1995. He also comments in detail on all of the articles of the 1979
Luxembourg law. More than eighty judgements delivered by the Court are
summarized in this complete manual which mainly addresses firms and their external
advisors.

554    **Die luxemburgische Sozialversicherung bis zum Zweiten
       Weltkrieg. Beiträge zur Wirtschaftsgeschichte.** (The Luxembourg
       social insurance up to the Second World War. Contributions to the
       history of economics.)
       Michael Braun.   Bamberg, FRG: Aku-Fotodruck, 1982. 666p.

Braun's study ranges from 1839, the year in which the Luxembourg state, as we know
it today, came into existence, up to the Second World War. Although the social
security system is already very much a subject of the first half of the 20th century, the
studies referring to it are only fragmentary. The beginning of the book deals with the
relationship between social policy and social security and defines the political and
economic frame in which the social security system was developed. The main part of
the study reports on the four social security branches that are illness, accident, age and
disability and pension insurance for employees. Finally, the last chapter summarizes
the results of Braun's research from historical and theoretical aspects.

# Finance and Banking

**555 Les assurances terrestres au Grand-Duché de Luxembourg.**
(Insurance in the Grand Duchy of Luxembourg.)
Pierre Weber.   Luxembourg: Editions Guy Binsfeld, 1985. 296p.
(Collection Fenêtres).

Pierre Weber, a lawyer in a firm which has worked in the field of insurance for twenty years, wrote this book to help the consumer understand more about the structure and mechanism of insurance activity. Beginning with a general survey of the sector, the volume goes on to analyse the role and control of the state and concludes by dealing with some specific forms of insurance such as personal insurance.

**556 Finanzplatz Luxemburg.** (The financial position of Luxembourg.)
Michael Bartsch, Jörg H. Wittenberg.   Landsberg-Lech, Germany:
Verlag Moderne Industrie, 1988. 2nd ed. 243p.

Luxembourg offers many advantages to the private investor and this volume sets out to show the reader the whole gamut of the country's various investment possibilities. After a short introduction to the country and its inhabitants, the reader will find general information on Luxembourg's financial position and especially on the importance of the Euro-market. In addition, the problems of property administration, the foundation of holdings and the banking sector are discussed, as are the fiscal aspects and regulations governing movements of capital. A final chapter provides practical advice in the way of a travel guide.

**557 Essai sur l'évolution bancaire dans le Grand-Duché de Luxembourg:
étude historique et économique.** (Essay on the evolution of banking in
the Grand Duchy of Luxembourg: a historical and economic study.)
Jérôme Anders.   Luxembourg: Editions luxembourgeoises, 1928.
100p.

Writing in 1928, Anders provides an account of the development of banking in the Grand Duchy of Luxembourg. In 1838 a great part of the capital invested in Luxembourg firms was of Belgian origin and the first bankers in the newly-independent country were all foreigners. With the extension of the railway system and the exploitation of mineral resources, banking activity developed. In 1856 the Banque Internationale (International Bank) was established in Luxembourg and a local banking system set up. The Banque Nationale du Grand-Duché (Grand Duchy National Bank) was founded in 1873, but on 26 September 1881 it went bankrupt. Anders' account goes up to the year 1927, which was marked by devaluation and feverish activity within companies, from which the banks greatly profited.

558 **Place financière de Luxembourg. Textes coordonnés et jurisprudence.** (Financial Centre of Luxembourg. Coordinated texts and jurisprudence.)
Luxembourg: Service central de législation, 1995. 323p. (Les Recueils de Législation).

The Service central de législation (Central Legislation Service) began publishing its series, *Les recueils de législation* (Legislation collections), to provide the general reader with a survey of, and convenient way of consulting, the various laws existing on a certain subject. This 1995 compilation gathers all the extant legislation on the supervisory authorities of the financial sector, the credit institutes and other professional organisms, the OPCs (Organismes de placement collectif – Collective investment organizations), the Stock Exchange, bonds and commercial securities, and the monetary statute of the Grand Duchy of Luxembourg. It is a useful source of information for Luxembourg professionals, foreign correspondents and investors alike.

559 **Struktur des Bankwesens in Luxemburg.** (The structure of banking organization in Luxembourg.)
Ulrich Meier. Frankfurt am Main, FRG: Knapp, 1975. 148p. (Struktur Ausändischer Banksysteme, 7).

After some preliminary remarks on Luxembourg's currency, banking history and holding societies, the author devotes individual chapters to: the banks' functioning as central banks, control forms and legislation, the private credit sector, the public credit sector, European institutions of finance, and other capital market institutions.

560 **La réglementation bancaire au Grand-Duché de Luxembourg.** (Banking regulation in the Grand Duchy of Luxembourg.)
René Link. Luxembourg: Editions Guy Binsfeld, 1980. 135p. (Collection Fenêtres).

Real banking activity developed in Luxembourg in about the middle of the 19th century. In 1970 there were 37 banks registered; by 30 June 1979 this number had gone up to 107. Link's concise and helpful guidebook sets out to familiarize the general reader with the economic and juridical infrastructure which enabled Luxembourg's quick development into an international banking centre. He deals with the public and private sectors, banking controls, bank secrets, various taxes, central bank functions and new banking legislation.

561 **The regulation of banks in the member states of the EEC.**
Inter-Bank Research Organization. Alphen aan den Rijn,
Netherlands: Sijthoff & Noordhoff, 1978. 331p.

Commissioned by the British Bankers' Association in order to analyse the methods
used by the various supervisory authorities to regulate banks in each of the EEC
member states, this volume also represents a valuable contribution to the continuing
debate on methods of banking surveillance and supervision, allowing easy comparison
between each country's arrangements in different areas of regulation. Each of the nine
chapters is devoted to the arrangements in one of the EEC states, and subdivided into
twenty-one sections relating to particular aspects of the regulatory system.
Luxembourg is dealt with in chapter seven (p. 188-210).

562 **Le secret bancaire en droit luxembourgeois.** (The banking secret
under Luxembourg law.)
Claude Schmit, Albert Dondelinger. In: *Le secret bancaire dans la
C.E.E. et en Suisse.* Paris: Presses Universitaires de Paris, 1973,
p. 139-76.

This is a national report from a conference organized by the International Centre of
Banking Economy and the University Study Centre of the European Communities at
the Université de Paris in October 1971. The authors conclude that although there
exists for the banker in Luxembourg law an obligation and a right to professional
secrecy, it is far from being absolute and unqualified.

563 **Mécanismes financiers des entreprises luxembourgeoises.** (Financial
mechanisms of Luxembourg companies.)
Alain Steichen. Luxembourg: Editions Emile Borschette, 1988. 552p.

Steichen's intention was not to theorize about the proverbial financial flair and
intuition of the managers but rather to assess them through a strict analysis of financial
mechanisms. However, first of all Steichen provides us with the basic accountancy
concepts before he examines the Luxembourg accountancy environment including the
legal background, for example, the fourth directive transposed into Luxembourg law
in 1984. The second chapter deals with financial mechanisms (the settlement of the
financial balance and financial tables) and the last part analyses the risks inherent in
all companies. Steichen's aim is to combine theoretical and practical information and
for that reason the text is followed by revised applications and technical notes that
deepen specific financial points.

564 **Le Luxembourg et sa monnaie.** (Luxembourg and its money.)
Paul Margue, Marie-Paule Jungblut. Luxembourg: Editions Guy
Binsfeld, 1990. 192p.

After a short historical introduction on money and its forms in general, and of
Luxembourg's monetary situation before 1839 in particular, the authors retrace the
economic and political history of the Grand Duchy from 1839 to the present day. They
deal with the monetary situation in Luxembourg under the German customs union up
to the creation of the economic union with Belgium (UEBL) after the First World
War, as well as with the monetary problems before, during and after the two world
wars and the origins of the banking centre that Luxembourg has become since the
1960s. Well illustrated, the book provides a good general overview of Luxembourg's
monetary history.

565 **Les relations monétaires entre la Belgique et le Grand-Duché de Luxembourg.** (Monetary relations between Belgium and the Grand Duchy of Luxembourg.)
Norbert Rollmann. Luxembourg: Imprimerie Saint-Paul, 1964. 124p. bibliog. (Université Catholique de Louvain. Collection de l'Ecole des Sciences Economiques, 89).

On 25 July 1921 long negotiations between Belgium and the Grand Duchy resulted in an economic union which contained some very important financial clauses. Rollmann sets out to analyse the monetary clauses, which were widely experimental, and attempts to evaluate them against a wider background. The author provides a chronological table which shows that, since the French Revolution, about eleven different monetary systems have been current in Luxembourg.

566 **Le système monétaire du Grand-Duché de Luxembourg.** (The monetary system of the Grand Duchy of Luxembourg.)
Paul Bastian. Luxembourg: Echo de l'Industrie, 1936. 61p.

Peculiarities of commerce, the geographical situation and political relations largely account for the complexity of the Luxembourg monetary system. Customs and excise duties are received in Belgian currency; and Luxembourg is forced to have several currencies circulating in its territory. Transactions within the country are made in Luxembourg money, but the Luxembourg franc has only territorial value, and it cannot be converted into gold.

567 **Monnaie et circuits financiers au Grand-Duché de Luxembourg.** (Money and financial channels in the Grand Duchy of Luxembourg.)
Ernest Muhlen. Luxembourg: Université Internationale de Sciences Comparées, 1968. 136p. bibliog. (Etudes Economiques Luxembourgeoises).

Muhlen's study comprises six chapters on Luxembourg's: monetary system; instruments of monetary policy (the roles of Belgium and Luxembourg and their common action); banking history, organization and legal status; saving and credit policy; other financial intermediaries; and role as an international financial centre. There are several appendixes on monetary parity, jobs in the banking sector, stock exchange figures, and assets of investment companies.

568 **Le marché financier luxembourgeois: étude historique et économique.** (The financial market in Luxembourg: a historical and economic study.)
Jérôme Anders. Brussels: Office des Editions Internationales, 1932. 168p.

Dealing with the history of Luxembourg's banks, joint-stock companies and stock exchanges in the interwar period, this study is interesting to compare with today's financial markets.

569  **Les sociétés holding au Grand-Duché de Luxembourg: aspects juridique, fiscal et comptable.** (Holding companies in the Grand Duchy of Luxembourg: juridical, fiscal and accountancy aspects.)
Guy Bernard.  Luxembourg: Institut Universitaire International, 1979. 139p. (Etudes Economiques Luxembourgeoises).

This is one of the best studies of holding companies in Luxembourg in the late 1970s. It describes the juridical and fiscal context of their development, expounds on some less well-known aspects of their activity, and considers contemporary criticisms of them and the fiscal measures taken by the government to control their future. In his conclusion, Bernard outlines the future for these companies in Luxembourg. Seven appendixes reproduce the text of important laws, instructions and administrative guidelines.

570  **Les sociétés 'holding' au Grand-Duché de Luxembourg: étude théorique et pratique de la loi du 31 juillet 1929.** (Holding companies in the Grand Duchy of Luxembourg: a theoretical and practical study of the law of 31 July 1929.)
Bernard Delvaux, Edmond Reiffers.  Paris: Sirey; Luxembourg: Buck, 1969. 5th ed. 461p. (Etudes Financières et Economiques de la Caisse d'Epargne de l'Etat du Grand-Duché de Luxembourg).

This study on the fiscal structure of Luxembourg's holding companies sets out to provide the interested reader with technical information on the subject.

571  **Les fonds d'investissement en droit luxembourgeois.** (Investment funds in Luxembourg's legislation.)
Aloyse Biel, Charles Stuyck.  Luxembourg: Institut Universitaire International, 1978. 58p. (Etudes Economiques Luxembourgeoises).

At the end of April 1977, eighty-six investment trusts, controlling a capital of more than eighty-six billion Luxembourg francs, were subject to Luxembourg law. Most of them date from the late 1960s. After describing the various types of trust, the authors examine Luxembourg's control systems and the official list kept by the bank control commissioner.

572  **Cent vingt-cinq ans de papier-monnaie luxembourgeois.** (One hundred and twenty-five years of Luxembourg paper money.)
Raymond Weiller.  Luxembourg: Imprimerie Joseph Beffort, 1981. 213p.

The 125th anniversary of the Luxembourg 'Banque Internationale' (Inernational Bank) was also the anniversary of the first bank note issued in Luxembourg. Weiller describes all of the notes that have been issued in Luxembourg, as far as they are known, in four chapters and parallel French, German and English columns. Even though this catalogue helps to illustrate the Grand Duchy's complex monetary evolution, it will mainly appeal to the collector.

573    **Une banque raconte son histoire.** (A bank tells its story.)
Christian Calmes.    Luxembourg: Imprimerie Saint-Paul, 1981. 575p.
(Au Fil de l'Histoire).

The Banque Internationale (International Bank) of Luxembourg is the country's oldest
limited company. Created in 1856, it has become an important bank among the more
than 200 that now exist in the country. The historian, Christian Calmes, presents a
reliable study on its first 125 years. He manages to set the bank's story in the political
and historical context of the time and objectively describes the realities of everyday
banking life.

574    **125e Anniversaire Caisse d'Epargne de l'Etat du Grand-Duché de
Luxembourg. Banque de l'Etat 1856-1981.** (The 125th anniversary
of the State Savings Bank of the Grand Duchy of Luxembourg. State
Bank 1856-1981.)
Pierre Guill.    Luxembourg: Imprimerie Saint-Paul, 1981. 189p.

Guill, the chairman of the State Savings Bank, did not intend this commemorative
volume to be a history of the bank which was established in 1856. Rather, he set out to
describe the institution's main lines of evolution and development. One chapter is
devoted to various kinds of figures concerning the bank, whereas the final section of
the volume contains only photographs.

575    **Cinquantième anniversaire.** (The fiftieth anniversary.)
Luxembourg: Banque Générale du Luxembourg, 1969. 146p.

On 29 September 1919 a new bank was etablished in Luxembourg, the Banque
générale du Luxembourg – société de droit belge, avec siège social à Arlon et siège
administratif à Luxembourg (General bank of Luxembourg – Belgian law firms, with
social headquarters at Arlon and administrative headquarters in Luxembourg). On the
occasion of its fiftieth anniversary in 1969, this bank (which soon became one of the
most important) published a luxurious brochure recalling its fast development and
important economic liaising role with Belgium. The book contains high-quality
photographic documentation of the town and the country, and includes six double-
page colour reproductions of famous water-colour paintings by Sosthène Weis.

576    **Banque Nationale du Grand-Duché de Luxembourg 1873-1881.
Eine Episode in der luxemburgischen Währungsgeschichte.**
(National Bank of the Grand Duchy of Luxembourg 1873-81. An
episode in Luxembourg's currency history.)
Jutta Jaans-Hoche.    Luxembourg: Imprimerie Saint-Paul, 1981. 237p.

Besides the State Savings Bank and the International Bank, the National Bank was
Luxembourg's third financial institution to be established in the 19th century.
Although it only existed from 1873 to 1881, the bank deeply influenced the financial
and political life of the Grand Duchy. Numerous reproduced documents complete the
analytical and descriptive part of the text.

# Business and Industry

577 **L'industrie au Département des Forêts: une statistique d'il y a cent ans.** (Industry in the Forestry Department: statistics from a hundred years ago.)
Antoine Funck. Luxembourg: Imprimerie Artistique Luxembourgeoise, 1929. 240p.

Deals with the industrial situation in the Forestry Department in 1811, as revealed by statistics produced in 1812. It also describes this department's participation in staging exhibitions of the products of French industry, that of the national exhibition of 1806, in particular.

578 **La politique industrielle au Luxembourg.** (Industrial policy in Luxembourg.)
Luxembourg: Institut Universitaire International, 1982. 348p.

Presents the proceedings of the February 1982 session of a winter postgraduate international seminar organized by the International Luxembourg University Institute. The fifteen contributions from local economists, bankers and foreign university lecturers describe the international context of research and development.

579 **Luxembourg: ideal location for your development plans. Management guide.**
Luxembourg: Chambre de Commerce du Grand-Duché de Luxembourg, 1979. 114p. 3 maps.

An excellent guide for firms considering setting up production or starting a business in Luxembourg. It describes economic and social conditions in Luxembourg and provides detailed information on the right of establishment, labour law, the taxation system, public aid for enterprises and investment and EEC aid. An appendix presents interesting maps, charts, basic statistics, procedures and regulations.

580 **Les multinationales au Luxembourg: le cas des firmes américaines.**
(Multinational concerns in Luxembourg: the case of the American
firms.)
Romaine Goergen. MA thesis, University of Toulouse-Le Mirail,
France: June 1982. 134p.

Through research at the Luxembourg Chamber of Commerce, analysis of some individual firms as well as the consultation of press articles, Goergen attempted to reveal the main aspects of the relationship between the multinational combine and the host country. The resulting work actually covers the basic policy of industrial diversification that Luxembourg has pursued since the early 1960s.

581 **Guide du marché luxembourgeois, 1979-80.** (Guide to the
Luxembourg market, 1979-80.)
Chambre de Commerce du Grand-Duché de Luxembourg.
Luxembourg: Imprimerie Bourg-Bourger, 1979. 319p.

This directory contains: an alphabetical index of products; a list of products according to the simplified EEC nomenclature for the community's external trade statistics; and an alphabetical list of firms, with descriptions of their activities. An appendix lists: banks in the Grand Duchy, Luxembourg chambers of commerce abroad, foreign chambers of commerce for Belgium and Luxembourg located in Belgium, and professional chambers, associations and federations in the Grand Duchy. An index of useful addresses concludes the appendix.

582 **Les industries minière et sidérurgique du Luxembourg au fil des
années.** (Mining and steel industries of Luxembourg through the
years.)
Marcel Steffes, Guy Steffes. Luxembourg: Imprimerie
Bourg-Bourger, 1962. 181p. bibliog.

After a geological and geographical survey of the mining fields, the authors provide a technical, well-illustrated description of the steelworks. One chapter is devoted to the pioneers and personalities of heavy industry in Luxembourg.

583 **Wirtschaftliche Entwicklung und Bedeutung der Gruben- und
Eisenindustrie im Grossherzogtum Luxembourg.** (Economic
development and the significance of the mining and steel industry in
the Grand Duchy of Luxembourg.)
Rolf Buehlmann. Luxembourg: Imprimerie Bourg-Bourger, 1949.
254p. bibliog.

Buehlmann's volume on Luxembourg's mining and steel industry is divided into five sections which deal with: the raw material; the economic history of Luxembourg; the large steel manufacturing companies; their national and international importance; and data on management and staff.

584 **D'Aarbecht an de Gallerien.** (The work in the mines.)
Norbert Quintus. Luxembourg: Imprimerie Saint-Paul, 1988. 189p.

Quintus provides a vivid pictorial overview of Luxembourg's mining industry, located in the south of the country, between Dudelange and Pétange. This well-illustrated souvenir book (containing 376 black-and-white photographs) shows us both the working conditions and the continuing evolution of the working method. The pictures make their point more efficiently than would a long description.

585 **Die Luxemburger Eisenindustrie: wirtschaftsgeschichtliche Abhandlung technischer Prägung in Wort, Bild und Zeichnung.**
(The Luxembourg iron industry: a technical, historical and economic survey in words, pictures and diagrams.)
Marcel Steffes. Esch-sur-Alzette, Luxembourg: Kremer-Müller, 1947. 2nd ed. 165p.

Steffes first provides the general reader with basic geological and geographical details about the Luxembourg mining areas, and discusses the modern developments of heavy metallurgical equipment such as blast furnaces, rolling mills and steel manufacturing machinery. He also deals with such links between agriculture, the building trade and industry as exemplified by the production of fertilizing slag (Thomasmehl) and cement. In addition he highlights the role of heavy industry in providing the local population with electricity. This well-informed work concludes with considerations of mergers and associations of steel companies around 1900, workshops, raw materials and scientific research.

586 **Die Wirtschaftsformation der Schwerindustrie im Luxemburger Minett.** (The economic formation of the steel industry in the Luxembourg Minette iron ore area.)
Heinz Quasten. Saarbrücken, FRG: Universität des Saarlandes, 1970. 268p. bibliog. (Arbeiten aus dem Geographischen Institut der Universität des Saarlandes, vol. 13).

Based on the situation in 1963, this is a methodical account of the geography of Luxembourg's steel industry, within the territorial frontiers to the south and west of the city. The work examines: the conditions for the implantation of heavy industry; the workers and their settlements; the transportation of goods; and the commuting of the workforce.

587 **La sidérurgie luxembourgeoise sous le régime du Zollverein et de l'union économique belgo-luxembourgeoise.** (Luxembourg's iron and steel industry under the 'Zollverein' and under the Belgian-Luxembourg economic union.)
Camille Wagner. Luxembourg: Imprimerie Artistique Luxembourgeoise, 1931. 207p.

Wagner explains that Luxembourg's heavy industrial equipment was developed as a result of the country's entry into the German Zollverein (1842-1918). Thereafter the Belgian-Luxembourg economic union inaugurated a new industrial and commercial policy. Luxembourg's steel industry has gone on to achieve international success and invest heavily in foreign companies.

588　La métallurgie du Luxembourg: étude de géographie physique, sociale et économique.
(Luxembourg's steel industry: a study in physical, social and economic geography.)
M. E. Faber.　Luxembourg: Hausemer, 1927. 156p.

Originally a doctoral thesis presented at the University of Lausanne, Switzerland, this work considers the conditions of metallurgical production, the production itself, and the trade in metallurgical products. An appendix contains historic photographs which show characteristic views of mines, surface mines and steelworks.

589　Die Entwicklungsgeschichte der Luxemburgischen Eisenindustrie im XIXten Jahrhundert. (History of the development of Luxembourg's iron industry in the 19th century.)
M. Ungeheuer.　Luxembourg: Kraus, 1910. 362p. 2 maps.

Represents an interesting, well-documented survey of the first phases of the slow development of Luxembourg's iron industry from 1815 to 1907.

590　Arbed.
Luxembourg: Aciéries Réunies de Burbach-Eich-Dudelange, 1971. 143p.

This is a brochure on the Arbed, one of the greatest European steel-producing companies, which was established in 1911; its full name is Aciéries Réunies de Burbach-Eich-Dudelange, as it resulted from the merger of three 19th-century companies. In 1967 the Arbed absorbed the Hadir, and in 1971 it became heavily involved in the Saar Stahlwerke Röchling Burbach Gmbh (Saar Steelworks of Röchling Burbach Ltd.).

591　Un demi-siècle d'histoire industrielle, 1911-1964. (A half-century of industrial history, 1911-64.)
Félix Chomé.　Luxembourg: Aciéries Réunies de Burbach-Eich-Dudelange, 1972. 401p.

This book is not intended for the general public, but for executive and management staff new to Arbed (Aciéries Réunies de Burbach-Eich-Dudelange) in order to familiarize them with the large company they are joining. It offers a concise survey of the company's historical, social, economic and financial role during fifty years of industrial development not only in Luxembourg, but also in the Arbed branches in the Saar and South America.

592　Arbed.
Luxembourg: Aciéries Réunies de Burbach-Eich-Dudelange, 1973. 80p.

This information and presentation brochure on the Arbed, a Luxembourg limited company and one of Europe's main steel firms, has already taken on a historical significance because it was published in 1973, when the full implications of the first petrol shock had not yet become apparent.

593 **Un siècle de hauts-fourneaux à Rodange, 1872-1972.** (A century of
blast furnaces at Rodange, 1872-1972.)
Paul Spang.   Rodange, Luxembourg: Minière et Métallurgique de
Rodange, 1972. 180p.

On the occasion of the centenary celebration of the Rodange steelworks, Spang (then
director of the State Archives) examined the firm's archives and published this well-
documented survey of its development and daily life. He describes the close
connections between the archaeological site of Rodange and the steel-producing
activities of the area; the first exploitation of iron ore here was in Celtic and Roman
times, and it has continued to develop since.

594 **Dudelange. L'usine centenaire.** (Dudelange. The 100-year-old
ironworks.)
Arbed.   Luxembourg: Imprimerie Victor Buck, 1982. 219p.

Provides an overview of the Grand Duchy's first integrated steelworks, created in
1882 in Dudelange. The text and illustrations which make up this commemorative
volume already have a historical significance, as now only some highly specialized
workshops and production units remain of the original plant.

595 **Cent ans Usine de Wecker.** (One hundred years of the Wecker
Factory.)
Léon-M. Duchscher, Lore Hasselmann, Johannes Plum, Herbert Vetter.
Wecker, Luxembourg: Usine de Wecker, 1972. 33p.

The period of rapid economic and industrial development that the Grand Duchy of
Luxembourg underwent after the Franco-Prussian War coincided with the foundation
of the Usine de Wecker (Wecker Factory) by André Duchscher (1841-1911). Early in
1873 he established a foundry plant for the manufacture of table utensils, together
with a small machining workshop. Also a successful poet and politician in his own
country, he created and developed his factory, which established a world-wide
reputation for its machinery for the oil industry, and blast-furnace epuipment, for
example. The volume's various contributions are accompanied by French, English and
German translations.

596 **Die Mühlen des Luxemburger Landes**. (The mills of the country of
Luxembourg.)
Emile Erpelding.   Luxembourg: Editions Emile Borschette, 1988.
800p.

Erpelding provides a geographic and economic listing of Luxembourg's mills,
classifying them according to type and function. The study sets out to describe the
manifold importance of the mills and to follow their development through the
centuries. The volume is more than a mere alphabetical list, as it offers rich
documentary details and illustrations. On the other hand, the appendix of the book is
composed of an alphabetical person, town and subject names' list.

597 **150 ans gaz à Luxembourg.** (150 years of gas in Luxembourg.)
Ville de Luxembourg. Luxembourg: Imprimerie Worré-Mertens,
1989. 95p.

Published on the 150th anniversary of the introduction of gas in Luxembourg, this
commemorative volume provides a good basic survey of gas from 1838, when
Luxembourg's first gasworks was opened, onwards. Illustrated with colour charts and
photographs, the brochure documents the development of the use of gas in the Grand
Duchy.

598 **SES 1908-1983.** (SES 1908-83.)
Syndicat des Eaux du Sud. Esch-sur-Alzette, Luxembourg: Editpress,
1983. 127p.

The SES (Syndicat des Eaux du Sud – Southern Water Union) has the double aim of
supplying the southern towns of Luxembourg with drinking water and supplying the
industry in the south with water. This commemorative brochure retraces the SES's
seventy-five years in text and pictures.

599 **Onse Be'er ass gudd! Bier und Brauwesen in Luxemburg.** (Our
beer tastes good! Beer and the brewing industry in Luxembourg.)
Gambrinus Bruderschaft. Esch-sur-Alzette, Luxembourg: Editions
Schortgen, 1993. 160p.

Luxembourg, with its five breweries and one of the world's highest rates of beer
consumption, enjoys a special status in the brewing world. This well-illustrated and
documented monograph deals with the history of Luxembourg's brewing industry as a
whole, so that it provides information on the different components of the beer, the
brewing process and all the objects that concern beer, including beer mats, beer
glasses and beer cans.

600 **La centrale nucléaire de Remerschen. Tout sur le projet
luxembourgeois le plus ambitieux du siècle.** (The nuclear power
station of Remerschen. Everything on the most ambitious Luxembourg
project of the century.)
Paul Kayser. Luxembourg: Imprimerie Centrale, 1992. 331p.

From 1973 to 1978, the project to build a nuclear power station in Remerschen (in the
extreme east of Luxembourg at the Luxembourg-French-German triangle) was one of
the main topics of debate in Luxembourg's social and economic milieus. Kayser (who
was at that time president of the inter-ministerial control commission investigating the
Remerschen plan, and expert on radiation protection at the ministry of health) takes
original documents and attempts to reconstruct the affair in as impartial a way as
possible. He therefore reproduces many of these documents and analyses the
economic, financial, political, environmental, technical, social, legal and international
aspects of the problem. Kayser contradicts the view that the Remerschen station was
not built in the end as a result of the construction of the French Cattenom nuclear
power station (only a few kilometres away from the Luxembourg border), arguing that
this parallel project had been planned long before.

601   **Les problèmes actuels de la distribution: structure et caractères de la distribution luxembourgeoise.** (Present-day problems of distribution: structure and features of Luxembourg distribution.)
Jules Stoffels.   Luxembourg: Université Internationale de Sciences Comparées, 1972. 87p. (Etudes Economiques Luxembourgeoises).

Deals mainly with the problem of concentration in distribution and with future prospects for supermarkets and retailers. Of course, the statistics and reports it contains are now rather dated.

602   **100 Joër Sankt Paulus Dréckerei 1887-1987**. (The 100 years of the Saint-Paul's printing office 1887-1987.)
Charles Jourdain.   Luxembourg: Imprimerie Saint-Paul, 1988. 210p.

This is a commemorative publication on one of Luxembourg's largest printers that issues the daily newspaper, *Luxemburger Wort* (Luxembourg Word), which has the widest circulation figures in the country. Jourdain, who was the administrative and staff manager in 1987, retraces the history of the *Luxemburger Wort* which began in 1848, a few days after the freedom of the press had been proclaimed. Only forty years later it had established its own publishing house. The work concludes with a detailed photographic and textual report on the internal celebration of the 100th anniversary.

603   **Training in the retail trade of the Grand Duchy of Luxembourg: report of the Force Programme.**
Nadine Spoden.   Berlin: CEDEFOP, 1994. 54p.

Force (Formation and continuous education) is the European Community's programme for the development of continuing vocational training. It is focused on companies, especially on small- and medium-sized companies, and promotes working partnerships in continuing training between companies, training bodies and public authorities. This study of the situation in Luxembourg was carried out within the scope of the European retail trade sector study as part of the EC Force Programme. Trends are analysed and two case-studies evaluated in detail, the firms Adler S. A. and Cactus S. A.

604   **La Grande Compagnie de Colonisation: documents of a new plan.**
Tom Palmer.   Worcester, Massachusetts: Clark University Press, 1981. 175p.

Translated from the original 1937 German text, *Dokumente eines grossen Planes* (Documents of a great plan) (Luxembourg: Malpartes Verlag, 1937. 140p.) and published along with related documents (several maps and a postscript including an interpretative essay by the Luxembourg historian, Christian Calmes). As the war was imminent, Tom Palmer, a pseudonym for the well-known Luxembourg-based businessman, Henry J. Leir, projected a view of how nations pursuing enlightened self-interest, could, with the most modern technology and managerial skills at their disposal, discover that peace means profit, prosperity and the improvement of human life. The meticulous attention to geographical detail, the illumination of geopolitical constellations and the imaginative use of documentary reportage, make this publication a unique utopian vision and afford the reader a global perspective.

605  **Le Parc des Expositions de Luxembourg.** (The exhibition park of
     Luxembourg.)
     Société des Foires Internationales de Luxembourg.    Luxembourg:
     Imprimerie Saint-Paul, 1981.

In order to satisfy the demands of exhibitors and visitors alike, and above all to
expand into the congress and conference sector, a new trade fair and conference centre
was opened in the spring of 1991, affording even greater, more advanced, and more
diverse facilities on the Kirchberg plateau (a suburb of the city of Luxembourg). This
catalogue, which consists mainly of colourful photographs, describes this entire
infrastructure and reports on Luxembourg's trade-fair tradition.

# Labour Movements and Trade Unions

606  **Le syndicalisme au Luxembourg et en Europe.** (Trade unionism in
Luxembourg and Europe.)
Jules Stoffels.   Luxembourg: Université Internationale de Sciences
Comparées, 1972. 339p. (Etudes Economiques Luxembourgeoises).
Presents a wide-ranging and solid study of various European countries': development
of workers' legislation and role of trade unions; theories of salaries and income
policies; decision-sharing and self-management; interpretations of politics and trade
unionism; and problems of syndical unity. The final chapter outlines important
present-day issues such as economic and industrial concentration, European limited
companies and economic planning.

607  **Cinquantenaire de la Chambre du Travail, Luxembourg.** (Fiftieth
anniversary of the Council of Labour.)
Luxembourg: Chambre du Travail, 1973. 162p.
The Luxembourg Council of Labour was created by law in 1924. This commemorative
book for its fiftieth anniversary contains contributions on the evolution of labour laws,
trade unions, industrial insurance and old age benefit, the standard of living of
Luxembourg's labour force and future perspectives.

608  **L'emploi et les migrations au Grand-Duché de Luxembourg.** (The
employment situation and migratory workers in the Grand Duchy of
Luxembourg.)
Claude Laby.   Luxembourg: Université Internationale de Sciences
Comparées, 1969. 92p. (Etudes Economiques Luxembourgeoises).
Presents the text of a series of lectures given in 1968-69. Although the statistics are
now dated, Laby provides a useful survey of the problems of the employment sector,
its policies and its executive organism, the National Labour Office. The final chapter
deals with different aspects of foreign labour immigration.

609  **75 Joër fräi Gewerkschaften. Contributions à l'histoire du mouvement syndical luxembourgeois.**
(Seventy-five years of free trade unions. Contributions to the history of the Luxembourg unionist movement.)
D. Scuto, R. Steil.  Esch-sur-Alzette, Luxembourg: OGB-L, 1992. 302p.

In 1991, the OGB-L (Onofhängegen Gewerkschafts Bond-Lëtzebuerg – Independent Trade Union Association – Luxembourg) organized the seventy-fifth anniversary celebration of free trade unions in Luxembourg and published this commemorative volume. The organization chose the two young historians, D. Scuto and R. Steil, to present specialized subjects on Luxembourgs' trade-union history and to revive almost forgotten facts, thereby providing the reader with new material for reflection and debate. The book dwells on the importance of trade-union development, the social achievements of the 20th century and the activities of the trade-union pioneers. The text is supplemented by an appendix which contains the labour chronicle of the OGB-L since its foundation in 1979.

610  **1912-1987: Fédération générale des fonctionnaires communaux (FGFC).** (1912-87: General Union of Municipal Employees.)
Luxembourg: FGFC, 1987. 231p.

Retraces the history of the municipal employees' trade union (FGFC) by reproducing documents and illustrations from its seventy-five-year history. At the end of the 1980s, this federation, which sets out to promote the interests of civil servants, had more than 2,000 members.

# Transport and Telecommunications

611 **L'accessibilité au Luxembourg. Transport individuel et transport collectif. Complémentarité et/ou concurrence?** (Accessibility in Luxembourg. Individual transport and collective transport. Complementary factor and/or competition?)
John Braun. Thesis for the degree in teaching, Luxembourg, 1994. 144p.

Braun's thesis compares the two most commonly used transport options in Luxembourg, namely public transport and the individual car. He questions, among other things, whether Luxembourg's public transport system is effective enough to allow convenient and fast travel and sufficient coverage of the whole of Luxembourg. The study begins by outlining theoretical aspects and the main characteristics of the traffic zones, while the maps included should be considered as arguments in themselves and not merely as illustrations.

612 **L'aviation luxembourgeoise: son passé, son avenir.** (Luxembourg aviation: its past, its future.)
Pierre Hamer. Luxembourg: Imprimerie Bourg-Bourger, 1978. 414p. maps. bibliog.

Hamer's wide-ranging report covers all aspects of the development of air traffic in Luxembourg, including air sports, commercial airway exploitation, organization and economic policies. Besides political declarations and public speeches, the book contains an appendix dealing with airmail stamps, air balloons and aeronautic legislation.

613 **Le pavillon maritime luxembourgeois.** (The Luxembourg maritime flag.)
Jean Brucher, Jean-Marie Bauler. Luxembourg: Banque Générale du Luxembourg, 1991. 37p.

The law creating Luxembourg's sea flag was passed in November 1990. It afforded the country the possibility of registering and managing a deep-sea-fleet under its

national colours, even though Luxembourg is a land-locked country. The authors'
intention was not to comment on each of the 128 articles of the 1990 law, but rather to
highlight the main features of Luxembourg's flag legislation.

614 **The Moselle river and canal from the Roman Empire to the
European Economic Community.**
Jean Cermakian.   Toronto; Buffalo, New York: University of Toronto
Press, 1975. 162p. maps. bibliog.

The author sets out to study a waterway which, for many, symbolizes the 'European
spirit'. He believes that only with the recent canalization (1956-64) of the Moselle
River can the building of a united Europe become a reality. To illustrate the historical
roots of the project with all its wars, quarrels, rivalries and feuds, the study relies
heavily on secondary sources and relegates economic and technical aspects to second
place. It is chronological rather than topical, and divided into five periods delineated
by certain key dates in European history. The discussion opens with the 'Geographica'
of Strabon (58BC-21BC), a famous Greek geographer, and terminates with some
considerations regarding the latest traffic developments on the Moselle. A statistical
appendix contains sixteen tables and an abstract in French and German.

615 **Aus der Geschichte der Moselschiffahrt.** (The history of the Moselle
navigation.)
Norbert Etringer.   Luxembourg: Krippler-Müller, 1978. 2nd ed. 217p.
map.

Provides an interesting account of various aspects of, and activities on, the Moselle,
such as: freight and passenger traffic, unusual forms of transport, war transport,
pleasure trips, rafting of timber, skippers' inns and clubs, inland navigation,
bargemen's dwellings, stables for towing horses, naval construction yards, customs
offices, the veneration of Saint Nicholas, types of barges, canalization projects, and
obstacles. It includes a twenty-five-page bibliography of books and periodical articles,
arranged alphabetically.

616 **La canalisation de la Moselle.** (The canalization of the Moselle.)
Jules Stoffels.   Luxembourg: Banque générale, 1984. 36p. (Réalités et
Perspectives, 1984/2).

Stoffels' study, backed up by all the relevant statistics and figures, shows that the
canalization of the Moselle River, which has its source in France and forms the border
between Luxembourg and Germany before flowing into the Rhine, is an economic and
political success that has not harmed the natural environment in a significant way.

617 **Eisenbahnen in Luxemburg.** (Railways in Luxembourg.)
Edmond Federmeyer.   Freiburg, FRG: Eisenbhan-Kurier, 1984. 575p.

Federmeyer's bibliographical description of Luxembourg's railway history explains
that although Luxembourg's network is one of the smallest in Europe, it has
experienced the most varied influences from its neighbouring countries due to events
such as the German annexation of Alsace and Lorraine between 1870 and 1918 and
the invasions of the Second World War.

618    **Les chemins de fer à section normale du Grand-Duché de
Luxembourg.** (Standard gauge railways of the Grand Duchy of
Luxembourg.)
Emile Majerus.    Luxembourg: Joseph Beffort, 1933. 146p.

Luxembourg's entry into the customs and trade union with Germany (Zoll- und
Handelsverein) made the construction of a railway system indispensable, and the
Luxembourg-Arlon and Luxembourg-Thionville lines were inaugurated in 1859. The
author deals with the history of the railway system up to 1930.

619    **Gares et haltes des Chemins de Fers Luxembourgeois. Bahnhöfe
und Haltepunkte der Luxemburger Eisenbahnen.** (Stations and
stops of the Luxembourg railway.)
'Les Cheminots – Philatélistes 61 Luxembourg'.    Luxembourg:
Imprimerie Saint-Paul, 1984. 349p.

For the 125th anniversary of Luxembourg's railway in 1984 this illustrated reference
book on the station buildings and stops was issued. Besides dealing with the
architectural characteristics of the buildings, the French-German comments emphasize
the contribution made by the railway to Luxembourg's industrial and economic
development.

620    **Schmalspurbahnen in Luxemburg.** (Narrow gauge railways in
Luxembourg.)
Edmond Federmeyer.    Luxembourg: Imprimerie Lux-Print, 1992-94.
2 vols.

Volume 1 describes the development of Luxembourg's secondary railways, canton
railways and municipal railways from 1882 until their nationalization in 1934. The
publication also deals with the narrow gauge railway law of 1911 and the French
Thionville-Mondorf railway, as well as the routes passing through the Belgian town of
Martelange on the Belgian-Luxembourg border. Reproductions of drawings, old maps
and authentic photographs make these two volumes a fascinating historical reference
work. The second volume discusses not only the renowned small trains named Jangeli,
Chareli and Benni (1934-55), which are still a current topic of discussion among
middle-aged people, but also provides detailed description of all the vehicles from
1882 onwards.

621    **125 Jahre Eisenbahnstrecke: Luxemburg-Wasserbillig.** (125 years
of railway lines: Luxembourg-Wasserbillig.)
'Les Cheminots – Philatélistes 61 Luxembourg'.    Luxembourg:
Imprimerie Saint-Paul, 1986. 247p.

This commemorative volume celebrates the 125th anniversary of the railway route,
Luxembourg-Wasserbillig, as well as the 25th anniversary of the railwaymen
philatelists. It discusses facts and stories concerning the two anniversaries. After a
historical review of the Luxembourg-Wasserbillig railway, the authors deal with
planned but unbuilt railways in Luxembourg, while the second part of the volume
provides some information on the stamp collectors' club and its congresses and
exhibitions since 1961.

622    **100 Joer Zuch op Woolz.** (The centenary of the train to Wiltz.)
       Luxembourg: Imprimerie Saint-Paul, 1981. 197p.

Published to commemorate the centenary of the Kautenbach-Wiltz line (1881-1981), this volume contains contributions which are so many examples of the importance of the development of the railway for the northern part of Luxembourg. The text is accompanied by reproductions of original documents, maps and photographs.

623    **Tramways municipaux. De Stater Tram 1875-1993.** (Municipal
       tramways. The tramway of the city 1875-1993.)
       J.-P. Hoffmann, Raymond Duhr, René Clesse, Marcel Balthasar.
       Luxembourg: Imprimerie Centrale, 1993. 259p.

Different contributions reconstruct the history (1875-1993) of the local passenger traffic of the city of Luxembourg. The study is noteworthy for its grasp of the social and historical significance of the tramway and its evaluation of the documentation. Concentrating not only on the tramway, the authors present a lively chronicle of all the city's public traffic, that is to say the horseway (1875), the tramway (1908-64) and the buses, which prevailed over the tramways after a parallel extension from 1926 to 1935. Numerous reproductions of photographs provide an idea of how Luxembourg and its suburbs looked in the past.

624    **Kommunikation – das gesellschaftliche Nervensystem. Die neuen
       Medien und ihre Bedeutung für Luxemburg.** (Communication – the
       social nervous system. The new media and their significance for
       Luxembourg.)
       Mario Hirsch.    Luxembourg: Administration des P. et T., 1984. 50p.

The journalist, Mario Hirsch, deals with the concept of the new media such as cable and satellite television, video and teletext. Although written in 1983 and outdated in the light of recent developments, the essay provides an easily comprehensible introduction to the subject.

625    **Les origines et l'extension du téléphone au Grand-Duché de
       Luxembourg.** (The origins and extension of the telephone in the Grand
       Duchy of Luxembourg.)
       Léon Bodé.    Luxembourg: Administration des P. & T., 1985. 268p.

For the centenary of the telephone service in Luxembourg, the Post Administration issued this book by Léon Bodé, one of its board inspectors. It describes the establishment and development of the service during the period 1884-1920. Many reproductions of contemporary photographs and original documents, and an appendix containing the names of the first subscribers, and a list of the public telephones, contribute to the vividness and interest of the account.

626    **Astra: Fernsehen ohne Grenzen. Eine Chronik.** (Astra: television
       without frontiers. A chronicle.)
       Wilfried Ahrens.    Düsseldorf, Germany: ECON Verlag, 1993. 255p.

Describes the recent but rapid rise of satellites, and specifically the Astra satellite that was first sent into orbit in 1989. Today more than forty million households all over Europe receive signals from the Grand Duchy, the home country of the private operating company, SES (Société Européenne des Satellites – European Satellite Society), which today runs a highly competitive technology centre. In addition to listing the television satellites over Europe, Ahrens describes the complex world of satellite technique in a comprehensive way, and reports on the success of the new technology from every angle.

# Planning

627 **Programme directeur de l'aménagement du territoire.** (Guidelines for regional planning.)
Luxembourg: Ministère des Finances, 1978. 361p. maps.

Assesses the human, natural, economic and cultural resources available to Luxembourg up to the year 1990. Besides the ruling principles laid down by the Interministerial Committee for Territorial Planning in November 1977, the volume contains the text of the guidelines decided upon by the committee, the report of 6 April 1978 of the High Council for territorial planning and that of the Economic and Social Council. A first law on territorial planning was passed on 20 March 1974.

628 **Quelques problèmes de l'aménagement du territoire au Grand-Duché de Luxembourg.** (Some problems of regional planning in the Grand Duchy of Luxembourg.)
Carlo Hemmer. Luxembourg: Université Internationale de Sciences Comparées, 1973. 107p. (Etudes Economiques Luxembourgeoises).

In 1970 the Luxembourg government proposed the first draft of a bill on town and country planning which was to revise previous legislation on the protection of natural sites and the planning of industrial areas (dating from 1927, 1937 and 1965). The volume is divided into five chapters which: set out the main problems; deal with the legislative context; analyse the first draft of the guidelines for regional planning; examine the problem raised by plans for new motorways; and discuss the protection and preservation of nature and the environment.

629  **Politique de structure et aménagement du territoire au Grand-Duché de Luxembourg.** (Structural policies and regional planning in the Grand Duchy of Luxembourg.)
Ernest Muhlen.  Luxembourg: Université Internationale de Sciences Comparées, 1971. 60p. (Etudes Economiques Luxembourgeoises).

After describing the objectives, ways and means of structural policies in general, Muhlen outlines the basic features of Luxembourg's specific situation, and considers the origins and implementation of this policy in the Grand Duchy.

630  **Quel Luxembourg pour demain? Esquisse structurelle d'aménagement du territoire.** (Which Luxembourg for tomorrow? Structural outline of town and country planning.)
Ministère de l'aménagement du territoire.  Luxembourg: Imprimerie Kremer-Müller et Cie, 1994. 91p.

This draft, containing numerous colour charts, tables and maps, is intended to trigger off new reflection on territorial planning before a new white book (draft version of new legislation) is put together and presented to the European Commission. Part of this outline deals with the catalogue of problems presented by the Luxembourg parliament's territorial planning commission before the vote took place which passed Luxembourg's first territorial planning law in 1974. It also presents attempts to formulate some rules, regarding long-term development and concerted regionalization, and some wider goals for future territorial planning policy.

631  **Luxembourg situation et défis. Vision pour demain.** (Luxembourg situation and challenges. A vision for tomorrow.)
Arthur Andersen.  Luxembourg: Imprimerie Victor Buck, 1993. 178p.

Arthur Andersen and Co. Ltd. belongs to the multinational offices of Arthur Andersen and Co. which have their head office in Geneva. The firm works in the area of auditing, management and financial consultancy. Using methods of strategical analysis as expounded by the private sector, the firm presents a rigorous balance sheet of Luxembourg's political, economic and social strengths and weaknesses and a future vision for the country. The research project that was undertaken to produce these findings, lasting eighteen months, was a collective work organized by Arthur Andersen and Co. which used skilled consultants who live in Luxembourg but come from ten different countries.

632  **L'état de l'environnement 1993.** (The state of the environment in 1993.)
Luxembourg: Ministère de l'Environnement Grand Duché de Luxembourg, 1994. unpaginated.

Published by the Ministry of Environmental Affairs, this report is an original and serious attempt to answer the questions raised both by national and international institutions and by the public. Well researched, it contains a wealth of information and studies in detail eight different themes such as air pollution, water and forests. Several illustrations are presented together with easily understandable explanations, maps and charts while the text is supplemented by a bibliography after each chapter.

633   **L'exclusion sociale et l'espace au Grand-Duché de Luxembourg.**
(Social exclusion and space in the Grand Duchy of Luxembourg.)
Claudia Hartmann-Hirsch in collaboration with Claude Gengler.
Luxembourg: Published by Claudia Hartmann-Hirsch, 1994. 72p.

The intention behind this work is, above all, to initiate town and country planning programmes and discussion on a national level, for although Luxembourg is a small country, it still faces the question of how its space can best be used. Problems arise continually due to the often conflicting interests of the environment on one hand, and humans and their activities on the other.

634   **Die Gemeindetechnik. Leitfaden für die Kommunalpolitik.**
(Municipal techniques. A practical guide to municipal policies and techniques.)
Léon Nilles.   Luxembourg: Imprimerie Saint-Paul, 1981. 300p.

Following a detailed description of the standards that city-planners and builders are expected to meet, the author deals with the existing legislation that politicians and administrations have to respect. He also introduces the reader to various specific aspects of planning such as land development and planning, water supply, parks and green belts.

635   **Circulation routière et génie civil à Luxembourg. Solution globale sans danger pour la zone verte du Grünewald.** (Road traffic and engineering in Luxembourg. Global solution protecting the green zone of the Grünewald.)
Roger Schmol.   Luxembourg: R. Schmol, 1994. 118p.

Roger Schmol is a civil engineer and independent researcher who drafted, at the request of Hilda Rau-Scholtus, municipal councillor of the city of Luxembourg, a thirty-seven-point plan concerning the west side of the capital and particularly the forest of the Grünewald. Nevertheless the government recently (February 1995) chose to opt for an alternative project involving numerous tunnels which reduces the forest by about 15 hectares.

# Agriculture

636 **L'agriculture.** (Agriculture.)
Charles Christians. Liège, Belgium: Séminaire de Géographie de
l'Université de Liège, 1977. 187p. maps. bibliog.

Lists facts and problems and analyses future agricultural planning perspectives in the
context of geographical factors. The report mainly covers the period from 1960 to 1974,
but has been updated to include 1976 and looks forward to the year 1990. Viticulture
is dealt with in a separate chapter and parallels are set up with the programmes
concerning tourism and the protection of nature and sylviculture. Suggested objectives
are based on the resolution of responsible authorities to safeguard and promote the
development of individual family smallholdings in a free farming organization.

637 **L'agriculture et la viticulture luxembourgeoise dans le Marché
commun.** (Luxembourg agriculture and viticulture in the Common
Market.)
Adrien Ries. Luxembourg: Université Internationale de Sciences
Comparées, 1973. 200p. bibliog. (Etudes Economiques
Luxembourgeoises).

Deals with contemporary national and European Community events on the agricultural
scene. Ries covers: the evolution of a common agricultural policy; the establishment
of common organizations for the wine and milk markets; monetary developments and
their repercussions on the common agricultural system; and the profound changes that
have taken place in Luxembourg's agriculture.

638 **1894-1994 100 Joër LUXLAIT. 100 Joër Mëllechwirtschaft zu
Lëtzebuerg.** (1894-1994 100 years LUXLAIT. 100 years of
Luxembourg milk economy.)
Luxembourg: Imprimerie Saint-Paul, 1995. 301p.

Retraces the centenary of LUXLAIT (Laiterie de Luxembourg), Luxembourg's
leading dairy since 1978. As approximately sixty per cent of the country's total

174

agricultural earnings come from milk production, it is easy to assess the importance of the milk economy for this sector in Luxembourg. The twelve contributions in this well-illustrated publication present a detailed account of the origin and development of the firm.

639  **Fédération Agricole. Allgemeiner Verband. 75/1909-1984.**
     (Agricultural Federation. General Association. 75/1909-84.)
     Luxembourg: Allgeménge Verband, 1984. 132p.

For its seventy-fifth anniversary (1909-84), the General Association of the agricultural goods cooperative society issued this commemorative volume which retraces the history of a supporting structure created by the farmers to help themselves.

640  **Das Weinbaugebiet der deutsch-luxemburgischen Obermosel.** (The wine-growing region of the German-Luxembourg upper Moselle.)
     Otmar Werle.   Trier, FRG: Geographische Gesellschaft, 1977. 210p. maps. bibliog.

Werle's study is based on field surveys and archival work undertaken between 1967 and 1970. It analyses and differentiates the ecological situation, the development of viticulture, physiognomic and functional structures of the present viticultural areas, and forms of production and marketing on either side of the Moselle.

641  **Aus der Geschichte des Luxemburger Weinbaus.** (From the history of Luxembourg viticulture.)
     Martin Gerges.   Wiesbaden, FRG: Gesellschaft für die Geschichte des Weines, 1977. 23p. map. bibliog. (Schriften zur Weingeschichte, No. 41).

This is the text of a talk given by the author at Remich, Luxembourg in September 1976. It is an interesting survey of the social, cultural and economic aspects of the Moselle Valley.

642  **The Luxembourg Moselle wines.**
     Luxembourg: Service Information et Presse, 1973. 24p.

Provides essential data on Moselle wines. Luxembourg's wine-producing areas cover around 1,200 hectares (3,000 acres), consisting of about 1,600 holdings which are essentially small family estates. The vineyards spread over the slopes exposed to the south, and run along the Moselle River for a distance of 42 km, from Lorraine to its entry into Germany. The varieties planted are Riesling-Sylvaner, Elbling, Riesling, Auxerrois, Pinot blanc, Pinot gris and Traminer. The production of sparkling wines increases continually. Six cooperative wineries group together about seventy per cent of the wine-growers. There exists a national trademark which classifies the wines and bestows quality-labels on the best such as *vin classé* (selected wine), *premier crû* (high quality wine) and *grand premier crû* (very high quality wine).

643 **La forêt du Grand-Duché de Luxembourg.** (The forest of the Grand
Duchy of Luxembourg.)
Administration des Eaux et Forêts.   Luxembourg: Imprimerie
Saint-Paul, 1971. 95p.

Deals with all the subjects connected with Luxembourg's forests, for example:
configuration and historical development; geographic, economic and legislative data;
protection; private and public ownership; exploitation of wood for industry; hunting;
hydrography; ecology; and future prospects. The brochure contains a useful glossary
of deer, game, fish and tree varieties to be found in the forest.

644 **Le Luxembourg et ses vétérinaires 1790-1990. De l'artiste
vétérinaire au docteur en médecine vétérinaire.** (Luxembourg and
its veterinary surgeons 1790-1990. From the veterinary artist to the
doctor in veterinary medicine.)
Georges Theves.   Luxembourg: Imprimerie Beffort, 1991. 310p.

When, in 1790, Nicolas Wagner was the first Luxembourger to benefit from the
veterinary schools that had been created all over Europe from 1750 onwards, a
tradition of over a thousand years came to an end: the passing down of the knowledge
and practical work of animal medicine from generation to generation. Theves provides
a survey of the achievements of the veterinary profession and its contribution to the
progress of agriculture and cattle breeding as well as its commitment towards
agricultural associations. This work fills a gap in national history studies, because
nobody before Theves had written such a historical overview on the evolution of
veterinary medecine. The volume is enriched by the numerous bio-bibliographical
references to Luxembourg's veterinary surgeons.

645 **La médecine vétérinaire au Grand-Duché de Luxembourg. Passé,
présent et avenir.** (Veterinary medicine in the Grand Duchy of
Luxembourg. Past, present and future.)
National trade union of Luxembourg veterinary surgeons.
Luxembourg: Imprimerie Beffort, 1992. 184p.

This is the second volume concerning veterinary medicine to be published in less than
two years; it was issued to celebrate the 200th anniversary of the national veterinary
surgeons' union. Whereas the first book on this subject (see preceding item) described
the evolution of the veterinary profession, this study includes various contributions
concerning the everyday activities of the profession. Finally, an appendix provides an
alphabetical index of all the veterinary surgeons in Luxembourg, which shows their
dates of birth, the universities they studied at as well as the dates they graduated.

# Cultural Life

646 **Sancti Willibrordi Venerantes Memoriam. Echternacher Schreiber und Schriftsteller von den Angelsachsen bis Johann Bertels.** (In memory of Saint Willibrord. Echternach scribes and authors from the Anglo Saxons to Johann Bertels.)
Michele Camillo Ferrari. Luxembourg: Cludem, 1994. 125p.
Ferrari first analyses the development of the Benedictine convent-library of Echternach (a town located on the German-Luxembourg border) from which some remarkable manuscripts of the early and late Middle Ages originate. In the second part of the work he reports on traces of the creative use of the written word by presenting texts drawn up in Echternach. Special attention is given to the 12th-century abbot, Thiofrid, because he somehow best expressed the traditions of Echternach in his works. Because of the wealth of surviving records (about 175 complete or fragmentary manuscripts) and the range of the time span covered, the author presented this overview as a research report. An important bibliography and more than thirty reproductions are included at the end of the volume.

647 **Luxemburgs Kulturentfaltung im neunzehnten Jahrhundert. Eine kritische Darstellung des literarischen und wissenschaftlichen Lebens.** (The cultural development of Luxembourg in the 19th century. A critical description of literary, artistic and scientific life.)
Pierre Grégoire. Luxembourg: Imprimerie Saint-Paul, 1981. 578p.
Following a short description of the international and national-political situation in the 19th century, Grégoire tackles the question of whether there exists a Luxembourg national culture and details the history of thought in Luxembourg during this decisive period.

648 **De la Société Archéologique à la Section Historique de l'Institut Grand-Ducal. Tendances, méthodes et résultats du travail historique de 1845 à 1985.** (From the Archaeological Society to the Historical Section of the Grand Ducal Institute.)
Joseph Goedert. Luxembourg: Imprimerie Beffort, 1987. 540p. (Publications de la Section Historique de l'Institut Grand-Ducal de Luxembourg, Vol. 101).

Represents a splendid piece of research work which traces the tendencies, methods and results of the historical work carried out over a period of 140 years by the honorary members of a learned society, the Archaeological Society, which later became known as the Historical Section of the Grand Ducal Institute. Joseph Goedert, one of the most accomplished historians of his generation, is the former Director of the National Library of Luxembourg (1961-72).

649 **Anthologie Nicolas van Werveke: publiée par les soins de la Société des Amis de Nicolas van Werveke.** (Anthology of Nicolas van Werveke: published through the efforts of the Society of the Friends of Nicolas van Werveke.)
Nicolas van Werveke. Luxembourg: Buck, 1956. 386p.

No other Luxembourg historian has been as prolific as van Werveke. In a bibliography published by Edouard Oster in *Les Cahiers Luxembourgeois*, vol. 2, no. 7 (1924-25), we find about ninety studies and dissertations on various historical, archaeological, numismatic or onomastic subjects. This anthology presents his main contributions under the following headings: documents, times of war, field names, state and urban organizations, jurisdiction, church and clergy, education, the traffic system, the health system, public funerals, life and crafts, trade and commerce, and hunting and fishing. Van Werveke was a popular lecturer and history teacher at the Ecole Industrielle et Commerciale (Industrial and Commercial School) who also enjoyed an international reputation.

650 **Mélanges offerts à Joseph Goedert.** (Miscellany offered to Joseph Goedert.)
Edited by Gilbert Trausch and Emile Van der Vekene. Luxembourg: Bibliothèque nationale, 1983. 396p.

For the seventy-fifth anniversary of Joseph Goedert, this commemorative volume was published. This former director of the National Library battled for the recognition of the institution which took on a new status under his direction. The library was transferred to another building and a Rare Collections Department was finally created in 1969, just before his retirement in 1972. Besides a bibliography of his publications, the volume consists of more than twenty contributions by well-known Luxembourg authors. The subjects mainly concern historical topics, but also include: a retrospective of the legal basis of the cultural institutes in Luxembourg by Paul Spang; a farce by Norbert Weber; and an essay on written Luxembourgish by Lex Roth.

## 651 Cultural life in the Grand Duchy of Luxembourg.
Ministry of Cultural Affairs.   Luxembourg: Service Information et
Presse, 1977. 56p.

Takes stock of what was going on in the field of culture in the late 1970s and
particularly emphasizes efforts to promote the arts in various contexts. It first presents
official institutions, then deals with theatrical, musical, cinematographic, photographic
and artistic life. Further headings survey literature, social and cultural promotion,
continuing education, scientific research and international contacts.

## 652 Petit guide pratique. (Little practical guide.)
Ministère des Affaires Culturelles.   Luxembourg: Imprimerie
Centrale, 1994. 64p.

Records the cultural activities of Luxembourg as promoted by the cultural institutions
of the state. The final pages of this brief, practical guide include more than 200
addresses of institutions and associations related to culture.

## 653 Grand-Duché de Luxembourg: Fleuron de Culture. (Grand Duchy
of Luxembourg: flower of culture.)
Luxembourg: Luxembourg 1995 – Ville Européenne de la Culture,
1995. 38p.

Published to celebrate Luxembourg's year as European City of Culture in 1995, this
volume offers a practical guide to arts, theatres, museums, and popular heritage events
all over the country, accompanied by a compendium of useful addresses and
publications.

## 654 Kultur im Karree. (Culture in the square.)
Edited by Alfred Diwersy, Rainer Silkenbeumer.   Lebach, Germany:
Hempel Verlag, 1989. 240p.

Saar-Lor-Lux is the term for the cross border area that includes the German Saar, the
French Lorraine and Luxembourg. Twenty critical contributions, including a
Luxembourg one by Guy Linster and Mars Klein, propose new ideas for the cultural
policy of this large region.

## 655 Drucker, Gazettisten und Zensoren durch vier Jahrhunderte
luxemburgischer Geschichte.
(Printers, gazetteers and censors through four centuries of Luxembourg
history.)
Pierre Grégoire.   Luxembourg: Sankt-Paulus-Druckerei, 1964-66.
5 vols.

Rather than offering a history of printing in Luxembourg, Grégoire examines the
development of censorship and the struggle of the first newspapers and magazines to
safeguard the freedom of the press.

656   **1792, Goethe in Luxemburg.**
Nikolaus Hein.   Luxembourg: Imprimerie Bourg-Bourger, 1961.
3rd expanded ed. 217p.

Presents an interesting literary and historical account of Goethe's stay in Luxembourg in 1792, when he was on his return from the campaign in France. Hein manages to convey the local and international background events very vividly by annotating and analysing Goethe's notes.

657   **Goethe in Trier und Luxemburg 1792-1992. 200 Jahre. Campagne in Frankreich. Ausstellungskatalog.** (Goethe in Trier and Luxembourg 1792-1992. 200 years. Campaign in France. Catalogue of the exhibition.)
Trier, Germany: Imprimerie Neu GmbH, 1992. 467p.

The exhibition that took place in 1992 to celebrate the 200th anniversary of Goethe's stays in Luxembourg and Trier also saw the publication of this catalogue that illustrates about 250 exhibits from Belgium, France, Luxembourg and Austria. Containing twenty-five contributions in French, Luxembourgish and German, this volume was issued by the National Library of Luxembourg and the municipal library of Trier.

658   **Colpach, édité par un groupe d'amis de Colpach.** (Colpach, edited by a group of its friends.)
Luxembourg: Amis de Colpach, 1978. 2nd ed. 292p.

In 1957, on the tenth anniversary of the death of Aline Mayrisch-de Saint Hubert, who was the wife of Emile Mayrisch, and a great personality and patron of art in Luxembourg, some friends decided to offer her a lasting homage in the form of this commemorative book. Colpach was the residence of Emile Mayrisch, the outstanding Luxembourg steel tycoon and philanthropist, who was the master-mind behind the Entente Internationale de l'Acier (International Steel Agreement) and the founder of the Comité Franco-Allemand d'Information et de Documentation (Franco-German Committee for Information and Documentation). He invited to his home leading French and German political, literary and artistic personalities and so contributed to the Franco-German *rapprochement* that was happening in the context of a new European constellation. André Gide, Walther Rathenau, Jean Schlumberger, Ernst-Robert Curtius, Paul Claudel, Jacques Rivière, Henry Michaux, Karl Jaspers, Jules Romains and Annette Kolb were all guests at Colpach. At her death, Mayrisch bequeathed her Colpach home to the Red Cross in Luxembourg.

659   **L'activité scientifique des Luxembourgeois à l'étranger: les professeurs d'université luxembourgeois de 1880 à nos jours.**
(Scientific activity of Luxembourgers abroad: Luxembourg university professors from 1880 to the present.)
Robert Stumper.   *D'Lëtzebuerger Land*, nos. 37, 38, and 47 (1970).

Stumper set out to show that many of his countrymen had excelled in higher learning and occupied prestigious academic posts at foreign universities, in spite of the absence of a university in Luxembourg (the Centre Universitaire de Luxembourg, the single academic institution to provide any university teaching, was only established in 1969). His list covers the years 1794 to 1937 and groups eighty-six Luxembourgers who taught at universities in twelve different countries.

660 **Luxemburger Wissenschaftler im Ausland.** (Luxembourg scientists abroad.)

Robert Stumper. Luxembourg: Editions Lëtzebuerger Land, 1962. 114p.

Stumper presents a portrait of thirty-five Luxembourg-born scientists who acquired fame abroad for their research and so contributed significantly to the progress of natural sciences, especially in chemistry and steel engineering.

661 **Lëtzebuerger Almanach '89.** (Luxembourg Almanac '89.)

Luxembourg: Editions Guy Binsfeld, 1989. 480p.

The almanac produced by the country's best-known publisher, Guy Binsfeld, was issued annually between 1986 and 1989 but unfortunately stopped after that period. Each volume included useful, informative, critical and interesting reports, thematic and topical analysis and a special retrospective of the year. This last volume of its publication contains more than forty contributions in which the authors express their views on contemporary themes of politics, history, society and culture.

662 **La vie scientifique.** (Scientific activity in Luxembourg.)

Jos A. Massard. In: *Mémorial 1989.* Edited by Martin Gerges.

Luxembourg: Les Publications Mosellanes, 1989, p. 408-40. bibliog.

This is by far the best and most recent survey of scientific activity in Luxembourg. The author first outlines the establishment of the different scientific societies and public institutions, before dealing with the domains of botany, zoology, geology, physics and mathematics. A final chapter is devoted to Luxembourg explorers.

663 **175e anniversaire de la respectable Loge 'Les Enfants de la Concorde fortifiée', 1803-1978.**

(The 175th anniversary of the Honourable Lodge 'Les Enfants de la Concorde fortifiée', 1803-1978.)

Grande Loge de Luxembourg. Esch-sur-Alzette, Luxembourg: Imprimerie A. Wagner, 1978. 158p.

On 22 November 1803 the Freemasons of the Grand Orient de France (The Great Orient of France) transferred their charter to the young Luxembourg Lodge, Les Enfants de la Concorde fortifiée (The Children of the Fortified Agreement). This commemorative anniversary brochure introduces the grades, activities and various sections of the Lodge to a wider public.

664 **Essai d'histoire de la franc-maçonnerie dans le Grand-Duché de Luxembourg.** (Tentative history of the Freemasonry of the Grand Duchy of Luxembourg.)

L. Schleich. Luxembourg: Buck, 1939. 160p.

The history of Luxembourg's Freemasonry is linked to that of the Austrian Netherlands. In 1770 the Marquis de Gages founded the first regular and settled lodge, 'la Parfaite Union' (the Perfect Union). However, in 1786 the first difficulties arose: an imperial decree of Joseph II limited masonic gatherings to provincial cities, and later only to Brussels. The French troops which entered Luxembourg in 1795 allowed the Freemasons to resume their meetings. After some false starts, the new civil lodge, Les Enfants de la Concorde fortifiée (The Children of the Fortified Agreement), was born.

# Folklore

665  **Altluxemburger Denkwürdigkeiten.** (Memorable facts and features
of old Luxembourg.)
Joseph Hess.   Luxembourg: Linden, 1960. 389p. bibliog. (Beiträge
zur Luxemburgischen Sprach-und Volkskunde, 7).

A fundamental reference book which groups fascinating facts and theories under the
following headings: the oldest records; law and what passes for law; superstitions;
popular medicine; religion and faith; the village; the peasant population; stages of life;
costumes and language; and the customs of the calendar year.

666  **Luxemburger Volksleben in Vergangenheit und Gegenwart.** (The
life of Luxembourg people in the past and in the present.)
Joseph Hess.   Grevenmacher, Luxembourg: Faber, 1939. 175p.

Hess was the country's greatest specialist in popular life, customs and traditions. In
this volume he attempts to analyse popular thinking about the past, examines the
documents and psychology of village life, work, art and communal customs and
traditions, and outlines modern ways of thought and feeling.

667  **Luxemburger Volkskunde.** (Luxembourg folklore.)
Joseph Hess.   Grevenmacher, Luxembourg: Faber, 1929. 318p.

The first inventory of surviving customs and traditions from Luxembourg's rural past.
Its intention is not to be exhaustive or scientifically systematic, but rather to raise a
wider interest in the moral and social values of the past.

668  **Luxemburger Sitten und Bräuche.** (Luxembourg manners and
customs.)
Edmond de La Fontaine.   Luxembourg: Imprimerie Saint-Paul, 1985.
new ed. 164p.

Presents an almost exact reprint of an original work by Edmond de la Fontaine
(Luxembourg: Peter Brück, 1883. 168p.), one of Luxembourg's most famous poets.

This new edition is illustrated by some pictures taken from National Library material. The first section covers customs and begins with the Christian year (from the time of Advent) whereas the second part deals with non-Christian practices. The volume would be improved by the inclusion of a short introduction defining the contemporary intellectual climate and describing Edmond de La Fontaine's personality.

669  **Luxemburg – Damals.** (Luxembourg – in those days.)
     Norbert Weins.   Luxembourg: Imprimerie Centrale, 1984. 167p.

This volume is an interesting report on the country from the 19th until the mid-20th century when the Grand Duchy was still a 'quiet fortress'. Weins includes some of his personal memories and the texts of well-known Luxembourg poets such as Batty Weber and Willy Goergen. The wealth of photographs and documents recreate the atmosphere of the period.

670  **Luxembourg, land of legends.**
     W. J. Taylor-Whitehead.   London: Constable, 1951. 144p. map.

The Grand Duchy is rich in colourful legends and tales of magic, devils and dream castles – but few of them have been recorded and documented. The author sets out to explore the early part of Luxembourg's history that provides the setting for most of the legends. In part one he describes the land and its people; part two deals with local tales and legends; and part three tells of the feats of some legendary heroes.

671  **The land of haunted castles.**
     Robert J. Casey.   New York: Century, 1921. 496p.

'If ghosts must walk the earth, they could find no spot on the globe where their appearance would be more natural or better understood', writes the author in his introductory chapter, called 'Grimm reality', for through Luxembourg have successively swept many groups of peoples including the Goths, the Visigoths, the Huns, the Romans, the Belgae, the Franks, the Gauls, the Spaniards, the Dutch, the Germans and the French. This academic and well-documented book is divided into thirty-two chapters devoted to regional and local tales.

672  **Sagenschatz des Luxemburger Landes.** (Treasury of Luxembourg legends.)
     Nicolas Gredt.   Luxembourg: Ministerium für Künste und Wissenschaften, 1963-67. rev. ed. 2 vols.

This is the authoritative collection of Luxembourg legends, collected by many primary-school teachers and school children from all parts of the country. The first edition appeared under the same title in 1883. Gredt has organized this vast corpus of material under an amazing number of specialized headings. Volume two consists of subject tables by Jean Dumont, Adolf Jacoby and Henri Rinnen.

673  **Von Tieren und Tierspuk.** (On animals and haunting animal apparitions.)
     Jean Haan.   Luxembourg: Edi-Centre, 1970. 147p. (Am Sagenborn des Luxemburger Volkes, No. 2).

Deals with supernatural beliefs in werewolves, apparitions of snakes, cats, horses, hares and other animal figures.

674 **Sagenumrankte Heimatburgen.** (Legendary castles.)
Jean Haan.   Luxembourg: Krippler-Müller, 1961. 95p. (Am
Sagenborn des Luxemburger Volkes, No. 1).

A collection of popular legends and tales concerning about sixty castles perched high
on Luxembourg's hills.

675 **Hexenwahn und Zauberei in Luxemburg.** (Witchcraft and magic in
Luxembourg.)
Theo Witry.   Luxembourg: Schroell, 1939. 254p.

Partly based on the acts of the Provincial Luxembourg Council, this volume provides
an account of witchcraft and the witch trials which reached a climax in the 16th and
17th centuries. It includes an index of places and persons.

676 **Von Hexen und wildem Gejäg.** (On witches and wild hunting.)
Jean Haan.   Luxembourg: Edi-Centre, 1971. 159p. (Am Sagenborn
des Luxemburger Volkes, No. 3).

In Luxembourg the obsessive belief in witches caused the deaths of about 30,000
people over 250 years; they were mostly burned at the stake. The first trial took place
in Luxembourg in 1372, with collective hysteria reaching its climax in the 16th and
17th centuries. At the beginning of the 17th century there were about 200 trials every
year. An ordinance of Louis XIV and energetic action by Empress Marie-Thérèse
caused this horror to be abolished.

677 **Die Hexenprozesse im Luxemburger Lande**. (The witch trials in
Luxembourg.)
Nicolas van Werveke.   Luxembourg: Schroell, 1900. 24p.

A summary survey about the cruel and inhuman witch-trial proceedings, which started
in about 1501, peaking in about 1585 and again around 1640. In the course of two
centuries not less than 500 'witches' were officially burnt. The main causes for these
evils can be found in the superstition and ignorance of the clergy, the social misery of
the people, greed and savage cruelty. Some of these trials are described in detail.

678 **Prophètes et sorciers dans les Pays-Bas, XVIe-XVIIIe siècle.**
(Prophets and sorcerers in the Netherlands, 16th to 18th centuries.)
Marie-Sylvie Dupont-Bouchat, Willem Frijhoff, Robert Muchembled.
Paris: Hachette, 1978. 366p. maps. bibliog.

An interesting study of popular culture and religion, this volume contains three
contributions which: deal with the repression of sorcery in the Duchy of Luxembourg
in the 16th and 17th centuries (p. 41-154), and analyse its ideology, mechanisms and
efficiency; cover the sorceresses of the Cambresis (area around Cambrai in northern
France); and examine prophecy and society in the United Provinces of the 17th and
18th centuries.

679 **Die Schobermesse. So war sie früher.** (The Schobermesse. In times past.)
Compiled by Norbert Etringer. Luxembourg: Imprimerie Saint-Paul, 1992. 197p.

Whereas Michel Pauly's *Schueberfouer 1340-1990* (see next item) is rather a historical study, Norbert Etringer's collected retrospects mainly concern the popular and anecdotal aspects of Luxembourg's Bartholomew fair which takes place each August in the city. A great number of photographs and documents convey to the reader a vivid impression of what the fair looked like a century ago.

680 **Schueberfouer 1340-1990. Untersuchungen zu Markt, Gewerbe und Stadt im Mittelalter und Neuzeit.** (Annual Fair 1340-1990. Research into market, industry and town in the Middle Ages and modern times.)
Edited by Michel Pauly on behalf of CLUDEM (Centre luxembourgeois de documentation et d'études médiévales auprès du Centre Universitaire). Luxembourg: Imprimerie Saint-Paul, 1990. 152p.

In 1990, Luxembourg celebrated the 650th anniversary of John the Blind's (King of Bohemia and Count of Luxembourg) foundation of 'Schueberfouer', the annual weekly fair that takes place in the city of Luxembourg. His intention was to create a distinct commercial and trading fair, although in the course of time it has become the fun fair we know today. The 'Schueberfouer' is one of Luxembourg's oldest and most vivid traditions, but historical studies on the subject are quite rare. The author therefore attempts to provide an academic interpretation of the fair, accompanying his account with documents and photographs. They describe the creation and role of this fair in Luxembourg's economic life in the Middle Ages and modern times, the prerequisites of the city trade in particular, the topographic and legal development of the city in general and the significance of the fair in the supraregional area.

# Religion

681 **Die Kirche in Luxemburg von den Anfängen bis zur Gegenwart.**
(The Luxembourg church from the beginnings to the present.)
Emile Donckel.   Luxembourg: Imprimerie Saint-Paul, 1950. 248p.
maps. bibliog.

Donckel's work is a very searching historical survey of the development of the Church of Luxembourg since early times, in the Middle Ages, under foreign rulers and after the foundation of a Luxembourg independent diocese under Bishop Nicolas Adames in 1870. It provides interesting details about the foundations of religious convents, cloisters and orders, and also deals with the life of the church under Nazi rule and during the reconstruction under Bishop Philippe and his newly-appointed coadjutor, Léon Lommel.

682 **L'érection de l'échêvé de Luxembourg**. (The setting up of the
Bishopric of Luxembourg.)
Nicolas Majerus.   Luxembourg: Imprimerie Saint-Paul, 1951. 605p.
map.

Deals with the negotiations which led to the creation of the Bishopric of Luxembourg, providing relevant documents. On 16 March 1861 the Apostolic Pro-Vicar, Nicolas Adames, was appointed Bishop in partibus; his nomination was acknowledged by the government on 11 August. An Apostolic decree of 30 March 1870 appointed Adames as the First Bishop of Luxembourg.

683 **Aspects de sociologie religieuse du diocèse de Luxembourg.**
(Aspects of religious sociology of the diocese of Luxembourg.)
André Heiderscheid.   Luxembourg: Imprimerie Saint-Paul, 1961-62. 2
vols. 89 maps. bibliog.

The first volume covers: the infrastructure of religious society; geography, demography and economic evolution; and the Luxembourg people, social evolution and political evolution. Volume two deals with: religious society and its confrontation with lay society; structural aspects of the diocese; the evolution of religious practice; other indications of religious vitality; the issue of vocation; the opposition of the two powers (church and state); sociological reflections on religious evolution and the present situation: sacerdotal callings in their sociological context; and the problems facing the church.

684 **Umfrage zur Luxemburger Synode: Uberblick über Ergebnisse und Motivzusammenhänge.**
(Public opinion poll on the occasion of the Luxembourg Synod: survey on results and motivational patterns.)
Institut für Demoskopie Allensbach. Allensbach: Luxembourg, 1973. 46p. + annexes.

In order to prepare for Luxembourg's church council, 225,521 questionnaires were distributed in 1971; 91,510 copies were sent back, but only 79,799 were fully valid and suitable for screening. Even so, this was an unusually high rate of participation. The questions and statistical tables deal mainly with church attendance, issues of faith, rituals, attitudes towards the church and missionary work. Fifty-three detailed tables provide a good picture of the situation of the Luxembourg church in the early 1970s.

685 **La communauté juive du Luxembourg dans le passé et dans le présent: histoire illustrée.**
(The Jewish community in Luxembourg past and present: an illustrated history.)
Charles Lehrmann, Graziella Lehrmann. Esch-sur-Alzette, Luxembourg: Imprimerie Coopérative Luxembourgeoise, 1953. 155p.

Considers the traditional characteristics of the Jews, the destiny of Jews all over the world, and their general history in the Luxembourg region. The six chapters deal with: the Jews from the Middle Ages to the French Revolution; the Jewish colony in Luxembourg enjoying 150 years of freedom, 1790-1940; the ordeals of the Second World War; the old and new buildings of the synagogue; the contribution Jews have made to the country of Luxembourg and the role of the most ancient families; and Jews as Luxembourg citizens and their relationships with Israel.

686 **La procession dansante d'Echternach: son origine et son histoire.**
(The dancing procession of Echternach: its origin and its history.)
Alex Langini. Echternach, Luxembourg: Société d'Embellissement et de Tourisme, 1977. 79p.

This guidebook provides essential data on the history of the abbey of Echternach and the life of St Willibrord, and studies the sacred processions. It describes the compulsory procession of 'the simple crosses' (des croix banales) which is the origin of the Echternach procession. In a final chapter Langini answers the traditional objections and criticisms raised against this religious manifestation, which has been performed since the end of the 11th century, and concludes that it is much more than a folkloristic pageant or a therapeutic physical exercise.

687 **Sankt Willibrord: sein Leben und Lebenswerk.** (Saint Willibrord: his life and his work.)
Camille Wampach. Luxembourg: Sankt-Paulus-Druckerei, 1953. 435p. 3 maps.

This is the basic documentary biography of the Irish missionary, St. Willibrord, born in about 658 in Northumberland, who first set out to convert the Frisians and later founded a monastery at Echternach. This was soon to become a missionary school and centre of Christian civilization, and of intellectual and artistic life. The author's interests range far beyond St. Willibrord's individual personality and he constructs an impression of the cultural and spiritual ethos of Europe in the 7th and 8th centuries.

688 **Die Echternacher und ihre Basilika.** (The people of Echternach and their basilica.)
Paul Spang. Luxembourg: Imprimerie Saint-Paul, 1988. 167p.

Spang's volume is not a commemorative volume, but is rather a dedication to the population of Echternach (a town located east of Luxembourg city, on the German border) who have always proudly defended their rich heritage, which consists mainly of the funeral church of Saint Willibrord, the basilica of Echternach. The account deals with the present situation although many pages are devoted to the almost total destruction of the church after the Second World War.

689 **Exposition Saint Willibrord: Abbaye d'Echternach 24 mai – 24 août 1958.** (Saint Willibrord exhibition: Abbey of Echternach 24 May – 24 August 1958.)
Luxembourg: Imprimerie Saint-Paul, 1958. 148p.

In order to celebrate the thirteenth centenary of the birth of Saint Willibrord (658-1958), the Anglo Saxon missionary who founded the abbey of Echternach in Luxembourg in 698, an exhibition was organized in 1958. It shows the perenniality and the spiritual impact of his extraordinarily rich works. Before describing all the documents and relics that the organizers were able to display for a short time, the volume provides an account of the life and the cult of Saint Willibrord which is still celebrated in the abbey town of Echternach.

690 **Echternach.**
Pierre Schritz. Luxembourg: Imprimerie Saint-Paul, 1981. 349p.

Published for the seventieth birthday of the teacher, Georges Kiesel (1911- ), who is known for his research on the Saint Willibrord cult (he has published articles in the *Luxemburger Wort* since 1945), this volume comprises contributions which deal with various themes concerning the abbey town of Echternach where Saint Willibrord is celebrated every year on Whitsun Tuesday. This luxurious edition also includes a biographical notice and a bibliography of Georges Kiesel.

691 **Traube und Rebe in der religiösen Kunst Luxemburgs.** (Grape and vine in religious art in Luxembourg.)
Norbert Thill, Michel Schmitt. Luxembourg: Imprimerie Saint-Paul, 1982. 202p.

Grape and vine are not only religious cult symbols but they are also the central point of creation in sacral art. In this photographic trip through Luxembourg's churches and chapels, the two authors offer the reader a modest insight into how architecture, sculpture, painting and iconography have dealt with the grape theme in the regional context in order to create an artistic world which, according to the authors, 'has not until now found the respect and acknowledgement it deserved'.

692 **D'Psalmen op Lëtzebuergesch.** (Psalms in Luxembourgish.)
Translated by Felix Molitor, Raymond Schaack, illustrations by Marc Chagall. Luxembourg: Actioun Lëtzebuergesch Eis Sprooch, 1996. 308p. (Eis Sprooch: Extra Serie, 18).

'Psalmein' in Greek means to play a string instrument, to accompany a song on the harp. The Book of Psalms is one of the most important books of the Holy Scripture and is highly estimated by both Jews and Christians. A great deal of the 150 psalms written for the religious service were written by King David (1000-961 BC) and King Solomon (961-31 BC). Others were added later. After the Babylonian Exile (586-35 BC), the book took on its present form. This Luxembourgish translation is based on the German translation by Martin Buber, the 'Bible de Jerusalem' (the Jerusalem Bible) and the German 'Einheitsübersetzung' (Standard version).

693 **De Mënsch schwätzt mam Härgott: 50 Psalmen op Lëtzebuergesch.** (Man speaks to God: fifty psalms in Luxembourgish.)
Alice Schroell, Gaby Schroell. Luxembourg: Joseph Beffort, 1979. 134p.

Alice and Gaby Schroell were the first laywomen to translate fifty psalms into Luxembourgish. They respected the dense Hebrew poetry while attempting to render its special characteristics in Luxembourgish.

694 **Pour que l'homme vive.** (So that man should live.)
The Congregation of apostolic life in Luxembourg. Luxembourg: Imprimerie Saint-Paul, 1995. 92p.

Published to support the exhibition, 'The congregations of apostolic life in Luxembourg', held from 29 April to 11 June 1995, this publication provides an illustrated and detailed overview of the social and educative contribution of the female congregations to the culture of Luxembourg in the 19th and 20th centuries.

695 **Les Capucins de Luxembourg.** (The Capuchins of Luxembourg.)
Pierre Hamer. Luxembourg: Imprimerie Saint-Paul, 1982. 276p.

This volume collects Hamer's studies on the Capuchins of Luxembourg, which cover their history, missions, chronicle, monastery and monastic life. The book is a monograph on the activities of this order in Luxembourg, Louisiana and Santo Domingo, Dominican Republic. Hamer also provides an account of the latest excavations on the site of the Capuchin church in Luxembourg and describes such personalities as Raphaël of Luxembourg, Jean-Guillaume Guerrier and Anselme d'Esch.

696 **Raphaël de Luxembourg: une contribution luxembourgeoise à la colonisation de la Louisiane.** (Raphaël of Luxembourg: a Luxembourg contribution to the colonization of Louisiana.)
Pierre Hamer. Luxembourg: Imprimerie Saint-Paul, 1966. 266p. bibliog. (Publication de la Section Historique de l'Institut Grand-Ducal).

Hamer traces the lives and works of ten Luxembourg Capuchin friars who contributed to the French colonization of the Mississippi valley and the northern shore of the Gulf of Mexico. Raphaël of Luxembourg was the outstanding figure among them because of his social ideas, his political activity for the people of Louisiana and his efforts to make the social order and administration more just.

697 **Anselme d'Esch: l'art de savoir bien mourir.** (Anselm of Esch: the art of knowing how to die well.)
Pierre Hamer. Luxembourg: Imprimerie Saint-Paul, 1977. 193p.

This is another volume by Hamer on the history of the Capuchin friars in Luxembourg and of outstanding Luxembourg monks. Anselm, who was never allowed to leave for the American missions, wrote a series of remarkable works in Latin, French and German and proved to be one of the most cultured men of 18th-century Luxembourg. The first part of this volume deals with the general background and organization of the cloister of the mendicant friars in Luxembourg, while the final pages present some extracts from Anselm's works.

698 **Camino de Santiago ein Pilgergang von Biwels nach Santiago de Compostela.** (Camino de Santiago, a pilgrim's walk from Biwels to Santiago de Compostela.)
Adrien Ries. Luxembourg: Imprimerie Saint-Paul, 1989. 248p.

On 1 May 1987, Adrien Ries began a long walk from his home town, Biwels, in Luxembourg (in the Oesling) to the pilgrim city of Saint Jacques of Compostela in the northwest of Spain, where he arrived ninety-nine days later, on 7 August 1987. Ries describes in detail his pilgrimage to Compostela, a city in which the mortal remains of the apostle, Jacques, were discovered and where a cathedral was built in the 11th and 12th centuries. The appendix includes a short French summary of the book which is entirely written in German.

699 **Sur le Chemin de Saint-Jacques de Luxembourg à Compostelle.** (On the way to Saint-Jacques from Luxembourg to Compostela.)
Maria-C. Haller. Luxembourg: Imprimerie Saint-Paul, 1984. 175p.

Although Haller did not undertake her trip to Compostela on foot, but by train and taxi, she joined a group of pilgrims in Moissac (near Toulouse, France) who were taking the historic road to Compostela, accompanied by a local expert on the area. She provides a historical overview and details on the regional sanctuaries.

700   **Auf Wegkreuzfahrt durch das Grossherzogtum.** (On the roadside
      calvary ride through the Grand Duchy.)
      Norbert Weins.   Luxembourg: Imprimerie Centrale, 1982-84. 6 vols.

Weins presents the findings of his extensive research work on the stone witnesses of
Christian belief in past centuries, that is to say the roadside calvaries which spread all
over the country. The six volumes reproduce numerous photographs and the
supplementary final volume includes a list of all the villages represented in the whole
work.

701   **Union Saint Pie X 1969-1994.** (Saint Pius X's Union 1969-94.)
      Edited by Roby Zenner.   Luxembourg: Imprimerie Saint-Paul, 1995.
      151p.

Published to commemorate the twenty-fifth anniversary (1969-94) of the Union Saint
Pie X, the umbrella organization of the Saint Cecilia Chorus, this volume provides a
photographic history of the association and regional sub-associations. It also includes
contributions such as short biographies of Pope Pius X and Saint Cecilia.

# Language

## General

702 **Grundlegung einer Geschichte des Luxemburgischen; Teil 1: Das Zeugnis der Geschichte; Teil 2: Das Zeugnis der Luxemburger Mundarten.** (Foundation for a history of Luxembourgish; Part 1: The evidence of history; Part 2: The evidence of the Luxembourg dialect.)
Robert Bruch. Luxembourg: Ministère de l'Education Nationale, 1953. 269p. 62 maps. bibliog. (Publications Littéraires et Scientifiques du Ministère de l'Education Nationale, No. 1).

Reveals previously unknown geographical dialect material on the history of Luxembourgish and considers the position of Luxembourgish within the framework of West Middle German dialects. It challenges the older views held by the Rhenish school under the leadership of Theodor Frings, and suggests that the linguistic history of the Rhineland was shaped by a powerful Frankish west-east expansion in Merovingian and Carolingian times. Bruch argues that Luxembourg's peripheral position has facilitated the survival of the language type which emerged from the linguistic symbiosis of the West Franks and Romans in northern Gaul after the Frankish conquest.

703 **Grundlegung einer Geschichte des Luxemburgischen; Teil 3: Das Luxemburgische im Westfränkischen Kreis.** (Foundation of a history of Luxembourgish; Part 3: Luxembourgish in the West-Franconian area.)
Robert Bruch. Luxembourg: Ministère de l'Education Nationale, 1954. 161p. map. (Publications Littéraires et Scientifiques du Ministère de l'Education Nationale, No. 2).

Sets the characteristic features of the Luxembourgish language in the context of Frankish linguistic evolution. The author defines the West Moselle Franconian relief

192

area as being enclosed by a belt of isoglosses running from the Franco-German linguistic frontier west of St. Vith in the Eifel, southeastwards towards Bitburg, from there southwards to west of Trier, and southwestwards to the Franco-German linguistic frontier southwest of Thionville in Lorraine. Breaking new ground in dialectology, this fundamental book is a landmark in Luxembourg's historic and descriptive linguistics. Several chapters, however, deal with highly specialized subjects and make for difficult reading for all but specialists.

704 **German dialects: phonology and morphology with selected texts.**
R. E. Keller. Manchester, England: Manchester University Press, 1961. 396p. map. bibliog.

Affords the student of German a descriptive phonological and grammatical survey of certain dialects. Keller devotes his chapters to the Schwytzertütsch, Alsatian, Darmstadt, Upper Austrian, Luxembourgish, Westphalian and North Saxon (lower Elbe) dialects. The chapter on Luxembourgish (p. 248-99) is subdivided into phonology, morphology, an extract from Michel Rodange's *De Renert* (The tale of the fox), notes and glossary. It offers a very proficient and systematic survey of the area, status and general characteristics of Luxembourgish. The whole book constitutes a unique comparative work and stimulating starting-point for further detailed study.

705 **Luxembourg and Lëtzebuergesch. Language and communication at the crossroads of Europe.**
Edited by Gerald Newton. Oxford: Clarendon Press, 1996. 286p.

This book is by far the best work currently available in English on Luxembourg and its language. Gerald Newton, a lecturer in Germanic studies at the University of Sheffield, a well known specialist on the dialectology of German and related languages, brought together commissioned contributions from Luxembourgish and English specialists. Newton himself presents the historical, linguistic and literary background; V. J. Russ contributes a remarkable linguistic study on the phonology, spelling and grammar of Luxembourgish; Fernand Hoffmann offers well-informed surveys on developments and desirabilities, the domains of Luxembourgish, and its stylistic levels and textual varieties; Jean-Paul Hoffmann covers the problems of a language which is in contact with two powerful competitors (German and French) and studies the usage of Lëtzebuergesch outside the boundaries of the Grand Duchy. An excellent bibliography and interesting text illustrations complete this high-ranking academic publication.

706 **Central Franconian.**
Gerald Newton. In: *The Dialects of Modern German. A linguistic survey*. Edited by Charles Russ. London: Routledge, 1990, p. 136-209.

Written by an English specialist, this chapter represents the most proficient study of the Central Franconian area. Sixty-five pages are devoted to Luxembourgish as such, with special attention given to phonological and grammatical features and interesting text extracts to illustrate the various points. An extensive bibliography completes this well-informed survey.

707  **Sprachen in Luxemburg.** (Languages in Luxembourg.)
Fernand Hoffmann. Luxembourg: Institut grand-ducal. Section de
linguistique, de folklore et de toponymie, 1978. 174p. (Beiträge zur
Luxemburgischen Sprach- und Volkskunde; no XII).

An authoritative description of a triglossic situation from a historical, literary and
linguistic point of view. In Luxembourg, people speak three different languages
(French, German and Luxembourgish), but each language has well-specified areas of
usage. This study is based on fieldwork undertaken by students at the Institut
Pédagogique de Walferdange (Walferdange Educational Institute).

708  **Gesammelte Aufsätze.** (Collected articles.)
Robert Bruch. Luxembourg: Bibliothèque Nationale, 1969. 245p.
maps. bibliog. (Luxemburgensia Anastatica, 1).

Introduced by Professor Walther Mitzka from Marburg, this volume contains the most
significant articles and essays by Robert Bruch, Luxembourg's greatest linguist, who
initiated a new period in Luxembourg dialectology. Divided into four parts, the
volume contains: a study of the problems of language and linguistics; a description of
Luxembourgish as a language of wine-growers and peasants; an interesting article on
Luxembourg railway semantics; and a presentation of the 'man who hides behind the
work'. The work concludes with a complete bibliography of Bruch's literary and
linguistic publications.

709  **Critères linguistiques de la nationalité luxembourgeoise.** (Linguistic
criteria of Luxembourg nationality.)
Robert Bruch. *Bulletin de Documentation Service Information et
Presse – Ministère d'Etat*, vol. 13, no. 1 (Jan. 1957), p. 1-17.

Consists of the text of a lecture concerning the relationship between the language and
the national character of Luxembourg people.

710  **We are what we speak: the psychology of the Luxembourger seen
through the evolution of his dialect, speech habits, proverbs and
sayings.**
Fernand Hoffmann. *Lore and Language,* vol. 2, no. 1 (July 1974),
p. 5-14.

The author draws the conclusion that Luxembourgish sayings and phrases are
characteristic of the Luxembourg people's history. As uninvolved witnesses of great
events, they use a rustic language whose syntax is elementary, whose morphology is
stunted and whose vocabulary is small. Yet the Luxembourg people love it, because it
mirrors their character and their past.

711  **Das Luxemburgische im Unterricht.** (Luxembourgish at school.)
Fernand Hoffmann. *Courrier de l'Education Nationale*, No. A7
(1969), p. 7-74.

Intended for the teacher who is in charge of a Luxembourgish class, this guide
provides basic information on the history of the language, its psychology and its
grammar and introduces the available teaching materials. An interesting didactic
chapter deals with the influence that Luxembourgish exerts on pupils' written

German. Hoffmann's analysis is based on abundant material supplied by Georges Milmeister.

712    **Glossarium Epternacense: spätalthochdeutsche Glossen aus Echternach; Tatsachen und Quellen, Wörter und Namen.** (The Echternach glossary: Old High German glosses from Echternach; facts, sources, words and names.)
Robert Bruch.    Luxembourg: Ministère des Affaires Culturelles, 1964. 173p. (Publications Nationales du Ministère des Affaires Culturelles).

Contains the first two parts of an uncompleted threefold project. The first part deals with facts and sources; the second covers words and names; while the final section analyses the forms and sounds of the Echternach codices, old cloister scripts in a West Frankish language which had developed from the old High German and showed some regional variants. This volume represents a significant step in the attempt to trace and establish scientifically the historical development of the Luxembourg tongue.

713    **Luxemburgischer Sprachatlas: Laut- und Formenatlas.** (Luxembourgish linguistic atlas: atlas of dialect sounds and forms.)
Robert Bruch.    Marburg, FRG: Elwert, 1963. 16p. 174 maps. (Publications Nationales du Ministère des Arts et des Sciences).

Bruch's atlas consists of 174 linguistic maps, providing the phonetic sounds recorded in response to a sample form. The basic map includes seventy-one villages in the Belgian province of Luxembourg in which residents used, or still use, the Luxembourg dialect, but does not include the southern villages in the French Thionville area where the dialect has survived among the older generation.

# Dictionaries and phrasebooks

714    **Luxemburger Wörterbuch.** (The Luxembourgish dictionary.)
Luxemburger Wörterbuchkommission.    Luxembourg: Linden, 1950-78. 5 vols. maps. bibliog.

In 1978 this first exhaustive Luxembourgish dictionary was completed, comprising four volumes and a supplement, and totalling 2,238 closely-printed pages. Explanations and comments on Luxembourgish phrases are in German. The first volume contains a linguistic, historical and phonetic introduction.

715    **Petit dictionnaire français-luxembourgeois.** (Concise French-Luxembourgish dictionary.)
Henri Rinnen, with the collaboration of Will Reuland.    Luxembourg: Imprimerie Saint-Paul, 1985. 2nd rev. ed. 309p.

This second edition of the concise French-Luxembourgish dictionary has been revised and augmented by about 1,000 new terms and is invaluable for new residents in Luxembourg.

716  **Dictionnaire français-luxembourgeois.** (French-Luxembourgish dictionary.)
Henri Rinnen.  Luxembourg: Imprimerie Saint-Paul, 1988. 1,171p.

A considerably extended version of the concise French-Luxembourgish dictionary by Henri Rinnen and Will Reuland (see preceding item), this provides many examples of idiomatic phrases and also includes a lot of useful technical terms from the domains of geography and geology, with special reference to Luxembourg's flora and fauna. It is the best compendium of present-day Luxembourgish to date.

717  **Kleines deutsch-luxemburgisches Wörterbuch.** (Concise German-Luxembourgish dictionary.)
Henri Rinnen, Will Reuland.  Luxembourg: Sankt-Paulus-Druckerei, 1979. 3rd ed. 178p.

A practical guide which fills a real gap for everyday use.

718  **Portugiesesch-Lëtzebuergeschen Dictionnaire.** (Portuguese-Luxembourgish dictionary.)
Lycée Michel Rodange, Luxembourg, collective work directed by Jul Christophory.  Luxembourg: Imprimerie Litho Bourg-Bourger, 1980. 204p.

This Portuguese-Luxembourgish dictionary is a collective work produced by 140 students and several teachers of the Lycée Michel Rodange (Michel Rodange High School) in Luxembourg. This pocket edition was not intended to be exhaustive but rather to offer a practical aid to Portuguese people living in the Grand Duchy.

719  **English-Luxembourgish dictionary.**
Lycée Michel Rodange, Luxembourg, collective work directed by Jul Christophory.  Esch-sur-Alzette, Luxembourg: Editions Schortgen, 1995. 288p.

Compiled and revised by over 300 pupils and several teachers of the Michel Rodange High School, this English-Luxembourgish dictionary is the result of work which began in 1979 and was first published in 1982. The selection of English words is based on the 35,000 headwords of the pocket edition of the *Langenscheidts Universal Wörterbuch Englisch* (Langenscheidts universal English dictionary) (Berlin: Langenscheidt, 1976). For the Luxembourgish language material, the authors drew on the *Kleines Deutsch-Luxemburgisches Wörterbuch* by H. Rinnen and W. Reuland (q.v.) and the official five-volume Luxembourgish dictionary, the *Luxemburger Wörterbuch* by the Luxemburger Wörterbuchkommission (Luxembourg: Linden, 1950-78. 5 vols. maps. bibliog.).

720  **6000 Wierder op Lëtzebuergesch: Français – Deutsch – English – Español – Português.** (6,000 words in Luxembourgish: French – German – English – Spanish – Portuguese.)
Collected by Jacqui Zimmer.  Luxembourg: Imprimerie Saint-Paul, 1993. unpaginated.

After publishing a provisional edition containing 1,500 words in 1988, Zimmer produced this five-language translation of the 6,000 most useful Luxembourgish words. The initiative has its origins in Luxembourgish classes taught at Luxembourg Accueil, the organization which welcomes foreign residents and arranges leisure activities.

721   **2500 Spréch a Spréchwierder**. (2,500 sayings and proverbs.)
Collected by Laure Wolter.   Luxembourg: Imprimerie Saint-Paul, 1986. 119p.

Wolter lists about 2,500 Luxembourgish sayings and proverbs, and includes some specific sayings from country life and meteorology at the end of her useful publication. Entirely written in Luxembourgish, these sayings provide an insight into the Luxembourg way of thinking.

722   **Steng fir lëtzebuergesch-franzéischen Dictionnaire**. (Building blocks for a Luxembourgish-French dictionary.)
Marie-Thérèse Kroemmer.   Luxembourg: Linden, 1989. 82p. (Extra Serie vun 'Eis Sprooch', 11).

Compiled by an author living in the Arlon region in the Belgian border area, this collection of 6,000 Luxembourgish words is an attempt to lay the foundation for a Luxembourgish-French pocket dictionary. It only partly succeeds because many of the reference words are used exclusively in the western border regions of the country in the 'pays d'Arlon' (Arlon region).

723   **Verhonziklopedi lëtzebuergesch-français franséisch-luxembourgeois**. ('Verhonziklopedi' Luxembourgish-French French-Luxembourgish.)
Pol Tousch.   Luxembourg: Imprimerie Centrale, 1995. 132p.

Tousch is interested in the history and folklore of simple people, especially those living in the Ardennes. The absurd title of this publication conceals a Luxembourgish-French, French-Luxembourgish dictionary of invective words and expressions accompanied by funny caricatures by Guy W. Stoos.

724   **Biller aus der Lötzeburger Sprôch: Riédensarten a Wirder zesummegesicht**. (Images from the Luxembourg language: sayings and expressions.)
Nicolas Pletschette.   *Revue Trimesterielle d'Etudes Linguistiques, Folkloriques et Toponymiques*, fascicule 35/36 (1950), p. 73-203.

An engaging compilation of picturesque or obsolete words, sayings, phrases, proverbs, expressions and metaphors in Luxembourgish, which reveals unexpected linguistic treasures in what was long supposed to be only a country dialect.

725 **Old and new imagery in Lëtzebuergesch.**
Jul Christophory. In: *Allegory old and new: creativity and continuity in culture. Colloque international, special number of Revue Luxembourgeoise de Littérature Générale et Comparée.*
Luxembourg: Sociéte luxembourgeoise de littérature générale et comparée, 1992, p. 61-87.

Represents an original study of the traditional pattern of idiomatic reference in a rural setting and of modern developments away from the agrarian context. An amazing renewal of imagery is illustrated by texts from Manderscheid and Rewenig which are characterized by a more refined psychology and a greater literary sensitivity.

726 **Luxemburger Pflanzennamen.** (Plant names in Luxembourgish.)
Henri Klees. Luxembourg: Institut grand-ducal, Section de linguistique, de folklore et de toponymie, 1974. 187p. bibliog.
(Beiträge zur Luxemburgischen Sprach- und Volkskunde, No. 8).

Klees records 1,111 German plant names, indicating their Latin and French versions and all Luxembourgish names and variants which appear in various local records and publications. The lay reader will be amazed by the number of popular names for one scientific variety. Klees considers his comprehensive record of names as a first step towards an overall popular taxonomy. Alphabetical indexes of the Latin, French and Luxembourgish names complete this reference book.

727 **Luxemburger Tiernamen.** (Animal names in Luxembourgish.)
Henri Klees. Luxembourg: Institut grand-ducal, Section de linguistique, de folklore et de toponymie, 1981. 131p. bibliog.
(Beiträge zur Luxemburgischen Sprach- und Volkskunde, No. XIV).

Drawing on newly available sources, charts and questionnaires, Klees revises, updates and completes the collection of animal names published in 1894 by Ferrant and Kraus (in the journal, *Fauna* [Luxembourg: P. Worré-Mertens], volume IV [1894]) under the title, 'Lokalnamen der einheimischen Thiere' (Local names of indigenous animals), which has long been out of print. Containing 605 entries in German, Latin, French and Luxembourgish, the work incorporates Rinnen's article, 'Luxemburger Vogelnamen' (Bird names in Luxembourgish) (q.v.).

728 **Luxemburger Vogelnamen.** (Bird names in Luxembourgish.)
Henri Rinnen. *Bulletin Linguistique et Ethnologique,* fascicule 15 (1969). 51p. bibliog.

An interesting multilingual catalogue of 285 varieties of birds arranged in alphabetical order of the German nomenclature. Besides the Latin, French, Dutch and English designations the author includes many regional and local Luxembourgish variants. Rinnen provides two alphabetical indexes of the Latin, French and Luxembourgish names.

# Grammars and guides

729 **Précis populaire de grammaire luxembourgeoise: Luxemburger Grammatik in volkstümlichem Abriss.** (Short version of Luxembourgish grammar.)
Robert Bruch. Luxembourg: Institut grand-ducal, Section de linguistique, 1973. 3rd ed. 123p. 16 maps. bibliog. (Beiträge zur Luxemburgischen Sprach- und Volkskunde, No. 10).

Represents a first attempt to catalogue and classify the fragmentary, impaired morphology and fickle syntax of spoken Luxembourgish. It is a landmark for all later systematic studies of the mechanism of the language. In a parallel German and French commentary, Bruch's intention was to avoid the scholarly language of grammarians and to expound concisely the basic features of spelling, morphology, syntax and linguistic geography of Luxembourgish. Students of the language will find this volume an indispensable reference guide.

730 **Mir schwätze Lëtzebuergesch. Nous parlons luxembourgeois. Abécédaire luxembourgeois. Guide bilingue de grammaire et de lecture.** (We speak Luxembourgish. Luxembourgish primer. Bilingual guide to grammar and reading.)
Jul Christophory. Luxembourg: Imprimerie Saint-Paul, 1974. 167p.

Written for the English- and French-speaking communities living in Luxembourg, this textbook complements the phrasebook, *Who's afraid of Luxembourgish?*, by the same author (q.v.).

# Literature

## General

731 **Who's afraid of Luxembourgish? Lëtzebuergesch? Qui a peur du luxembourgeois?**
Jul Christophory.   Luxembourg: Imprimerie Bourg-Bourger, 1979. 120p.

About a third of Luxembourg's population consists of foreigners. This Luxembourgish phrasebook, a new edition of *Sot et op Lëtzebuergesch* (Say it in Luxembourgish), contains English and French translations and was compiled for English- and French-speaking people living in Luxembourg. By presenting dialogues and vocabulary for about thirty everyday situations, it provides an insight into Luxembourgish as spoken by the average inhabitant.

732 **Langues et littératures du Luxembourg.** (Luxembourg language and literature.)
Fernand Hoffmann.   In: *Luxembourg.*   Edited by Christine Bonneton. Le Puy, France: Christine Bonneton, 1984, p. 169-217.

Five Luxembourg specialists contributed to a splendid scholarly volume on Luxembourg's culture and traditions. Fernand Hoffmann offers a brief review of fascinating aspects of the language situation and of the three literatures of the country.

733 **Die drei Literaturen Luxemburg. Ihre Geschichte und ihre Problematik.** (The three literatures of Luxembourg: their history and problems.)
Fernand Hoffmann.   In: *Mémorial 1989.*   Edited by Martin Gerges. Luxembourg: Les Publications Mosellanes, 1989, p. 467-518.

In this celebratory compendium edited by Martin Gerges to mark the 150th anniversary of the independence of Luxembourg, Fernand Hoffmann deals at length with the history and the problems of the three literatures in Luxembourg – French, German and Luxembourgish. He paints lively portraits of the main representatives of each language and evaluates their most essential works.

734 **Standort Luxemburg.** (Vantage-point Luxembourg.)
Fernand Hoffmann. Luxembourg: Sankt-Paulus-Druckerei, 1974.
317p.

This collection of Hoffmann's articles and essays, most of which have been previously published in the *Luxemburger Wort* and elsewhere, focuses on various aspects and personalities of Luxembourg. The author presents a well-informed account in a readable, journalistic style.

735 **Mëscheler: Luxemburgisches am Rande vermerkt.** (Miscellany: Luxembourg marginal notes.)
Fernand Hoffmann. Luxembourg: Sankt-Paulus-Druckerei, 1968.
268p.

Represents a rather heterogeneous collection of Hoffmann's articles and essays which deal with concepts of Luxembourg and Luxembourg identity. The first part sketches portraits of some Luxembourg poets and scholars, whilst the second tackles the problems of language and culture. The final two chapters contain social observations and personal reminiscences.

736 **La vie littéraire.** (Literary life.)
Nicolas Ries. In: *Le Luxembourg. Livre du centenaire.* (Luxembourg. Centenary book.) Luxembourg: Imprimerie Saint-Paul, 1949,
p. 283-310.

Ries contributes a brilliant survey of Luxembourg's literature in French, German and Luxembourgish up to 1940.

737 **Zur Literaturgeschichte Luxemburgs.** (Contribution to the literary history of Luxembourg.)
Pierre Grégoire. Luxembourg: Sankt-Paulus-Druckerei, 1959. 122p.
(Das Wartejahrbuch, 1959).

Reflects on Luxembourg's cultural situation and its lack of great achievement in the literary field. It represents a somewhat digressive analysis of the Luxembourg intellectual's situation as that of a passive observer separated from French and German ways of thinking.

738 **Luxemburgische Literaturgeschichte.** (History of Luxembourg literature.)
Victor Delcourt. Luxembourg: Sankt-Paulus-Druckerei, 1992. 324p.

Delcourt briefly describes forty-nine Luxembourg writers, among whose work we find the country's three languages represented. In citing significant extracts from their writings, this survey is a subjective anthology of Luxembourg literature as well as a practical work of reference.

739 **Luxembourg literature today.**
Rosemarie Kieffer. *Books Abroad*, Summer 1974, p. 515-19.
Kieffer's short article is an account of the Luxembourg literary scene, which takes note of writing in all three of the country's languages: French, German and Luxembourgish.

740 **Littératures du Grand-Duché de Luxembourg.** (Literatures of the Grand Duchy of Luxembourg.)
Annette Berger, Cornel Meder, Michel Raus. Virton, Belgium: Origine-Dryade, 1976. 39p.
Comprising the texts of three presentations held at the Château du Pont d'Oye on the Belgian-Luxembourg frontier by three Luxembourg poets on 28 September 1975, this volume surveys the dialectal, French- and German-writing Luxembourg authors, analysing the leading figures and their successes and failures. A recurring point is that provincialism need not necessarily be a handicap, if it is articulated and tackled by real literary talent, instead of being rejected or snobbishly ignored. As a rule, German-writing authors are more politically committed than those writing in French, who tend to be more interested in fine arts and perfect literary form.

741 **LSV: Lëtzebuerger Schrëftstellerverband. D'Memberen.**
(Luxembourg Writers' Association. The Members.)
Luxembourg writers' association. Esch-sur-Sûre, Luxembourg: Op der Lay, 1991. 118p.
This short reference book represents a first attempt at creating a lexicon of Luxembourg authors. Sixty authors are featured with their full biographical and bibliographical data and others are just listed. Unfortunately this inventory was compiled without any criterion of quality, so that the representative value of the cited authors remains questionable.

742 **Poesia Liuksemburga.** (Luxembourg poetry, an anthology.)
Translated by Waldemar Weber, Tatiana Klinva. Moscow: Raduga, 1988. 504p.
This is a superb anthology of Luxembourg poetry (French, German and Luxembourgish) translated into Russian, which opens with a proficient synopsis of the language and literature situation in Luxembourg (p. 5-30). In all, nearly 500 poems translated into Russian attempt to convey Luxembourg feelings and landscapes.

743 **Anthologie '95 intercity.** (Anthology '95 intercity.)
Lëtzebuerger Schrëftstellerverband. Luxembourg: Editions Phi – Op der Lay, 1995. 175p.
In launching its inter-regional literary contest, the Luxembourg writers' association wanted to discover what represents the literary characteristics of the Belgian, German, French and Luxembourg border area. This anthology presents the thirty-two best authors from the 211 entries.

# French

744 **Anthologie des écrivains luxembourgeois de langue française.**
(Anthology of Luxembourg authors writing in French.)
*Les Cahiers Luxembourgeois*, vol. 14, nos. 3-4 (1937), p. 299-479.
This collection of selected texts is introduced by two articles, the first by Joseph Hansen on the French language as the active leaven of Luxembourg's intellectual life, and the second on the Society of French-Writing Luxembourg Authors (SELF) by its secretary, Mathias Tresch.

745 **Anthologie française du Luxembourg.** (French anthology of Luxembourg.)
Marcel Gérard.   Luxembourg: Imprimerie Saint-Paul, 1960. 328p.
This is a selection of texts written in French by Luxembourgers for secondary-school students. It mainly includes literary texts, but also contains some pages of a historical, folkloristic, artistic or moral character. The first section deals with poetry (p. 1-46), the second with theatre (p. 47-70) and the third covers prose under the following headings: folklore, travelling, school, tales and anecdotes, landscapes, difficult times, literary criticism of novels, meditation and perspectives. Short bibliographical notes conclude this useful work.

746 **Le roman français de chez nous: romanciers luxembourgeois d'expression française.** (French novels written by Luxembourgers: the Luxembourg novelists writing in French.)
Marcel Gérard.   Luxembourg: Imprimerie Saint-Paul, 1968. 378p.
Analyses the works of about a dozen novelists which have been published since Luxembourg became independent in 1839, including: Félix Thyes, Etienne Hamélius, Mathias Esch, Nicolas Ries, Willy Gilson, Nicolas Konert, Joseph Leydenbach, Paul Palgen and Albert Borschette.

747 **Littérature luxembourgeoise de langue français.** (Luxembourg literature written in French.)
Edited by Rosemarie Kieffer.   Sherbrooke, Canada: Naaman, 1980. 174p. bibliog. (Littératures, 6).
The main chapters of this volume are devoted to the novel, short story, poetry, theatre essay, youth literature, women writers, the press and the teaching of French in Luxembourg. Full-blooded novelists are rather rare, with most Luxembourg authors who write in French preferring either personal poetry or the short literary essay. The introduction and conclusion stress Luxembourg's particular historical role in the field of literature as being that of a mediator, a unifying and conciliatory force between diverging cultures and conflicting interests in the heart of Europe.

748 **Pays clément dans la fureur des vagues – les femmes écrivent au Luxembourg.** (Mild country in the fury of the waves: women writing in Luxembourg.)
Anthology compiled by Rosemarie Kieffer and Danièle Medernach-Merens, cover and illustrations by José Ensch.   Luxembourg: Ministère des Affaires Culturelles, 1993. 436p.

The two compilers have grouped – in chronological order – extracts from sixty-one Luxembourg women authors who express themselves in French. They represent the pioneers of a new domain who were already publishing at around the beginning of the 20th century, sometimes hiding behind a masculine pseudonym.

749 **Etudes sur la littérature luxembourgeoise de langue française.** (Studies on Luxembourg literature in French.)
Frank Wilhelm.   PhD thesis, l'Université de Paris IV – Sorbonne, 1991. 327p.

Reviews the full range of Luxembourg literature written in French, gathering a number of articles, essays and studies – both new and previously published. The remarkable corpus of literary and bibliographical information collected here makes this work by far the best source of reference currently available on the subject.

750 **Le Grand-Duché de Luxembourg dans les carnets de Victor Hugo.** (The Grand Duchy of Luxembourg in the notebooks of Victor Hugo.)
Complete edition, with commentary and annotations by Tony Bourg and Frank Wilhelm.   Luxembourg: RTL Edition, 1985. 343p. bibliog.

Victor Hugo, one of the most famous French writers of the 19th century, visited Luxembourg (and especially Vianden) five times. This volume, which is annotated by two Luxembourg professors who teach French, reproduces the travel note-book kept by Victor Hugo during his visits to Luxembourg. These writings contain political testimonies (he was a refugee during the 1870-71 Franco-Prussian war), historical reflections as well as thoughts of a more personal or tourist nature. The editors consider this study as a valuable contribution to the strengthening of French-Luxembourg relations.

751 **Recherches et conférences littéraires.** (Literary research and lectures.)
Tony Bourg.   Luxembourg: Imprimerie Saint-Paul, 1994. 799p.

Alongside his teaching career, Tony Bourg published numerous studies and gave many literary lectures concerning the stays of French and other writers in Luxembourg, with a preference for two topics: the international influence of the Mayrisch family and the visits and stays of Victor Hugo in the Grand Duchy. This volume includes some articles and lectures by Tony Bourg, his bio-bibliography and an important appendix which includes some correspondence and iconographic documents.

752 **Villerouge sur Caille.**
Fernand Lorang.   Luxembourg: Imprimerie Linden, 1983. 450p.

Lorang's novel describes the small events of everyday life in a straggling fictional village called Villerouge sur Caille, which might be any smart countryside village of the Luxembourg mining basin. Through his fanciful and figurative narration of the way of life of imaginary Luxembourg miners and peasants, the author succeeds in drawing a valid portrait of the traditions and folklore of the mining basin.

# German

753 **Luxembourg: identity and creative distances.**
Basil Mogridge. *Carleton Germanic Papers*, vol. 6 (1978), p. 57-87.
Mogridge takes a sympathetic short-cut through Luxembourg's contemporary literature in German, with a personal interpretation of selected poems by Pierre Puth, Cornel Meder, Charles Bintz, Fernand Muller, Roger Manderscheid, Guy Rewenig and Anise Koltz. The author set out to show that the art of poetry is very much alive in Luxembourg and to illustrate that a concern with identity may be successfully combined with the distance, or objectivity, necessary for true poetic achievement.

754 **Dichter unseres Landes, 1900-1945.** (Luxembourg poets, 1900-45.)
Albert Hoefler. Luxembourg: Hémecht, 1945. 175p.
Hoefler evaluates the works of nineteen Luxembourgers who wrote in German: Nikolaus Welter, René Engelmann, Batty Weber, Joseph Tockert, Nikolaus Hein, Joseph Funck, Wilhelm Weis, Peter Faber, Jacques Kintzelé, Alex Weicker, Bernard Simminger, Marie-Henriette Steil, Jean-Pierre Erpelding, Paul Henkes, Pierre Grégoire, Jean-Pierre Decker, Jacques Meyers, and Frantz Clément. Finally, Léopold Hoffmann assesses Hoefler's own writing.

755 **Nachrichten aus Luxemburg: Deutschsprachige Literatur in Luxemburg.** (News from Luxembourg: Luxembourg literature written in German.)
Edited by Carlo Hury. Hildesheim, FRG: Olms, 1979. 305p. bibliog. (Auslandsdeutsche Literatur der Gegenwart, Bd. 11).
Comprises contributions by authors whose work has been published since 1944, including texts from books, collected works, yearbooks and quarterlies. No newspapers or poorly-accessible periodical articles were considered. Within their genres, the texts are grouped first in alphabetical order and then in chronological order of publication. The preface analyses Luxembourg's literary and psychological scene, and the economic background of the country's publishing. Thirty-two authors are represented in all.

756 **Lyrik in Luxemburg: eine Anthologie. Band 1: bis 1940.** (Lyrical poetry in Luxembourg: an anthology. Vol. 1: before 1940.)
Fernand Hoffmann, Joseph-Emile Müller, Nic Weber. Luxembourg: Grossherzogliches Institut von Luxembourg. Abteilung für Kunst und Literatur, 1979. 153p. bibliog.
Covers Luxembourg lyric authors who wrote in German since about 1900. The following authors are represented by extracts from their works: Hermann Berg (i.e.

Wilhelm Weis), Jean-Pierre Decker, Nikolaus Hein, Paul Henkes, Albert Hoefler, Pol Michels, Joseph-Emile Müller, Gregor Stein (i.e. Pierre Grégoire), and Nikolaus Welter.

757 **Schriftbilder: Neue Prosa aus Luxemburg.** (Scripts: new prose from Luxembourg.)
Edited by Rolf Ketter and Georges Hausemer. Luxembourg: Editions Guy Binsfeld, 1984. 234p.

Small countries like Luxembourg often have a literature which is largely unknown outside the country itself. Moreover, they have to fight against a lot of stereotyped ideas. This collection provides information on the position of German-language literature in Luxembourg (in 1984) by presenting original contributions written exclusively in German by twenty authors from Luxembourg.

758 **Über sich selbst: Autobiographisches.** (About himself: autobiographical notes.)
Batty Weber. Luxembourg: E. Kutter, 1977. 232p. (Gesammelte Werke, 2).

Batty Weber (1860-1940) was a well-known journalist and dramatist who published in three languages. He was most famous for his daily newspaper columns, popular dramas, and the novel, *Fern Kass*. This volume contains some of his autobiographical writings which include his memories of Dicks (Edmond de la Fontaine), the great national playwright and poet.

759 **Jahreszeiten und Allerlei, 1913/1914: Abreisskalender.** (Seasons and miscellany, 1913-14: daily calendar notes.)
Batty Weber. Luxembourg: E. Kutter, 1977. 319p. (Gesammelte Werke, 1).

Batty Weber, a well-known editor and columnist, published his first diary column on 15 September 1913 in the liberal paper, *Luxemburger Zeitung* (Luxembourg Newspaper), his last note appearing on 13 December 1940. In all he published about 7,500 of these columns, which were to become part of Luxembourg's cultural heritage. This first volume includes 147 pieces from 1913-14.

760 **Lebendige Mosel; Melodien einer Landschaft.** (Living Moselle; melodies of a landscape.)
Selected and arranged by Martin Gerges. Luxembourg: Imprimerie Bourg-Bourger, 1960. 179p. (Schwebsinger Moselpublikationen, 8).

Celebrates the natural and cultural excellence of the Moselle river and valley in yearly publications. It refers to passages concerning the river in the writings of famous foreign and Luxembourg writers, including Maurice Barrès, François-René de Chateaubriand, Victor Hugo and the Luxembourgers, Pierre Frieden, Pierre Grégoire, Nikolaus Hein, Paul Noesen, Batty Weber and Nikolaus Welter.

# Luxembourgish

761  **Grossherzogins Geburtstag: 34 ironische Geschichten.** (The
birthday of the Grand Duchess: thirty-four ironic stories.)
Adrien Ries.  Luxembourg: Imprimerie Victor Buck, 1983. 92p.

Ries's volume of thirty-four ironic stories, accompanied by fourteen drawings by the
caricaturist, Roger Leiner, is a refreshing, funny and clever report on Luxembourg
people and their way of life.

762  **Geschichte der Luxemburger Mundartdichtung.** (History of
Luxembourgish dialect literature.)
Fernand Hoffmann.  Luxembourg: Ministère des Arts et des Sciences,
1964-67. 2 vols. bibliog. (Publications Nationales du Ministère des
Arts et des Sciences).

Represents the standard reference work on Luxembourg's dialect literature. Volume 1
covers the beginnings (1827) up to Michel Rodange (1876). The first part presents the
first documents in Luxembourgish and the founders of the Luxembourgish literature
(p. 5-213); the second and major part is an anthology of collected texts (p. 221-591).
Volume II surveys the period from Andrei Duchscher (1840-1911) to 1966 under the
headings: theatre, lyrics, prose, epics and books for young people, translators and
historians of the dialect (p. 3-295). The major part of this volume (p. 305-905) is taken
up by a comprehensive anthology. Both volumes include a systematic bibliography
compiled by Carlo Hury.

763  **A short history of literature in Luxembourgish.**
Jul Christophory.  Luxembourg: Bibliothèque nationale, 1994. 168p.

Luxembourg's literature consists of three different branches, using either German,
French or Lëtzebuergesch (Luxembourgish) as its means of expression. Written
evidence of a literature in Luxembourgish can be traced back to the mid-1820s. This
volume surveys the slow development of the different literary forms over the last 170
years of Luxembourg history. Besides the traditional genres, it deals with non-fiction
prose, films in Luxembourgish, translation from, and into, Luxembourgish, research,
dictionaries, and spelling. An appendix provides sixteen pages of bibliographical
references. The running text is interspersed with numerous illustrative examples,
portraits and sketches.

764  **Das Luxemburgische und sein Schrifttum.** (Luxembourgish and its
literature.)
Nikolaus Welter.  Luxembourg: Joseph Beffort, 1947. 189p.

The writer and statesman, Nikolaus Welter, outlines the basic features of
Luxembourgish and defines the identity of the Luxembourger. In chapter II he
analyses the beginnings of Luxembourgish literature and the first evidence of a real
dialect literature in Anton Meyer's poetry work, 'E Schrék op de Lëtzebuerger
Parnassus' (A step towards the Luxembourg Parnassus). More significant works
followed between 1829 and 1848 under the influence of the liberal policy of William
I. Chapter III deals with the prime of Luxembourgish poetry and the works of Michel
Lentz, Edmond de la Fontaine and Michel Rodange, while chapter IV surveys the
contemporary scene. A standard reference book, it was the first and best attempt at

# Literature. Luxembourgish

classifying authors and assessing their literary merits before Fernand Hoffmann published his systematic history of Luxembourgish dialect literature (q.v.).

765 **Die Dichter der luxemburgischen Mundart.** (The writers of Luxembourg dialect literature.)
Nikolaus Welter.   Diekirch, Luxembourg: Das Luxemburgische und sein Schrifttum, 1947. rev. ed.

Welter discusses dialect and High German literature in Luxembourg. His work is a contribution to the intellectual and cultural history of the Grand Duchy.

766 **Mir wëlle schreiwen wéi mir sin Band I – 13. Jahrhundert bis um 1920.** (We want to write how we are volume I – 13th century to 1920.)
Fernand Weirich.   Luxembourg: Imprimerie Kremer-Müller, 1984. 250p. (Chronik der Luxemburger Lyrik).

This volume on Luxembourgish poetry covers some forty of the best-known poets with a representative choice of their works from the 13th century up to the 20th century. It also lists the newspapers and magazines which deal with poetry.

767 **Lëtzebuergesch Texter fir 7e a 8e.** (Luxembourgish texts for forms 7 and 8.)
Luxembourg: Ministère de l'Education Nationale, 1990. 3rd ed. 402p.

This is the third edition of a selection of interesting texts chosen from Luxembourgish literature to be read in the single weekly period set aside for the study of Luxembourgish in the first two years of secondary school. A final chapter offers a useful introduction to the particular problems of contact languages and sociolinguistics. It also offers valuable material for practical exercises. The first edition of this book appeared in 1978, the second in 1982.

768 **Les Luxembourgeois par eux-mêmes; The Luxembourgers in their own words; d'Lëtzebuerger am Spigel vun hirer Sprooch. I: Recueil de textes luxembourgeois avec traduction française et anglaise; Selected texts in Luxembourgish with English and French translation. II: Portrait d'un petit pays et de sa langue; The anatomy of a small country and its language.**
Edited by Jul Christophory.   Luxembourg: Imprimerie Bourg-Bourger, 1978. 382p.

Divided into two sections, this work is intended to complete and expand on the author's previous volumes (q.v.) and to provide both the beginner and advanced student of Luxembourgish with interesting and substantial reading material. Part I is an anthology of classical and modern Luxembourgish texts, as well as tales and anecdotes, satirical verse, literary cabaret and revue songs to illustrate typical aspects of Luxembourg life. Part II, on the other hand, is entirely in English and includes critical and explanatory articles and comments on the psychology of the people, their international and patriotic attitudes, social structure, culture and humour.

769 **Das 'Yolanda' Epos.** (The 'Yolanda' epic poem.)
Pierre Grégoire. Luxembourg: Sankt-Paulus-Druckerei, 1979. 339p.

Yolanda (1231-83), born the daughter of a count at the castle of Vianden (northeast of Luxembourg) joined the Dominican order. She was prioress for twenty-five years and although she experienced temptation, she remained faithful to the vocation of the Dominicans. Brother Hermann's poetry on the life of Yolanda is said to be the first extensive poetry of German-Luxembourgish literature. It has been translated into German, verse by verse, by Pierre Grégoire, who also provides an interesting historical and literary introduction.

770 **Gesamtwierk.** (Collected works.)
Michel Lentz. Luxembourg: Krippler-Müller, 1980-81. 2 vols.
(Klassiker vun der Lëtzebuerger Literatur, Bd. 3).

Volume I presents miscellaneous poems and the collected verse, *Spaass an Ierscht* (Fun and Earnestness) (Luxembourg: Victor Buck, 1873. 319p.), published by Michel Lentz, a man who was soon considered as the national poet, because his sentimental and patriotic vein perfectly expressed the general mood of the average contemporary Luxembourg citizen. Volume II offers the poems published in *Hierschtblummen* (Luxembourg: Joseph Beffort, 1887. 381p.) and *Wantergréng* (Winter green) (Luxembourg: Worré-Mertens, 1920. 53p.), a complete index of works, anthologies and secondary literature.

771 **Gesamtwierk.** (Collected works.)
Dicks (Edmond de la Fontaine). Luxembourg: Krippler-Müller, 1981-84. 4 vols.

Four volumes, introduced by Pierre Grégoire and Carlo Hury, present a complete set of Dicks' (Edmond de la Fontaine's) works, poems, dramas, songs, and prose essays on subjects including: linguistic problems; Luxembourg legends and customs; and local historical problems concerning Stadtbredimus and Vianden, for example. A complete bibliography and a full set of reference indexes compiled by Carlo Hury illustrate the diversity of Dicks' talents and interests.

772 **Dicks oder Aufstieg und Abstieg des Edmond de La Fontaine: Leben und Schaffen eines Nationaldichters.** (Dicks or the rise and fall of Edmond de La Fontaine: The life and works of a national poet.)
Fernand Hoffmann. Luxembourg: Imprimerie Saint-Paul, 1991. 146p.

Although Edmond de la Fontaine will be remembered forever as the creator of drama in Luxembourg, in the mid-1850s, he also played a significant part in the development of forms such as lyric poetry, satire, popular song and chanson. With reference to existing archive material, Fernand Hoffmann provides a comprehensible and accurate portrait of the Luxembourg national poet, Edmond de la Fontaine, also known as Dicks. The author shows the interrelations between the poet's work and life and sets his various pieces within their historical and social context.

773 **Gesamtwierk.** (Collected works.)
Michel Rodange, edited by Cornel Meder. Luxembourg: Krippler-
Müller, 1974. 846p. bibliog. (Klassiker vun der Lëtzebuerger Literatur,
Bd. 1).

The year 1972 was the centenary of the publication of the national animal epic, *De Renert* (The Fox), by Michel Rodange. To commemorate the occasion this impressive three-part volume of Rodange's works was published. Part I comprises a chronological table and texts written in Luxembourgish (p. 31-389); part II contains the texts in German (p. 393-607); and an appendix (p. 611-837) consists of annotations, prefaces and glossaries to certain texts, written by Joseph Tockert, Henri Rinnen, Cornel Meder, Fernand Hoffmann and Jean Weber. The work also contains an extensive Rodange bibliography prepared by Carlo Hury. Prefaced by Pierre Goedert, the then headmaster of the Michel Rodange High School in Luxembourg, this is a monumental work which sets new standards in editorial and critical excellence.

774 **Livre d'or édité à l'occasion du 150e anniversaire de la naissance
du poète national Michel Rodange et du 75e anniversaire de la
Fanfare de Waldbillig.** (Golden book published on the occasion of the
150th anniversary of the birth of the national poet Michel Rodange and
of the 75th anniversary of the Fanfare de Waldbillig.)
Waldbillig, Luxembourg: Fanfare de Waldbillig, 1977. 538p.

Published on the 150th anniversary of the national poet, Michel Rodange, in 1977, when a fortnight's cultural festival was organized in his home village to mark the occasion and assess the poet's lasting impact.

775 **De Renert.** (The tale of the fox.)
Michel Rodange. Complete edition with historical and political
explanations by Romain Hilgert. Luxembourg: Editions Guy
Binsfeld, 1987. 254p.

One of the numerous *De Renert* editions that have been published since Michel Rodange wrote his great animal epic poem in 1872 epitomizing the history and character of the Luxembourger. Nevertheless this book differs from others in at least two aspects. Hilgert, through his historical and political observations, attempts to help the reader to understand the spiritual and social climate of a period (1867-72) which is often seen as one of the most confused in Luxembourg's history. In addition, Hilgert reproduces those parts of the poem which were often censored.

776 **Gesamtwierk.** (Collected works.)
Willy Goergen, edited by Emile van der Vekene. Luxembourg:
Krippler-Müller, 1987-92. 5 vols. (Klassiker vun der Lëtzebuerger
Literatur, Bd. 7).

Willy Goergen (1867-1942) was born in Steinsel, Luxembourg, the son of a village peasant. He went to the universities of Bonn, Louvain and Strasbourg, qualified as a secondary-school language teacher in 1895 and settled in Luxembourg with his wife and children in 1898. His natural context remained the farming world of his native village. At the age of thirty-four he published his first volume of poems in Luxembourgish, *Hémechtstéin* (Homely tunes), which was to be followed by a stream of others until a year before his death in 1942.

777 **Gesamtwierk.** (Collected works.)
Max Goergen. Edited by Carlo Hury. Luxembourg: Krippler-Müller, 1985. 2 vols. (Klassiker vun der Lëtzebuerger Literatur, Bd. 5).

The complete works of Max Goergen (1893-1978) are compiled in these two volumes. Because this Luxembourg poet, playwright and writer was very reserved and often worked under pseudonyms, it is impossible to trace all his plays. The first volume includes fourteen of his plays whereas the second volume contains his prose texts.

778 **Gesamtwierk.** (Collected works.)
Auguste Liesch. Edited by Carlo Hury. Luxembourg: Krippler-Müller, 1979. 439p. bibliog. (Klassiker vun der Lëtzebuerger Literatur, Bd. 2).

This volume of Auguste Liesch's work comprises 150 pages of poems and anecdotes in Luxembourgish, 2 short stories and 1 novel (*Im Schatten des Eichenhofes* [In the shade of the Eichenhof]) in German and 4 short stories in French. The author is the master of a special blend of Luxembourg satire and social criticism. In skilful sketches he demystifies pompous language and behaviour. His masterpiece is *d'Maus Ketti* (Ketti the mouse) (Luxembourg: Soupert, 1936. 12p.) which transposes the Aesopian fable of the country-mouse's visit to the town-mouse into a Luxembourg setting. His satirical vein is most remarkable in the parodies he wrote of *Der Taucher* (The diver) by Friedrich Schiller and of *Des Sängers Fluch* (The curse of the singer) by Ludwig Uhland. Auguste Liesch was born in Mondorf in 1874 and died in 1949 as a result of his deportation by the Nazi régime. He was a long-serving judge before he became the director of the customs administration.

779 **Literarescht Wierk.** (Literary works.)
Demy Schlechter, edited by Evy Friedrich. Christnach, Luxembourg: Editions Emile Borschette, 1988. 251p.

Demy Schlechter (1884-1923) is the author of some colourful prose sketches which figure in most primary-school textbook editions and anthologies. This collection is compiled and edited by Evy Friedrich and specially bound by Pe'l Schlechter.

780 **Gesamtwierk.** (Collected works.)
Adolf Berens. Luxembourg: Krippler-Müller, 1986-88. 2 vols. (Klassiker vun der Lëtzebuerger Literatur, Bd. 6).

Adolf Berens (1880-1956) will be remembered as the author of *D'Kerfegsblo'm* (Cemetery flower), an abortive attempt to create a great historical novel about events during the revolutionary wars of the 1790s in the Moselle town of Grevenmacher (Part I – Grevenmacher, Luxembourg: Faber, 1921. 40p.; Part II – Luxembourg: Worré-Mertens, 1925. 156p.). He also tried his hand at iambic tetrameters to produce a rather nationalistic verse called *De grousse Kaeser – Nationalepos vum Gilliüs Döll* (a pseudonym) (The great imperial national epic poem by Gilliüs Döll) (Luxembourg: Worré-Mertens, 1948-53. 269p.).

781 **Méi wéi honnert Pärelen.** (More than one hundred pearls.)
Pir Kremer. Edited by Nic Weber. Luxembourg: Editions des
Cahiers Luxembourgeois, 1994. 126p.

The name of Pir Kremer is well known in Luxembourg. This poet, author, political
satirist and revue artist, whose popular weekly radio programme 'Um Stamminet'
(Café), has delighted listeners for years, celebrated his seventy-fifth birthday in 1994.
This commemorative volume, compiled by some old friends, gathers about 100 of his
best texts, poems and satires.

782 **Schacko Klak.**
Roger Manderscheid. Luxembourg: Rapidpress, 1988. 353p.

Roger Manderscheid established his reputation in the early 1960s with his radio plays
and critical essays in German, while his earlier works announced a talent capable of
grasping a substantial piece of reality in a new way. This promise is masterfully
fulfilled in the novel, *Schacko Klak*, in which the author describes, through the eyes of
a five-year-old child, his memories from the immediate pre-war period and early war
years in his native village of Itzig, Luxembourg. The onomatopoeic title evokes the
soldier's helmet (French *chacot*) and the French collapsible top hat (*chapeau claque*).

783 **Schacko Klak de Film.** (*Schacko Klak* the film.)
J. P. Thilges. Luxembourg: Rapidpress, 1990. 101p.

*Shacko Klak* is also the name of the widely acclaimed film inspired by Roger
Manderscheid's autobiographical novel.

784 **Hannerwëtz mat bireschnëtz: Lëtzebëtz.** (Cunning with pear
snippets: Lux-residues.)
Roger Manderscheid. Luxembourg: Graphic Press, 1991. 138p.

Roger Manderscheid belongs to a new group of Luxembourg writers of the late 1960s
who are more influenced by the Luxembourg literary tradition but who are not
uncritical of it. The author has included in this volume more than eighty short poems
in Luxembourgish, accompanied by original illustrations by Renée Weber.

785 **Elektra (an onser Sprooch).** (Electra in our language.)
Camille Lamboray. Luxembourg: Imprimerie Saint-Paul, 1991. 131p.

Sophocles wrote 133 dramas. Camille Lamboray translated *Elektra*, one of his best-
known tragedies, into Luxembourgish. The Greek versification is a real test-case for
the flexible Luxembourg language. Lamboray manages to avoid most of the potential
pitfalls involved in translating this work and so brilliantly meets the challenges he set
himself.

786 **Wanns de laanscht gees, bleif dach stoen!** (If you pass, please stop!)
Compiled by Andrée Collignon. Luxembourg: Imprimerie La
Frontière; Esch-sur-Alzette, Luxembourg: Rémy Quintus, 1995. 103p.

Contains a collection of more than fifty Russian poems, by poets ranging from
Puschkin to Wissotzki, which are admirably translated into Luxembourgish in the
parallel column.

787 **Macbeth – Mäcbess.**
William Shakespeare, translated by Jean-Michel Treinen.
Esch-sur-Sûre, Luxembourg: Op der Lay, 1996. 160p.
In the 1990s the stage manager, Claude Mangen, put on a Luxembourgish version of Shakespeare's *A Midsummer Night's Dream* in Esch-sur-Sûre. In July 1996 he produced *Macbeth* in Luxembourgish in an open-air theatre near Berdorf. Both plays were remarkable achievements and announced a real dramatic breakthrough for the Luxembourgish language which proved strong enough to carry the heavy semantic load of Shakespearian vocabulary and metrics. The juxtaposition of the English and Luxembourgish texts in this volume demonstrates the great talent of the translator, Jean-Michel Treinen. His delicate feeling for Shakespeare's subtle connotations and dense textual structure overcomes all the obstacles and pitfalls of the project.

788 **D'Manifest vun der Kommunistescher Partei. Eischt Lëtzebuergesch Editioun.** (The manifesto of the Communist Party. First Luxembourg edition.)
Karl Marx, Friedrich Engels, translated by Romain Hilgert.
Luxembourg: COPE, 1983. 62p.
First published in London in 1848 and existing in thousands of editions and more than a hundred languages, the Communist manifesto now also exists in Luxembourgish. It was translated by Romain Hilgert according to the German text of 1890 and was published in the centenary year of Karl Marx's death. Friedrich Engels' notes and explanations (to the English publication of 1888 and the German one of 1890) are included in this Luxembourg edition.

789 **Die zeitgenössischen luxemburgisch- und deutschsprachigen Autoren im Areler Land.** (The contemporary Luxembourgish- and German-speaking authors in the Arlon region.)
Michèle Leonard. Thesis, Louvain-la-Neuve, Belgium, 1981. 115p.
Leonard set out to discover, with the aid of a questionnaire, the Luxembourgish- and German-speaking authors from an area which now borders the Grand Duchy but which formerly belonged to the Luxembourg duchy until 1839.

# Education

## General

790 **Aperçu sur un siècle et demi d'enseignement supérieur et moyen.**
(Survey on a century and a half of higher and secondary instruction.)
Michel Schmit. In: *Mémorial 1989.* Luxembourg: Les Publications
Mosellanes, 1989, p. 395-407.

Michel Schmit, a former Government Councillor at the Ministry of Education, offers a brief survey of the legislative work supporting Luxembourg's secondary-school system and first-year university studies at the Centre Universitaire. Since 1989, however, some significant new reforms have been introduced. Nevertheless, this essay, which is supplemented by an essential bibliography, remains a useful source of reference.

791 **L'enseignement technique et professionnel.** (Technical and
professional instruction.)
Vic Diederich. In: *Mémorial 1989.* Luxembourg: Les Publications
Mosellanes, 1989, p. 369-94.

Represents the best survey currently available on the complex structure of vocational training in Luxembourg, with its manifold private and public branches, national and regional institutions. Diederich includes a concise bibliography.

792 **Notre enseignement primaire.** (Our primary schools.)
Vic Diederich. In: *Mémorial 1989.* Luxembourg: Les Publications
Mosellanes, 1989, p. 337-68.

Diederich's exemplary historical essay, which contains an excellent bibliography, retraces the development of primary-school instruction in Luxembourg from its beginnings in 1815 after the Congress of Vienna to the present. Important stages in its long evolution include: the laws of July 1843; the 1881 Kirpach law (which

214

introduced compulsory school attendance); the reforms of 1912 and 1921; the
unfortunate war years under German legislation; and the more recent reforms of 1963
and 1983.

793 **Projet Periclès. La qualité de l'enseignement.** (Pericles project. The
quality of the teaching.)
Colloquium of 12 March 1994 at the C.U.L. (Centre Universitaire
Luxembourg – Luxembourg University Centre). Luxembourg:
Ministry of Education, 1994. 47p.

In 1989, a law was passed in Luxembourg which modified the upper levels (fifth and
sixth forms) of secondary teaching. The resulting new structures raised such questions
as what was the best way to reconcile the needs of those students who required to
specialize in their studies with a general curriculum which would be accessible to all
secondary-school pupils. This document was published in the run-up to the first
colloquium of the Pericles programme, which was held in March 1994, and sent to all
of the 150 participants, who included professors, headmasters and public sector
employees. It should be seen as the starting-point of research setting out to clarify the
final years of secondary-school teaching in Luxembourg.

794 **L'enseignement universitaire et la recherche scientifique au
Luxembourg.** (University teaching and scientific research in
Luxembourg.)
Jul Christophory, Paul Kintziger, et al. Unpublished working
document, 1984. Xerox copy available at the National Library of
Luxembourg. 46p.

Although Luxembourg possesses several public scientific institutes, it does not have
any complete university curriculum. The various contributions compiled together in
this document discuss this situation and cite examples of the backwardness of the
Grand Duchy as compared to other countries while proposing solutions which would
not require too substantial financial means to be realized.

795 **Notre loi scolaire: aperçu publié à l'occasion du soixantenaire de la
loi du 10 août 1912 concernant l'organisation de l'enseignement
primaire.** (Our school law: a survey on the occasion of the sixtieth
anniversary of the law concerning the organization of the primary
school system.)
Victor Diederich. Luxembourg: Association des Instituteurs Réunis,
1973. 159p.

Diederich provides a historical outline of the laws governing primary-school
education in Luxembourg which begins with 1817 when, after the Congress of Vienna
(1815), the new Dutch régime introduced new regulations. The first chapter deals with
the situation following the law passed in 1881, while the last chapter analyses the
modifications applied to the 1912 law and provides biographical sketches of the
politicians involved.

796 **Histoire de l'instruction publique dans le Grand-Duché de Luxembourg: Recueil de mémoires publiés à l'occasion du troisième centenaire de la fondation de l'Athénée grand-ducal de Luxembourg.** (History of public instruction in the Grand Duchy of Luxembourg: a collection of papers published on the occasion of the third centenary of the foundation of the Athénée grand-ducal de Luxembourg.)
Nicolas van Werveke, Jules Wilhelm, Martin d'Huart.   Luxembourg: Joseph Beffort, 1904. 677p.

This commemorative volume consists of five contributions: Nicolas van Werveke's 'Summary history of schooling and instruction in Luxembourg'; Jules Wilhelm's 'The convent school of Altmunster'; and 'Commentarius de erectione et gestis Collegii Societatis Jesu Luxemburgensis, 1570-1608' (Commentary on the building and running of the College of Jesuits at Luxembourg, 1570-1608); 'The foundation of the ancient College of Jesuits at Luxembourg'; and 'The curricula of studies at the ancient College and the Athénée de Luxembourg from 1602 to 1903', all by Martin d'Huart.

# Secondary and higher

797 **Le Centre Universitaire de Luxembourg.** (Luxembourg University Centre.)
Luxembourg: Service Information et Presse, 1976. 35p.

The Centre Universitaire de Luxembourg (Luxembourg University Centre), the only academic institution which provides university teaching in the country, was created on 18 June 1969. It comprises three departments: the Department of Law and Economic Sciences, the Department of Arts, and the Department of Sciences. It offers a first-year university syllabus geared to the pursuit of second-year studies in France, Germany, Belgium and Great Britain. There are also departments for professional development and postgraduate courses, practical work experience and guided research work.

798 **The Luxembourgers and the idea of a university.**
Jul Christophory.   In: *Les Luxembourgeois par eux-mêmes.* (The Luxembourgers in their own words.)   Luxembourg: Imprimerie Bourg-Bourger, 1978, p. 335-40.

The author takes stock of the controversy and traditional arguments in favour of establishing a university in Luxembourg. These latter arguments cite the development of favourable conditions for intellectual work and scientific research, close contact with foreign universities and the alleviation of the financial burden on parents whose children must study abroad, while the main arguments against derive from philistinism and dilettantism. Christophory suggests new forms of university studies and research work that would be accessible and suitable to Luxembourg's modest possibilities.

799  **University studies in Luxembourg and abroad.**
Jul Christophory.  *Luxembourg Weekly Review*, no. 35-36 (Sept.
1975), p. 12-14.
Deals with Luxembourg's particular graduate and postgraduate situation and provides
1974 statistics about the foreign universities and departments most popular with
Luxembourg's students who can attend only a first-year undergraduate course in their
own country.

800  **Cent cinquante ans de dissertations.** (150 years of dissertations.)
Jean-Pierre-Roger Strainchamps.  *Courrier de l'Education Nationale*,
May 1988. Special issue. 301p.
This special edition is a bibliography of the dissertations that have been written since
1837 in order to obtain the degree in secondary-school and tertiary teaching. The list
goes up to 1987 and is arranged according to subjects. An alphabetical list of the
authors is included to allow the reader to research the particular field of study of an
individual teacher. Pending a new edition, the author intends to publish such a
supplementary catalogue every two years.

801  **Les dissertations de programmes de l'enseignement moyen
luxembourgeois (1837-1939): Répertoire bibliographique.**
(Dissertations on the curricula of Luxembourg secondary schools,
1837-1939: bibliographical index.)
Gaby Waxweiler.   Dissertation l'IPERB de Liège, Belgium, 1984-85.
112p.
This is a bibliographical index of the dissertations written by a teacher from each
school in Luxembourg that were published between 1837 and 1939 in the secondary
schools' statistical annuals on curricula, staff and pupils. In addition to this list
Waxweiler's work contains information on the subjects taught in all the classes and
the number of pupils per class, as well as essays concerning literary, historical,
scientific or pedagogical subjects. Most of the works mentioned in this bibliographical
index are not mentioned in the Luxembourg collection catalogue of the National
Library and so this work makes these publications accessible to a larger audience.

802  **Athénée grand-ducal de Luxembourg: trois cent cinquantième
anniversaire de sa fondation.** (Athénée grand-ducal of Luxembourg:
350th anniversary of its foundation.)
Luxembourg: Imprimerie Bourg-Bourger, 1955. 457p.
The Athénée, Luxembourg's first classical grammar school, was founded by the
Jesuits in 1603 as their convent school. This book describes present-day aspects of the
school's teaching as well as its history. The many excellent contributions are from
headmasters and teachers in Luxembourg.

803 **Athenaei discipuli meminerunt. Les Anciens Athénéens se souviennent.** (The former pupils of the Athenaeum remember.)
Amicale des Anciens de l'Athénée. Luxembourg: Imprimerie Saint-Paul, 1992. 456p.

Since 1964, the history of the Athenaeum has been divided, as it was moved into a new building in Merl (a suburb of Luxembourg city). The Athenaeum's former building near the cathedral now houses the National Library. Contributions on this move and other aspects of the Athenaeum's history, followed by individual contributors' personal recollections of the Second World War, portraits of teachers, poems and satirical songs of the pupils, make this commemorative volume, published for the tenth anniversary of the former pupils' association, a lively account of the institution.

804 **Lycée de Garçons Luxembourg 1892-1992.** (Luxembourg Boys' Secondary School 1892-1992.)
Editorial committee of the Lycée de Garçons Luxembourg.
Luxembourg: Imprimerie Saint-Paul, 1993. 389p.

Just after the Second World War, the 'Industrial and Commercial School' became the 'Lycée de Garçons' (Boys' Secondary School), but today the school is coeducational in spite of its name. This commemorative volume, published on the occasion of the school's centenary, opens with a historical account of the school with contributors including the well-known historians, Gilbert Trausch and Paul Dostert. The collection compiles texts written by, and about, the school's present and former headmasters, professors and students together with lots of photographs of sporting events, the building itself and portraits of celebrated alumni.

805 **Lycée Michel Rodange Luxembourg: 25e anniversaire.** (Michel Rodange Secondary School Luxembourg: twenty-fifth anniversary.)
Editorial committee of the Lycée Michel Rodange. Luxembourg: Imprimerie Reka, 1993. 541p.

This is a vivid and well-illustrated report of the twenty-fifth anniversary celebrations of the Michel Rodange secondary school that was built in 1968 next to the 'Nouvel Athénée' (the Athenaeum school which was moved to a new building in 1964). The book retraces the school's twenty-five years of history and contains contributions from headmasters, students and teachers, past and present.

806 **Livre d'or du Lycée classique de Diekirch.** (Golden book of the Diekirch Grammar School.)
Editorial committee of the Lycée classique de Diekirch.
Luxembourg: Imprimerie Saint-Paul, 1992. 735p.

This commemorative volume on the Diekirch Grammar School allows all those interested to gain valuable information on more than 150 years of public instruction and national education in the northern region of Luxembourg. Up to the 1970s this school was the only state secondary school in the north of the country. The first part of the volume includes a chronicle of more than 150 years (1830-1992) which is divided into different periods of development. A second part of the book, entitled 'Nos anciens élèves se souviennent' (Our former students remember) compiles anecdotal stories concerning school life. Chapter three is made up of various studies and essays whereas the last chapter provides an account of the school's cultural life throughout this period.

807   **75 ans ingénieur technicien 1916-1991.** (Seventy-five years of technical engineering, 1916-91.)
Editorial committee of the Institut Supérieur de Technologie.
Luxembourg: Imprimerie Saint-Paul, 1992. 239p.

Besides recording the commemorations of the seventy-fifth anniversary of the professional training of technical engineers in Luxembourg, this brochure also constitutes a useful document for all those who are interested in the evolution of that educational process throughout the history of what is now called the 'Institut Supérieur de Technologie' (Higher Institute of Technology). It not only describes the different stages of its evolution, but also includes reflections on current problems faced by the institution as well as considerations concerning the job of a technical engineer.

808   **1914-1989: Institut Emile Metz. Lycée Technique Privé.** (Emile Metz Institute. Private Technical High School.)
Editorial committee of the Institut Emile Metz.   Luxembourg: Imprimerie Saint-Paul, 1989. 193p.

When the Emile Metz Institute was founded in 1914, there was such a need for technical instruction due to the Grand Duchy's large but unfulfilled industrial potential, that the school became devoted to technical instruction. Published for the school's seventy-fifth anniversary, this volume includes contributions which retrace, in summarized form, its construction, geographical environment, and its professional, technical, cultural and sporting activities.

809   **CEMPE – LTETT 1969-1994: 25e anniversaire du Lycée Technique d'Ettelbruck.** (CEMPE – LTETT 1969-94: twenty-fifth anniversary of the Technical Secondary School of Ettelbruck.)
Editorial committee of the Lycée Technique d'Ettelbruck.
Luxembourg: Imprimerie Watgen, 1994. 192p.

Today the Technical Secondary School of Ettelbruck (30 km north of Luxembourg) offers a large choice of educational possibilities in line with the provisions of the 1990 law on secondary technical education. This law involved a complete reshuffling of the curricula so as to allow a greater spectrum of optional subjects and personal choice. To celebrate the twenty-five-years (1969-94) existence of the Ettelbruck school which nowadays attracts about 1,200 students, this commemorative brochure was published. The volume contains photographs and covers the history of the school, provides information about the different clubs and associations and deals with the transborder educational projects and international contacts of the 'Lycée Technique d'Ettelbruck'.

810   **Ecole privée Fieldgen: 1891-1991.** (Fieldgen Private School: 1891-1991.)
Editorial committee of the Ecole privée Fieldgen.   Luxembourg: Imprimerie Saint-Paul, 1991. 229p.

To celebrate the centenary of its existence, the Catholic private high school for young girls, 'Fieldgen', compiled this commemorative volume. It comprises different historical contributions from the time of the school's foundation onwards, when the boarding school first had the role of an agricultural school of domestic science. Other accounts deal with people involved with the school who had an impact on its evolution, offer a retrospective of its 100-year-old history, and describe the launching of the educational project of the early 1980s. This latter project organized different fund-raising activities to finance efforts to fight illiteracy and build schools in developing countries.

811　**Lycée technique privé Sainte Anne: 1852 Ettelbruck 1992.** (The Saint Anne Private Technical High School: 1852 Ettelbruck 1992.) Editorial committee of the Lycée technique privé Sainte Anne. Luxembourg: Imprimerie Saint-Paul, 1992. 267p.

A century ago, this private school was one of the first attempts at educational diversification, being the first school devoted to the education of girls. For 140 years the sisters of the Christian Doctrine have been active in Luxembourg and for more than a century they have been in charge of the education of future women. Richly illustrated with past and present photographs, this commemorative publication provides a history of the institution.

812　**Lycée technique Nic Biever 1968-1993.** (Nic Biever Technical High School, 1968-93.) Editorial committee of the Lycée technique Nic Biever.　Luxembourg: Imprimerie Hengen, 1993. 335p.

Among the festivities for the twenty-fifth anniversary of the existence of the 'Lycée technique Nic Biever' (Nic Biever was a former minister and parliamentarian who was born in Dudelange), an editorial committee took the decision to publish this commemorative volume on the school. It retraces the school's history by describing various initiatives (such as the school newspaper and the Christmas fair), by publishing pupils' short stories and poems and by providing information about different projects that concern the school. One of these projects is PETRA, the European Commission action programme for the vocational training of young people and their preparation for adult and working life. Interlarded with numerous photographs and documents, this is a vivid report of a promising school.

# The Arts

## Painting and sculpture

813 **L'art au Luxembourg: Premier volume; Des origines au début de la Renaissance.** (Art in Luxembourg: first volume; from its origin to the Renaissance.)
Ministry of Arts and Sciences. Luxembourg: Imprimerie Saint-Paul, 1966. 632p. 4 maps. bibliog. (Publications Nationales du Ministère des Arts et des Sciences.)
This luxurious and lavishly illustrated prestige publication from the Ministry of Arts and Sciences is a compilation of the work of different contributors: Joseph Meyers on prehistory and Roman times (p. 15-109); Paul Spang on the Frankish period (p. 109-23); Richard Maria Staud on religious pre-Romanesque architecture (p. 125-53); Joseph-Emile Müller on illuminated manuscripts from Echternach (p. 153-87); Albert Nothumb on religious architecture in Gothic times (p. 187-275) and on fortified castles and towns (p. 275-333); Edmond Goergen on mediaeval and Renaissance mural paintings (p. 333-91); and Georges Schmitt on Roman and Gothic sculpture.

814 **L'art au Luxembourg.** (Art in Luxembourg.)
Albert Nothumb. In: *Le Luxembourg livre du centenaire.*
(Luxembourg centenary book.) Luxembourg: Imprimerie Saint-Paul, 1949, 2nd ed., p. 335-93.
The Luxembourg arts remained for a long time the privilege of religious centres. The abbey of Echternach was the guiding light in the 9th and 10th centuries, especially in the illumination of manuscripts and in Romanesque architecture, before later centuries saw the rise of military architecture. The 18th century brought many baroque churches and interesting decorative painting. In 1845 the Society for the Research and the Conservation of Ancient Monuments was founded. Its efforts were continued after 1928 by the Commission of Art Sites and National Monuments.

815 **Le monde et le marché de l'art au Luxembourg.** (The art world and
its market in Luxembourg.)
Henri Entringer. Luxembourg: H. Entringer, Banque et Caisse
d'Epargne de l'Etat, 1991. 259p.

Because publications which analyse artistic activity in its sociological, economic and
financial aspects are quite rare, Entringer's study mainly concentrates on describing
the presence of plastic art in contemporary Luxembourg society. The reader will find
in this work a wide range of information on aesthetic concepts, the world art market,
measures taken by the European Community in the visual art field, as well as the
concept of the Luxembourg art sector, the price of paintings and cultural policies. This
research represents a useful complement to the existing monographs on contemporary
Luxembourg painters and sculptors.

816 **Portraits d'artistes.** (Portraits of artists.)
Liliane Thorn-Petit. Luxembourg: RTL Edition, 1982-92. 3 vols.

The title of this publication, 'Portraits d'artistes', used to be a television programme
where Liliane Thorn-Petit, a well-known Luxembourg journalist, presented famous
artists to the public. In 1982, she decided to publish a systematic inquiry into modern
art which took its inspiration from the show. Five years later, there was a second, and
in 1992 a third, publication so that the three volumes introduce the works of more than
140 different painters (e.g. Delvaux, Klee, Brandy), sculptors (e.g. Wercollier) and
architects (e.g. Hundertwasser). The aim of the author was above all to portray the
artists and their works and to communicate what they had to say about themselves and
their creations. Well illustrated (by at least one work from every artist) and presented
in a luxurious manner, these three volumes represent more of an intimate conversation
with the artists concerned rather than a mere anthology of individual statements.

817 **Regard sur deux siècles de création et d'éducation artistique au
Luxembourg.** (A look at two centuries of artistic creation and
education in Luxembourg.)
Association des professeurs d'éducation artistique de l'enseignement
secondaire et supérieur (A.P.E.A.). Luxembourg: Imprimerie Saint-
Paul, 1987. 332p.

For the twentieth anniversary of the A.P.E.A. (Association des professeurs d'éducation
artistique de l'enseignement secondaire et supérieur – Association of art teachers in
secondary and higher education) this publication pays testimony to the contributions of
fine arts teachers in the Grand Duchy's secondary schools over more than a century and
a half. An alphabetical list contains the names of all of these teachers (such as
Wercollier, Tissen, Leyder, Unden and Kraus), together with the main details on their
professional careers. Full of reproduced drawings and paintings, this commemorative
volume covers the period from 1848 the date when secondary education got a legal basis.

818 **Anthologie des arts au Luxembourg.** (Anthology of fine arts in
Luxembourg.)
Lambert Herr. Luxembourg: Imprimerie Linden, 1992. 464p.

To reflect the varied artistic tendencies present in the Grand Duchy, Lambert Herr
chose a neutral, objective and encyclopaedic approach. He set out to list all
Luxembourg artists, in alphabetical order (from 1544 onwards), famous and unknown

alike. Therefore, poor information on a particular artist does not necessarily signify that his or her works are of little quality.

819   **Regard sur la création au Luxembourg.** (A look at artistic creation in Luxembourg.)
Wolfgang Osterheld.   Luxembourg: Imprimerie Kremer-Müller, 1995. 260p.

This black-and-white picture album presents Luxembourg artists from all fields of artistic creation, including plastic artists, writers, poets, musicians and composers. Osterheld's intention was not to provide a hall of fame of the best artists but to write a personal and anecdotal account of Luxembourg's art scene, based on personal meetings and friendships.

820   **Collections privées au Luxembourg.** (Private collections in Luxembourg.)
Musée National d'Histoire et d'Art Luxembourg.   Luxembourg: Imprimerie Centrale, 1995. 441p.

This is the catalogue which was issued on the occasion of an exhibition held at the National Museum of History and Fine Arts in April 1995. While it briefly explains and illustrates nearly all of the 237 objects, the catalogue, and correspondingly the exhibition, set out to reflect the passion, the engagement and the taste of some art lovers and collectors who live in Luxembourg. Although the selection is mainly limited to French paintings and sculptures dating from the 20th century, the works of some contemporary German and Austrian artists are also represented.

821   **Anciennes vues de Luxembourg. Alte Luxemburger Stadtansichten.** (Ancient views of Luxembourg.)
J.-P. Koltz.   Luxembourg: Paul Bruck, 1982. 97p.

This trilingual (French, German and English) album includes forty-eight views of the capital of Luxembourg throughout four centuries. Each view is briefly described and falls into one of several categories: needle or dry-point engravings, etchings or aquatints, lithographs and wood engravings (xylographs).

822   **Gravures Luxembourgeoises.** (Luxembourg engravings.)
Bibliothèque Nationale de Luxembourg.   Luxembourg: Imprimerie Centrale, 1991. 207p.

This catalogue includes more than eighty reproductions of engravings by Luxembourg and foreign artists living in Luxembourg. The works are classified according to the birth date of the artists. An appendix provides an alphabetical list.

823   **La sculpture et les origines de la sculpture au Luxembourg à l'époque de la Renaissance.** (Sculpture and the origins of sculpture in Luxembourg during the age of the Renaissance.)
Joseph Walentiny.   Luxembourg: Imprimerie Saint-Paul, 1986. 314p. (Publications Nationales du Ministère des Affaires Culturelles).

Joseph Walentiny's PhD thesis (presented at the University of Nancy II) fills a gap by providing an overall view of the funeral sculpture of the Grand Duchy during the age of the Renaissance. It systematically lists and describes the origins of these art-monuments in Luxembourg. Furthermore Walentiny analyses the five large workshops that influenced the development of this art in Luxembourg, such as the Hieronymus or Bildhauer's workshop at Treves.

824 **Der heilige Willibrord im Zeugnis der bildenden Kunst: Ikonographie des Apostels der Niederlande, mit Beiträgen zu seiner Kultgeschichte**. (Saint Willibrord in the plastic arts: an iconography of the apostle of the Netherlands with contributions to his cultural history.)
Georges Kiesel.   Luxembourg: Ministère des Arts et des Sciences, 1969. 553p. map. (Publications Nationales du Ministère des Arts et des Sciences).

The main parts of this imposing study deal with: the life and personality of the saint; the memory of St. Willibrord in his cult; the contribution of the Abbey of Echternach; the cult of the saint in the Netherlands; and a complete iconography of the saint (from 990 to 1800). A comprehensive catalogue of works existing in Luxembourg, the Netherlands, Belgium, Germany, France, Austria, and Switzerland is included, together with 256 splendid plates.

825 **Lucien Wercollier.**
Joseph-Emile Müller.   Paris: ARTED, 1976. 49p.

This is a splendid art book on the works of the most important contemporary Luxembourg sculptor, Lucien Wercollier (1908-   ), written by the renowned Luxembourg art critic, Joseph-Emile Müller. Wercollier began by producing figurative bronze pieces, but he also likes to sculpt in marble, alabaster and onyx. In 1952 he began to express himself in a more abstract way. His temperament is essentially anti-romantic and anti-baroque, with the forms he creates being at once personal and subtly monumental. This book contains eighty photographic reproductions of his most important works. Eight years after the publication of this volume, Joseph-Emile Müller issued another excellent book of the same title on Wercollier (Luxembourg: Imprimerie Saint-Paul, 1983. 132p.) which reviews more than thirty-five years of his work (from 1947 to 1982). The 214 photographs (15 of which are in colour) are intended to provide a vivid idea of the artist's work, while the short annotations indicate what were, and what remain, his major preoccupations.

826 **Auguste Trémont.**
Georges Schmitt, photographs by Marcel Schroeder.   Luxembourg: Section des arts et des lettres de l'Institut grand-ducal, 1980. 141p. bibliog.

Trémont is the most famous animal painter and sculptor Luxembourg has ever known. He was born in Luxembourg in 1892, but spent most of his life in Paris. In his artistic development he was influenced by the great French *animalier*, François Pompon, but after 1930 he went his own way, creating splendid specimens of wild beasts. He also excelled as a portraitist, a medal-maker and a modeller of rare talent. His works figure in the greatest art museums of the world. An art book of superlative quality, this publication contains twelve colour plates and about eighty black-and-white plates.

827 **Greeff: Un atelier luxembourgeois de sculpture au 18e siècle.**
(Greeff: a Luxembourg sculpture workshop in the 18th century.)
Théophile Walin, Lily Thill-Beckius, Norbert Thill-Beckius.
Luxembourg: Imprimerie Saint-Paul, 1992. 368p.

The most important Luxembourg sculpture workshop of the 18th century belonged to
the Greeff family of Altwies (near Mondorf). The workshop created a prolific number
of sculptures, which were rare in the Luxembourg region in that they were of the
baroque style. This book provides the reader with an almost exhaustive and
abundantly illustrated inventory of the family's work, comprising mainly religious
sculptures (including altars, statues and ornaments) which decorated numerous
churches in the Saar-Lor-Lux region.

828 **Madones au Luxembourg.** (Madonnas in Luxembourg.)
Georges Schmitt, photographs by Marcel Schroeder. Luxembourg:
Ministère des Arts et des Sciences, 1966. 112p. (Publications
Nationales du Ministère des Arts et des Sciences).

This album features 112 colour and black-and-white photographs of the Virgin Mary
as represented in Luxembourg's churches and chapels. The plates are accompanied by
French and German annotations.

829 **Vierges de pitié luxembourgeoises.** (Luxembourg *pietàs*.)
Joseph Hirsch. *Hémecht,* vol. 19, no. 3 (1967), p. 295-397; vol. 20,
nos. 2-3 (1968), p. 117-379.

These *pietàs*, pictures or sculptures of the Virgin Mary holding the dead body of
Christ on her lap, originated in Germany. In Luxembourg, what is known in French as
the *vierge de pitié* is often described as *Mater dolorosa*. The author lists 160 of these
*pietàs* which are to be found in Luxembourg churches in alphabetical order of the
villages in which they are located. Individual photographic plates are accompanied by
detailed technical and artistic commentary.

830 **Le Cercle Artistique de Luxembourg 1893-1993.** (The Artists'
Society of Luxembourg 1893-1993.)
Edmond Zwank. Luxembourg: Imprimerie Centrale, 1993. 333p.

Zwank's book, published to mark the 100th anniversary of the artistic society of
Luxembourg, is a reference document which is intended to simplify research work. It
describes the main historical events of the society with much reference to the authors
and protagonists of the circle, even if, as the author admits himself, 'the art history of
Luxembourg does not entirely correspond to the history of the association'. Another
volume celebrating this anniversary, which documents the exhibition held for the
occasion, is *Cercle artistique de Luxembourg – rétrospective. Cent ans d'art
luxembourgeois 1893-1993* (q.v.).

831  **Cercle artistique de Luxembourg – rétrospective. Cent ans d'art luxembourgeois 1893-1993.** (Artistic society of Luxembourg – retrospective. 100 years of Luxembourg art 1893-1993.)
Cercle artistique de Luxembourg.   Luxembourg: Imprimerie Lux-Print, 1993. 2 vols.

This association of high repute was founded with the support of the former Grand Duchess Marie Adelaïde, who was herself passionately fond of painting. To celebrate the centenary of an association that assembles together Luxembourg's most important painters and sculptors, a retrospective exhibition was held and this sumptuous work was published. The publication includes a list of the presidents and members of the association throughout its history. Each of the artist-members of the association, which aims to promote artistic creation in Luxembourg, is represented through information on their work, former exhibitions and a reproduction of one of their works.

832  **Etapes de l'art luxembourgeois: des impressionnistes aux expressionnistes.** (Stages of Luxembourg art: from the impressionists to the expressionists.)
Luxembourg: Musée d'Histoire et d'Art, 1963. unpaginated.

This is the catalogue of an exhibition which took place at the Luxembourg Museum in June and July 1963. In his preface, the art critic, Joseph-Emile Müller, assesses the following impressionist artists of Luxembourg who adopted this style and technique much later than their French neighbours, mostly only after 1900: Frantz Seimetz, Jean-Pierre Beckius, Dominique Lang, and the visionary Sosthène Weis. The first artists to move away from this school appeared after the First World War and included Nico Klopp, Joseph Kutter and Michel Stoffel, who, after 1949, all turned to abstract art. The catalogue also presents drawings by Berthe Brincour and animal sculptures, paintings and drawings by Gustave Trémont. 134 exhibits are represented in the catalogue.

833  **Peintures et dessins luxembourgeois. Collection du Musée d'Histoire et d'Art/Luxembourg.** (Luxembourg paintings and drawings. Collection of the Luxembourg History and Art Museum.)
Jean-Luc Koltz.   Luxembourg: Imprimerie Bourg-Bourger, 1979. 77p.

This catalogue lists the names and reproduces some works of the most important Luxembourg artists, or foreign artists living in Luxembourg, who exert a real artistic influence in the Grand Duchy.

834  **Album de Redouté; with 25 facsimile colour plates from the edition of 1824 and a new Redouté bibliography.**
Sacheverell Sitwell, Roger Madol.   London: Collins, 1954. 20p.

Pierre Joseph Redouté (1759-1840), the French painter who was born in the former Duchy of Luxembourg, was the portraitist of Queen Marie Antoinette. He specialized in the delicate representation of flowers, fixing their forms and species in an infinite range of subtle colour shades and variegated design. His individual plates decorated the salons and boudoirs of Napoleon, Charles X and Louis-Philippe.

835 **J. K.: la vie et l'oeuvre de Joseph Kutter.** (J. K.: the life and works
of Joseph Kutter.)
Frédéric Humbel. Luxembourg: Imprimerie Kremer-Müller, 1994.
96p.

Frédéric Humbel, a young art historian, provides an account of the fascination of
Joseph Kutter (1894-1941), one of the greatest Luxembourg painters; a fascination he
still exerts today, although he died in 1941 at the age of forty-six. It is even possible
that his most important works have never been discovered. Humbel reassesses Kutter
from a fresh perspective. He qualifies some of the praise formerly dedicated to the
artist, questioning the real nature of his talent and analysing the degree to which he
was successful in creating a specifically Luxembourg art. A detailed chronological
biography is followed by an analysis of his works accompanied by about thirty
unpublished plates from the album of the Kutter family, most of which were taken by
the painter himself while staying abroad on his numerous trips. The young author has
also included a bibliography containing the most interesting books and articles as well
as a catalogue of Kutter's works which refers to about 300 paintings and drawings.

836 **Joseph Kutter.**
Introduced by Joseph-Emile Müller. Luxembourg: E. Kutter, 1967.
unpaginated. bibliog.

Kutter is Luxembourg's greatest expressionist painter who has enjoyed an international
reputation on the basis of his remarkable landscapes, expressive portraits and clowns.
This publication presents colour reproductions of fifty of the artist's works, with text
on Kutter's life and art.

837 **Kutter 1894-1941.**
Edited by the Musée Nationale d'Histoire et d'Art, with contributions
by Jean Luc Koltz, Edmond Thill and Robert Wagner. Luxembourg:
Imprimerie Saint-Paul, 1994. 163p.

Joseph Kutter (1894-1941) was surely one of the most famous Luxembourg painters.
His paintings dominated the inter-war years, even if his works were not appreciated by
everyone during his lifetime. This catalogue, which reproduces his most well-known
paintings, was issued in time for the exhibitions held in Luxembourg during December
1994 and January 1995 and in Berlin in 1995. Yet this brochure is not merely a
catalogue because it contains, besides a short bibliography, French and German
contributions on subjects such as Joseph Kutter as seen by the Luxembourg press
(1914-46), and Kutter and European expressionism.

838 **Jean-Pierre Beckius.**
Madeleine Frieden-Kinnen, Gaston Mannes. Schwebsange,
Luxembourg: Les Publications Mosellanes de Schwebsange, Entente
des communes et des syndicats d'initiative de la Moselle
luxembourgeoise, 1977. 156p. bibliog. (Publications Mosellanes de
Schwebsange, 20).

This book deals with one of the most famous Moselle painters, Jean-Pierre Beckius,
who was born in the village of Mertert in 1899 and died there in 1946.

839   **Joseph Probst.**
Joseph-Emile Müller.   Luxembourg: Edouard Kutter, 1979. 148p.
bibliog.

Joseph Probst (1911-   ) is a contemporary painter who was born in Vianden. He is one of the most important living painters, who switched from figurative representation to geometric abstraction in the direction of what the author calls 'a mood of lyrical abstraction'. The author is an internationally-known Luxembourg art critic. His luxurious monograph is a collection of various articles in French and German, illustrated by eighty-three splendid black-and-white and colour reproductions.

840   **Frantz Seimetz, ein Künstlerleben.** (Frantz Seimetz, the life of an artist.)
Robert Stumper.   Schwebsange, Luxembourg: Les publications mosellanes de Schwebsange, 1973. 100p. (Publications Mosellanes de Schwebsange, Vol. 16).

Frantz Seimetz is the oldest of the so-called Moselle painters. He was born in Grevenmacher in 1858 and he died in Luxembourg in 1934. A great traveller, he explored many different techniques of drawing and painting, but his favourite genres remained portraits and landscapes. The book also contains extracts from the *Feuersalamander* (Spotted salamander) (Luxembourg: Linden & Hansen, 1931-34. 4 vols.), the painter's excellent collection of anecdotes, pamphlets and aphorisms.

841   **Nina et Julien Lefèvre. Deux artistes, une oeuvre.** (Nina and Julien Lefèvre. Two artists, one work.)
Nina Lefèvre, Julien Lefèvre.   Luxembourg: Imprimerie Saint-Paul, 1978. 251p.

The married Lefèvre couple practised nearly every style of painting or graphic art. This album enabled them to open their workshop to a larger audience and show their rich and manifold works. The reproductions of their work in this volume demonstrate more effectively than any theoretical thesis the value of the two artists. While Julien Lefèvre (1907-84) is better known for his precise drawings of Luxembourg coins and paper money, his wife, Nina (1904-81), specialized in paintings of flowers, landscapes and portraits of ladies.

842   **Jean-Pierre Lamboray.**
Joseph Hirsch.   Luxembourg: Imprimerie Saint-Paul, 1986. 201p.

There are more than eighty of Lamboray's paintings in this catalogue. This Luxembourg painter, who was born in 1882 and died in 1962, was best known for his landscapes of the Ardennes.

843   **Bertemes.**
Nic Klecker.   Luxembourg: Institut grand-ducal. Section des arts et des lettres, 1984. 40p.

Nic Klecker describes the painting style of the Luxembourg artist, Roger Bertemes (b. 1927). He tells us more about Cézanne and Kutter, the foreign and Luxembourg painters whom Bertemes admired and who influenced him. Finally, the author presents Bertemes' previously unpublished diary and a biographical note on the painter before concluding with reproductions of thirty-six examples of his work.

844 **Nico Klopp (1894-1930).**
Musée National d'Histoire et d'Art. Luxembourg: Editions G. Klopp, 1994. 214p.

Painting Moselle villages, willow-lined rivers, the water and reflections on the water as well as the passing seasons were the major themes of Nico Klopp (1894-1930), the painter and engraver, who had learned these techniques in Weimar Germany. To commemorate the 100th anniversary of his birth, the National History and Art Museum of Luxembourg presents the largest retrospective ever devoted to this artist. The account is written in three languages (French, English and German) and interlarded with reproductions of Klopp's paintings and drawings while a running text describes his life up to his tragically premature death in 1930.

845 **Emile Kirscht.**
Guy Wagner. Esch-sur-Alzette, Luxembourg: Editpress, 1987. 141p.

This volume was published to celebrate the seventy-fifth anniversary of the Luxembourg painter, Emile Kirscht (1913-94), with the simultaneous aim of making his works better known to a larger public. The works of Kirscht, a self-educated and very discreet painter, are represented in more than fifty illustrations. Kirscht found the necessary time to paint despite working shifts in a factory until he retired.

846 **François Gillen un artiste: Echternach eine Stadt.** (François Gillen an artist: Echternach a town.)
Lucien Kayser, Paul Spang. Luxembourg: Imprimerie Centrale, 1995. 93p.

François Gillen (1914- ), one of the main contemporary Luxembourg artists was born in Echternach. This is an annotated collection of his works supplemented by an essay that provides a descriptive cultural tour of his native town where a lot of his creations have been brought together.

847 **Mett Hoffmann.**
Fernand Hoffmann. Luxembourg: Institut grand-ducal de Luxembourg, 1984. 42p.

Fernand Hoffmann is in fact a homonym of Mett Hoffmann (1915-94), the Luxembourg painter. This volume describes the life and particularly the works of this artist and insists on the constant change of style in his artistic development. Reproductions of thirty-eight of his paintings can be found at the end of the volume.

848 **Unger: Encres.** (Unger: Inks.)
M. Arnault. Luxembourg: Imprimerie Saint-Paul, 1982. unpaginated.

Arthur Unger (born in 1932) is a Luxembourg painter who has developed a very personal technique of painting by the handling of acidulated liquids and fire on the electrolytic copper plates that he uses as a creative surface. From 1978 onwards he also produced an important series of ink-drawings that are presented in this album, together with a short biographical account.

849 **Foni Tissen.**
Edited by Paul Tousch, Baba Tissen. Luxembourg: Imprimerie Centrale, 1987. 131p. (Publications Mosellanes).

Foni Tissen (1909-75) surely belongs to the most noteworthy Luxembourg artists of the postwar years. His paintings, which have such a personal style, are difficult to classify because he is at once a realist and a surrealist. Many of his works can be linked by oneirology and most of the time he drew laughing autoportraits. This monograph includes different contributions which attempt to define the colourful personality of Foni Tissen, expressed in his life and paintings.

850 **Robert Brandy.**
Echternach, Luxembourg: Editions Phi, 1982. 113p.

Robert Brandy is perhaps the most popular contemporary Luxembourg painter. His fresh approach also brought him some success abroad. With seven French contributions (accompanied by English translations) by different people that describe and discuss his personal style, the publication also includes reproductions of some of his paintings.

851 **Robert Brandy.**
L. Kayser, C. Lorent, J.-P. Schneider, J. Sorrente. Echternach, Luxembourg: Editions Phi, 1991. 142p.

Robert Brandenbourger (b. 1946) – known as Brandy – is a famous contemporary Luxembourg modern art painter. To celebrate the twenty years of his painting career, this commemorative volume, which was published in 1991, includes colour photographs of his works and contributions from four different authors. An appendix contains a short biography whilst the text sets out to link the painter's life with his artistic evolution. The French text is followed by a German translation and an English contribution, but the three parts are each illustrated with different paintings.

852 **Wou d'Rief laascht d'Musel doftech bléit.** (Where fragrant Moselle vineyards amply blossom.)
Mars Schmit. Pétange, Luxembourg: G. Kieffer, 1987. 80p. (Nos Cours d'Eau).

Mars Schmit (1931-90) is a Luxembourg painter whose work has embraced, over the years, landscapes and figurative subjects as well as more airborne abstractions. His aim is to communicate, through his paintings, the story of Luxembourg's natural and architectural heritage. He is particularly successful in capturing the atmosphere of small towns, streets, castles, mediaeval seignorial residences and rivers. Having written works on the Alzette – *Wou d'Uelzecht durech d'Wisen zéit* (Where the Alzette winds across the meadows) (Pétange, Luxembourg: G. Kieffer, 1985. 80p.) – and the Sura (the Sûre) – *Duurch d'Fielsen d'Sauer brêcht* (Where the Sura breaks through the rocks) (Pétange, Luxembourg: G. Kieffer, 1987. multiple pagination.) – this work of Schmit's contains rough outlines, Indian ink-drawings and water-colour paintings of the Moselle area.

853 **Goethes Luxemburger Zeichnungen.** (Goethe's Luxembourg drawings.)
Joseph Kohnen. Luxembourg: Imprimerie Saint-Paul, 1980. 142p.
Johann Wolfgang von Goethe (1749-1832), one of the most popular German writers of all time, stayed in the fortress of Luxembourg for a short period in 1792. During his visit he made sketches and drawings to perpetuate the views of the city that impressed him most. For the first time, twenty of his works are collected in a de luxe edition. Analytical comments together with a bibliography, pictorial evidence and photographs of Luxembourg 'Goethe-sites' make this publication one of the most interesting recent studies on the subject.

854 **Victor Hugo au Luxembourg. Vues et Visions.** (Victor Hugo in Luxembourg. Views and visions.)
Joseph-Emile Müller. Luxembourg: Imprimerie Saint-Paul, 1982. 145p.
Between 1862 and 1871, the famous French writer, Victor Hugo, visited Luxembourg five times. This luxurious publication by the art critic, Joseph-Emile Müller, provides an account of those visits. The text is interlarded with reproductions of seventy-five drawings that Victor Hugo made during his stays.

855 **J. M. W. Turner. The Luxembourg watercolours.**
Luxembourg: Imprimerie Centrale, 1995. 59p.
This is the catalogue of the water-colours of Luxembourg by the famous English landscape painter, J. M. W. Turner, which were put on display in Luxembourg in January and February 1995 as a contribution to 'Luxembourg: European city of culture 1995'. The classical and romantic painter visited Luxembourg twice (in 1824 and in 1839) and painted parts of the city in which the rock of the Bock, the fortress dominates.

856 **Munkacsy und Luxemburg.** (Munkacsy and Luxembourg.)
Joseph Kohnen. Luxembourg: Imprimerie Saint-Paul, 1984. 200p.
Michály Munkacsy (1844-1900) was a famous Hungarian painter who first stayed in Luxembourg in 1871 after having made the acquaintance of Baron Edouard de Marches. In 1874 he married Cecile Papier, the Baron de Marches' widow, and he stayed in Colpach, Luxembourg until 1896. Munkacsy died in Paris in 1900. In order to revive the memory of a great artist who made a contribution to Luxembourg's cultural history and who is still underrated, Kohnen presents a selection of the artist's paintings, sketches and drawings. These reproduced works are preceded by a detailed biography which describes Munkacsy's contacts with Luxembourg.

857 **Spottbilder aus der Geschichte Luxemburgs.** (Caricatures from the history of Luxembourg.)
Pol Tousch. Luxembourg: Musée d'Histoire et d'Art, 1979. 143p. (Karikatur in Luxemburg, Vol. 2).
Caricatures are undeniably a factor of cultural life and a faithful reflection of its atmosphere. Tousch offers a panoramic view of the works of about twenty well-known and influential artists in this field and in doing so reviews many critical and

controversial moments from Luxembourg's public and political life. Tousch is also the author of *Albert Simon: Luxembourg's 'Schnellkarikaturist'* (Albert Simon: the fast caricaturist of Luxembourg) (q.v.).

858    **Joseph et Ria Hackin: Couple d'origine luxembourgeoise au service des arts asiatiques et de la France.** (Joseph and Ria Hackin: couple of Luxembourg origins in the service of Asian arts and of France.)
Emile Mayrisch.    Esch-sur-Alzette, Luxembourg: Imprimerie Kremer-Müller, 1987. 143p.

The Guimet museum in Paris is one of the most important Asiatic art museums of France, and with its exhibition, 'Paris-Tokyo-Begram', it paid a tribute to its curator and restorer, Joseph Hackin (1886-1941). Because of his Luxembourg origins, the exhibition was also held in Luxembourg from November 1987 to January 1988. The research work of Joseph Hackin and his wife, Ria Hackin, was mainly centred around Grecian-Buddhist art. This publication includes: a catalogue of the exhibits; a bibliography of works written by, and about, Hackin; and an essay on Aline Mayrisch-de Saint-Hubert, wife of the famous captain of industry, Emile Mayrisch, and her cultural efforts: she arranged a lecture on Joseph Hackin, for example, in Luxembourg in 1927.

859    **Faïences fines de Septfontaines. Décors et styles de 1767 au début du XIXe siècle.** (Fine china from Septfontaines. Decorations and styles from 1767 to the beginning of the 19th century.)
Jean-Luc Mousset.    Luxembourg: Imprimerie Saint-Paul, 1991. 257p.

This presents photographs of a selection of more than 200 unknown pieces of fine china from the Manufacture Boch sise à Septfontaines (Boch factory located at Septfontaines), which was founded by the Boch brothers in 1766 and trades under the name, Villeroy Boch. This factory was the oldest in the Austrian Netherlands and it was able to thrive because it was spared any foreign competition thanks to the protectionism of Vienna. This catalogue was issued at the same time as the exhibition of fine china in Luxembourg and Brussels in 1991. It is composed of two different parts: the reader can admire the beauty of the different types of ornament and also discover the stylistic evolution of production in Septfontaines from 1767 to 1925.

860    **Faïences fines.** (Fine china.)
Anne-Marie Mariën-Dugardin.    Brussels: Musées Royaux d'Art et d'Histoire, 1975. 2nd ed. 279p.

This catalogue is published by the Royal Museums of Art and History in Brussels. It forms part of a series which illustrates the collections of the ceramic section. Chapter III (p. 118-68) deals with Luxembourg and provides a detailed description of interesting items made by: the Manufacture Boch sise à Septfontaines (Boch factory located at Septfontaines), founded by the Boch brothers in 1766; the Faïencerie d'Echternach (Echternach ceramics factory) founded in 1797 by Jean-Baptiste Dondelinger and later managed by Jacques Lamort (1845-56); and the Manufacture d'Eich (Eich factory), founded in 1830 by Guillaume and Théodore Pescatore.

861 **Earthenware from Septfontaines. Floral decorations dating from 1767 through the early 19th century.**
Jean-Luc Mousset. Luxembourg: Banque générale, 1989. 107p.
Villeroy Boch is the trade name of the large porcelain factory in Septfontaines which can trace its origins back to the end of the 18th century. The Boch family left their native Lorraine and resettled at the gates of the Luxembourg fortress in order to introduce the first commercial production of porcelain to the Austrian Netherlands in 1766. This catalogue, which was published to accompany an exhibition in Luxembourg in 1989, describes some 120 porcelain show-pieces which represent this decorative industry. Unfortunately, because this catalogue is a companion volume to the exhibition, it does not contain photographs, but only short descriptions.

# Music

862 **La vie musicale.** (Musical life.)
Joseph Meyers. In: *Le Luxembourg. Livre du centenaire.*
(Luxembourg centenary book.) Luxembourg: Imprimerie Saint-Paul, 1949, 2nd ed., p. 393-447.
Apart from some Roman mosaic figures which feature musical instruments, there are no documents of musical life in Luxembourg in the first centuries AD. It was only with Charlemagne and the revival of organ music that the monasteries became centres of Gregorian chant. Meyers traces the remains and documents of musical activity in Luxembourg through the ages. He emphasizes the amazing number of good choirs and local brass bands, the international status of the symphonic orchestra of Radio-Télé-Luxembourg, and the professional Musique Militaire (Military Band) which serves as a school for local conductors.

863 **Luxemburger Komponisten heute.** (Luxembourg composers today.)
Guy Wagner. Echternach, Luxembourg: Editions Phi, 1986. 187p.
(Reihe: Musik).
This publication provides an overall view of some thirty-five Luxembourg composers from Jules Krüger (born in 1899), who was the first composer who subsequently turned to symphonic, as opposed to popular brass-band music, to Pierre Nimax jr. (born in 1961). The author examines their works as well as their importance for the cultural life of the country. Guy Wagner's intention was not to present a critical evaluation of today's composers, but to provide a short portrait of each of them. At the end of the book there is a detailed catalogue of works by these composers.

864 **Lëtzebuerger Komponisten. 125 Joer Lëtzebuerger Stadmusek.**
(Luxembourg composers. 125 years of Municipal Music in Luxembourg.)
Léon Blasen. Luxembourg: Imprimerie Saint-Paul, 1988. 423p.
This book, published on the occasion of the 125th anniversary of the Luxembourg city brass band, is a real monument to Luxembourg's composers and brass bands. It

provides a detailed chronicle of the society, and offers biographical data on all the major composers. In addition there is a remarkable contribution in French by Guy Jourdain, entitled 'La musique au Luxembourg' (Music in Luxembourg) (p. 195-208). The author also includes an alphabetical list of fact sheets on all the town and village brass bands (p. 209-367).

865 **Conservatoire de Musique de la Ville de Luxembourg. Soixante-quinzième anniversaire.**
(Music academy of Luxembourg city. Seventy-fifth anniversary.)
Luxembourg: Imprimerie Saint-Paul, 1981. 210p.

The seventy-fifth anniversary (1906-81) of the music school of Luxembourg city was celebrated just one year after the municipal council had decided to build a new conservatoire on the outskirts of the city, at Merl-Belair. This volume includes different contributions on the history of the former music academy (located in the heart of Luxembourg city) and the people that shaped it, as well as texts on musical education in general.

866 **Conservatoire de Musique Esch-sur-Alzette.** (Music School of Esch-sur-Alzette.)
Esch-sur-Alzette, Luxembourg: Imprimerie La Frontière-Quintus, 1993. 83p.

This book was issued on the occasion of the opening festivities of the new school of music at Esch-sur-Alzette, second town of the country. The school, which was originally founded in the 1920s, was transferred in 1993 to a historic building which formerly belonged to the Luxembourg steel company, ARBED. Following the traditional preamble, the volume provides a short historical review of the school before dealing with the architectural concept of its new building and presenting the programme of the 1993 festivities.

867 **Das Luxemburger Rundfunkorchester 1933-1940/1946-1958.**
(The Luxembourg radio orchestra 1933-40/1946-58.)
Loll Weber. Luxembourg: Imprimerie Saint-Paul, 1993. 428p.

By means of historical evidence, Loll Weber attempts to contradict those who still believe that the serious cultural activities of the Luxembourg Radio Orchestra only took place in the 1960s and 1970s. The author discusses the activities, concerts and studio productions of the Luxembourg Radio Orchestra over the years 1933-40 and 1946-58, while it was under the direction of the conductor, Henri Pensis. Even if two serious crises threatened the existence of the orchestra (in 1939 and in 1947/48), the detailed documentation, in the form of concert programmes which highlight the involvement of national and international guest performers, should provide lasting evidence of the orchestra's high standard of performance.

868   **Cent trente-cinquième anniversaire de la Musique Militaire
Grand-Ducale.** (The 135th anniversary of the Grand-Ducal Military
Band.)
Musique Militaire Grand-Ducale.   Luxembourg: Commandement de
l'Armée Luxembourgeoise, 1977. 536p.

On 29 December 1842 the Grand Duchy's first military brass band was created, with
twenty-nine musicians. Today the Musique Militaire Grand-Ducale (Grand-Ducal
Military Music) comprises sixty-one professional musicians. It constitutes a unit in the
Luxembourg army; besides the concerts the band performs, the unit has to take part in
all military parades and official ceremonies. This commemorative illustrated volume
reconstructs the most important moments of this glorious formation, which is a
cornerstone of Luxembourg's official, social and artistic life.

869   **150 Joër Maîtrise vun der Kathedral 1844-1994.** (150 years of the
master choir of the cathedral 1844-1994.)
Luxembourg: Imprimerie Saint-Paul, 1994. 251p.

To commemorate its 150th anniversary, the Saint Cecilia master choir of the Notre
Dame cathedral presents a vivid, well-illustrated account. It includes a short summary
of the first 125 years, a review of the years 1940-45 as well as a survey of the
concerts, masses and auditions held since 1968. Other contributions deal with the
cathedral's life and treasures and the famous fire that destroyed the old west tower in
1985.

870   **Orgeln und Orgelbau in Luxemburg.** (Organs and organ building in
Luxembourg.)
Norbert Thill.   Christnach, Luxembourg: Editions E. Borschette,
1993. 502p.

This lavishly-illustrated reference book does not only retrace the history (from the
17th century to the present) of Luxembourg's organs, but it also provides an account
of the activities of the different organ workshops and their influence on the local organ
scene. By describing, in alphabetical order, all the church and concert organs across
the country as well as those in studios and homes, the publication constitutes a
practical guide for every organist.

871   **La chanson populaire luxembourgeoise.** (Luxembourg folk songs.)
Mathias Tresch.   Luxembourg: Buck, 1929. 307p.

'Only a dozen of our songs can really be called popular', writes the author, who sets
out to link Luxembourg's folklore with that of the Germanic east and the Gallic west,
the Lorrainese south and the Walloon north. The songs are in Luxembourgish, German
and French. The value of the book lies in its reproduction of the lyrics and tunes,
which are accompanied by translations by the author.

872  **Singendes Volk: Volkslieder aus Luxemburg gesammelt und herausgegeben.** (A singing people: popular songs from Luxembourg collected and edited.)
Mathias Thill.   Esch-sur-Alzette, Luxembourg: Imprimerie Kremer-Müller, 1937. 675p. bibliog.

The majority of the 306 folk songs presented in this volume are of German origin; they have survived generations through oral tradition, sometimes appearing in a Luxembourgish version. The rest of the songs are Luxembourgish and French. The first part deals with half-forgotten songs of yesteryear, whilst the second part assembles the songs which originated after 1870. For each song, Thill provides variant forms, records the year and place of notation, and the name of the singer; a complete bibliographical index of Luxembourg collections of popular songs is to be found on p. 639-40. Mathias Thill, who lived from 1880 to 1936, was a primary-school teacher in Esch-sur-Alzette.

873  **De Wilhelmus.** (The Wilhelmian song.)
Paul Ulveling.   Esch-sur-Alzette, Luxembourg: Editpress, 1984. 67p.

'De Wilhelmus' is a very special hymn for the Luxembourg population as it is the anthem of the Luxembourg grand ducal family. However, other versions of this hymn exist as in, for example, the Dutch national anthem, although the original melody seems to stem from a French military song. The author has therefore considered it interesting to inquire into the history of this song and he provides an account with a commentary that runs in four parallel languages: Luxembourgish, Dutch, French and German.

874  **Laurent Menager (1835-1902).**
Luxembourg: Chorale Sang a Klang, 1985. 215p.

This biography of Laurent Menager, the founder of the Chorale Sang a Klang (Song and Sound Choir), is a tribute to a man who was one of the most famous people in Luxembourg during his lifetime, but who has almost fallen into oblivion since. Laurent Menager gave the nation something that it did not have before: songs of its own to sing and music of its own to play. This publication has an additional historical angle in its analysis of the development of patriotism.

875  **Mélanges Jos Kinzé.** (Miscellany Jos Kinzé.)
Compiled by André Bauler.   Diekirch, Luxembourg: Town of Diekirch, 1995. 141p.

With this book, the town of Diekirch honours one of its outstanding citizens, the composer and musical director, Jos Kinzé. Born in Essen (Germany), the young organist and choirmaster settled in Diekirch in 1952 to take over the church organ, to teach music in the local grammar school and other regional schools and to direct some reputed local choirs like the 'Dikricher Sängerbond' (Diekirch Singers' Circle) and the 'Solschlösselcher' (Sol Clefs) and other well-known choirs in Bettembourg, Ettelbruck and Vianden. At the end of the book Jean-Claude Moris, the curator responsible for music at the National Library, presents a most impressive catalogue of forty pages of Jos Kinzé's music, ranging from instrumental and vocal music to special music for theatre.

876   **Mäi Land, mäi Lidd.** (My country, my song.)
Pierre Nimax.   Luxembourg: Imprimerie Saint-Paul, 1984. 67p.
This song-book includes nearly fifty Luxembourg classical songs collected by the
Luxembourg composer and musician, Pierre Nimax, who adapted them for the piano.

877   **Lëtzebuerger Lidderbuch.** (Luxembourg song-book.)
Guillaume Stomps.   Luxembourg: Editions Krippler-Müller, 1982.
217p.
This is a reprint of 101 Luxembourg songs compiled and edited by the publisher,
Guillaume Stomps, in the year 1898.

878   **Luxemburger Gaudeamus. Taschenliederbuch für sangesfreudige
Luxemburger.** (Luxembourg 'Gaudeamus'. Pocket song-book for
Luxembourg people keen on singing.)
Compiled by Nic Biwer.   Luxembourg: M. Huss, 1925. 318p.
Reprinted, Luxembourg: Imprimerie Saint-Paul, 1982. 371p.
This publication is an exact reprint of the third edition of the pocket song-book which
first came out in 1925. It includes a rich choice of Luxembourg, German and French
folk songs with text and notes.

879   **Lëtzebuerger Rocklexikon; erweitert auf pop, folk, country, jazz
und jazz-rock.** (Luxembourg rock encyclopaedia; extended to pop,
folk, country, jazz and jazz-rock.)
Luke Haas.   Echternach, Luxembourg: Editions Phi, 1988. 191p.
This encyclopaedia, written by the Luxembourg singer, Luke Haas, contains short
descriptions of each performer's or group's origin and evolution, accompanied by
their photographs and discography. Since it was published in 1988, the material is now
in need of updating.

# Theatre

880   **Theater in Luxemburg von den Anfängen bis zum heimatlichen
Theater 1855.** (Theatre in Luxembourg from the beginnings to the
national theatre 1855.)
Joseph Hurt.   Luxembourg: Administration Communale, 1989. 166p.
Hurt's work, which was originally published in 1938 as a special issue of *Jong
Hémecht* (Young Homeland), describes the development of theatre in Luxembourg.
Republished in 1989 to celebrate the twenty-fifth anniversary of the Municipal Theatre
of Luxembourg, the information is now clearly arranged in six chronological chapters,
and covers the period up to 1855.

881    **Triviales Theater: Untersuchungen zum volkstümlichen Theater am Beispiel des luxemburgischen Dialektdramas von 1894-1940.** (Popular theatre of entertainment: investigations into the popular theatre, as exemplified by the Luxembourg dialect drama from 1894 to 1940.)
Pit Schlechter.   Luxembourg: Imprimerie Bourg-Bourger, 1974. 349p. bibliog.

Schlechter's very serious and systematic MA thesis, produced for the Luxembourg Secondary School Teaching Diploma, focuses on the genres, styles, plots, heroes, titles, and means of production of popular theatre and an analysis of the social and moral values transmitted by it. This indispensable basic work aids our understanding of the development and aspects of the village stage and its archetypal figures. Also included is an extensive reference glossary with a substantial bibliography.

882    **Théâtre Municipal Luxembourg 1964-1989.** (Luxembourg Municipal Theatre 1964-89.)
Luxembourg: Imprimerie Saint-Paul, 1989. 191p.

With its more than 5 million visitors and about 5,000 performances in 25 years, the Municipal Theatre of Luxembourg has surely become of national importance. The more than thirty contributions included in this commemorative volume attempt to retrace the history (1964-89) of the theatre that was newly built for Luxembourg's millennium in 1963. This luxurious book also includes photographs of the most successful performances, and of the visits of personalities as well as reproductions of posters announcing some of the highlights.

883    **Tun Deutsch, 1932-1977: dem Schauspieler und Freund, die Freunde. Souvenirs et témoignages des amis.** (Tun Deutsch, 1932-77: to the actor and friend from his friends.)
Edited by Alice Deutsch-Kinnen.   Junglinster, Luxembourg: A. Deutsch-Kinnen, 1979. 121p.

This commemorative volume is devoted to a great actor and highly popular innovator of Luxembourg theatre. Tun Deutsch was only forty-five when he died in 1977. His fertile career as an actor, stage-director, reciter of poems, cabaret show-master, lecturer on dramatic art and founder and mastermind of the Centre grand-ducal d'art dramatique (Kasemattentheater – Grand-ducal centre of dramatic art) opened new modernistic perspectives for Luxembourg's semi-professional and amateur theatre. He conducted poetry recitals in German, French, English and Luxembourgish with equal mastery. The album comprises contributions from Deutsch's friends, an introduction by Nic Weber, general documentation by Pierre Capésius, and a graphic presentation by Frantz Kinnen, Tun Deutsch's father-in-law.

884    **De Cabaret zu Letzebuerg. Eng Analyse.** (The revue in Luxembourg. An analysis.)
*Galerie*, no. 3 (1983/84). 48p.

Issued after the first Luxembourg Revue Days (held in Bourglinster in June 1983), this publication was intended to be the starting-point of more theoretical discussions.

885 **Luxemburgs Pioniere der leichten Muse.** (The Luxembourg pioneers of light entertainment.)
Roger Spautz. Luxembourg: RTL Edition, 1983. 317p.

This collection of pre- and postwar memories focuses on light entertainment, especially from RTL (Radio-Télé-Luxembourg), which turned Luxembourg into a genuine entertainment centre. It also evokes the up until now more or less ignored cultural contribution of the writers, musicians and actors who stayed in Luxembourg for some time in the 1930s after having left Hitler's Germany.

886 **Die Entertainer der Nationallotterie.** (The entertainers of the National Lottery.)
Roger Spautz. Luxembourg: Imprimerie Centrale, 1983-84. 3 vols.

Since its foundation in 1950, the revue company (variété-ensemble) of the National Lottery has numbered nearly seventy members. Roger Spautz deals with sixty-two of them in three volumes classified according to the specificity of their performance. The first volume deals with reciters and cabaret artists, the second volume with actors, illusionists and comedians, while the third volume lists acrobats, ballerinas and chorus girls.

# Cinema

887 **Le cinéma et la télévision au Luxembourg.** (Cinema and television in Luxembourg.)
Luxembourg: Ministère des Affaires Culturelles, 1989. 205p.

To celebrate the European year of cinema and television, this volume publishes articles on cinema, television, telecommunications politics and European financial stakes in Luxembourg's telecommunications industry. It also provides a list of the main bodies, institutions and producers in the audiovisual field and other useful information.

888 **Lebende Bilder. Aus Luxemburgs guter alter Kinozeit.** (Living pictures. Luxembourg's good old cinema era.)
Norbert Etringer. Luxembourg: Imprimerie Saint-Paul, 1983. 124p.

In a nostalgic review, Etringer introduces the reader to the early history of Luxembourg cinematography at the turn of the 20th century.

889 **Zelluloid Cowboy. Die Filme von Andy Bausch.** (Celluloid Cowboy. The films of Andy Bausch.)
Edited by Richard Roderes. Luxembourg: Rapidpress, 1993. 199p.

A team of nine journalists and writers followed the career of the Luxembourg film maker, Andy Bausch, from his short film beginnings up to his mature, committed cinema films. Richly documented with more than 250 photographs, this book is an indispensable source of reference for every film fan.

890 **Germaine Damar. Ein luxemburger Star im deutschen Film der 50er Jahre.** (Germaine Damar. A Luxembourg star in the German films of the 1950s.)

Dudelange, Luxembourg: Centre national de l'audiovisuel, 1995. 63p.

This brochure provides an account of the life and career of Germaine Damar, the dancer and acrobat who was born in Pétange (Luxembourg) in 1929. She was introduced into an acting career by Zarah Leander, a popular German singer in the 1950s, in 1952, and in ten years she performed in twenty-eight revue films, usually in the lead role, together with the musical and comedy stars of the day.

# Photography

891 **The Family of Man.**

Edward Steichen. New York: Museum of Modern Art, 1988. 192p.

'The Family of Man symbolizes the universality of human emotions' (wrote the *New York Times* about Steichen's exhibition in 1977). That is exactly how this thirtieth-anniversary edition of Steichen's classic book of photography, created for the Museum of Modern Art (New York), can be described. It includes selected photographs taken all over the world, representing the human life cycle from birth to death, with emphasis on the daily relationships of man with himself, his family, the community and the world he lives in. In all, the book contains 503 pictures from 68 countries, taken by 273 men and women, both unknown amateurs and renowned professionals.

892 **Photos.**

Edward Steichen, text by Ruth Kelton. Munich, FRG: Rogner & Bernhard, 1977. 96p. (Photo-Galerie, Vol. 3).

Edward Steichen, the famous photographer, director of the Museum of Modern Art in New York, organizer of the unique exhibition, 'The Family of Man', and founder of the Photo-Secession Galleries, was born in Luxembourg on 27 March 1879. His family emigrated to Hancock, Michigan, where his father worked in a copper mine. When he was fifteen, his family settled in Milwaukee, where he began his apprenticeship in a lithographic institution. It was the beginning of a glorious career. This album reproduces about forty of his most famous photographs, with a short German introduction by Ruth Kelton. *Edward Steichen: selected texts and bibliography*, edited by Ronald J. Gedrim (Oxford: ABC-Clio; New York: G. K. Hall, an imprint of Simon & Schuster Macmillan, 1996. 225p. bibliog.) is another excellent volume which includes a bibliography of the literature relating to Steichen's life and work.

893 **Steichen, the master prints, 1895-1914: the symbolic period.**

Edward Steichen, Alfred Stieglitz. London: Thames & Hudson, 1978. 180p. bibliog.

Comprises seventy-two plates of Steichen's prints with notes and comments on letter-print by Steichen and Alfred Stieglitz and their contemporaries, and a description of

Steichen's printing techniques. The works reproduced are drawn from five museums and two private collections.

894   **The Family of Man: Témoignages et documents.** (The Family of
      Man: witness reports and documents.)
      Edited by Jean Back and Gabriel Bauret.   Dudelange, Luxembourg:
      Centre national de l'audiovisuel; Luxembourg: Ministère des affaires
      culturelles, 1994. 222p.

The Centre national de l'audiovisuel (National Audiovisual Centre) published this work on the occasion of the opening of the new museum, 'The Family of Man', in 1994, at the Castle of Clervaux, Luxembourg which provided a permanent home for Steichen's original 1977 exhibition in New York. It brings together twenty-four authors, photographers, journalists, art historians and friends of Edward Steichen who recount, analyse and present their impressions of the most famous exhibition that ever toured the world.

# Architecture

895   **Die Parler und der Schöne Stil, 1350-1400: europäische Kunst
      unter den Luxemburgern.**
      (The Parlers and the 'pretty style': European art under the
      Luxembourgers.)
      Edited by Anton Legner.   Cologne, FRG: Schnütgen-Museum,
      1978-80. 5 vols.

This is the guidebook to a great exhibition which took place in Cologne in 1979 to celebrate the golden age of sculpture and architecture in Prague under the 14th-century Holy Roman Emperor Charles IV from the House of Luxembourg. The Parlers were a great dynasty of sculptors and architects of that period. Three more volumes on the Parlers followed this work but they do not directly concern Luxembourg.

896   **L'historicisme à Luxembourg. Historismus in Luxemburg.**
      (Historicism in Luxembourg.)
      Robert L. Philippart.   Luxembourg: Imprimerie Saint-Paul, 1989.
      157p.

Philippart presents a historical introduction to the architecture of Luxembourg at the turn of the 20th century (between 1850 and 1918), showing extant buildings irrespective of their artistic value. The text of the book runs in four languages (French, German, English and Japanese; the French and German versions, however, are more detailed). Each building is illustrated together with some essential data (such as current addresses, original function and name of the architect) and, whenever it is of special interest, the original plan or project has been provided in order to show the complete architectural concept.

897 **Plateau Bourbon und Avenue de la Liberté. Späthistorische Architektur in Luxemburg.** (The Bourbon Plateau and Liberation Avenue. Late-historical architecture in Luxembourg.)
Antoinette Lorang. Luxembourg: Imprimerie Linden, 1988. 401p. (Publications de la Section Historique de l'Institut Grand-Ducal. Vol. 103).

This study by Antoinette Lorang is the MA thesis she presented to the Art History Institute at the University of Heidelberg, Germany. Containing more than 160 photographs, the work is above all an attempt to investigate historicism in Luxembourg and to provide documentary evidence as exemplified by one Luxembourg-city district: the Bourbon Plateau and Liberation Avenue in the Quartier de la gare (Station district). Urbanism, together with architecture and theory forms one of the three main sections of the book. The author discusses: the conditions for the enlargement of the city; the urbanization projects; and the state concept. The second chapter provides an architectural and historical description of Liberation Avenue together with a detailed examination of construction techniques, including possible sources of inspiration. The theoretical part provides the reader with a detailed analysis of the individual buildings in order to determine the theoretical architecture basis.

898 **Mascarons de Luxembourg.** (Mascarons from Luxembourg.)
Nelly Moia. Esch-sur-Alzette, Luxembourg: Polyprint, 1995. 207p.

Fantastic stone faces perched on the dull, 'bourgeois' façades of the towns of Luxembourg and Esch look down on passers-by. Some of them resemble political personalities, while others represent princes, gods, mythological or allegorical figures of beauty and prosperity. The attentive reader and observer will encounter fascinating, often exotic discoveries and unexpected meetings.

899 **Luxembourg, la capitale et ses architectes.** (Luxembourg, the capital and its architects.)
Pierre Gilbert. Luxembourg: Imprimerie Saint-Paul, 1986. 220p.

This publication is not a book on architecture, but rather an inventory of the architecture built in Luxembourg city since 1870 that is still standing, as well as an observation of the evolution of the city's built environment. Gilbert attempts to demonstrate to the reader through a series of photographs that the unique character of the city is in danger of being lost by the construction of recent buildings. The pictures of each building are accompanied by the names of the architects, whose portraits figure at the end of the volume.

900 **Rob Krier – Architecture and Urban Design.**
London: Academy Editions; Berlin: Ernst & Sohn, 1993. 144p. (Architectural Monographs, 30).

The buildings and projects of the well-known Luxembourg artist, Rob Krier, are invariably informed by his views on the nature of urban space, which derive from the traditional city and the notion of a 'res publica' or civic realm. Whether house, tenement block or public structure, his work always refers to his desire to create space and communal focal points that are invested with the sort of functions indispensable to the idea of neighbourhood and community. Beginning with his earliest projects of the late 1960s, this comprehensive portfolio (containing over 500 illustrations, most of which are in colour) of his work throws light on one of today's most creative and indefatiguable traditionalists, covering his larger creations in Berlin and the master-plan for the city of Amiens as well as the more recent proposals for the Hague and San Sebastian in Spain.

901  **Les châteaux historiques du Luxembourg.** (The historic castles of Luxembourg.)
Jean-Pierre Koltz, photographs by Tony Krier.   Luxembourg: Imprimerie Saint-Paul, 1975. 231p. bibliog.

On the occasion of the European Architectural Heritage Year in 1975, the photographer, Krier, and the local historian and fortress specialist, Koltz, compiled a luxurious album containing the most beautiful views of seventy-six castles that still exist in the present Grand Duchy, and mentioning many more which are either in ruins or have completely disappeared. They are presented in alphabetical order; first-class historical comments and reference data make this a unique album.

902  **Du château du Bock au Gibraltar du Nord. Luxembourg et sa forteresse.** (From the castle of the Bock to the Gibraltar of the North. Luxembourg and its fortress.)
Gilbert Trausch.   Luxembourg: Banque de Luxembourg, 1994. 40p.

Published by the Banque de Luxembourg and written by the historian, Gilbert Trausch, this well-illustrated brochure presents the genesis and evolution of the fortress of Luxembourg and highlights its importance for the capital, and also for the country. It is an essential part of the collective memory of the Luxembourg population and its architectural inheritance.

903  **Die Bautätigkeit der Abtei Echternach im 18. Jahrhundert (1728-1793): ein Beitrag zur Geschichte des luxemburgischen Bauwesens im Barockzeitalter.** (The building activities of the Echternach abbey in the 18th century, 1728-93: a contribution to the history of the Luxembourg building trade and architecture in the baroque age.)
Michel Schmitt.   Luxembourg: Ministère des Arts et des Sciences, 1970. 229p. bibliog. (Publications Nationales du Ministère des Arts et des Sciences).

The first part of Schmitt's work shows the imperial abbey as a building sponsor active in civil engineering and the building trade in the 18th century, whilst part II presents the abbey constructions in Echternach and such masterbuilders as the Lorrainese Benedictine architect, Léopold Durand, and the Mungenasts builder family. Part III surveys the abbey's building activities outside Echternach, delineates the importance of church construction within the baroque Echternach building trade, emphasizes the influence of Austrian legislation on clerical architecture and building projects, and explains the relationship of Echternach tithe churches to the ecclesiastical architecture of the 18th century. A final part describes the importance of the rural villas and tithe farms for the abbey building trade. This solid study is rounded off by 143 splendid photographs.

904   **La Cathédrale Notre-Dame de Luxembourg.** (The Cathedral of Our
Lady of Luxembourg.)
Luxembourg: Imprimerie Saint-Paul, 1964. 148p.

When Luxembourg was made a diocese in 1870, the Cathédrale Notre-Dame, the
former 17th-century Jesuit church, was chosen as the seat of the bishopric. On the
occasion of the millennium of the town of Luxembourg in 1963, a solemn
consecration of the newly-renovated cathedral took place. This work commemorates
that occasion, and is based on articles previously published in the *Luxemburger Wort*.

905   **Maison de Raville. Ein Zeitdokument: Luxemburger Geschichte
um ein Renaissance-Haus.** (The house of Raville. A time document:
Luxembourg history around a Renaissance house.)
André Haagen, Jean-Pierre Koltz, Paul Margue.   Luxembourg:
Banque UCL; BfG Luxemburg, 1981. 120p.

Published by the UCL (Union des Consommateurs Luxembourgeoise – Luxembourg
Consumers' Union) bank, this brochure contains reports, in pictures and text, of the
dismantling and subsequent restoration and reconstruction of a 400-year-old house,
which is now the head office of that same bank. The main part of the publication
nevertheless provides insights into: Luxembourg social history (by Paul Margue);
currency circulation and monetary policy in Luxembourg during the second half of the
16th century (by Raymond Weiller); and the building history of the 16th century (by
Jean-Pierre Koltz).

906   **Bekannte und verborgene Schönheiten in Luxemburg. Vol. I.**
(Known and hidden beauties in Luxembourg. Vol. 1.)
Norbert Thill.   Clairefontaine, Luxembourg: Verlag Heimat und
Mission, 1995. Various pagination.

*Heimat und Mission* (Homeland and Missionary Work) is a monthly journal which
presents interesting documentary files on the architectural and artistic local heritage of
Luxembourg, and provides basic documentation on social, economic and religious
topics. Some issues of the series were conceived from 1991 to 1994 as monographs on
certain Luxembourg villages, and illustrate both reputed and largely unknown
treasures from local churches, castles, or simple farmhouses. The success gained by
these special issues prompted the publisher to assemble a series of special issues into
several volumes of monographs in order to reach a larger public. The first volume
covers the remarkable cultural heritage of the following villages: Asselborn,
Brachtenbach, Eischen, Gilsdorf, Mondorf and Oberwiltz. Most of the contributions
are from the reputed art photographer and cultural globe-trotter, Norbert Thill, others
by Edy Ahnen and Jengi Ney.

907   **Vianden in seinen Kirchen, Kapellen und sakralen Kunstschätzen.**
(Vianden in its churches, chapels and sacral art treasures.)
Pierre Bassing.   Luxembourg: Imprimerie Saint-Paul, 1983. 247p.

The Vianden 'Friends of History' have set out, since their foundation, to inventorize
and analyse the works of art of their town (northeast of Luxembourg city). Pierre
Bassing is the first to deal with the religious art of Vianden. His detailed and well-
illustrated study also includes an appendix on the former goldsmith's workshop and its
work.

908 **Rindschleiden: Monographie de l'église paroissiale.** (Rindschleiden:
a book of the parish church.)
Blanche Weicherding-Goergen.    Luxembourg: Imprimerie Saint-Paul,
1974. 88p. map. bibliog.

Rindschleiden, a hamlet tucked away in a remote Ardennes region, has a church
whose beautiful architecture and mural paintings make it one of the country's art
treasures. Most of the ceiling frescoes were discovered and restored by Edmond
Goergen in 1952. The text is accompanied by thirty-five photographic plates.

# Cuisine

909   **Luxemburg bei Tisch.** (Luxembourg at table.)
Fernand Hoffmann.   Luxembourg: Imprimerie Saint-Paul, 1988.
4th ed. 339p.

This is the fourth, completely revised and enlarged edition since the volume's successful first publication in 1963. Hoffmann draws a portrait of Luxembourg cuisine including the popular white wines and the typical fruit spirits. His intention was not to provide a traditional cookery book or even a gastronomic guide, but above all to entertain.

910   **Le livre de la cuisine luxembourgeoise. Das Kochbuch aus Luxemburg.** (The book of Luxembourg cooking.)
Pol Tousch.   Luxembourg: Pol Tousch, 1980. 143p.

Luxembourg cooking has been influenced by the economic constraints of the past. Therefore it is simple, and makes use of regional products. This publication, with its more than 100 recipes which range from starters to desserts, encourages the reader to try some old and typical Luxembourg recipes in this era of fast food and the microwave.

911   **A matter of taste. A selection of favourite recipes from the hearts and homes of the members of the American Women's Club of Luxembourg.**
Compiled and edited by the Cookbook committee of the American
Women's Club of Luxembourg.   Luxembourg: American Women's
Club, 1994. 313p.

Represents an inspiring and out-of-the ordinary cookbook, for which a large number of contributors have participated in the collection, taste-testing and selection processes. The most interesting pages are those on 'Regional Cuisine' because here the reader will find the preparation of typical Luxembourg dishes explained in the English language, which is hard to find elsewhere.

912 **Kachen a Brachen: Aus der Luxemburger Küche.** (Cooking and
pottering about in the kitchen: about Luxembourg cuisine.)
Tun Nosbusch. Luxembourg: Editions Guy Binsfeld, 1992. 145p.

This colourful cookery book addresses people who consider cooking as a hobby. By
explaining every recipe in detail, the author's aim is to make sure that the dish can be
cooked without any previous knowledge. The book contains more than 200 recipes
which are often illustrated and are typical of current Luxembourg cuisine.

913 **Die Weisswein-Küche.** (White-wine cooking.)
Paul Thiltges, Gaston Junck. Luxembourg: Editions Guy Binsfeld,
1987. 173p.

Presented in an original format (with a corkscrew inside), this publication was issued
after a public competition organized by the cooperative wine cellars of
Wormeldingen. The participants had to send in recipes which used Luxembourg wine.
The reader will find exactly 173 recipes which range from starters to desserts.

# Sport and Recreation

914  **Ligue des Associations Sportives Estudiantines Luxembourgeoises (L.A.S.E.L.) 1938-1988.**
(League of the Luxembourg Students Sport Associations [L.A.S.E.L.] 1938-88.)
Edited by Laurent Fautsch.   Luxembourg: Imprimerie Saint-Paul, 1988. 458p.

For the L.A.S.E.L.'s fiftieth anniversary (1938-88), this commemorative volume was published. It chronicles the outstanding events that contributed to the birth, development and evolution of school sports. This vivid report is illustrated with numerous photographs.

915  **Spill a Sport. Ligue des associations sportives de l'enseignement primaire (LASEP).** (Play and sport. League of the Sport Associations of Primary Schools [LASEP].)
Luxembourg: Imprimerie Centrale, 1989. 156p.

This commemorative publication of the LASEP (Ligue des associations sportives de l'enseignement primaire – League of the Sport Associations of Primary Schools) summarizes the objectives the founders had in 1964. It is useful above all for gym teachers and coaches, as it presents many illustrated exercises that can be carried out without any large effort or expense. While the first part of this guide concerns physical games in general, the second part demonstrates and explains the basic movements in different sports, such as soccer, basketball and swimming.

916  **Fédération Luxembourgeoise de Football 1908-1983.** (Luxembourg Soccer Federation 1908-83.)
Luxembourg: Imprimerie Saint-Paul, 1983. 309p.

Luxembourg's most important sport federation celebrated its seventy-fifth anniversary by issuing this commemorative volume. Besides reviewing the federation's history and classifications since the first national championship in the 1909-10 season, the volume also includes numerous illustrations from past and present.

917  **75 ans: Fédération du sport cycliste luxembourgeois 1917-1992**.
(Seventy-five years of the Luxembourg cycling sport federation
1917-92.)
Luxembourg: Imprimerie Watgen, 1992. 208p.

Cycling holds an important place in Luxembourg's sporting history. This
commemorative volume which celebrates the seventy-fifth anniversary of Luxembourg's
cycling federation (1917-92) recounts, after a short, historical introduction, the past
successes of Luxembourg cyclists such as Nic Frantz, Charly Gaul and Elsy Jacobs,
while providing detailed information on the federation and its members.

918  **Tour de Luxembourg 1935-1990**. (The Luxembourg race, 1935-90.)
Gast Zangerlé, Fernand Thill, Raymond Elcheroth, Henri Bressler.
Luxembourg: Imprimerie Saint-Paul, 1990. 255p.

This collective volume, issued by the same authors that wrote the volumes of
*Sternstunden des Luxemburger Sports* (Highlights of Luxembourg sport) (q.v.)
reviews the forty-nine races of the 'Tour de Luxembourg'. Well illustrated, the book
particularly addresses those who want to recapture the legs they followed on the road
or while listening to the radio. An appendix lists the final classifications since 1935
and the racing cyclists who have won the most legs since this race began.

919  **50e Anniversaire 1932-1982. Fédération Luxembourgeoise de
Canöe-Kayak.** (Fiftieth anniversary 1932-82. Luxembourg canoe and
kayak federation.)
Luxembourg: Fédération luxembourgeoise de Canoë-Kayak, 1982.
unpaginated.

To celebrate its fiftieth anniversary (1932-82) the Luxembourg canoe and kayak
federation issued this commemorative publication. Besides a historical overview, it
briefly describes its member clubs.

920  **Fédération luxembourgeoise de basketball: Lëtzebuerger
Basketballverband 1933-1993. 60 Joër.** (Sixty years of the
Luxembourg Basketball Federation, 1933-93.)
Fédération luxembourgeoise de basketball.  Luxembourg: Imprimerie
Print-Service, 1993. 240p.

To commemorate its sixtieth anniversary, the Luxembourg basketball federation
published this vivid pictorial account of its success story. Founded in 1933, the
association's numbers had swelled to nearly 4,000 members by 1993 when this sport
was becoming one of the most popular in Luxembourg. This volume includes scoring
tables of national championships from 1933-93, and contributions on referees, the
training centre, the federation and its organs as well as one aspect that has determined
the marketing of this sport since the 1960s: the participation of foreign players.

921  **75 Joër 1919-1994 Lëtzebuerger Scouten.** (Seventy-five years,
1919-94, of the Luxembourg boy scouts.)
Luxembourg: Imprimerie Saint-Paul, 1994. 216p.

This commemorative volume was published for the seventy-fifth anniversary (1919-
94) of Luxembourg's boy scouts, a Catholic association that united with

Luxembourg's girl guides in 1994. It recounts the eventful history of that association and includes, among other things: a report on the chief scout Robert Baden Powell's stay in Luxembourg in 1929; a short chronological review of the institution's seventy-five-year history; and contributions from the association's sections and groups all over the country. The book is well illustrated and entirely written in Luxembourgish.

922 **Sternstunden des Luxemburger Sports.** (Highlights of Luxembourg sport.)
Armando Bausch, Gaston Zangerlé, Pol Schmoetten, Henri Bressler, Gaston Hoffmann, Jean-Paul Kolbusch.    Luxembourg: Imprimerie Saint-Paul, 1988-95. 4 vols.

Like the Luxembourgish language, sport in Luxembourg is often seen as an important factor in reinforcing the unity of the Grand Duchy. By an overall review of the sportsmen and teams that have created Luxembourg's sporting history, the authors have set out to perpetuate the great moments, but also to stimulate future generations to create new sporting highlights which become rarer and rarer. The times when Josy Barthel, Charly Gaul and others were able to compete with sportsmen all over the world are definitively over. The work is richly illustrated with photographs from the archives of the Ministry of Sports or from various national and international newspapers. The first volume provides a portrait of Luxembourg sportsmen who have won gold medals at either the Olympic Games, world or European championships or who have broken world or European records. The second volume describes outstanding performances by Luxembourg soccer teams and Luxembourg professional players abroad. Another section in the second volume provides an account of performances in professional athletics and gymnastics. In 1990 the third volume appeared, which deals with cycling, walking, athletics and fencing. Volume four, which deals with more recent, mostly post-war disciplines, was published in 1995.

923 **Josy Barthel: la fameuse histoire d'une consécration olympique.**
(Josy Barthel: the great story of an Olympic consecration.)
Gaston Zangerlé.    Luxembourg: Imprimerie Saint-Paul, 1992. 128p.

The day a Luxembourg sportsman wins an Olympic Gold Medal is a historic date for the whole nation. The first, and so far only time that this occurred was at the Olympics in Helsinki in 1952, when Josy Barthel won the 1,500m race. This publication retraces the life and professional career of Barthel, who died prematurely in 1994. The historic 1,500m race held in Helsinki is narrated in detail and the book, which is available in French and German, is illustrated with numerous pictures.

924 **Charly Gaul: der Engel der Berge und seine Zeit.** (Charly Gaul: the angel of the mountains and his time.)
Gaston Zangerlé.    Luxembourg: Imprimerie Saint-Paul, 1988. 128p.

Charly Gaul is Luxembourg's most popular and successful professional cyclist. His elegant style of climbing made him one of the foremost mountain specialists of all time. Zangerlé sets out to record his career which began in 1949, came to a climax in 1958 when he won the 'Tour de France' and finally ended in 1965. The book addresses both those who want to remember the performances of Gaul and a younger public, who are interested in finding out more about him.

925 **L'ange de la montagne. Charly Gaul: la véridique histoire.**
(The angel of the mountain. Charly Gaul: the true history.)
Jean-Paul Ollivier.   Paris: Editions Glénart, 1993. 250p.

Jean-Paul Ollivier, a French journalist and expert on cycle racing, highlights the epic dimension of Luxembourg's greatest cyclist, Charly Gaul, who is also known as the angel of the mountain. The author quotes from interviews he had with the former champion and vividly recounts the different stages of his career as well as his most outstanding performances. The appendix lists the prizes won by Charly Gaul from 1949 to 1965.

926 **L'ange qui aimait la pluie.** (The angel who enjoyed the rain.)
Christian Laborde.   Paris: Editions Albin Michel, 1994. 199p.

No other cyclist climbed mountains in such a way as Luxembourg's specialist cycle-racer, Charly Gaul. The author of this book chose the form of the novel to commemorate this exceptional sportsman. He draws a memorable portrait of this most enigmatic member of the main bunch and allows the reader to experience the fabulous peripeteias of Gaul's outstanding performances, such as in the 1958 Tour de France.

# Libraries, Archives and Museums

927 **Les instituts culturels.** (Cultural institutes.)
Jul Christophory. In: *Mémorial 1989.* Luxembourg: Les
Publications mosellanes, 1988, p. 395-407.

Presents a historical survey of the material and scientific development of the main
cultural institutions of the Luxembourg state over a century and a half, accompanied
by charts and diagrams.

928 **Dokumentation in Luxemburg.** (Documentation in Luxembourg.)
Jul Christophory. In: *Nationalbibliotheken im Jahr 2000: Festgabe
für Günther Pflug zum 65. Geburtstag.* (National libraries in the year
2000: festivities for the sixty-fifth birthday of Günther Pflug.)
Frankfurt, GDR: Deutsche Bibliothek, 1988, p. 65-79.

Provides a general survey of the library situation in Luxembourg in the late 1980s.

929 **Répertoire des bibliothèques scientifiques ou populaires au
Grand-Duché de Luxembourg.** (Repertory of scientific and popular
libraries in the Grand Duchy of Luxembourg.)
Emile van der Vekene. Luxembourg: Imprimerie Saint-Paul, 1973.
2nd ed. 69p.

This directory lists forty-three libraries, in each case indicating the name, address,
owner, type, stocks and collections, purchase capacities, name of the chief librarian,
opening hours, conditions of access, rules of usage, catalogues, year of foundation and
publications. There is an index of the range of the collection under subject headings.
In 1973 Luxembourg had only one library counting 480,000 volumes or more, three
with 60,000 volumes or more, one with 50,000, two with 40,000, one with 30,000, and
three with 20,000 volumes or more. There were in all about 1,100,000 volumes,
seventy-four per cent of which being located in Luxembourg city. This volume
represents the only precise description of the library situation for the period.

930 **Guide des bibliothèques luxembourgeoises.** (Guide to Luxembourg's libraries.)
Emile Thoma, Pascal Nicolay. Luxembourg: Bibliothèque nationale, 1995. 2nd rev. ed. 220p.

In 1990, on the occasion of the first 'Journée des Bibliothèques Luxembourgeoises' (Luxembourg Library Day) at Bourglinster, the national library published a provisional edition of such a guide to Luxembourg's libraries which met with an enthusiastic reponse in professional circles. This new version, based on a recent questionnaire, takes stock of the current situation on the Luxembourg information market and provides full details on the collections and services of: state and municipal libraries; foreign cultural centre libraries; the European Union libraries at Kirchberg; public and private specialized libraries; and about thirty-two secondary-school libraries. This very useful compendium also includes a select bibliography.

931 **Répertoire et étude des bibliothèques de l'enseignement secondaire et secondaire technique au Grand-Duché de Luxembourg.** (Repertory and study of secondary and technical secondary school libraries in the Grand Duchy of Luxembourg.)
Pascal Nicolay. Degree in librarianship thesis, L'Institut d'Enseignement Supérieur Social des Sciences de l'Information et de la Documentation de la Communauté Française de Belgique, Brussels, 1994. 258p. bibliog.

Nicolay's thesis is an interesting and exhaustive synopsis of the library situation in public and private grammar schools and vocational post-primary institutions.

932 **Luxembourg.**
Martha Brogan. In: *Research guide to libraries and archives in the Low Countries.* New York: Greenwood Press, 1991, p. 476-96.

Represents the best English-language guide currently available on the Luxembourg library scene, based on personal interviews and data collected from 1987 to 1989.

933 **Les origines de la Bibliothèque nationale du Grand-Duché de Luxembourg.** (The origins of the National Library of the Grand Duchy of Luxembourg.)
Alphonse Sprunck. Luxembourg: Imprimerie Saint-Paul, 1954. 61p.

The suppression of the Jesuits in 1773 entailed an auction of their library stock of about 4,000 books. The annexation of Luxembourg to the French Republic in 1795 meant the confiscation of all the books belonging to religious institutions for the benefit of the central administration. In 1798 all these books were brought together in the library of the newly created Central School, which served as the basis of the present National Library.

934 **La Bibliothèque nationale de Luxembourg: son histoire, ses collections, ses services.** (The National Library of Luxembourg: its history, its collections, its services.)
Luxembourg: Imprimerie Centrale, 1994. 103p. bibliog.

After a general statement of the National Library's situation at the beginning of 1995 and a short historical overview, each of the different services offered by the National Library to its readers are dealth with, such as the general and Luxembourg stock, the international lending department and, available since 1993, the media library. The numerous photographs, which show the building and its premises together with the quotations throughout the book, bear testimony to the convivial atmosphere inside this cultural institution.

935 **La Réserve Précieuse 1970-1980.** (The Rare Collection Department 1970-80.)
Bibliothèque Nationale. Esch-sur-Alzette, Luxembourg: Editpress, 1981. 151p.

Published on the occasion of an exhibition at the National Library, this catalogue provides a general overview of the 1970-80 acquisitions made by the curator of the Rare Collections Department, Emil van der Vekene. As a mirror and display case of the National Library, this department also created new collections such as portraits, posters and precious book-bindings.

936 **Archives de la Section historique de l'Institut grand-ducal. Tome 1.** (General Description of the Holdings kept at the National Archives of the Grand Duchy of Luxembourg and at the Historical Section of the Grand-Ducal Institute. Vol. 1.)
Paul Spang. Luxembourg: Imprimerie Beffort, 1995. 754p.
(Publications de la Section Historique de l'Institut Grand-Ducal: 112).

Paul Spang, former director of the State Archives, compiled this first volume of an overall inventory of the holdings and collections kept at the National Archives (its new name since December 1988). It will be completed by a second volume in the prestigious series of the 'Publications de la Section Historique de l'Institut Grand-Ducal de Luxembourg' on the occasion of the 150th anniversary of this institute. The introduction is entitled, 'Quand les Archives racontent les archives' (When Archives tell the history of the archives). It is followed by an explanation of the different classification systems whilst the last part takes stock of the present situation and briefly presents the different administrative and political files, charts and papers according to their origin, mainly cloisters, convents and noble families.

937 **Les Archives du Gouvernement du Grand-Duché de Luxembourg: inventaires sommaires.**
(The Archives of the Government of the Grand Duchy of Luxembourg: summary inventories.)
Pierre Ruppert. Luxembourg: Bück, 1910. 328p.

Ruppert's work is chronologically ordered, and then grouped according to subject matter, with an index of headwords. The appendix contains a summary survey of the documents referring to Luxembourg that are kept in the State Archives of Belgium and France and in the Archives of the historical section of the Institut Grand-Ducal. References are made in footnotes to legal, constitutional and administrative history.

938 **Les Archives de l'Etat du Grand-Duché de Luxembourg et l'histoire locale.** (State Archives of the Grand Duchy of Luxembourg and local history archives.)
Antoine May. *Hémecht*, vol. 16, no. 2 (1964), p. 111-53.

Written by the State archivist, this is a short guide to the amazing riches of the archives, which contain: early documents that refer to the country as a duchy; material concerning the former provincial and departmental administration; 19th-century documents on the government of the Dutch kings; and more recent documents on Luxembourg's national dynasty. Depositories hold material from abbeys, convents, cloisters, seigniories and justices, localities and families. In addition to the technical services it offers, the State Archives also runs an educational service, which is intended to familiarize the young generation with the documents of the past.

939 **Les archives du Conseil de Luxembourg. Etude archivéconomique.** (The archives of the Governing Council of Luxembourg.)
Antoine May. Luxembourg: Archives de l'Etat, 1967. 119p. (Etudes Archivéconomiques, 1).

The Provincial Council was the most important institution of the ancient Duchy of Luxembourg and County of Chiny. For three and a half centuries it was the highest administrative and judicial authority of the Duchy of Luxembourg, which covered four times the area of the present-day Grand Duchy. Originating from a council of vassals, its influence grew from the second half of the 13th century onwards. In 1444 Philip the Good set up a new council; in 1531 Charles V reorganized it completely as the Provincial Council. Local documents usually refer to it as the Council of Luxembourg. It was suppressed in 1795 by the armies of the French Republic, but its archives survive and are described in this book.

940 **Répertoire analytique des pièces de procédure fournies par inventaire (1724-1795).** (Analytical index of documents of proceedings provided by inventory, 1724-95.)
Antoine May. Luxembourg: Archives de l'Etat, 1964. 125p. (Inventaire des Archives du Conseil Provincial et Souverain, I).

This is a catalogue of documents which form part of the Archives of the Council of the Duchy of Luxembourg. The collection is made up of 220 bundles of holdings. May's book is a parallel work to Marcel Bourguignon's *Inventaires du Conseil de Luxembourg. II. Procès. 1720-1795* (Inventories of the Council of Luxembourg. II. Cases. 1720-95) (Brussels: Archives Générales du Royaume, 1961), which catalogues the papers stored in Arlon, Belgium (part of the former Duchy of Luxembourg). These documents include title-deeds, procurations, replications and rejoinders of prosecutors and lawyers, inventories, reports of proceedings and records of evidence. An index of places, persons and subject matter is provided.

941 **Regesten des Archivs der Herren von Bourscheid.** (Archived excerpts from the Lords of Bourscheid.)
François Decker.   Bourscheid, Luxembourg: Les Amis du château de Bourscheid, 1989. 3 vols.

The sphere of activity of the lords of the Bourscheid castle (40km to the north of Luxembourg) concerned not only the area around Bourscheid, but also the Duchy of Luxembourg and Jülich, the Ahr valley and the region around the Moselle, Saar and Rhine. The first two volumes of this work, which cover the periods 1224-1558 and 1558-1626, contain rare and often unique documents whereas the third volume is a name and town register. The work contains the archive material (documents, records, certificates, papers and deeds) that were moved from Bourscheid to Gemünden in the Hunsrück in 1802 before being examined in detail in 1962. These mediaeval documents have a lasting value because they should be able to provide answers to numerous questions and therefore make people more aware of their history and its relevance to everyday life, in this case in the Moselle area.

942 **Trésors du Musée national d'histoire et d'art.** (Treasures from the National Museum of History and Art.)
Luxembourg: Musée national d'histoire et d'art, 1989. unpaginated.

The first medal cabinet was created in 1839, but there was no museum to house it until 1939 when the Musée d'histoire et d'art (Museum of History and Art) was lodged in the building it currently occupies on the corner of Fishmarket Square. In 1988, a definitive statute gave the museum its autonomy, which it had had to share with the Museum of Natural Sciences for decades, and it became officially known as the Musée nationale d'histoire et d'art (National Museum of History and Art). The collections are displayed in more than 150 rooms, many of which are located in aristocratic houses dating from the 17th to the 19th centuries. Its main sections are Pre- and Protohistory, Gallo-Roman and Merovingian Antiquities, Fine Arts, Decorative and Popular Arts and Numismatics.

943 **Musée National d'Histoire et d'Art Luxembourg.** (National Museum of History and Fine Art, Luxembourg.)
Musée National d'Histoire et d'Art Luxembourg.    Tielt, Belgium: Lannoo, 1990. 128p. (Musea Nostra).

The 'Musea Nostra' series has already published a series of volumes about various museums all over Belgium. This sumptuous illustrated volume concerns the Museum of History and Fine Arts in Luxembourg. After a historical survey by its director, Paul Reiles, the various sections of the institution are dealt with, such as the archaeological section with its important prehistoric collections and the holdings of the Medal Cabinet, introduced by the internationally renowned expert, Raymond Weiller. The largest section of the volume provides an account of the 'Vie Luxembourgeoise' (Life in Luxembourg) section that illustrates the economic, artistic, social, religious and intellectual aspects of the life of Luxembourgers from the 16th century to the beginning of the 20th century.

944 **National Museum of History and Fine Arts Luxembourg.**
Edited by the Museum Education Service of the National Museum for
History and Fine Arts.   Luxembourg: Joseph Beffort, 1984. 47p.

This thin English guidebook shows the way through the various departments of the
National Museum and highlights the most important objects displayed in the rooms.
The National Museum of History and Fine Arts is located on the corner of Fishmarket
Square, which was the centre of the early mediaeval settlement, and it presents the
rich and varied history of the country from prehistoric times to the 20th century.

945 **Peinture sous verre.** (Underglass painting.)
Luxembourg: Musée d'Histoire et d'Art, 1977. 111p.

With its 386 pieces, the collection of underglass painting in the Luxembourg Museum
of History and Fine Arts (which became the National Museum of History and Fine
Arts in 1988) is one of the richest in western Europe, although none of these pictures
was actually made in Luxembourg. They originate mainly from Upper Bavarian,
Southern German, Black Forest and Alsatian workshops. The oldest picture dates from
1710 and represents the Immaculate Conception. Another old stained glass dates from
1769 and portrays Pope Clement XIV. Most of the popular paintings belong to the first
half of the 19th century. The pictures are classified by region, by place and, where
possible, by workshop.

946 **Les époques gallo-romaine et mérovingienne au Musée d'Histoire
et d'Art, Luxembourg.** (The Gallo-Roman and Merovingian periods
in the Museum of History and Art of Luxembourg.)
Gérard Thill.   Luxembourg: Marché-aux-Poissons, 1972. 2nd ed. 35p.

The Roman occupation of Luxembourg lasted about five centuries, from 53 BC until
the Frankish invasion of the 5th century AD. There are still many remains of that long
period in Luxembourg. Discoveries at ancient sites reflect the daily life, economy,
religion and funerary customs of Luxembourg's Gallo-Roman ancestors. The Frankish
period also lasted nearly five centuries, ending in the 10th century with Sigefroi, the
first count of Luxembourg. The remains of the Frankish epoch are less numerous than
those of the Gallo-Roman time: the Franks' wooden houses disappeared without
leaving traces but some large cemeteries have been discovered. The artefacts found in
these graves include typical weapons, some household equipment and, more rarely, a
beautiful brooch or a piece of adornment. This booklet, which includes eighty-eight
black-and-white photographs, is a short guide to the departments of Gallo-Roman and
Frankish antiquities in the Luxembourg Museum. It provides a detailed commentary in
French and summaries in German and English.

947 **Pierres sculptées et inscriptions de l'époque romaine: catalogue.**
(Sculptured stone-work and Roman inscriptions: catalogue.)
Eugénie Wilhelm.   Luxembourg: Musée d'Histoire et d'Art, 1974.
160p. map.

Luxembourg once abounded with sculptured stones and monuments which Roman
landowners erected in their fields and living places. In the Middle Ages most of these
monuments were damaged or destroyed. Nevertheless, the Luxembourg Museum is
extremely rich in such artefacts of the Gallo-Roman past. This systematic inventory of
its collections represents a valuable contribution to the international archaeological
*Corpus Signorum Imperii Romani* (Inventory of Imperial Roman Inscriptions).

948 **La verrerie de l'époque romaine au Musée d'Histoire et d'Art, Luxembourg.** (The glassware of the Roman period in the Museum of History and Art, Luxembourg.)
Eugénie Wilhelm. Luxembourg: Musée d'Histoire et d'Art, 1969. 84p.
This exhibition catalogue describes glass works from the first four centuries AD. They originate from the Mediterranean area and were found mostly on the territory of the Grand Duchy, especially in the 'Gutland' (the southern area). In 1968 the remnants of an ancient glassware factory were discovered at Titelberg: it was probably worked for the Gallic aristocracy. This catalogue offers a detailed description of 131 finds, with 5 colour photographs and many black-and-white reproductions.

949 **Bronzes figurés de l'époque romaine au Musée d'Histoire et d'Art, Luxembourg.** (Bronze statuettes and figurines of the Roman period in the Museum of History and Art of Luxembourg.)
Eugénie Wilhelm. Luxembourg: Marché-aux-Poissons, 1971. 59p.
Most of the artefacts found in Luxembourg are products of provincial craftsmanship. Besides human figures, they represent the lion, panther, goat, cock, dog, eagle and dolphin. One single statuette represents the Gallic goddess, Epona. Unfortunately, many interesting Luxembourg finds of the past century are now in foreign museums, such as that of Mainz, Germany. In this catalogue, Wilhelm provides a detailed description of 124 pieces, and mentions some interesting objects which are now held abroad or in private collections. She also provides a survey of zoomorphous fibulae accumulated in the Luxembourg Museum. Black-and-white photographs reproduce the objects in natural size.

950 **L'industrialisation du Luxembourg de 1800 à 1914. Musée d'Histoire et d'Art – Luxembourg.** (The industrialization of Luxembourg from 1800 to 1914. History and Art Museum – Luxembourg.)
Jean-Luc Mousset. Mamer, Luxembourg: Graphic-Press, 1994. 2nd ed. 175p.
In order to deepen the subject concerning the industrialization of Luxembourg from 1800 to 1914, Jean-Luc Mousset decided to issue a guide and catalogue extending the limits imposed by a permanent exhibition held in the History and Art Museum in Luxembourg. After a short historical summary of the most important stages of Luxembourg's industrialization in the 19th and early 20th centuries, the author describes, one by one, in text and illustrations, each of the objects shown at the exhibition.

951 **145 musées dans la région européenne. Grand-Duché de Luxembourg, Lorraine, Sarre, Rhénanie-Palatinat et Sud-Est de la Belgique.** (145 museums in the European region. Grand Duchy of Luxembourg, Lorraine, Sarre, Rhineland-Palatinate and southeast of Belgium.)
Antoinette Lorang. Luxembourg: Editions Guy Binsfeld, 1988. 168p.
This museum guide presents 145 museums from all over Luxembourg, a part of Germany (the Saarland and Rheinland-Pfalz), three French 'départements' (the

Meuse, Moselle and Meurthe et Moselle) and, finally, the three Belgian 'provinces' of Liège, Namur and Luxembourg. In addition to practical information, the reader will find precise descriptions of small local historical museums and specific collections as well as the well-known art, and regional history, museums. This guide, in handy paperback format, was conceived to introduce the regional museums to a larger public.

952 **Tous les musées de Belgique et du Grand Duché de Luxembourg.**
(All the museums of Belgium and of the Grand Duchy of
Luxembourg.)
Brigitte Monneaux. Brussels: Le Cri, 1989. 383p.

Monneaux's useful guide lists all the Belgian and Luxembourg museums and also includes a brief, sixteen-page (p. 252-68) non-illustrated summary from Antoinette Lorang's guide, *145 musées dans la région européenne. Grand-Duché de Luxembourg, Lorraine, Sarre, Rhénanie-Palatinat et Sud-Est de la Belgique* (145 museums in the European region. Grand Duchy of Luxembourg, Lorraine, Sarre, Rhineland-Palatinate and southeast of Belgium) (q.v.).

953 **Kulturrouten durch das Grossherzogtum Luxemburg.** (Culture
routes through the Grand Duchy of Luxembourg.)
Christoph Becker and Georges Calteux. Luxembourg: Imprimerie
Saint-Paul, 1994. 144p.

A useful guide to the cultural identity of some regions of Luxembourg. Each of the eleven routes described (eight routes can be made on foot and three by cycle) focuses on a particular cultural area, usually concerning architecture or relics. With subjects such as Roman buildings, the extension of the Maria Theresian style and industrial culture, this pocket guide conveys the importance of the architecture of the countryside in Luxembourg. This volume also contains small colour photographs, reproductions of regional maps and an appendix containing literature related to the routes presented.

# Manuscripts and Rare Books

954 **Bertels Abbas Delineavit 1544-1607. Les dessins de l'abbé Bertels.**
(The drawings of the abbot Bertels 1544-1607.)
Paul Spang. Luxembourg: Imprimerie Saint-Paul, 1984. 255p.

Spang presents reproductions of all the known drawings of Jean Bertels (1544-1607)
that are held in Luxembourg. Considered the first historian of Luxembourg, Bertels
was appointed abbot of the historic Saint Willibrord abbey in Echternach by King
Philippe II of Spain in 1595. Jean Bertels created paintings which depict the
Luxembourg towns and everyday life of the period. This publication contains a
French/German biography and makes the unique, iconographic documentation
available to a wider audience.

955 **Handschriften und ihre Schreiber: ein Blick in das Scriptorium
der Abtei Echternach.** (Manuscripts and their writers: a glance at the
scriptorium of the abbey of Echternach.)
Paul Spang. Luxembourg: Imprimerie Bourg-Bourger, 1967. 95p.
bibliog.

Spang outlines the history of the Echternach library and describes the work that went
on in the scriptorium and cloister library. The volume illustrates the production of a
mediaeval manuscript from the preparation of the parchment to the detailed craft of
the writer. The final chapter provides a pictorial account of life in the first half of the
11th century.

956 **Das Goldene Evangelienbuch von Echternach.** (The Golden Gospel
Book of Echternach.)
Egon Verheyen, edited by Ludwig Grote. Munich, FRG: Prestel,
1963. 96p. (Bilder aus der Deutschen Vergangenheit, 22).

For 250 years the *Codex aureus* was the property of the imperial abbey of Echternach.
In 1795 the monks had to flee the French Revolution, taking along their most precious
manuscripts, thus the *Codex* came to the Benedictines at Erfurt and was later sold to

Duke Ernst II von Sachsen-Gotha-Altenburg. In 1955 the Germanisches National-museum acquired the precious piece. In 1956 the Prestel publishing company published the *Codex* in the form of an art book, a masterpiece of Salian illumination and mediaeval theology. This book is a shorter and smaller version of the original publication, with reproductions in colour and black-and-white.

957  **Katalog der Inkunabeln der Nationalbibliothek Luxemburg.**
(Catalogue of the incunabula of the National Library of Luxembourg.)
Emile van der Vekene.   Luxembourg: Sankt-Paulus-Druckerei, 1970.
81p.

This catalogue, with 21 photographic plates, records 132 titles, providing details on their owners and origins, and briefly describing the particular features of each. Today, the National Library stores 140 incunabula.

958  **Copie ou fac-similé?** (Copy or facsimile?)
Bibliothèque Nationale de Luxembourg.   Esch-sur-Alzette,
Luxembourg: Kremer-Müller, 1988. 163p.

Modern reproduction techniques nowadays make possible the creation of facsimiles (exact reproductions of an original written document or printed book) that can scarcely be distinguished from the original. These facsimiles not only allow better conservation of the original manuscript, but they open up the beauty of ancient and mediaeval art to a wider public. In this catalogue, Emile van der Vekene, curator of the Rare Collections department at the National Library, presents ninety facsimiles of important manuscripts or rare prints.

959  **Bemerkenswerte Einbände in der Nationalbibliothek zu
Luxemburg, ausgewählt un beschrieben.** (Remarkable bookbindings at the National Library in Luxembourg, selected and described.)
Emile van der Vekene.   Luxembourg: Nationalbibliothek, 1972. 142p.
bibliog.

The author presents in chronological order sixty-two old bindings, of which the oldest date from the early 16th century. Most come from French and German workshops. Van der Vekene could not trace any typical Luxembourg style of bookbinding, although most convent libraries had their own binding workshops. However, two remarkable volumes from the ateliers of J.-B. Beffort (1878) and of Jean Harles (1926) testify to high standards of local craftsmanship. The photographic plates are accompanied by short, bilingual captions in French and German.

960  **Reliures d'art du XXe siècle.** (Fine bookbindings of the 20th century.)
Bibliothèque nationale de Luxembourg.   Luxembourg: Imprimerie
Linden, 1994. 164p.

For more than twenty years, Emile van der Vekene, curator of the Rare Collections department of the National Library, has been collecting the most beautiful specimens of bookbindings from Luxembourg and the surrounding countries. This volume presents 70 illustrations in chronological order, selected from the National Library's collection of about 300 art and history bookbindings. Published at the same time as an exhibition organized for the fourth international fine bookbinding forum in April

1994, held in the National Library, the catalogue provides a short survey of the state of this fine art in the 20th century.

961 **Cent livres illustrés de l'époque 1890-1990.** (One hundred illustrated books from the period 1890-1990.)
Compiled by Emile van der Vekene. Luxembourg: Bibliothèque nationale, 1990. unpaginated.

This luxurious catalogue illustrates a selection of about 200 artists' illustrated books over a time span of 100 years (1890-1990). The books are presented in chronological order of their publication, although the first part of the century is poorly represented. Emile van der Vekene has added some bibliographical notes for each publication, as well as references to other bibliographies and exhibition catalogues.

962 **Les manuscrits à peintures de la Bibliothèque nationale de Luxembourg: catalogue descriptif et critique.** (The illuminated manuscripts of the National Library of Luxembourg: descriptive and critical catalogue.)
Blanche Weicherding-Goergen. *Publications de la Section Historique de l'Institut G.-D. de Luxembourg*, vol. 83 (1968). 140p.

The National Library of Luxembourg holds about twenty illuminated manuscripts ranging from the 11th to the 16th century. Most of them came from the famous abbeys of ancient Luxembourg – Echternach and Orval – while some were acquired by purchase and others were bequeathed. This book deals with the truly mediaeval illuminations, those dating from the 11th to the 15th century. The present stores go back to 1795: an inventory in 1798 mentions 224 manuscripts, but another in 1806 refers to only 137. By the beginning of the 19th century the National Library retained only a small part of its former riches. It slowly tried to make up for the losses by making astute purchases, and today it has 350 volumes of manuscripts, including modern ones. This catalogue is divided into three parts, covering the illuminations from Echternach and Orval, those of unknown origin and those from various donations.

963 **150 manuscrits précieux du 9e au 16e siècle conservés à la Bibliothèque nationale de Luxembourg.** (150 precious manuscripts from the 9th to the 16th century kept at the Luxembourg National Library.)
Jul Christophory. Luxembourg: Bibliothèque nationale, 1989. 311p. bibliog.

The Luxembourg National Library holds about 800 important manuscripts today, of which 150 date from the 9th to the 16th century and show interesting initials, miniatures or illuminations. Forty-eight of these works come from the renowned scriptorium of the abbey of Echternach, and seventy-three originate from Orval. Eighty-one Echternach codices and three Orval codices were taken away by the French occupants in 1802 and are kept at the Bibliothèque nationale de Paris. After a general introduction on the history and typology of the remaining collections, this catalogue presents, in chronological order, each manuscript and its technical particularities. Numerous statistical data, comparative tables, diagrams and colour reproductions convey a vivid impression of the wealth and splendour of this collection.

964   **De Vésale à Laënnec: Médecine et pharmacie dans les collections de la Bibliothèque nationale.** (From Vésale to Laënnec: medicine and pharmaceutics in the collections of the National Library.)
Edited by Claude Weber and Michael Walenta with the collaboration of Berthe Schneider.   Luxembourg: Bibliothèque nationale, 1995.
246p.

This splendid illustrated exhibition catalogue contains contributions from reputed specialists on the history of medicine and pharmaceutics, and emphasizes the richness and variety of the 'Fonds Ancien' of the National Library in Luxembourg. Bibliographical description and expert comment on the exhibits help to familiarize the reader with the great minds of the medical and pharmacological sciences from the 16th century to the beginning of the 19th century.

# Mass Media

## Newspapers and periodicals

965 **The Germanic press of Europe: an aid to research.**
Icko Iben. Münster, FRG: Fahle, 1965. 146p. maps. bibliog.
(Studien zur Publizistik: Bremer Reihe, Bd. 5).
The section on the Luxembourg press (p. 31-37) includes a table of Luxembourg holdings, primarily those of the Bibliothèque nationale, of ten newspapers. The first date of publication, owners, editors and circulation are provided in each case. Secondary literature is listed on p. 34-35. The first Luxembourg newspaper, *La Clef du Cabinet des Princes, un Recueil Historique et Politique sur la Matière du Temps* (The Key to the Cabinet of Princes, a Historical and Political Collection on the Subject of Time) began publication in 1704.

966 **Zeitung in Luxemburg: chronologischer Uberblick.** (Newspapers in Luxembourg: a chronological survey.)
Evy Friedrich. Luxembourg: Imprimerie Bourg-Bourger, 1975. 31p.
Friedrich deals with the Luxembourg newspapers that appeared from 1704 to 1848 in some detail whilst only summarily sketching the rest in this booklet. This volume's coverage is to be completed by a second part which will list all the publishers, titles, periods of publication, printers and publishers. In 1848 press censorship was abolished, allowing for the development of newspapers in Luxembourg. The author does not claim that the volume's reference lists are exhaustive, as the National Library and the State Archives do not have complete collections of all the items. Friedrich based his work on Martin Blum's *Geschichtlicher Rückblick auf die im Grossherzogtum Luxemburg bisher erschienenen Zeitungen und Zeitschriften. Ein Beitrag zur Kulturgeschichte des Luxemburger Landes* (Historical survey of the newspapers and periodicals published in the Grand Duchy of Luxembourg. A contribution to the cultural history of Luxembourg) (Luxembourg: Worré-Mertens, 1899-1901. 2 vols.).

967 **L'économie de la presse écrite au Grand Duché de Luxembourg.**
(The economy of the written press in the Grand Duchy of
Luxembourg.)
Adrien Ries. Luxembourg: Imprimerie Saint-Paul, 1983. 131p.
The object of this study is to provide factual information on a little-known sector of
the Luxembourg economy: the paper, printing and publishing industry of Luxembourg
at the beginning of the 1980s.

968 **Eis Press: le journalisme en Luxembourg. Documents, 1925-75.**
(Our Press: journalism in Luxembourg. Documents, 1925-75.)
Association luxembourgeoise des journalistes. Esch-sur-Alzette,
Luxembourg: Imprimerie Coopérative Luxembourgeoise, 1975. 121p.
On the fiftieth anniversary of their association, Luxembourg journalists published this
commemorative brochure. It includes a wide spectrum of professional and literary
contributions, all concerned with interesting aspects of Luxembourg's press activities
in times of war and peace. On pages 120-21 is a list of the present members of the
association. Pages 11-21 contain the text of the press law of July 1869, which was
modified and completed by grand-ducal decrees in July and September 1945.

969 **125 Jahre *Luxemburger Wort*: Verjüngung und Strahlung; Vom
Wirken und Wachsen der Zeitung in den verflossenen 25 Jahren.**
(125 years of *Luxemburger Wort* [Luxembourg Word]: revival and
radiance; its activities and development over the last 25 years.)
Marcel Fischbach. Luxembourg: Sankt-Paulus-Druckerei, 1973.
220p.
This commemorative publication introduces the management and staff of
Luxembourg's Catholic daily, the *Luxemburger Wort* (Luxembourg Word) which
enjoys the greatest circulation figures in the country (c. 85,000). Fischbach considers
the following topics: the newspaper and the church; the development of the firm and
the modernization of its equipment and organization; the influence of the daily; and
the social solidarity of the *Luxemburger Wort* employees. The work concludes with a
detailed textual and photographic report on the company's celebration of its 125th
anniversary. Fischbach was a former editor of the *Luxemburger Wort*, before he
became a minister and ambassador of the Luxembourg government.

970 **Hundert Jahre *Luxemburger Wort*.** (The centenary of the
*Luxemburger Wort*.)
Pierre Grégoire. Luxembourg: Sankt-Paulus-Druckerei, 1948. 138p.
Grégoire's work is devoted to the changes brought about in the *Luxemburger Wort* by
the events of the Second World War, which caused great losses among its leading
personalities. The editors were arrested and sent to the concentration camp of
Oranienburg or Dachau, where in September 1942 Jean Origer and Jean-Baptiste Esch
lost their lives.

Mass Media. Newspapers and periodicals

971 **Das 'Luxemburger Wort für Wahrheit und Recht'. Die Geschichte einer Zeitung in der Geschichte eines Volkes.** (The *Luxembourg Word for Truth and Justice*: the history of a newspaper in the history of a people.)
Pierre Grégoire. Luxembourg: Sankt-Paulus-Druckerei, 1936. 288p.

On 20 March 1848 the government proclaimed the freedom of the press. Three days later the first issue of the *Luxemburger Wort* (Luxembourg Word) appeared. The newspaper's editor of the time, Grégoire, recounts the main stages of the newspaper's development, stressing the political and intellectual role of the Catholic daily. He also discusses the main editors, the importance of the staff, and the composition of the governing board.

972 **Schriftleiter-Silhouetten: Luxemburger Wortführer der Wahrheit.**
(Profiles of editors: Luxembourg spokesmen for truth.)
Pierre Grégoire. Luxembourg: Sankt-Paulus-Druckerei, 1973. 167p.

Grégoire commemorates some remarkable defenders of truth in the history of the Luxembourg press. He sketches portraits of seven leading editors of the *Luxemburger Wort*, the motto of which is 'For truth and justice'. He published this book for the 125th anniversary of the 1848 foundation of the newspaper. The seven personalities described are Edouard Michelis, Jean-Nicolas Breisdorff, Jean-Baptiste Fallize, André Welter, Charles Lessel, Jean Origer and Jean-Baptiste Esch. The latter two died in German concentration camps.

973 **Tageblatt und Genossenschaftsdruckerei: 25 Jahre.** (*Tageblatt* [Daily Sheet] and the Cooperative Printing Office: twenty-five years.)
Esch-sur-Alzette, Luxembourg: Genossenschaftsdruckerei, 1953. 208p.

This book, published on the occasion of the twenty-fifth anniversary of the socialist daily paper, *Tageblatt* (Daily Sheet), offers a retrospective survey of the management and staff of the printing shop and sketches the highlights of its political and ideological commitment to the freedom of the press and to cooperative solidarity.

974 **40 Joer: Zeitung vum Lëtzebuerger Vollek.** (For forty years: newspaper of the Luxembourg people.)
Luxembourg: Coopérative Ouvrière de Presse et d'Editions, 1986. 83p.

The Luxembourg Communist Party newspaper was issued for the first time just after the Second World War in 1946. For its fortieth anniversary, which was celebrated in 1986, the editors decided to publish a brochure featuring articles and extracts originally included in the *Zeitung vum Lëtzebuerger Vollek* (Newspaper of the Luxembourg People) of the 1940s to 1980s. These articles provide an insight into how the historical events were described and interpreted in the Luxembourg Communist press.

975 **D'Wäschfra: Histoire d'un journal satirique.** (The Washerwoman: history of a satirical weekly.)
Marc Thiel. Luxembourg: Editions Forum, 1993. 302p.

*D'Wäschfra* (The Washerwoman – the name of the famous old gossiper), published between 1868 and 1884, was the first Luxembourg satirical weekly. This publication was known for its virulent anti-clericalism on the one hand and for the support it gave to civil servants and teachers on the other. In this study, the young historian, Marc Thiel, retraces the history of this weekly and describes the economic, political and social aspects of the situation in the Grand Duchy during the second part of the 19th century. By relating details about the publication's founder, Thiel reveals *D'Wäschfra's* background. With a foreword by Gilbert Trausch and more than sixty reproductions of the most representative caricatures from the magazine, this book is the first academic study of satirical literature in Luxembourg.

976 **Luxemburger Wort für Wahrheit und Recht.** (Luxembourg Word for Truth and Justice.)
   Luxembourg: Sankt-Paulus-Druckerei, 1848- . daily.
The first edition of this oldest Luxembourg daily, the Catholic and conservative *Luxemburger Wort*, carries the date of 23 March 1848. It appeared three days after the freedom of the press was proclaimed by Grand Duke William II. At the outset it was published twice-weekly only. It was founded by the merchant, J. P. C. Würth, Karl Gerard Eyschen and Michel Jonas. Circulation in 1954 was 62,000; in 1961 this figure had reached 70,000; in 1979 it was 77,000; and by 1995 the figure was about 85,000. The newspaper is printed by the Imprimerie Saint-Paul, a stock company which combines all functions pertaining to the production and distribution of the newspaper and is the biggest printing firm in Luxembourg. The *Luxemburger Wort* addresses a very wide audience in the German and French languages and devotes special pages to culture (daily) and financial life (once-weekly) in Luxembourg. Its special weekly literary supplement, which has appeared since 1948, is called *Die Warte* (The Watchtower).

977 **Tageblatt, Zeitung fir Lëtzebuerg.** (*Tageblatt*, paper for Luxembourg.)
   Esch-sur-Alzette, Luxembourg: Editions Edi-print, 1913- . daily.
*Tageblatt* (Paper for the Day) was first published in 1913 by P. Schroell. It is the unofficial paper of the Luxembourg Socialist Party, and has been printed since 1927 by the Luxembourg Workers' Trade Union. Leading editors have included Hubert Clément, Pierre Krier and Jängi Fohrmann. Circulation in 1995 was 28,000. With its young and militantly progressive approach, the *Tageblatt* uses an often polemic and provocative style and has greatly increased its audience over the last years.

978 **Lëtzebuerger Journal.** (Luxembourg Journal.)
   Luxembourg: Imprimerie Centrale, 1880- . daily.
The *Lëtzebuerger Journal* was first published in 1880 under the name of *Obermoselzeitung* (Upper Moselle Paper). In 1945, the newspaper took on its present name. It is the mouthpiece of the Democratic Party. The circulation figure in 1961 was 10,000. More recently, in 1995, this figure was about 8,000. Printed by the Imprimerie Centrale S. A., it has a small but handy format of sixteen daily pages.

979 **Zeitung vum Lëtzebuerger Vollek.** (Paper of the Luxembourg people.)
   Luxembourg: COPE, 1946- . daily.
This is the official mouthpiece of the Luxembourg Communist Party (PCL), of strict Moscow obedience until November 1981. It was first published in 1946 and has a circulation of about 5,000 copies.

980   **Le Républicain Lorrain-Luxembourg**. (The Lorraine Republican –
      Luxembourg edition.)
      Metz, France: Le Républicain (group), 1961- . daily.

This regional edition from a French newspaper company based in Metz is the only
Luxembourg daily written entirely in French and has appeared since 1961. It is also
the only neutral, non-party-bound paper. It has local offices in Luxembourg and Esch,
but its headquarters are in Metz, France. Its circulation in Luxembourg is about 18,000
and it also publishes a special Sunday edition. Through its sensationalist reporting and
heavy pictorial coverage of local events, it now enjoys a regular and faithful audience.

981   **d'Letzebuerger Land.** (The Country of Luxembourg.)
      Luxembourg: Imprimerie Centrale, 1954- . weekly.

This sixteen- to twenty-page magazine, issued on Fridays and printed by the
Imprimerie Centrale S. A., is reputed for its well-informed political background
analysis and witty final page of humour and satire. This 'independent weekly for
politics, economy and culture' staunchly defends free enterprise, liberal market
policies and progressive liberalism in culture and art.

982   **Grénge Spoun: Zeitung fir Eng ekologesch a Sozial Alternativ.**
      (The Green Chip: Journal for an Ecological and Social Alternative.)
      Luxembourg: Grénge Spoun Soc. Coop., 1988- . weekly.

A monthly at the outset, this alternative publication became a weekly in 1993. Through
its serious research and independent inquiries, it has gained a growing audience.

983   **Revue: d'Lëtzebuerger Illustréiert.** (Revue: the Luxembourg
      Illustrated Magazine.)
      Luxembourg: Editions Revue S.A., 1945- . weekly.

This independent weekly, written in German, is a very popular illustrated magazine. It
covers local events, but also features critical columns on society and politics, economy
and education. Considerable space is devoted to entertainment and radio and
television programmes.

984   **Télécran.** (Telescreen.)
      Luxembourg: Imprimerie Saint-Paul, 1978- . weekly.

Sponsored by the *Luxemburger Wort* and printed at the Imprimerie Saint-Paul, this
radio and television listings magazine has, since its first publication in 1978, gained a
wide audience and has recently even outrivalled its older competitor, the *Revue*
(1945-48. bi-weekly; 1948- . weekly).

985   **Lëtzebuerger Sonndesblad.** (Luxembourg Sunday Paper.)
      Luxembourg: Editions Saint-Paul, 1869- . weekly.

This popular and edifying Catholic magazine, which places its emphasis on moral and
religious spirituality, has undergone an interesting face-lift over recent years. Its new
columns on travelling, youth activities and local heritage have gained it new readers
and it currently circulates around 10,000 copies.

# Radio and television

### 986 Radio Luxembourg.
*Les Cahiers Luxembourgeois*, Christmas issue (1954). 231p.

An illustrated and well-documented technical and literary publication on Luxembourg's powerful radio station, which serves central Europe with multilingual programmes and popular and classical music. It was in 1930 that the station's first transmitting stations were created on the plateau of Junglinster, Luxembourg.

### 987 Radio and Television. Radio Luxembourg 1933-1993.
Denis Maréchal.   Nancy, France: Presses Universitaires; Metz, France: Editions Serpenoise, 1994. 266p.

Maréchal's work is the first history of Radio Luxembourg, the communications group set up in 1933. It is a well-documented account which has been written from research in numerous private and diplomatic archives.

### 988 Radio-Télé-Luxembourg: 30e anniversaire; au carrefour de l'Europe. (Radio-Télé-Luxembourg: thirtieth anniversary; at the crossroads of Europe.)
*Les Cahiers Luxembourgeois*, nos. 5-6 (1961). 205p.

Presents a splendid collection of articles on music, information, publicity and television.

### 989 Radio Luxembourg – the Station of the Stars: an affectionate history of 50 years of broadcasting.
Richard Nichols.   London: W. H. Allen, 1983. 192p.

Written in English, this book retraces the history of Radio Luxembourg from the beginning, in 1933, when the station began its first test transmissions on 1,191 metres long wave. It provides an account of the new station that soon flourished and could even be said to have set the trend after the Second World War.

### 990 RTL Télévision c'est nous! (RTL Television it's us!)
Jacques Navadic.   Luxembourg: Imprimerie Centrale, 1985. 286p.

Creator of the news programmes of Luxembourg television (Télé Luxembourg), Jacques Navadic presents portraits of the broadcasters that made the station a success. Navadic's tribute is more an anecdotal chronicle of the ten-year story (1975-85) than a historical review. Written in colloquial language and accompanied by numerous interview extracts, the intention behind the publication is to entertain.

# Specialist Periodicals

991  **ALEA News.**
Luxembourg: ALEA, 1987- . quarterly.

*ALEA News* is published by the ALEA (Association luxembourgeoise des enseignants d'anglais – Luxembourg Association of English Grammar-school and Technical High School Teachers). This association was founded in 1980 in order to defend the interests of English teaching in the curricula of post-primary and post-secondary schools in Luxembourg.

992  **Les Amis de l'Histoire.** (The Friends of History.)
Luxembourg: Les Amis de l'Histoire, 1957- . irregular.

This historical publication by the Association des Amis de l'Histoire features French and German articles that deal mainly with national history.

993  **Annuaire Statistique: Identité d'une Région Transfrontalière = Statistisches Jahrbuch: eine Europäische Grossregion zeigt Profil.**
(Statistical Annual, Identity of a European Transborder Area.)
Luxembourg: STATEC; Saarbrucken, Germany: Statistisches Amt, Saarland, 1993- . annual.

Published jointly by the Saarland and Luxembourg Statistical Offices, this publication is a statistical yearbook which illustrates the profile of a central European region.

994  **ARBED News: Périodique d'Entreprise d'ARBED Luxembourg.**
(ARBED News: ARBED Luxembourg's Business Review.)
Luxembourg: ARBED, 1988- . semi-annual.

A semi-annual information magazine published by the large steel concern, ARBED, to inform its staff and customers about current production figures, development projects and market orientations.

995 **Annuaire de l'ALUC.** (Annual of the Luxembourg Association of
Catholic University Graduates.)
Luxembourg: ALUC, 1978- . annual.

This is the yearly publication of the ALUC (Association luxembourgeoise des
universitaires catholiques – the Luxembourg Association of Catholic University
Graduates), the powerful intellectual movement which was founded at the beginning
of the 20th century and which has since wielded an important influence in the
political, social and religious domains of Luxembourg's cultural life.

996 **Brennpunkt.** (Focus.)
Luxembourg: Action Formation de Cadres – Solidarité Tiers-Monde,
1973- . bimonthly.

Issued by Action Formation de Cadres – Solidarité Tiers-Monde (Organization for the
training of officials –Third-World Solidarity), this publication is a bimonthly on the
problems of developing countries, with articles in French and German. Its previous
title was *Brennpunkt Dritte Welt* (Focus – Third World).

997 **The Bulge.**
Luxembourg: Cercle d'Etudes sur la Bataille des Ardennes, 1972- .
quarterly.

Published by the Cercle d'Etudes sur la Bataille des Ardennes (Battle of Ardennes
Study Circle) this periodical includes articles in English, French and German on
Second-World-War history.

998 **Bulletin de Documentation.** (Documentation Bulletin.)
Luxembourg: Information and Press Service, 1949- . irregular.

Currently published four times a year by the Information and Press Service of the
Ministry of State, this series presents general information on political, economic and
cultural activities, new legislation, official ceremonies and important events, from
both foreign and national sources.

999 **Bulletin de l'APESS.** (APESS Bulletin.)
Luxembourg: APESS, 1909- . quarterly.

Originally called the *Journal des Professeurs* (Teachers' Journal), this quarterly is
published by APESS (Association des professeurs de l'enseignement secondaire et
supérieur – the Association of Secondary School and University Teachers).

1000 **Bulletin de l'Association des Instituteurs Réunis du Grand-Duché
de Luxembourg.** (Bulletin of the United Association of Teachers of
the Grand Duchy of Luxembourg.)
Luxembourg: Association des instituteurs réunis du Grand-Duché de
Luxembourg, 1949-73. monthly.

A publication for teachers from the Association des instituteurs réunis du grand-duché
de Luxembourg (United Association of Teachers of the Grand Duchy of
Luxembourg). From 1974 onwards this monthly continued as a quarterly publication,
entitled *Ecole et Vie* (q.v.).

1001 **Bulletin de la Société des Naturalistes Luxembourgeois.** (Bulletin of the Luxembourg Naturalists' Society.)
Luxembourg: Société des naturalistes luxembourgeois, 1908- . quarterly.

This quarterly is published by Luxembourg's Botanic and Naturalist Society.

1002 **Bulletin de la Société des Sciences Médicales du Grand-Duché de Luxembourg.** (Bulletin of the Society of Medical Sciences of the Grand Duchy of Luxembourg.)
Luxembourg: Société des sciences médicales, 1864- . semi-annual.

This publication presents articles in French and English for medical doctors.

1003 **Bulletin des Antiquités Luxembourgeoises.** (Luxembourg Bulletin of Antiquity.)
Luxembourg: Société des antiquités nationales, 1969- . quarterly.

Publishes articles in French and German on archaeology.

1004 **Bulletin du STATEC.** (STATEC Bulletin.)
Luxembourg; STATEC, 1963- . 8-9 issues per year.

Issued by STATEC (Service central de la statistique et des études économiques – Central Statistical and Economic Studies Service), with eight or nine issues per year, this series publishes various statistical items.

1005 **Bulletin Linguistique et Ethnologique.** (Bulletin of Linguistics and Ethnology.)
Luxembourg: Institut grand-ducal, 1935- . quarterly.

Issued by the Institut grand-ducal, Section de Linguistique, de Folklore et de Toponymie (Grand-ducal Institute, Linguistic Section, Folklore and Toponymy), this quarterly publishes articles in French, German and Luxembourgish (sometimes also in English) on linguistics and ethnology.

1006 **Cahiers Economiques.** (Economic Folios.)
Luxembourg: STATEC, 1951- . annual.

This publication provides important economic surveys and up-to-date bibliographies.

1007 **Les Cahiers Luxembourgeois.** (Luxembourg Notebooks.)
Luxembourg: Raymon Mehlen, 1923-64. 6-8 issues per year;
Luxembourg: Nic Weber, 1988- . 6 issues per year.

From 1923 to 1965 the *Cahiers Luxembourgeois* represented Luxembourg's cultural life. In 1988 it was relaunched with four yearly issues, and it is currently published six times per year.

1008   **Carrière: Éischte Lëtzebuerger Fraëmagazin.** (Carrière: First
       Luxembourg Women's Magazine.)
       Luxembourg: Monique Mathieu, 1988- . quarterly.

An interesting publication written for, about, and by, women. The main columns deal
with the world of travelling, art, fashion, employment and health.

1009   **Courrier de l'Education Nationale.** (National Educational News.)
       Luxembourg: Ministry for National Education, 1952- . quarterly.

Containing mainly articles in French, with some in German, this publication enjoys
quite a wide circulation and occasionally devotes a special issue to a topical subject.

1010   **Ecole et Vie.** (School and Life.)
       Luxembourg: Association des instituteurs réunis du Grand-Duché de
       Luxembourg, 1974- . quarterly.

Previously entitled *Bulletin de l'Association des Instituteurs Réunis du Grand-Duché
de Luxembourg* (q.v.), this pedagogical journal publishes articles in French, German
and English.

1011   **Eis Sprooch.** (Our Language.)
       Luxembourg: Actioun Lëtzebuergesch, 1952- . irregular.

Written entirely in Luxembourgish, this periodical is irregularly published by Actioun
Lëtzebuergesch (Luxembourg Action), which works for the promotion and expansion
of the Luxembourg language.

1012   **Estuaires.** (Estuaries.)
       Luxembourg: Ligue luxembourgeoise pour le secours aux enfants et
       aux adultes mentalement et cérébralement handicapés, 1986- .
       quarterly.

Launched in 1986 by Emile Hemmen, Nic Klecker and René Welter, this literary
magazine presents the work of both Luxembourg and foreign authors in the field of
poetry and essays.

1013   **Journal of European Integration History.**
       Luxembourg: Centre Robert Schuman, 1995- . irregular.

The aim of the *Journal of European Integration History*, under the direction of
Professor Gilbert Trausch, is to promote the analysis and understanding of all aspects
of European integration and interdependence, particularly, but not exclusively, since
1945. It encourages contributions on diplomatic, economic, cultural, social and
technological aspects of the field. Each issue contains specialized and general articles,
as well as reviews of major relevant publications. Contributions are published in
English, French or German.

1014 **Europerspectives.**
Luxembourg: Association d'information européenne, 1981- .
quarterly.

Published by the *Association d'information européenne* (European Information
Society), this periodical deals with European issues. It provides an interesting
bilingual platform for analysing the role of Luxembourg within Europe and European
activities in Luxembourg.

1015 **Forum fir Kritesch Informatioun an Politik, Kultur a Religioun.**
(Forum for Critical Information on Politics, Culture and Religion.)
Luxembourg: Forum a.s.b.l., 1967- . quarterly.

Presents interesting documentary reports on political, cultural and religious topics.
Prepared by a young and dynamic editorial board, it publishes in French and German.

1016 **Galerie.** (Gallery.)
Differdange, Luxembourg: Centre Culturel de Differdange, 1982- .
quarterly.

This literary and pedagogical magazine was founded by Cornel Meder in 1982. It is
characterized by its thorough archival and documentary research, its clear and
systematic layout, its regional concern and its deep interest in the local heritage, i.e.
that of southern Luxembourg and the magazine's home-town of Differdange.

1017 **Heimat und Mission.** (Homeland and Missionary Work.)
Clairefontaine, Luxembourg: Ecole Apostolique Clairefontaine,
1927- . monthly.

A monthly journal on missionary activities, presenting interesting documentary files
on social, cultural, economic and religious problems.

1018 **Hémecht, Zeitschrift für Luxemburger Geschichte.** (Homeland:
a journal of Luxembourg history.)
Luxembourg: Imprimerie Saint-Paul, 1895- . quarterly.

Publishes articles in French and German on Luxembourg's national history. Founded
by Martin Blum in 1895, the publication carried the title, *Ons Hémecht* (Our
Homeland) until 1939. After the Second World War, the periodical resumed
publication as *T'Hémecht* (The Homeland) (1948-63). In 1962, however, not a single
issue appeared. The publication has been known by its current name since 1964. A
three-volume index exists for the periods 1895-1973, 1974-82 and 1893-1992,
compiled by Alphonse Eichhorn, Joseph Maertz and Paul Medernach.

1019 **Journal des Instituteurs.** (Teachers' Journal.)
Luxembourg: Fédération générale des instituteurs luxembourgeois,
1905- . bimonthly.

This educational magazine for teachers is published by the Fédération générale des
instituteurs luxembourgeois (General Federation of Luxembourg Teachers).

1020 **De Kéisécker. Bulletin de 'Jeunes et Environnement'.** (The Hedgehog. Bulletin of 'Youth and the Environment'.)
Luxembourg: Jeunes et environnement, 1972- . bimonthly.
This bimonthly periodical is published by a section of the ecological movement called Mouvement écologique.

1021 **De Lëtzebuerger Bauerekalenner.** (The Luxembourg Farmers' Calendar.)
Luxembourg: Centrale Paysanne, 1949- . annual.
Issued by the Centrale Paysanne, this yearbook specializes in publishing material on agricultural problems and modern farming life.

1022 **d'Lëtzebuerger Dueref.** (The Luxembourg Village.)
Luxembourg: Kathoulesch Aktioun vum Dueref, 1946- . monthly.
Written in German, this periodical is published for young farmers by Kathoulesch Aktioun vum Dueref (Catholic Action in the Village).

1023 **De Lëtzebuerger Jéer.** (The Luxembourg Hunter.)
Luxembourg: Fédération des chasseurs luxembourgeois, 1979- . bimonthly.
Represents the periodical of the Fédération des chasseurs luxembourgeois (Luxembourg Hunters' Association). It addresses, beyond the hunting world, all friends of nature and the environment.

1024 **Luxembourg News Digest.**
Luxembourg: Pol Wirtz, International City Magazines s.a.r.l., 1981- . weekly.
This English-language weekly has appeared since 1981. It addresses the international community of Luxembourg and provides it with necessary background information and a calendar of local events in its 'What's on' column.

1025 **Luxemburger Marienkalender.** (The Luxembourg Holy Mary Calendar.)
Luxembourg: Imprimerie Saint-Paul, 1877- . annual.
A most popular calendar-book which offers miscellaneous instructive and amusing articles and retrospectives, the latest information on public life and staff lists of government departments. It is a widely-used source of reference for practical and up-to-date facts, figures and general information.

1026 **Mémorial – Journal Officiel du Grand-Duché de Luxembourg.** (Memorial – Official Journal of the Grand Duchy of Luxembourg.)
Luxembourg: Ministère d'Etat, Service central de législation, 1816- . irregular.
Luxembourg laws and ministerial regulations are only valid if they have been published in this official government series, published by the Service Central de législation (Central Law Office) under the Ministry of State. It has been published in three

different volumes since 1962. Volume A: *Recueil de législation* (Legislation) contains legislative texts (laws and decrees). Volume B: *Recueil administratif et économique* (Administrative and economic measures) lists official acts since 1962 such as the appointment and resignation of civil servants, and information of general interest in almost every field of administrative activity. Volume C: *Recueil spécial des sociétés et associations* (Special collection on companies and associations) lists all the acts to be published in fulfilment of the laws concerning companies and associations, such as acts of incorporation, the names of senior management and all changes in appointments, balance-sheets and notices of shareholders' meetings. This latter part of the *Mémorial* is the most substantial. For each volume, good annual indexes facilitate consultation.

1027 **Nos Cahiers. Lëtzebuerger Zäitschrëft fir Kultur.** (Our Folios.
A Luxembourg Magazine for Culture.)
Luxembourg: Imprimerie Saint-Paul, 1980- . quarterly.

A cultural journal edited by a board of Catholic intellectuals. Issues contain bibliographies of cultural publications and magazines.

1028 **Nouvelles Pages de la SELF.** (The New Pages of the SELF.)
Luxembourg: SELF, 1952- . annual.

SELF (the Société des écrivains luxembourgeois de langue française) regularly publishes a kind of literary yearbook, which either takes the form of an anthology of selected texts or groups various texts focusing on a particular topic. This publication was renamed the *Nouvelles Pages de la Société des Ecrivains Luxembourgeois de Langue Française* (The New Pages of the Society of Francophone Luxembourg Writers) in 1973. The appendix includes a bibliographic survey of periodicals written in French, French plays being staged in Luxembourg, French lectures, and publications by members of SELF.

1029 **Ons Stad.** (Our Town.)
Luxembourg: Ville de Luxembourg, 1979- . quarterly.

*Ons Stad* is a well-illustrated documentary quarterly on the town of Luxembourg which is published by the municipality. Contributions are in French, German and Luxembourgish, while special pages provide useful administrative information in four languages (French, German, Italian and Portuguese).

1030 **Pizzicato.**
Luxembourg: Jeunesses Musicales, 1991- . quarterly.

This musical journal addresses mainly students and musicians, keeping them informed of the main events and highlights of the music scene. It also reviews the most recent products on the CD market.

1031 **Publications de l'Institut Grand-Ducal. Section des Sciences
Morales et Politiques.** (Publications of the Grand Ducal Institute.
Section of Moral and Political Sciences.)
Luxembourg: Institut grand-ducal, Section des sciences morales et politiques, 1970- . irregular.

Comprises features, essays and communications of a highly literary and philosophical nature, written in French.

1032 **Publications de la Section Historique de l'Institut Grand-Ducal de Luxembourg.** (Publications of the Historical Section of the Grand Ducal Institute.)
Luxembourg: Institut grand-ducal, Section historique, 1845- . annual.
This annual publication covers all aspects of the history of Luxembourg and all auxiliary historical disciplines, with articles in French and German.

1033 **Rappel.** (Reminder.)
Luxembourg: Ligue luxembourgeoise des prisonniers politiques et déportés, 1946- . monthly.
Deals with various aspects of the Second World War, resistance and deportations, local history and neo-Nazism.

1034 **Récréation. Association des Professeurs de l'Enseignement Secondaire et Supérieur.** (Recreation. Society of Teachers in Secondary and Higher Education.)
Luxembourg: APESS, 1986- . annual/semi-annual.
Published once or twice a year by the Association of Secondary School and University Teachers, this literary and cultural magazine is mainly devoted to literature and fine arts, but occasionally includes articles of a more trade-unionist nature.

1035 **Rendez-vous Lëtzebuerg: le Journal des Manifestations Culturelles.** (Rendez-vous Luxembourg: the Journal of Cultural Events.)
Luxembourg: Ville de Luxembourg, 1992- . monthly.
A glossy monthly magazine about the cultural events in Luxembourg's municipal theatres and galleries which produces a special yearly programme booklet of performances at the Théâtre Municipal (Municipal Theatre) and the Théâtre des Capucins (Capuchin Theatre).

1036 **Revue Gastronomique.** (Gastronomic Review.)
Luxembourg: Regipress, 1979- . monthly.
Provides a monthly guide to Luxembourg food, restaurants and hotels.

1037 **Revue Luxembourgeoise de Littérature Générale et Comparée.** (Luxembourg Review of General and Comparative Literature.)
Luxembourg: Société luxembourgeoise de littérature générale et comparée, 1987- . irregular.
Represents an innovative literary magazine in the field of comparative literature which is published once or twice a year by the Société luxembourgeoise de littérature générale et comparée (Luxembourg Society of General and Comparative Literature), a society that was founded in the mid-1980s on the periphery of language teaching at the Centre Universitaire de Luxembourg (Luxembourg University Centre) and which is eager to establish international exchanges with foreign sister associations and to organize specialized colloquia.

1038    **Revue Technique Luxembourgeoise.** (Luxembourg Technical
        Review.)
        Luxembourg: Association luxembourgeoise des ingénieurs et
        industriels, 1901- . quarterly.

This quarterly publication on technology, architecture and the arts is issued by the
Association luxembourgeoise des ingénieurs et industriels (Luxembourg Engineering
and Industrial Society) and contains articles in French, German and English.

1039    **Tabou.** (Taboo.)
        Luxembourg: Tabou s.à.r.l., 1991- . bimonthly.

*Tabou* is an interesting cultural magazine which covers transborder affairs and
supranational concerns of the Saar-Lor-Lux region. The wide-ranging calendar of
events and highly professional commentaries and reviews are the distinctive features
of this publication.

1040    **Utopia Graffiti.**
        Luxembourg: Utopia s.à.r.l., 1987- . monthly.

This publication is an unconventional movie news feature magazine which presents
the programmes of the two main cinemas in Luxembourg: Utopia (five screens), and
the newly-opened UTOPOLIS centre (ten screens) at Kirchberg. The magazine
includes details of new films, with reviews, interviews and photographs.

1041    **Vis a Vis: das Saar-Lor-Lux Magazin.** (Face to Face, The
        Saar-Lor-Lux Magazine.)
        Koblenz, Germany: Haselbauer & Partner, 1992- .

A sixty-page magazine for tourists written in German, which covers the central region
of the Lorraine, the Saarland and Luxembourg from a social, political, economic and
cultural point of view.

1042    **Voilà Luxembourg.** (That's Luxembourg.)
        Luxembourg: Service information et presse du gouvernement,
        1991- . irregular.

A highly interesting and well-illustrated information magazine published at irregular
intervals by the government's information and press service, and freely distributed to
embassies, news agencies, tourist offices and subscribers abroad. It represents a
splendid show-case for Luxembourg life and culture. So far seven numbers have
appeared, in three languages: English, French and German. On the occasion of the
Seville World Fair, a special issue also came out in Spanish.

# Directories

### 1043 Living in Luxembourg.
Luxembourg: American Women's Club of Luxembourg, 1993.
12th ed. 332p.

The first edition of this practical handbook was published in 1959 by the American Women's Club of Luxembourg (AWCL), which was founded in 1958. The handbook has evolved and improved over the years thanks to the ideas and experiences of many people. It represents a major source of information for new Anglo-American settlers in Luxembourg and contains plenty of practical advice on living, housing, furnishing and travelling as well as good tips on administrative procedures. The AWCL is a member of the Federation of American Women's Clubs Overseas (FAWCO) which consists of clubs in all five continents working together to achieve common goals.

### 1044 La Ligne Bleue – Les Pages Jaunes. (The Blue Line – The Yellow Pages.)
Luxembourg: Editus Sàrl, 1995. 12th ed. 1,184p.

All crafts people, industrialists, business people or independent people who practise a professional activity are able to profit from a free insertion of their address in one of several thousand specialized columns of this directory which is distributed, free of charge, to every household. It contains alphabetical indexes to trademark headings and companies, as well as street plans of main towns.

### 1045 Ons Stad: Services. (Our City: Services.)
Luxembourg: Imprimerie Centrale, 1993. 109p.

Contains useful information about the services the city of Luxembourg is able to offer its inhabitants and visitors. In addition to a historical and statistical overview, the guide informs the reader about issues of general interest and provides detailed information about general regulations.

### 1046 The Golden Book of Luxembourg.
Luxembourg: Agence européenne de communication, 1995. 142p.

This glossy magazine-style book is intended to meet the needs of business people, visitors and residents who want to learn about the various aspects of the Grand Duchy Setting out to provide entertainment and information in an attractive format, its largest target group seems to be hotel owners, tourist managers, bankers and industrialists, who could offer the directory to their clients as a gift. Concise text, splendid illustrations and attractive layout make for enjoyable reading or browsing.

### 1047 Business Guide to Luxembourg and the Interregion.
Luxembourg: Groupe Press Consultant International, 1993/94. 744p.

This directory is the successor to the *Businessman's Guide to Luxembourg* which first appeared in 1990 and soon became an indispensable bilingual annual for business people, a useful working tool and a reliable reference guide. Describing the existing infrastructures and explaining who does what, how and where, it has gradually enlarged its scope to cover the greater region it now deals with. Since April 1993 there also exists a 'Business Guide-Electronic Information Bank', an electronic database connected to Infopartners Serveur II. It is consulted by the sixty-two most industrialized countries in the world and is written in the official languages of the EU.

### 1048 Directory.
Luxembourg: ABBL, 1991. unpaginated.

This annual directory is published by the ABBL (Association des banques et banquiers luxembourgeois – Luxembourg Bankers' Association). It is a useful guide to the country's 220 banks and more than 1,000 holding societies and insurance companies.

### 1049 Developping [sic] firms in Benelux.
Lyon, France: Editions Juris Service, 1995. 415p.

Presents a bilingual business guide in the series, 'Doing Business in Europe', published by ICC Law (Inter Continental Consultants Law). It addresses all business people, lawyers and investors who need a general view of business law as practised in Belgium, the Netherlands and Luxembourg. The guide has been written by experienced lawyers, who are all members of the international organization, ICC Law, within which they have developed specialized professional skills. This mutual knowledge allowed them to coordinate their approaches and terminology. Pages 117-63 (in French) and 321-69 (in English) describe Luxembourg's situation under the headings of 'Legal Requirements', 'Employment Law' and 'Economic Environment'.

# Bibliographies

1050   **Luxemburgensia: eine Bibliographie der Bibliographien.**
(Luxemburgensia: a bibliography of bibliographies.)
Carlo Hury.   Munich, FRG: Saur, 1978. 2nd ed. 352p.

The term *Luxemburgensia* refers to: works printed in Luxembourg; works written by Luxembourgers; and works dealing with Luxembourg by foreign authors. This volume records general bibliographies, biographies, grammars, dictionaries, anthologies, collections of documents and sources. Almost all the titles are annotated and a very comprehensive subject, person and place index is provided.

1051   **Bibliographie luxembourgeoise ou catalogue de tous les ouvrages ou travaux littéraires publiés par des Luxembourgeois ou dans le grand-duché actuel de Luxembourg.** (Luxembourg bibliography or catalogue of all literary works published either by Luxembourgers or in the present Grand Duchy of Luxembourg.)
Martin Blum.   Luxembourg: Imprimerie Bourg-Bourger;
Worré-Mertens, 1902-32. 2 vols.

Only these two volumes appeared in this attempt to provide an all-embracing, retrospective national bibliography of authors in the alphabetical order of their names, with their works in chronological order of publication. A short biography of each author, an index of pseudonyms and occasional explanatory details about titles are provided. The holdings of the National Library are marked by asterisks.

1052   **Bibliographie luxembourgeoise.** (Luxembourg bibliography.)
Luxembourg: Bibliothèque nationale, 1946- . annual.

This is the official current Luxembourg bibliography, which lists books published since 10 September 1944. It lists publications printed in Luxembourg and those published by Luxembourgers or concerning Luxembourg. Since 1958 it has also included important newspaper and magazine articles and essays in collected works. The fiftieth volume in the series appeared in December 1995. The directory is structured according to subject, and within each group according to authors or titles when the author of the work is anonymous.

1053    **Luxemburg / Rheinland: eine Bibliographie zur Sprach-und Mundartforschung in chronologischer Anordnung.**
(Luxembourg/Rhineland: a bibliography of linguistic and dialectological research in chronological order.)
Compiled by Gerald Newton.   Luxembourg: Institut grand-ducal, Section de linguistique, folklore et de toponymie, 1993. 160p.
(Bulletin Linguistique et Ethnologique, fascicule 25).

This collection of 2,098 texts on linguistics and dialectology in Luxembourg and the Rhineland is based on a reference bibliography which the author compiled for his contribution on 'Central Franconian' in the volume, *The Dialects of Modern German*, edited by Charles Russ (London: Routledge, 1990, p. 136-209). The chronological arrangement allows a clear insight into the gradual development of Luxembourg and Rhineland linguistics and so clearly reveals striking features of similarity and regional differentiation in scholarly approach and methodology.

1054    **Bibliographie juridique luxembourgeoise.** (Luxembourg bibliography of law.)
Georges Krieger, Dean Spielmann, Claudine Graas-Lorang.
Brussels: Editions Nemesis, 1989. 267p.

This bibliography of Luxembourg law is based on a first bibliography produced in 1967 with the Brussels publisher, Larcier, by a team of Luxembourg lawyers, which listed 780 bibliographic records. The authors of the 1989 volume, three young Luxembourg lawyers, set out to update and complete this specific survey of Luxembourg law. They introduce their work with statements on the evolution of the various kinds of law (commercial, fiscal, penal, public, administrative, constitutional and international). They divide 1,535 publications between fifteen main chapters, arranging the titles in alphabetical order, and conclude with an author and subject index. This highly specialized bibliography is a very useful handbook for students and young practitioners of national legislation.

1055    **La Commune de Hosingen.** (The Commune of Hosingen.)
Joseph Goedert.   Hosingen, Luxembourg: Administration communale, 1984. 116p. (Bio-bibliographie du Canton de Clervaux).

From 1982 to 1992, the author published in the regional cultural journal, *De Cliärrwer Kanton*, detailed bio-bibliographical records about a number of communes of the Canton of Clervaux which cover all the interesting aspects of village and municipal life. This publication gathers all the contributions covering the commune of Hosingen. For each locality the author divided the material between the same categories, which included archaeological discoveries, social and political events and religious life.

1056　**Bernhard von Luxemburg um 1460-1535**. (Bernhard of
Luxembourg, c.1460-1535.)
Emile van der Vekene.　Hürtgenwald, FRG: Guido Pressler Verlag,
1985. 59p.

To commemorate the 450th anniversary of the death of Bernhard of Luxembourg in
1985, Emile van der Vekene published an annotated, improved second edition of the
bibliography of Bernhard's printed works. This publication appeared when the
National Library of Luxembourg displayed his works in an exhibition. Bernhard of
Luxembourg (1460-1535), who was a member of the Dominican order and belonged
to the committee of doctors at the University of Cologne, wrote numerous religious
tracts as well as pamphlets.

1057　**Bibliographie de l'Imprimerie Saint-Paul 1886-1986**.
(Bibliography of the Saint-Paul printing-house 1886-1986.)
Gast Zangerlé.　Luxembourg: Imprimerie Saint-Paul, 1988. 281p.

This commemorative volume (1886-1986) fills a gap by listing, in chronological
order, all the books and brochures, newspapers, magazines and other periodical
Luxembourg publications that have been issued by the Imprimerie Saint-Paul (Saint
Paul printing house) since its foundation in 1886.

1058　**Emil van der Vekene: Bibliographie der Jahre 1961-1992**. (Emil
van der Vekene: Bibliography of the years 1961-92.)
Hürtgenwald FRG: Guido Pressler Verlag, 1993. 122p.

For the sixtieth birthday of Emile van der Vekene, the curator of the Rare Collections
Department of the National Library, this commemorative volume was issued. It includes
a bibliography that attempts to compile his publications, contributions and lectures
from the years 1961-92, which represent so many examples of a rich working life.

# Indexes

There follow three separate indexes: authors (personal and corporate); titles; and subjects. Title entries are italicized and refer either to the main titles, or to many of the other works cited in the annotations. The numbers refer to bibliographical entry rather than page numbers. Individual index entries are arranged in alphabetical sequence.

# Index of Authors

Faber, R. 53
Fally, V. 522
Fanfare de Waldbillig 774
Fanfare Concordia
  Bauschelt 353
Fanfare Troisvierges 351
Fautsch, L. 914
Fayot, Ben 226, 460-61
Fédération agricole
  (Luxembourg) 639
Fédération des chasseurs
  luxembourgeois 1023
Fédération du sport
  cycliste luxembourgeois
  917
Fédération générale des
  fonctionnaires
  communaux
  (Luxembourg) 610
Fédération générale des
  instituteurs
  luxembourgeois 1019
Fédération
  luxembourgeoise de
  basket-ball 920
Fédération
  luxembourgeoise de
  canoë-kayak 919
Fédération
  luxembourgeoise de
  football 916
Fédération nationale
  des Corps de
  Sapeurs-Pompiers du
  Grand-Duché de
  Luxembourg 454
Federmeyer, E. 617, 620
Ferrari, M. C. 646
Ferraris, Joseph de 71
Fiedler, J.-P. 330
Fisch, R. 358
Fischbach, Marcel 969
Fischbach, V. 41
Fischer, Batty 326
Flesch, C. 384
Fletcher, W. A. 242
Flies, J. 334
Flower, J. 96
Fodor, Eugen 99
Folmer, N. 134
Franck, F. 369
Franck, M. 495
Frank, J. 451

Frank, R. 396
Franke, P. R. 52
Fresez, J. B. 27-29
Frieden-Kinnen, M. 398,
  838
Friedrich, E. 104, 106,
  268, 604, 966
Frijhoff, W. 678
Froehling, F. 508
Frommes, B. 413
Funck, A. 577

## G

Gade, John A. 162
Galler, B. 223
Gallion, Roger 302
Gallo, B. 442
Gambrinus Bruderschaft
  599
Gaul, R. 276, 282-83
Gedrim, R. J. 892
Gehring, J. M. 1, 49
Geister, J. 79
Gengler, C. 3, 450, 633
Gengler, Gast 331
Gérard, Luss 372
Gérard, M. 745-46
Gerges, M. 61, 641, 760
Gilbert, P. 899
Glaesener, J.-P. 159
Glastra van Loon, J. F.
  474
Goedert, J. 160, 345, 648,
  1055
Goedert, P. 773
Goergen, E. 813
Goergen, M. 777
Goergen, R. 580
Goergen, W. 776
Gonner, A. 435
Gonner, N. 434-35
Goolrick, W. K. 273
Graas-Lorang, C. 1054
Grande Loge de
  Luxembourg 663
Graulich, P. 474
Gredt, N. 672
Grégoire, P. 11, 173, 187,
  400, 418, 647, 655, 737,
  769, 970-72
Gross, B. 25

Grote, L. 956
Groupe de liaison des
  professeurs d'histoire
  auprès de la
  Commission européenne
  1015
Guill, P. 574
Guillite, P. 474

## H

Haagen, A. 905
Haan, J. 673-74, 676
Haas, A. 485
Haas, Luke 879
Hakimi, J. A. P. 35
Haller, M.-C. 699
Hamer, J. 233
Hamer, P. 157, 417, 612,
  695-97
Hanff, G. 463
Harmonie grand-ducale
  municipale Wiltz 348
Harpes, J. 325, 443
Hartmann-Hirsch, C. 633
Hary, A. 81
Hasselmann, L. 595
Hauffels, G. H. 507
Hausemer, G. 757
Hearl, D. 465
Heiderscheid, A. 430,
  683
Hein, N. 656
Heisbourg, G. 244, 272
Heischling, F. 295
Hemmen, E. 1012
Hemmer, C. 2, 31-32, 100,
  107, 534, 628
Henzig, J. 384
Herchen, A. 153
Hermann, L. 401
Herr, J. 132, 355
Herr, L. 818
Hess, G. 134
Hess, J. 431, 665-67
Heuertz, M. 128
Heyen, F. J. 170
Hilgert, E. 45
Hilgert, R. 358, 775,
  788
Hirsch, J. 360, 829, 842
Hirsch, M. 471, 624

Hoefler, A. 754
Hoffmann, A. 343
Hoffmann, F. 1, 11, 707,
710-11, 732-35, 756,
762, 772-73, 847,
909
Hoffmann, G. 922
Hoffmann, J.-P. 623
Hohengarten, A. 250-51,
253, 259-60, 300
Holzmacher, G. 295
Hommel, L. 542
Houtsch, A. 64
Hoyois, G. 545
Huart, Martin d' 796
Hugo, Victor 34
Humbel, F. 835
Hurt, J. 880
Hury, C. 11, 321, 435,
755, 771, 773, 777-78,
1050
Huss, M. 27

I

Iben, I. 965
Imedia 41
Information and Press
Service 20, 109
INSEE Lorraine 531
Institut Emile Metz 808
Institut für Demoskopie
Allensbach 684
Institut grand-ducal.
Section de linguistique,
de toponymie et de
folklore 427, 1005
Institut grand-ducal.
Section des sciences
politiques et morales
441, 524, 1031
Institut grand-ducal.
Section historique
1032
Institut Supérieur de
Technologie 807
Institut Universitaire
International
(Luxembourg) 578
Instituteurs réunis du
Grand-Duché de
Luxembourg 1010

Inter-Bank Research
Organization 561
IREP (Grenoble) 429

J

Jaans-Hoche, J. 576
Jacoby, L. 252, 404
Jaeger, V. 510
Javeau, Cl. 12
Jeunes et environnement
(Luxembourg) 1020
Jeunesses musicales de
Luxembourg 1030
Joset, Camille P. 166-67
Jost, P. 132
Jourdain, Ch. 602
Junck, G. 913
Jungblut, Marie-Paule 564
Jungerius, P. D. 82

K

Karen, F. 283
Kariger, M.-Th. 407
Kartheiser, F. 310
Kartheiser, J. 451
Kathoulesch Aktioun vum
Duerf 1022
Kauffmann, J. 341
Kauthen, P. 361
Kayser, E. M. 205
Kayser, G. 139
Kayser, L. 846, 851
Kayser, P. 600
Kayser, R. 287
Keipes, G. 352
Keller, R. E. 704
Kelton, R. 892
Ketter, R. 757
Kieffer, Rosemarie 398,
739, 747-48
Kiesel, G. 824
Kill, J. 154
Kinnen, F. 317, 883
Kintziger, P. 794
Kirchner, E. J. 465
Klarsfeld, S. 289
Klecker, N. 843, 1012
Klees, H. 1, 427, 726-27
Klein, F. W. 436

Klein, M. 519
Klinva, T. 742
Klopp, E. 261
Klopp, J. M. 68
Knepper, A. 255-56
Koch-Kent, H. 129, 227,
230-31, 233, 241, 245,
250-51, 304
Kodisch, N. 375
Koerperich, L. 337
Kohl, N. 140
Kohnen, J. 361, 853, 856
Kolbusch, J.-P. 922
Koltz, A. 753
Koltz, J.-P. 93, 158, 314,
320, 327, 821, 901, 905
Koltz, Jean-Luc 833
Kommunistische Partei
Luxemburgs see Parti
communiste
luxembourgeois
Konzem, W. 292
Krantz, R. 102, 337-38
Kremer, M. 290
Kremer, N. 294
Kremer, P. 781
Krieger, G. 1054
Krieps, Roger 433
Krier, A. 462
Krier, E. 2
Krier, Tony 901
Kroemmer, M.-T. 722
Kugener, H. 39, 420
Kuhn-Regnier, J. 408
Kunitzki, Norbert von
516, 541

L

La Fontaine, Edmond de
668, 771
Laborde, C. 926
Laby, C. 608
Lacaf, R. 84
Lahr, E. 54
Lamboray, C. 785
Lamesch, M. 127, 323
Lammar, D. 451
Langini, A. 686
Lannay, J. de 403
Lascombes, F. 315-16
Lathuilière, B. 79

Lefebvre, L. 209
Lefèvre, J. 841
Lefèvre, N. 841
Lefort, A. 198
Legner, A. 895
Lehrmann, C. 685
Lehrmann, G. 685
Leider, J. 307
Leipold, L. E. 86
Lemaire, G. 194
Lemogne, N. 386
Lenertz, M. 386
Lentz, M. 770
Léonard, M. 789
Lepthien, E. U. 37
Lëtzebuerger Natur- a
  Vulleschutzliga 122
Lëtzebuerger
  Schrëftstellerverband
  (Luxembourg) 741-42
Letzebuerger Scouten 921
Levert, Th. W. M. 82
Leyder, M.-A. 419
Liesch, A. 778
Liez, N. 27, 29
Ligue des associations
  sportives de
  l'enseignement primaire
  (Luxembourg) 915
Ligue des Associations
  sportives estudiantines
  luxembourgeoise 914
Ligue luxembourgeoise
  des prisonniers
  politiques et déportés
  1033
Ligue luxembourgeoise
  pour l'étude et la
  protection des oiseaux
  124
Link, R. 504, 560
Loos, V. 369
Lorang, A. 448, 851,
  897
Lorang, F. 234, 298,
  752
Lorent, C. 851
Loutsch, J.-C. 382, 386
Lucius, M. 76-78
Ludwig, M. 357
Luxembourg 1995 653
Luxembourg writers'
  association 741

Luxemburger Verband
  für Vogelschutz und
  Vogelkunde 123
Luxlait (Luxembourg)
  638
Lycée classique de
  Diekirch 806
Lycée de garçons
  (Luxembourg) 804
Lycée Michel Rodange
  (Luxembourg) 718-19,
  805
Lycée technique
  Ettelbruck 809
Lycée technique Nic Biver
  (Dudelange) 812
Lycée technique privé
  Sainte-Anne
  (Ettelbruck) 811

M

Madol, R. 834
Maertz, J. 274, 1018
Maîtrise de la Cathédrale
  Notre-Dame
  (Luxembourg) 869
Majerus, E. 543, 618
Majerus, M. 486
Majerus, N. 475, 489,
  682
Majerus, P. 218, 491-92
Manderscheid, R. 753,
  782, 784
Mannes, G. 838
Maréchal, D. 987
Margue, M. 180
Margue, N. 8, 153
Margue, P. 1, 163, 168,
  512, 564, 905
Mariën-Dugardin, A.-M.
  860
Martin, K. C. 390
Marx, Karl 788
Massard, Jos. A. 662
Mathieu, D. 108
Mathieu, F. 365
Mathieu, P. 108
May, A. 151, 182-83, 315,
  938-40
May, G. 17, 143, 331
Mayrisch, E. 858

Meder, C. 405, 512, 740,
  753, 773
Medernach, P. 1018
Medernach-Merens, D.
  748
Medinger, P. 374
Meier, U. 559
Meintz, C. 405
Melchers, E. T. 228-29,
  285
Mersch, Félix 317
Mersch, François 19, 26,
  319
Mersch, J. 388
Metzler, J. 134-35
Metzler, L. 477
Meyer, M. 119
Meyers, J. 153, 374, 421,
  813, 862
Miles, B. 88
Millman, R. 216
Milmeister, J. 114, 278,
  346-47
Ministère d'Etat
  (Luxembourg) 57
Ministère de
  l'aménagement du
  territoire (Luxembourg)
  630
Ministère de l'Education
  nationale (Luxembourg)
  69, 767, 1009
Ministère de
  l'environnement
  (Luxembourg) 632
Ministère des Affaires
  culturelles
  (Luxembourg) 57, 66,
  651-52, 887
Ministère des arts et
  sciences (Luxembourg)
  813
Ministère des finances
  (Luxembourg) 627
Ministère des Sports
  105
Ministère du Tourisme
  105
Ministry of State
  (Luxembourg) 384
Mitchell-Thomé 82
Mogridge, B. 753
Moia, N. 898

# Index of Titles

301

303

311

312

315

# Index of Subjects

# Map of Luxembourg

This map shows the districts, main towns and other features.

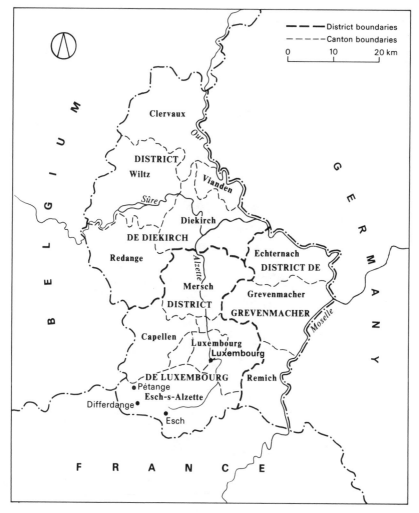

# ALSO FROM CLIO PRESS

## INTERNATIONAL ORGANIZATIONS SERIES

Each volume in the International Organizations Series is either devoted to one specific organization, or to a number of different organizations operating in a particular region, or engaged in a specific field of activity. The scope of the series is wide-ranging and includes intergovernmental organizations, international non-governmental organizations, and national bodies dealing with international issues. The series is aimed mainly at the English-speaker and each volume provides a selective, annotated, critical bibliography of the organization, or organizations, concerned. The bibliographies cover books, articles, pamphlets, directories, databases and theses and, wherever possible, attention is focused on material about the organizations rather than on the organizations' own publications. Notwithstanding this, the most important official publications, and guides to those publications, will be included. The views expressed in individual volumes, however, are not necessarily those of the publishers.

## VOLUMES IN THE SERIES

1  *European Communities*,
    John Paxton
2  *Arab Regional Organizations*,
    Frank A. Clements
3  *Comecon: The Rise and Fall of an
    International Socialist
    Organization*, Jenny Brine
4  *International Monetary Fund*,
    Anne C. M. Salda
5  *The Commonwealth*, Patricia M.
    Larby and Harry Hannam
6  *The French Secret Services*, Martyn
    Cornick and Peter Morris

7  *Organization of African Unity*,
    Gordon Harris
8  *North Atlantic Treaty Organization*,
    Phil Williams
9  *World Bank*, Anne C. M. Salda
10 *United Nations System*, Joseph P.
    Baratta
11 *Organization of American States*,
    David Sheinin
12 *The British Secret Services*, Philip
    H. J. Davies
13 *The Israeli Secret Services*, Frank
    A. Clements